A Theology of Power and Privilege

A Theology of Power and Privilege

An Evangelical Perspective on Race

Joseph Caldwell

LEXINGTON BOOKS/FORTRESS ACADEMIC
Lanham • Boulder • New York • London

Published by Lexington Books/Fortress Academic
Lexington Books is an imprint of The Rowman & Littlefield Publishing Group, Inc.
4501 Forbes Boulevard, Suite 200, Lanham, Maryland 20706
www.rowman.com

86-90 Paul Street, London EC2A 4NE, United Kingdom

Copyright © 2024 by The Rowman & Littlefield Publishing Group, Inc.

All rights reserved. No part of this book may be reproduced in any form or by any electronic or mechanical means, including information storage and retrieval systems, without written permission from the publisher, except by a reviewer who may quote passages in a review.

British Library Cataloguing in Publication Information Available

Library of Congress Cataloging-in-Publication Data

Names: Caldwell, Joseph, 1964– author.
Title: A theology of power and privilege : an evangelical perspective on race / Joseph Caldwell.
Description: Lanham : Lexington Books, Fortress Academic, [2024] | Includes bibliographical references and index. | Summary: "A Theology of Power and Privilege is an antiracist evangelical theology that examines critiques of white theology by Black theologians. It explores biases in the White theological tradition, evaluates the tradition historically, engages biblical text around questions of liberation, and offers a biblically grounded treatment of the doctrine of God"— Provided by publisher.
Identifiers: LCCN 2024013892 (print) | LCCN 2024013893 (ebook) | ISBN 9781978716506 (cloth) | ISBN 9781978716513 (epub)
Subjects: LCSH: Power (Social sciences)—Religious aspects. | White people—Race identity—Religious aspects. | Evangelicalism. | Anti-racism. | Black theology.
Classification: LCC BL65.P7 C23 2024 (print) | LCC BL65.P7 (ebook) | DDC 230.089/09—dc23/eng/20240509
LC record available at https://lccn.loc.gov/2024013892
LC ebook record available at https://lccn.loc.gov/2024013893

To Marva, Josh, and Chris, whose experience speaks louder than any argument made in this book. This is for you in the hope of a brighter tomorrow.

Contents

Acknowledgments ix

Introduction 1

PART I: AN EMPATHETIC-ANALYTICAL READING OF JAMES CONE 7

Chapter 1: Cone's Theological Agenda and Rhetorical Persona 9

Chapter 2: Influences on Cone's Body of Work 31

PART II: EVALUATING THE EVANGELICAL THEOLOGICAL TRADITION 45

Chapter 3: Methodology for Evaluating Evangelical Theology 47

Chapter 4: John Calvin and Racist Logics 57

Chapter 5: Jonathan Edwards and Racist Logics 81

Chapter 6: Charles Hodge and Racist Logics 103

Chapter 7: Carl F. H. Henry and Racist Logics 119

PART III: EXPLORATION OF THE BIBLICAL TEXT 145

Chapter 8: Exegetical Methodology and Text Selection 147

Chapter 9: Luke 4:14–30: Exegesis and Theology 151

Chapter 10: Luke 4 in Conversation with Romans 13 and the Household Codes 185

Chapter 11: The Theological Use of Luke 4:16–30 211

PART IV: DOCTRINAL AND ETHICAL CONSTRUCTION — 223

Chapter 12: Constructive Theological Methodology — 225

Chapter 13: Revelation — 227

Chapter 14: Providence — 261

Chapter 15: The Person of God — 285

Chapter 16: Toward a Theology of Power: Dialogue with the Biblical Text and Ethical Appropriation — 311

Bibliography — 323

Index — 333

About the Author — 335

Acknowledgments

Anyone who attempts to do theology is a debtor from the first argument they formulate to the last word they put on the page. They are indebted to centuries of scholars who have worked diligently before them. They are in debt to the numerous teachers who have trained them and mentored them along the way. Most importantly they are in debt to the communities they hope to affect through their writing. If theologians owe a debt, then I am to be counted as the chief of debtors. There is no way to acknowledge everyone whose work I drew inspiration from although I have tried diligently to cite their work throughout. As for my teachers, I have to mention Dr. Caroline Seed and Professor Rickus Fisk. This work was first conceived as a doctoral dissertation under their supervision. It owes much to their encouragement and constructive criticism. I deeply appreciate the work of Jeanette Redmond who helped with editing and the overall format of the book. I owe my interest in theology to three seminary mentors at Golden Gate Baptist Seminary who taught me the importance of thinking theologically about the world we live in. Dr. Dwight Honeycutt, Dr. Stan Nelson, and Dr. Rick Melick all had a profound influence on my theological formation. That said, I would be remiss if I did not recognize the one person who first taught me the importance of critical thinking and who first flamed the fire of learning in my heart and mind. I am forever in debt to Mr. Walter Hoover who saw possibility in me and inspired me to think better about the world.

Introduction

American theologian James Cone offers a salient critique of White theology in which he repeatedly calls White theologians to see their theological and exegetical work as grounded in biases derived from White power. White theologians have largely ignored this critique. White evangelical theologians, in particular, have failed to engage in constructive projects that make race and power the centerpiece of theological reflection. One key reason is that propositional evangelical theology has lacked the methodologies to generate a theology of power capable of both maintaining the centrality of Scripture and integrating critics, like Cone, as theological conversation partners. This book aims to develop a theology of power that can be faithful to Cone's critique and still recognizable as an evangelical theology.

This thesis I present here relates to a strand of North American evangelicalism that culminates with Carl F. H. Henry, whose work affirms the centrality of biblical authority in theological development. I also affirm John Sailhamer's argument that the evangelical view of Scripture is by nature precritical. He references[1] Hans Frei's identification of three aspects of this view: a belief that the Bible is referential and describes actual historical events; the idea that if the biblical world is a single world, then by extension it must include a single identifiable story; and the belief that the one biblical story includes the contemporary world as well.[2] Thus, evangelicalism at its core subscribes to a view that God's self-revelation lies within Scripture, which includes a realistic reading that makes the text referential, canonical, and sufficient for contemporary application.

Because this study aims at an evangelical theology of power, it presupposes the above definition of precritical realistic reading. The text spends little effort on defending this view, even though both modern and postmodern biblical criticism take issue with it. This research assumes instead that theological reassessment and restatement must proceed from a strict definition of biblical realism and reference to be appropriate to evangelicals. Unless the text directs the doctrine, the task of "revisioning" evangelical doctrine would be called into question.

This aim does not imply that this book's textual interpretation will follow a biblicist approach. My approach prefers literary analysis, in contrast to sociocultural and historical analyses of the text; recognizes that the text's final form is authoritative; and understands that Scripture can be communicated in ways that speak to the contemporary condition.

This text-based approach also implies that theology is the act of making God's revelation in Scripture intelligible to the contemporary situation. That means theology and theological method are ultimately hermeneutical. As Dan Stiver[3] asserts, hermeneutics and theology have an "unusual affinity"; and both Kevin Vanhoozer[4] and Anthony Thiselton[5] engage systematic theology and doctrine using a hermeneutical process. Thus, one can envision a theological method that follows a primarily hermeneutical method, conceivably giving a crucial role to Cone and also a governing role to evangelical concerns about the primacy and authority of Scripture.

This theological approach is possible because hermeneutical method assumes Hans-Georg Gadamer's notion of the separation between the horizons of the interpreter and of the text.[6] Before textual interpretation can begin, the interpreter must first understand and delineate the presuppositions she brings to the text.

My research tests whether bringing Cone's critique into conversation with the horizon of a White evangelical theologian, at various stages of a text-based interpretive process, can produce an evangelical theology of power that substantively differs from current evangelical systematics. This research requires a hermeneutical process that brings together critical reflection on evangelical presuppositions with the textual analysis of Scripture.

A HERMENEUTICAL PROCESS IN FOUR MOVEMENTS

This book's methodology follows four movements. Movement One entails illuminating and challenging the author's presuppositions as a starting point. In this movement, a researcher engages with an alternative tradition in conducting an empathetic-analytical reading. He seeks to understand the rational arguments made by others who oppose his position, in a way that allows for identifying errors in his argument, cohering ideas that he may not have considered, or identifying unwanted influences that correlate with his own ideas.

In Movement Two, the researcher conducts critical analyses of his historical theological tradition to understand the presuppositions he brings to the biblical text.[7]

Movement Three consists of eight detailed steps. First, recognizing that biblical text selection has hermeneutical issues, the researcher must clearly define the reasons for selecting particular texts. The second step involves a critical textual analysis, following Sailhamer, with attention to the text's final form, literary context, relation to the canon, genre, and "what it meant."[8] Any intertextual relationships are explored. Contra G. K. Beale,[9] this project adopts a minimalist approach to intertextuality. Where a clear connection exists between biblical texts—through a direct quote or incontrovertible allusion or echo—the discussion analyzes the differences and similarities between the texts' meanings and considers how these might affect the interpretation of the text under consideration. The researcher avoids using New Testament texts to interpret Old Testament texts. Once the textual analysis is complete in this second step, the scholar can make a preliminary interpretation.

Step three consists of challenging the researcher's preliminary findings with alternative interpretations of the text. Osborne describes this as the deductive stage of biblical interpretation.[10] Step four delineates secondary findings based on interaction with alternative interpretations.

Step five in Movement Three moves from textual interpretation to understanding the text's theological meaning and its broader significance for biblical-theological categories. The researcher must identify the text's primary theological foci based on the theological position of the biblical author or of the specific book where the text appears.[11] Step six places the text in dialogue with other texts in the canon that seem to oppose or alter the meaning of the core text.[12] The seventh step considers alternative theological assessments derived from the text, including its uses in theological reflection and its interpretation and place in comprehensive biblical theologies. Combining steps five through seven, the eighth and final step of Movement Three delineates the theological meaning of the chosen text in its biblical context.

Then Movement Four moves from understanding the biblical theology of selected texts to doing the constructive work of systematic theology.[13] This work places standard doctrinal categories in conversation with contemporary issues and makes ethical appropriations based on doctrinal conclusions. First, the researcher must determine which dogmatic categories speak most directly to the contemporary issue under consideration and delineate which traditional approach to the doctrine, of several options, he will place in dialogue with alternative voices. Next, the scholar places the chosen doctrines and traditional views in dialogue with alternative views that illuminate the contemporary issue being studied. The third step of Movement Four places the understanding of individual doctrines (derived from steps one and two) in conversation with the biblical study derived from Movement Three—allowing Scripture to play a "norming" role in the way doctrine is expressed. Step four accounts for the individual doctrines deriving from all the work up to this point.

The final step in Movement Four involves analyzing how the doctrines envisioned above can meet the requirements of appropriation. This step takes into account the final phase of Ricoeur's Hermeneutical Arch, David Clark's and Kevin Vanhoozer's discussion of the importance of sapientia in systematic theology, and Anthony Thiselton's use of "questions from life."[14] All of these considerations derive in some way from Gadamer, particularly his understanding of experience.[15] The primary work of Movement Four thus evaluates the degree to which the doctrine(s) can be appropriated and how their appropriation suggests their validity and sufficiency regarding the contemporary context.

This four-movement methodology is represented graphically in Table 0.1.

Table 0.1

Movements	Steps	Current Project	Part/Chapter Correlations
Movement One: Challenge presuppositions.	Engage with alternative tradition in empathetic-analytical reading.	Conduct empathetic-analytical reading of James Cone.	Part I
Movement Two: Challenge historical tradition.	Conduct critical analytical reading of presuppositions through personal identification and historical analysis.	Engage with reformed evangelical tradition using historical case studies: John Calvin, Jonathan Edwards, Charles Hodge, and Carl F. H. Henry.	Part II
Movement Three: Apply enlarged horizon from first two movements to chosen biblical text.	1. Select text.	Explain selection of Luke 4:16–30.	Part III, Chap. 8
	2. Conduct critical analysis of chosen biblical text.	Conduct analysis of Luke 4:16–30.	Part III, Chap. 9
	3. Challenge preliminary findings with alternative interpretations.	Offer alternative interpretations of Luke 4:16–30.	Part III, Chap. 9
	4. Conduct initial interpretation.	Offer preliminary interpretation of Luke 4:16–30.	Part III, Chap. 9
	5. Identify primary theological foci and significance of text.	Identify theological significance of Luke 4:16–30 in context of Lukan theology.	Part III, Chap. 9
	6. Place text in dialogue with other texts that indicate different theological perspectives or interpretive suggestions	Create dialogue between Luke 4:16–30, Household Codes (Ephesians 5:22–6:9, Colossians 3:18–4:1) and Romans 13.	Part III, Chap. 10

Movements	Steps	Current Project	Part/Chapter Correlations
	7. Consider theological interpretations in light of assessment of alternative biblical theologies.	Examine theological interpretations of the biblical texts placed in dialogue with Luke 4:16–30.	Part III, Chap. 11
	8. Reach final interpretation of theological and overall significance of biblical text for a canonical biblical theology.	Evaluate biblical interpretation from steps 1–7 and its relevance for an overall understanding of power and racism.	Part III, Chap. 11
Movement Four: Progress from biblical meaning to doctrinal and ethical constructions. (Note: Steps 2–4 in this study are not sequential; they are conducted simultaneously in chaps. 13–15 as each doctrinal category is considered.)	1. Select doctrines that relate to contemporary question and delineate those doctrines from perspective of researcher's tradition.	Examine doctrine of God in light of evangelical tradition that includes Calvin, Edwards, Hodge, and Henry.	Part IV, Chap. 12
	2. Place traditional understanding of each doctrine in dialogue with alternative views.	Place doctrinal tradition (identified in step 1) in dialogue with Cone.	Part IV, Chaps. 13–15
	3. Bring findings of steps 1–2 into conversation with biblical work of Movement Three, allowing biblical understanding to "norm" and mediate understanding derived thus far in Movement Four.	Place the conclusions of steps 1–2 of this movement in dialogue with biblical conclusions of Movement Three.	Part IV, Chaps. 13–15
	4. Use conclusions from steps 1–3 to articulate understanding of doctrine.	Examine conclusions of steps 1–3 for significance for theology of power and racism.	Part IV, Chaps. 13–15
	5. Delineate in what way the theology emerging from this analysis can be appropriated into church's life and work, how to move beyond theory to praxis, and how its implementation will bear witness to its own internal truth.	Address the ethical applications of the theology of power identified in step 4 of this movement.	Part IV, Chap. 16

This methodology is extensive, and the selection of verses, historical case studies, and doctrines cannot be fully comprehensive. For this reason, the work attempts to move toward a theology of power through intense interaction with a smaller set of scriptural, historical, theological, and philosophical data, demonstrating how these interpretative choices might generate new ways to construct a theology of power doctrinally and systematically. I hope that the methodology, interpretative choices, conversation partners, and their correspondence to the resulting doctrinal and systematic choices are so clear that other evangelical theologians can join a dialogue that adds to, clarifies, refutes, and elucidates the response of evangelical theology to the global issue of White supremacy.

With that in mind, part I turns to the work of Movement One: an empathetic-analytical reading of James Cone.

NOTES

1. Sailhamer, J. 1995 *Introduction to Old Testament Theology: A Canonical Approach.* Grand Rapids: Zondervan. 37.
2. Frei, H. 1974. *The Eclipse of Biblical Narrative: A Study in Eighteenth and Nineteenth Century Hermeneutics.* New Haven: Yale University.
3. Stiver, D. 2003. "Theological Method" in *Cambridge Companion to Postmodern Theology.* Edited by K. Vanhoozer. Cambridge: Cambridge University Press. 178.
4. Vanhoozer, K. 1994. "From Canon to Concept: 'Same' and 'Other' in the Relation Between Biblical and Systematic Theology." The Finlayson Memorial Lectures. 205.
5. Thiselton, A. 2007. *The Hermeneutics of Doctrine.* Grand Rapids: W. B. Eerdmans.
6. Gadamer, H. 2004. *Truth and Method.* 2nd Ed. New York: Continuum. 268–371.
7. Osborne, G. 1991. *The Hermeneutical Spiral: A Comprehensive Introduction to Biblical Interpretation.* Downers Grove: InterVarsity. 404–5.
8. Sailhamer, J. 1995: 36–187.
9. Beale, G. 2008. *We Become What We Worship: A Biblical Theology of Idolatry.* Downers Grove: IVP. 27–36.
10. Osborne, G. 1991: 12–14.
11. Osborne, G. 1991: 201–85.
12. Vanhoozer, K. 2005. *The Drama of Doctrine: A Canonical Linguistic Approach to Christian Theology.* Louisville: Westminster John Knox Press. 270–78; 1994: 105–10.
13. Vanhoozer, K. 1994: 96–124; Osborne, G. 1991: 286–317; Thiselton, A 2007: 3–109.
14. Ricoeur, P. 1996. *Interpretation Theory: Discourse and the Surplus of Meaning.* Fort Worth: Texas Christian University. 80–88; Clark, D. 2003. *To Know and Love God: Method for Theology.* Wheaton: Crossway. 87–88; Vanhoozer, K. 2005: 307–62; Thiselton, A. 2007: 3–109.
15. Gadamer, H. 2004: 341–55.

PART I

An Empathetic-Analytical Reading of James Cone

Chapter 1

Cone's Theological Agenda and Rhetorical Persona

The first movement toward an evangelical theology of power entails challenging the bias of evangelical theology through an empathetic-analytical reading of James Cone. Much in Cone's writing is antithetical to orthodox evangelical theology. His view of revelation, Christology, and soteriology may seem at direct odds with evangelical conceptions of the same. Given these and other differences, one might be tempted to launch into a critical debate with Cone that only serves to defend White evangelical theology against his attacks. However, bias is not challenged when evangelical theology moves to a defensive posture immediately.

A credible approach to this project attempts to understand Cone's position vis-à-vis Cone himself, his influences, and his conversation partners. Doing so does not require complete acquiescence to Cone's views, but those views must be understood first, for their potential to challenge the a priori views of evangelicalism that might impede an accurate interpretation of Scripture and a nuanced statement of evangelical doctrine. At this stage, however, examining Cone to challenge bias demands that a critical assessment of his theology must wait until later in this project. That is why I describe the approach as an empathetic instead of a critical analysis.

Because Cone frequently challenges White academics, how does this project engage Cone? Cone chastises White scholars for both their critical analysis of his work and their efforts to do Black Theology. This project attempts to turn Cone's critique inward to assess White evangelical theology, not to assess Black Liberation Theology per se. The work is intended to be what Cone himself might term an antiracist White evangelical theology.[1] Therefore, it pretends to be neither a work of Black theology nor a critical apologetic in opposition to it. Critical assessments of the compatibility of Cone's theology with White evangelical dogmatics occur later in this study, but these assessments reflect on the inner dynamics and definitions of White evangelical theology; they are not a direct attack on or acquiescence to the validity of Black theology. Ultimately the success or failure of this project rests on the degree to which Cone functions as a foil to evangelical bias, as opposed to being the source of an all-encompassing system into which evangelical theology is absorbed. An empathetic-analytical assessment of Cone and his work is the first step in this process.

Before analyzing Cone's views on doctrine, one must understand his broader agenda and his prominent rhetorical persona. These features drive both the way he is perceived and the way he envisions his theological work. This analysis helps challenge initial evangelical bias toward Cone.

Finally, Cone's theology cannot be understood apart from his interactions with his critics and conversation partners, in two respects. First, Cone's work often arises in response to the work of others and can only, therefore, be understood in light of these broader conversations. Second, as a founder of academic Black Liberation Theology, Cone deals with broad outlines and seldom gets distracted by details. He leaves to others the task of filling out his critique and moving it in constructive directions.

CONE'S AGENDA

Many scholars have misinterpreted the directness of Cone's agenda as evidence that his work is ideological. For example, Eric Lincoln, Herbert Edwards, Frederick Herzog, Paul Lehmann, and Helmut Gollwitzer—at a symposium on Cone's "Black Theology on Revolution, Violence, and Reconciliation"[2]—accused Cone of making ideological rather than theological arguments.[3] Much criticism revolves around Cone's political framing of his attack on racism. But Cone's point is that racial politics equals theology.

Because racial politics and theology are the same for Cone, he remains faithful to two parallel commitments: (1) his fight against White supremacy and (2) his efforts to create an apologetic for a Black theology. Cone works out this approach as an answer to Black nationalism, historians of Black religion, the prevailing myth of a universal theology, and a developing outline for a uniquely Black theology. Cone's fight against White supremacy and his apologetic for a Black theology began with his 1969 publication of *Black Theology and Black Power* and culminated in the 2018 posthumous publication of *Said I Wasn't Gonna Tell Nobody: The Making of a Black Theologian*. Because of their enduring nature, both of Cone's commitments require further consideration.

An Effort to Transform White Society

One can easily assume that Cone has nothing to say to White society. His critics often imagine Cone as a Black nationalist who has no intention of addressing White theologians.[4] This image should be dismissed for two reasons. First, Black theologians who have critiqued Cone's work see his definite attempt to reach back and address White audiences. Indeed, they are critical of his use of White theologians,[5] systematic schemas, and neo-orthodox methodology[6] and—per Black historians of religion and Black nationalists—of his too-adamant defense of Christianity as a Black religion. And second, Cone himself affirms that he is addressing White society. In his introduction to *Black Theology and Black Power*, he states, "This is a word to the oppressor, a word to Whitey."[7]

Both the recognition of Cone's critics and his own affirmation demonstrate that Cone's work was not limited to the Black community; he also had hopes of transforming White society. He remained skeptical about having any positive effect on the latter. Regardless, Cone continued to call White theologians to see the detrimental effects of White supremacy on both the White supremacist and the oppressed Black community. Critically, then, Cone did have something to say to Whites and therefore cannot be ignored on the grounds that he has relevance only to Black Americans.

White Church as Antichrist

Not only did Cone address White society in his attack on White supremacy, but he also challenged White supremacy within the White Church. Cone identifies the White Church as the "antichrist."[8] Before moving to his broader argument, consideration should be given to how Cone defines "antichrist."[9]

Cone identifies as antichrist any institution that "is the enemy of Christ" and equates it loosely with the biblical concept of "the principalities and powers."[10] Cone's use of the term mirrors its use by the early reformers and Anabaptists. Martin Luther, for example, often referred to the pope and the Catholic Church as the "antichrist," while Anabaptists tended to consider individuals and institutions as "guilty by association" with Satan, the "antichrist." In both instances, the antichrist is a real, current evil: one of the principalities and powers of this world.[11] What is noteworthy is that "antichrist" has a distinctly non-eschatological meaning for Cone.

He further defines the "enemy of Christ." Cone considers Christ's position as a suffering Jew to be hermeneutically equivalent to the oppression of Black people. Through this distinction, Cone identifies the Church of Christ as ontologically Black. If Christ is Black, and his church is Black, then the White Church's racism identifies it as an enemy of Christ. Within Cone's logical framework, at least, this argument justifies applying the label "antichrist" to the White Church.[12]

Once Cone's use of "antichrist" is understood, one can understand how he can argue that the White Church has an errant ecclesiology, ethics, and history. These arguments further Cone's critique of White supremacy in the White Church.

White Church as Anti-Church

Cone defines the Church as "the people of God, whose primary task is that of being Christ to the world by proclaiming the message of the gospel (kerygma), by rendering services of liberation (diakonia), and by being itself a manifestation of the nature of the new society (koinonia)."[13] Elsewhere he identifies how the White Church violates all three functional criteria.

First, he says the White Church fails to proclaim the true message of the gospel. Cone understands the Church's kerygma to be the message of *Christus Victor*: Christ victorious, through his death on the cross, over the evil powers oppressing the world. Thus, he argues that the Church is required to preach freedom to the oppressed and to proclaim that "the old powers of white racism are writhing in final agony."[14] He sees the White Church's failure as resulting both from its periodic preaching in support of White supremacy and from its continued silence about racism. For Cone, preaching must require its hearers to take a side; there can be no room for equivocation on issues of justice if the message is truly kerygmatic.[15]

His second argument is that the White Church fails in its service. Diakonia, he says, consists in the Church "joining Christ in his work of liberation."[16] For this Cone leans heavily on his understanding of atonement. Christ's victory over evil is significant as an act of liberation for those who suffer from the evil of oppression. If Jesus focuses his work on liberation, then the Church's service must mirror Christ's in liberating the oppressed from the old evil powers. The primary contemporary context of the Church as racism arising from White supremacy. Thus, the Church's diakonia must entail service that attacks racism at its source and places the Church in solidarity with the oppressed Black community. This service is made all the more important by the fact that the war against evil continues.[17]

Finally, Cone argues that the White Church fails in its fellowship. He envisions koinonia as fellowship that projects what the Church proclaims to do and "what it hopes to accomplish" in the world. For Cone, "the Church's preaching and service are meaningful only insofar as the Church itself is a manifestation of the preached Word."[18] Therefore, for a church to be an expression of the true Church, it must ensure the holiness of all its members. Cone defines "holy" is "a community that has accepted Christ's acceptance of us," implying a church that can accept all people. This definition is evident from his previous identification of the Church as "not bounded by standards of race, class, or occupation. . . . Rather the Church is God's suffering people." For the Church to be the Church, its fellowship must include the oppressed and those who have found solidarity with the oppressed.[19]

To maintain the holiness of this fellowship, the Church must ask, "Who in the community does not live according to the Spirit of Christ?"[20] In its application of discipline, Cone says, the White Church has too quickly defined unholy acts in terms of culturally bound views of individual morality—but seldom defines them in terms of racism. The continued existence of racists in White congregations means that the White Church is tainted by the unholiness of racist members and its refusal to deal with them.[21] Thus, Cone finds the White Church in violation of all three functions required of a true Church: kerygma, diakonia, and koinonia.

Cone further argues that the White Church is lacking both ethically and historically. Ethically the White Church has "enshrined immorality" in its defense of and silence about racism. Cone emphasizes both ethical praxis and latent racism in claiming that the White Church has failed to exercise "moral leadership and moral example" beyond passing a few resolutions. The White Church, he says, also has such a long history of racism that immoral practices have become latent within ecclesial structures. Thus, Cone concurs with Kyle Haselden: "We must ask whether our morality is itself immoral, whether our codes of righteousness are, when applied to the Negro, a violation and distortion of the Christian ethic."[22]

White Church as Racist

The latent racism and ethical immorality within the contemporary White Church directly result from a pattern of White supremacy throughout its history. Cone mounts his fullest assault here. He points out that White Church leaders wrote books defending slavery and that even abolitionist churches did not accept Blacks as equal to Whites. He also points out that many early preachers and missionaries owned slaves.

During the Civil Rights era, the Church did little better, preferring gradualism and status quo arguments over supporting Martin Luther King Jr. Those who joined the movement did so belatedly. While many White churches eventually came around to King, they did so only after the Black Power Movement arose. When Cone was writing *Black Theology and Black Power*, the White Church continued to oppose Black freedom: for example, by condemning the violence of rioters in Detroit and LA without offering sustained criticism of the violence Whites had perpetrated against Blacks during slavery, Jim Crow, the long reign of lynching laws in the South, and the abject poverty and ghetto culture imposed on northern Blacks by housing discrimination and city policies. Cone contends that this continued pattern of support for the "rule of law," calls for gradualism, and direct participation in racist acts have become so ingrained in the White Church that it fails to recognize what they are—forms of antichrist-like behavior.[23]

Cone concludes that the White Church "is a chaplaincy to sick middle-class egos. It stands (or sits) condemned by its very whiteness."[24] Therefore, he has built a case demonstrating not only that society is racist but that the very essence of the contemporary White Church is racist.

White Theology as Racist

Cone does not stop there. He also finds racism rooted in White theology and its formulations.

Cone's first reason for believing that White theology reflects White supremacy is that White theologians remain silent on issues of race. Their silence reflects several realities. White theologians can practice their profession without having to deal with race, in either their work or their lives. Dealing with race also stirs up uncomfortable guilt among White theologians. Similarly, Cone believes that many White theologians will not engage on questions of race because they are uncomfortable dealing with "Black Rage." Finally, most White theologians are not ready to discuss the radical "redistribution of wealth and power" that honest theological engagement with racism would demand.[25]

Ultimately, for Cone, silence about race is the most egregious error found in White theological discourse. If truly faithful theology speaks to the Church about its own practices in contemporary society, then White theology cannot be described as faithful theology when it remains silent on the question of race.[26]

White theology's close identification with social structures is another reason that Cone offers to substantiate how White supremacy is embedded in White theology. Cone is not the only scholar to make this claim. Similar claims are found in Nathan Hatch's *The Democratization of American Christianity*, Mark A. Noll's *God and Race in American Politics*, Simon Maimela's essay "Theology and Politics in South Africa: A Black Critique" (in *Proclaim Freedom to My People*), and Walter Brueggemann's essay "Relinquishing White Supremacism" (in *Tenacious Solidarity: Biblical Provocations on Race, Religion, Climate, and the Economy*).[27] Cone cites two factors underlying support for the social status quo: (1) "law and order" as a religious moral standard and (2) the compartmentalization of American theology. Regarding the former, Cone asserts, "In a culture which rewards 'patriots' and punishes 'dissenters,' it is difficult to be prophetic and easy to perform one's duties in the light of the objectives of the nation as a whole."[28] As for the latter, he argues that White theologians compartmentalize and avoid contemporary political issues because of anxiety about appearing to be dissenters. If they can justify focusing on the latest European philosophical-theological trend, they can justify race as being unrelated to contemporary theological pursuits.[29]

Another reason Cone claims that White theologians perpetuate racist systems is the inconsistency of White theologians who occasionally deal with race. This inconsistency is particularly true of theologians who support gradualism.[30] As a group, such theologians gravitate toward compromised solutions or paternalistic pity. Cone lists James Herzog as "a prominent exception" to the rule, but on the whole, his critique of White theologians hardened over time.

Cone also argues that White theology remains beholden to White supremacy because it has failed to engage with Black theologians and culture. He despairs, "There are almost no references to Black scholars or other people of color in any of the writings of major White theologians"; as an example, he points to Reinhold Niebuhr, who "did occasionally talk about race" but who does not cite Black intellectuals in his work. Cone does not ask White theologians to always agree with Black scholars, but he does insist they include Black intellectuals in the discussion. Doing so would foster greater empathy for both the arguments of Black intellectuals and the suffering of the Black poor.[31]

Focus also underpins racism in White theology. According to Cone, White theologians who take an interest in the oppressed have pointed their critique at class and economics and away from race. They have tended to prefer conversations with Latin American liberation theologians versus engaging with Black theology. As a result, they often overlook the racist elements of their theological traditions.[32]

Cone objects to the way White theology leans toward philosophical abstraction and away from concrete contemporary issues. He mentions how White theology in the 1960s and 1970s obsessed over questions of "the Death of God" but displayed almost total disregard for the question of race. He also disparages White theology's insistence on splitting theology from ethics in a way that suggests that ethical discourse is not theology—thus relegating theology to abstraction and casting ethics down to a lower level of intellectual respectability.

Finally, Cone sees a lack of praxis-focused theology as central to racism in White theology. He asserts that a new White theology must "come out of an antiracist political struggle,"[33] and he envisions theology as focused on "doing," both on behalf of and with the oppressed community. White theology's insistence on universal theology and objections to a particular theology of oppressed Black people are symptomatic of the racist afflictions of contemporary White theologians. Specifically, Cone critiques the many times White theology has abandoned its historic commitment to objectivity to use theological and doctrinal rhetoric to defend racist acts. These acts condemn White theology by placing it on the side of the oppressor, emphasize the hypocrisy of its claims to objectivity, and moot its opposition to theology derived from a politically focused praxis.

All of these factors, Cone says, point to a critical failure on the part of White theology. It has failed to generate an antiracist theology that sharply corrects its past errors. Cone asserts, "The development of a hard-hitting antiracist theology by White religion scholars is long overdue."[34] He calls on White theologians to engage with his work toward developing this antiracist theology. His critique suggests that evangelical theology should examine the extent to which it has been silent on race and has acquiesced to evangelical doctrine in defense of racism; it should also examine the degree to which evangelical doctrine might be subverted in this way. Should this analysis determine that Cone's critique is true for evangelicalism, then evangelical theologians should further ask to what degree an antiracist agenda might inform the broader evangelical theological enterprise.

The latter point is crucial for insisting on a reexamination of evangelical doctrine in light of power, privilege, and White supremacy—and a reexamination of doctrinal formulas in light of past misuse for racist purposes and how their resulting churches do not personify an antiracist theology or praxis. While one may not commonly think of doctrinal integrity as being proven by practical applications, evangelical scholars have suggested this connection. Kevin Vanhoozer and Anthony Thiselton are just two examples.[35] Thiselton argues that doctrine, to be functional, must be considered from the standpoint of "questions that arise" and is therefore primarily a hermeneutical task. If Vanhoozer and Thiselton are correct in stressing the importance of doctrine's connection to its real-life applications. In that case, one might suggest that doctrinal statements used for racist ends might either lack a proper language flowing out of "questions that arise" or in fact might not have the proper articulation, internal focus, or systematic distinctions to generate an "antiracist" theology. If so, further exploration is not only helpful but necessary to understand Cone's assumptions about the connections between White evangelical theology and racism, as well as the ways evangelical doctrine might be better articulated, systematized, and applied to exclude racist and White supremacist praxis.

An Apologetic for a Truly Black Christianity

Cone's critique of White supremacy is not his only focus. He also articulates an apologetic for a Black Christianity.

What White theologians often miss is Cone's attempt to preserve Black Christianity for a new generation of Black Americans. The Black Power Movement, along with other countercultural movements of the 1960s and 1970s, launched a direct attack on Christianity and the Church. The Black Church and its White counterparts faced a similar problem during this time: both struggled to avoid losing a new generation that was gravitating increasingly toward either atheism or other countercultural forms of religious expression. Some elements of the White Church engaged with the 1960s drug culture and participated in the emergence of the Jesus People Movement, embodied in the founding of Calvary Chapel and the emergence of the contemporary megachurch movement within North American evangelicalism.[36] Following the lead of the National Conference of Colored Churchmen, Cone launched an apologetic project that asserted a truly Black Christianity against the Black Power Movement's insistence that Christianity was "the white man's religion."[37] He did so in conversation with Black nationalists and historians of Black religion, and in opposition to Black self-hate.

Answering Black Nationalism

As Cone worked to affirm the Christian nature of Black power, he immediately confronted Black nationalists' vehement opposition to Christianity. The Black Power Movement saw abandoning Christianity as necessary to the revolution. The movement's early antecedents (like Franz Fanon and Malcolm X) and later popularizers (like Stokely Carmichael, the Black Panther Party, and the Black Arts Movement) were unanimous in opposing Christianity. Malcolm X followed this belief into the Nation of Islam, while Fanon and many Black Panthers embraced socialist Marxism. Black Arts Movement followers often preferred to recover African religions and moved toward Pan-Africanism. By 1969, when Cone wrote *Black Theology and Black Power*, the Black Power Movement was emerging as the new strategy for Black liberation—eclipsing and rejecting the Civil Rights Movement and its connections to organized Christianity.

The sentiments of the Black Power Movement are captured succinctly by Don Lee in a work of Black literary criticism. Lee's 1971 *Dynamite Voices: Black Poets of the 1960s* showcases emerging Black poets and illustrates their connection to the contemporary concerns of young Blacks who saw themselves as part of a revolutionary struggle for Black liberation. Lee's work establishes the difficulty Cone faced in defending Black Christianity at the time. Describing the work of Norman Jordan, Lee states that "No Hiding Place" reflects the poet's thought on the castration of the Black man while he prayed to an alien God:

> I Kneeled
> to pray
> and split
> the seam
> in the rear
> of my pants
> Letting God see
> The blood stain
> In the crotch
> Of my
> God-Damn shorts.

Lee sums up the common opinion of the Black Power Movement: "Traditionally, Blacks have looked to the 'living Word' for hope and consolation, while the man used it as proof that 'whatever is, is right.' Blacks have been admonished to absolve themselves of all evil—What evil? Whose evil? We all know what adherence to this philosophy led to: Christianization, then enslavement and death."[38]

This emerging anti-Christian element in Black nationalism led Cone to develop an apologetic defense of the role of Christianity in the Black struggle for freedom.[39] His approach accepts without argument all of the Black Power Movement's social strategies and nationalistic philosophies while arguing that the liberation of Black people is central to a uniquely Black Christianity and that this Black Christianity has a uniquely Black theology. He bases his argument on the historical development of Black Christianity, the identification of a theology "from below," and an insistence on the particularity of theology.

Cone views the unique context of slavery and Jim Crow segregation as critical in understanding the distinction between Black and White forms of Christianity. He primarily asserts that as Blacks encountered the Gospel, they interpreted it in a way unique to their circumstances. Oppressed Black slaves rightly understood the Gospel as a gospel of liberation. White Christians, situated in the role of oppressor, missed this essential element in Christianity. Black Christianity is thus distinct from White Christianity. Therefore, Christianity, as understood by the Black Church, cannot be viewed as the "white man's religion"; rather, it is consistent with the Black Power Movement.[40]

Cone further argues that a methodology recovering theology as a theology "from below" is essential to the theologian's task. Note that Cone's concept of theology "from below" is similar to that found in Baptist, Evangelical, Pietist, Anabaptist, and other Free Church traditions, which rely on sermons, confessional statements, hymnody, and other popular religious material to ascertain their group's theological distinctions. A theology "from below" was a critical argument in defeating the idea that Black Christianity was an outgrowth of White American and European professional "theologies of power." Many thought the Black Church lacked theology—that either it was purely a folk religion[41] or it had adopted White European theology without question or variation. Cone argues that because theology is often embedded in the ecclesial practices of faith communities, a unique theology can be recovered from the Black Church's music, poetry, art, sermons, and speeches; such a theology is independent of and distinguishable from White theology. In this way, Cone posits a truly Black theology independent of White theology and subverts the argument that the Black Church is enslaved to an oppressive White theological system.[42]

Cone also pushes against the commonly held notion of a universal theology and directly attacks the myth of theological universalism in favor of particularity. Cone argues that what is called "theology" and assumed to apply to all Christianity, regardless of race or culture, is the particular theology of White Americans and Europeans. Cone denies White theology any privileged status as the universal, objective expression of Christianity that must therefore be the theology of both the Black and White Churches. Therefore, both Black and White theologies are indebted to their own racial and cultural backgrounds and form distinct theologies. Far from insisting that both are therefore true, relative to their context, Cone contends that Black theology comes closer to the Gospel's truth than White theology because the Bible itself records the life of an oppressed people delivered by an oppressed Savior. Thus, true theology must come from oppressed communities. In this way, Cone counters Black nationalist arguments by asserting that the Black Church's particular theology is distinct from "universal theology" because of the location and interpretation of the oppressed Black community. Black theology is real, distinct, true, and therefore capable of moving forward the Black Power Movement and the liberation of Black people.[43]

Cone's apologetic was not merely an intellectual exercise; he worked it out in actual dialogue with Black nationalists within the Black Power Movement. He met with members of the Black Panther Party and, at the request of LeRoi Jones (Amari Baraka), led a workshop on religion at the Congress of African Peoples.[44] Cone was vigilant in presenting his apologetic for a uniquely Black Christianity; however, most Black nationalists remained unconvinced.

Answering Historians of Black Religion

If Black nationalists remained unconvinced, so did Black historians of religion. Members of the Society for the Study of Black Religion, including its preeminent founder, Charles H. Long, were critical of Cone's work. Cone summarizes Long's criticism: "Theology is a Western concept, created by Europeans to dominate and denigrate non-Western peoples, and is completely alien to the black religious experience."[45] Cone sees this position as shared by other members of the society, including J. Deotis Roberts and Gayraud Wilmore.

Cone's main rebuttal insists that Black theology differs from White theology in not only content but methodology. He affirms that "Black theology is a language about God that comes out of Black experience, and its meaning is found in its style. This marks the difference from White methodology."[46] Cone argues that Black theology is unique in privileging Black experience and Black forms of speech and in using a writing style unique to Black culture. Out of the latter Cone develops the idea that form equals content.[47] Thus, in both style and content, Black theology is methodologically distinct and owes nothing to European theology. Additionally, Cone criticizes Black historians of religion for focusing too intently on esoteric definitions of theology and religion and forgetting their subjects, the oppressed Black community.[48]

Answering Black Self-Hate

Cone's apologetic moves beyond academic debate to include the whole Black community. He developed Black theology to attack self-hate within the community: "I wasn't writing for rational reasons based on library research." He says, "I was writing out of my experience, speaking for the dignity of black people in a white supremacist world. I was on a mission to transform self-loathing Negro Christians into black-loving revolutionary disciples of the Black Christ."[49]

Cone's attack on Black self-loathing begins by assuring Blacks that they do not need to aspire to be White to be genuinely Christian.[50] He also affirms that God privileges the oppressed Black community over White oppressors and loves Black people because of, not despite, their blackness.[51]

Not only does God love Black people; but God has intentionally, through the suffering of Jesus, identified with their suffering. In this way, Jesus and God have become ontologically Black. One must avoid prejudging this argument; I only mention it at this point to highlight Cone's use of a Black Christ to thwart some Blacks' understanding that God is primarily White and must therefore love Whites more than Blacks. Cone attempts to break the prevailing imagery of a White God who privileges Whiteness over Blackness by instead giving the Black community a way to see God that fully affirms who they are in their Blackness.

White theologians can miss these apologetic elements of Cone's theology if they fail to understand that at least some of what they oppose in Cone's theology was necessary to preserve Christianity for future Black leaders and to help Blacks take pride in both their Blackness and their Christianity. Cone's efforts are similar to evangelical efforts to defend evangelical beliefs against both secular humanism and liberal Christianity, as well as attempts to argue for a distinct evangelical worldview to encourage evangelicals to persevere in their faith against attacks from outside groups. Seen in this way, evangelicals should at least sympathize with Cone's apologetic agenda, if not its actual content.

CONE'S RHETORICAL PERSONA

Having identified Cone's primary theological agenda as fighting White supremacy and creating an apologetic for a uniquely Black Christianity, I offer one further matter critical to an empathetic analysis of Cone. This section examines the revolutionary rhetorical persona he employs to execute his theological project.

Prophetic

Only Andre Johnson directly considers Cone's rhetorical persona.[52] An academic rhetorician, Johnson identifies Cone's rhetoric as directly connected to a prophetic rhetorical style within the Black prophetic tradition. Thus, for Johnson, Cone takes on the persona of a prophet. Johnson defines prophetic rhetoric: "What I mean by prophetic rhetoric is discourse grounded in the sacred, rooted in a community experience that offers a critique of existing communities and traditions by charging and challenging society to live up to the ideals they espoused, while offering celebration, encouragement and hope for a brighter future."[53]

Johnson's assessment does fall short in two important ways. First, if prophetic rhetoric is directed at critiquing an existing community, then Johnson's definition would only halfway apply to Cone's work. Cone, no doubt, is attacking the White community and White supremacists, and perhaps his work is prophetic in that way. However, the White community is not his only audience. One struggles to see how Cone's work is prophetic for the Black community. He offers no sustained critique of the Black community, so his prophetic persona only emerges if his work is read as primarily directed at the White community. Cone's persona, if it exists at all, must be found in a character that both critiques White society and liberates the Black community.

Second, Johnson deals with rhetorical patterns but avoids clearly defining what he means by "persona." Johnson's argument makes no clear distinction between argumentation patterns and Cone's portrayal of himself as a particular role or persona. Parts of Cone's arguments fit Johnson's prophetic style, but they lack any cohesive pattern that would suggest Cone is trying to project the persona of a prophet. While Cone does fit at least some of Johnson's prophetic criteria, one finds it hard to demonstrate that these touchpoints translate into a prophetic persona. For Johnson's work to hold up, it would need a formal framework for determining the use of persona, which it lacks.

Revolutionary

While not dealing with Cone at all, B. L. Ware and William A. Linkugel[54] do give a formalistic definition of a rhetorical persona and use it successfully to demonstrate that Marcus Garvey adopted the persona of Moses to advance his Black nationalist campaign. Their categories, when applied to Cone, suggest not a prophetic persona but a revolutionary persona.

Ware and Linkugel define rhetorical persona as consisting of two main forms—the immanent and the transcendent—from which the persona arises. The immanent form considers how the person (or the person's actions) can be compared to something else. One fits into the category shared by the persona one portrays. The transcendent form is how the persona brings to mind or identifies with a particular archetypal image.

Beyond the comparative nature of these forms are the particulars of speech and argumentation by which the person accesses the persona: phrases, words, idioms, or actions that relate the actor to the character and thereby subsume the actor and animate the character. Finally, participation refers to how the actor uses the forms and the particulars to bring the character to life in their rhetorical work. This understanding from Ware and Linkugel suggests ways that Cone uses a revolutionary persona to advance his rhetorical style.

Immanent Form

If the immanent form requires first that the actor, in this case Cone, be concretely identifiable as like the thing they wish to personify, then an academic theologian might seem as far away from a revolutionary as anyone can get. However, this assumption fails to understand the various ways in which individuals participated in the Black revolution.

Peniel E. Joseph's article "The Black Power Movement: State of the Field" assesses the current state of research into the Black Power Movement and Black revolutionary nationalism in the late 1960s and 1970s.[55] Joseph recognizes a growing consensus that Black revolutionary nationalism was more diverse than previously understood and that followers found varying ways to identify with the movement. The most prominent differences were between political revolutionary movements like the Black Panthers and cultural revolutionary groups like the Black Arts Movement. The former created programs and took action to assert Black power and Black self-determination. The Panthers' breakfast programs, Black consciousness educational classes, and political actions, including the carrying of guns into the California State Assembly, exemplified this type of Black revolutionary.

Black cultural revolutionaries, however, created specific Black spaces within cultural disciplines to reclaim those spaces. James T. Stewart, in an essay entitled "Black Revolutionary Artists," makes the case for the revolutionary nature of Black cultural nationalism:

> The point of the whole thing is that we must emancipate our minds from Western values and standards. . . . We must try to shape the thinking of our people. We must goad our people by every means, remembering as Ossie Davis stated: that the task of the Negro [sic, black] writer is revolutionary by definition. He must view his role vis-à-vis white Western civilization, and from this starting point in his estrangement begin to make new definitions founded on his own culture—on definite black values.[56]

Don Lee also affirms the Black Arts Movement's attempt to carve out a separatist space for Black Americans: "We've always had writers who happened to be Black, but the Sixties brought a new and universal definition of the Black man who chooses words as part of his lifestyle. Lifestyle is essentially what the new writers are about, a quest to legitimize and define their place and space."[57] Both Lee and Stewart highlight the degree to which Black cultural nationalism was both separatist and revolutionary. The artists of the Black Arts Movement saw themselves as revolutionaries who were very much part of the Black Power revolution.

By understanding the revolutionary nature of cultural Black nationalism, one can then compare Cone's efforts to create a Black theology with Black artists' efforts to create revolutionary Black poetry, theater, music, and literature. Cone was contemporaneous with a cultural movement that viewed participants as revolutionaries. If theology, philosophy, and other liberal arts form part of culture, then Cone's efforts in theology are like LeRoi Jones's and Lee's efforts in poetry. Black revolutionary artists like Jones and Lee also figure directly in Cone's theological work; he quotes Lee's *Dynamite Voices* and authors from Jones' edited anthology *Black Fire*.[58] In this way, Cone participates in the immanent form of a Black revolutionary.

Transcendent Form

If Cone fits the definition of the immanent persona, does he then connect with the transcendent notion of a revolutionary? Cone fits the transcendent revolutionary image through connections with two sources that define the archetype of the rebel in his day: Fanon and Camus, both of whom Cone quotes extensively.[59] Quoting Fanon ties Cone into a literature of rebellion that was central to both the political and cultural arms of the Black Power Movement. Pan-Africanism, African liberation movements, and Fanon's writing formed the central image of what rebellion could be, in America and on the African continent. Cone's use of Fanon tied Cone directly to the pan-African revolution in the same way that visions of Fanon tied the Black Panthers, Malcolm X, and other Black revolutionaries to actual revolution. By summoning Fanon into their cultural canon, American Black revolutionaries—including Cone—participated in the Black African freedom fighter archetype.

On the other hand, Camus provides the very definition of a rebel in his work by the same name.[60] Camus and French existentialism had only minor influence on Cone's work, which only substantiates his use of Camus to create a persona rather than building a fully engaged, theological dialogue with Camus' philosophy of absurdity. Cone quotes the definition of a rebel from early in Camus' work and does not reflect Camus' subsequent focus or conclusions on revolution. Otherwise, Cone uses Camus to obtain quotes from Fyodor Dostoevsky; Cone mentions the philosophy of absurdity just once, and then only negatively, as lacking any real answers to the human predicament. Cone's existentialism is evident, but he develops it by way of Paul Tillich's theological existentialism, not French existentialism. For example, Cone mentions Jean-Paul Sartre but does not deal with his philosophy. Like those of other theologians, Camus' ideas serve as prooftexts for Cone.

That said, by using Camus' definition of the rebel to assert that the Black man must rebel and that Black theology must support this rebellion, Cone places himself squarely among intellectual rebels who appear throughout Camus' lengthy literary treatise on revolt. Cone's use of Camus, like his use of Fanon, places Cone not in the archetypal prophet role but that of the rebel who, in Camus' words, "experiences a feeling of revulsion at the infringement of his rights and a complete and spontaneous loyalty to certain aspects of himself. Thus, he implicitly brings into play a standard of values so far from being gratuitous that he is prepared to support it no matter what the risks."[61] Camus' words could easily be appropriated for Cone; to the extent that Cone lives into the archetypal image of the rebel, he can be said to embrace the revolutionary persona.

Then how does Cone's persona fit the particulars of a revolutionary, albeit the cultural revolutionary type identified above? Where "revolutionary" has a purely political and militarized connotation, one finds it difficult to identify Cone as a revolutionary. While the political nature of revolution is apparent in Cone's work, he makes no distinction between the political and the theological; he views the writing and teaching of Black theology as a liberating political act, even in its purest academic form. See, for example, Cone's article "Christian Faith and Political Praxis."[62]

Cone as Revolutionary Archetype

To suggest that Cone exhibits both immanent and transcendent forms of the revolutionary persona is only partially helpful. He also must exhibit particular forms that identify him with the persona. Camus' definition, with assistance from Fanon, identifies three essential criteria that identify rebels: (1) righteous indignation at the violation of their rights; (2) self-awareness that overcomes a false self-image that previously allowed oppression; and (3) an alternate concept of life beyond oppression that validates using all necessary means to violently break from the present system toward self-determination.

Black revolutionary nationalism is best understood in the context of Fanon's work and its subsequent popularization in the pan-African liberation movements of the 1960s and 1970s. His vision passed on genetically through the US Black Power Movement's reading and appropriation of his work. His vision, therefore, in specific ways, shapes Camus' general rule that the revolutionary envisions a different future. For Cone's generation, the revolutionary vision is Fanon's, encapsulated in his conclusion to *The Wretched of the Earth*: "For Europe, for ourselves and for humanity, comrades, we must make a new start, develop a new way of thinking, and endeavor to create a new man." Fanon suggests that the task is nothing short of "starting over a new history of man."[63] For Cone's audience, the revolutionary was someone who completely rejected the status quo and offered that new "history of man," that "new way of thinking." The revolutionary was also willing to achieve this task "by any means necessary."

Fanon would not have approved of Cone's insistence on maintaining Christianity within his theological system. In fact, Fanon called for the abandonment of all religions in the interest of his new humanity. But Cone's departure from Fanon does not mean that Cone is not adopting a revolutionary persona. His insistence on the uniqueness of Black theology, despite the many White and Black scholars who objected to his logic, is further evidence of his attempt to hold on to the Black revolutionary persona at all costs. However, it might be more accurate to state that Cone wielded the persona of a revolutionary, albeit with a forced logic at times that rendered his participation in the persona suspect within the Black revolutionary movement.

How then does Cone fit the three particulars of the revolutionary archetype? First, the vast majority of his work identifies his righteous anger and revulsion at White supremacy and racism; the theme defines and unifies his entire intellectual corpus. Second, Cone's work illuminates both the awakening of his Black consciousness and the need to build the self-consciousness of the entire Black community. Finally, Cone's demarcation of a Black theology, wholly independent of White European theology or history, is consistent with Fanon's call to create completely new systems of thinking.

If Cone fits these criteria, what indications of clear intentionality or argumentation indicate that Cone is knowingly playing the role of revolutionary? Space does not permit going through each of Cone's writings. However, Cone's assessment of his theological legacy in *Said I Wasn't Gonna Tell Nobody* creates a window into his thoughts on this matter.

In that work, he clarifies his participation in the first two categories shaping the revolutionary persona. He recounts his righteous indignation early in his autobiography: "Detroit exploded and so did I. My explosion shook me at the core of my racial identity, killing the 'Negro' in me and resurrecting my black self. I felt a *black fire* burning inside me, so hot I couldn't control it any longer."[64] By referring to "black fire" and using italics, Cone seems to associate himself with *Black Fire: An Anthology of Afro-American Writing*, edited by Amiri Baraka and Larry Neal.[65] Cone knew Baraka personally and quoted from this work, an extensive collection of the writings of cultural and political Black power revolutionaries. Alluding to the title suggests that at the earliest part of his career, Cone was not only assessing but identifying with the Black Power movement.

He also clearly articulates this explosive energy using language that elicits Black revolution and his particular role in it:

> I knew that Black Power advocates, like Stokely Carmichael, and militant black ministers, like Albert Cleage, had no interest in debating white religious scholars or well-schooled white ministers. But I did! It was time for me to join my black brothers and sisters in the fight for justice. . . . It was time to turn white man's theology against him and make it speak for the liberation of black people. Militant Negro ministers needed a theology that could liberate their minds from any dependence on white theology.[66]

Cone's anger—his sense that he had to "join my black brothers and sisters" in the revolution—fit Camus' first criterion of what it takes to create a rebel.

Cone also shows his understanding of Camus' second criterion: self-consciousness and the pursuit of others' self-consciousness. In Cone's chapter titled "Removing My Mask"—a likely reference to Fanon's *Black Skins, White Masks*[67]—Cone references the emergence of his Black consciousness. He also recognizes his responsibility for instilling Black consciousness in the Black community. "Now with Black Power," he writes, "everything was at stake—the affirmation of black humanity in a white supremacist world. I was ready to die for black dignity." Camus' fully self-conscious and self-affirming rebel is part of Cone's rhetorical repertoire.

Cone also intentionally engages in Camus' final criterion, a complete remaking of the system oppressing the rebel: "I was not interested in making an academic point about theology; rather, I was issuing a manifesto against whiteness and for blackness in an effort to liberate Christians from white supremacy." In Black theology, Cone primarily sought to create a theological space, adrift from White European theology, to recast the Gospel in the image of the Black Church and create a mirror for White Christians to see how White supremacy is embedded within the White Church. Cone uses the language of "antichrist," claims that salvation comes only through the oppressed, envisions a Black Christ, and condemns White theologians for racism even while using their arguments to his advantage. Whether critics accept that Black theology represents a uniquely separatist space within theological discourse is inconsequential, because Cone intends to portray it as such. Cone's Black theology holds a strategic place similar to that of the Black Arts Movement in carving out room for Black thought and suppressing White supremacy.

In this way, Cone embodies the final criterion of a rebel. He is creating a new world: "a new humanity" and a "new way of thinking" that reverses the power structures in academic theology and creates a place where White theologians cannot dominate the discourse or methods. Cone's Black theology might be one of the most effective and enduring strategies within the pantheon of Black cultural revolutionary action. His work has outlasted the Black Arts Movement by several decades—at least as an intentionally separatist space—and birthed other intellectual movements dedicated to theological assessments of power, including womanist theology, queer theology, and other particularist theological pursuits.

If these examples fitting Camus criteria still leave room for doubt, perhaps Cone's own words bolster the argument: "It is incumbent upon us as black people to become 'revolutionaries for blackness,' rebelling against all who enslave us. With Marcus Garvey, we say: 'any sane man, race or nation that desires freedom must first of all think in terms of blood.'"[68] Cone was unlikely to self-identify as a prophet. But his work reiterates both his support of and his place in the Black cultural revolution.

Ware and Linkugel's formalistic approach to persona readily identifies Cone as a revolutionary, in both the imminent and transcendent forms. And he fits the particulars of the rebel archetype as articulated in Camus and Fanon, as demonstrated by his direct participation in these particulars in his theological writing.

A BLACK REVOLUTIONARY AND WHITE EVANGELICAL THEOLOGIANS

The question that remains is how Cone's revolutionary persona is important to White evangelical theology. White evangelical theologians must understand that Cone's language and participation in revolutionary rhetoric and movements form part of a nuanced, often overlooked perspective. His work serves purposes both apologetic and practical. His apologetic purpose was to salvage the Christian faith within the emerging Black power culture, and his practical purpose was to isolate White supremacy within the White Church and to hold up the alternative model of the Black Church. He also intended in a real way to speak to the lies of Black inferiority found within the Black community. However, Cone's revolutionary persona can dissuade evangelical theologians from considering his theological arguments, leading them to miss the benefits of his critique.

NOTES

1. Cone, 2004: 151.
2. Cone, J. "Black Theology on Revolution, Violence, and Reconciliation." *Union Seminary Quarterly Review* 31 (Fall, 1975): 5–14.
3. Cone, J. "The Content and Method of Black Theology." *The Journal of Religious Thought* 32, no. 2 (1975): 90–103.
4. Greeley, 1971.
5. Wilmore, 1998.
6. Cone, J. 1986. *My Soul Looks Back.* Nashville: Abingdon Press. xi.
7. Cone, J. 1997. *Black Theology and Black Power.* New York: Harper and Row. 3.
8. Cone, J. 1997. *Black Theology and Black Power.* 73.
9. See Cone, J. 2018. *A Black Theology of Liberation.* Maryknoll: Orbis. 51–53; 2011. *The Cross and the Lynching Tree.* Maryknoll: Orbis. 60–61.
10. Cone, J. 1997. *God of the Oppressed.* New York: The Seabury Press. 73.
11. See Luther, M. 1959. *Luther's Works Vol. 1.* Translated by J. Doberstein. Philadelphia: Fortress Press. 80; Williams, G., and A. Mergal. 1957. *Spiritual and Anabaptist Writers.* Philadelphia: Westminster Press. 42.
12. Cone, J. 1997. *God of the Oppressed.* 69.
13. Cone, J. 1997. *God of the Oppressed.* 71.
14. Cone, J. 1997. *God of the Oppressed.* 67.
15. Cone, J. 1997. *God of the Oppressed.* 69, 71–74.
16. Cone, J. 1997. *God of the Oppressed.* 67.
17. Cone, J. 1997. *God of the Oppressed.* 67.
18. Cone, J. 1997. *God of the Oppressed.* 70.
19. Cone, J. 1997. *God of the Oppressed.* 65, 70.
20. Cone, J. 1997. *God of the Oppressed.* 70.
21. Cone, J. 1997. *God of the Oppressed.* 71.
22. Cone, J. 1997. *God of the Oppressed.* 72.
23. Cone, J. 1997. *God of the Oppressed.* 74–80.
24. Cone, J. 1997. *God of the Oppressed.* 80.

25. Cone, J. "Theology's Great Sin: Silence in the Face of White Supremacy." *Black Theology: An International Journal* 2 (2004), no. 2: 144–50.
26. Cone, J. 1997. *Black Theology and Black Power.* 89.
27. Hatch, N. 1991. *The Democratization of American Christianity.* New Haven: Yale University Press; Noll, M. 2008. *God and Race in America.* Princeton: Princeton University Press; Maimela, S. 1987. *Proclaim Freedom to My People.* Braamfontein: Skotaville Publishers. 1–24; Brueggemann, W. 2018. *Tenacious Solidarity: Biblical Provocations on Race, Religion, Climate, and the Economy.* Minneapolis: Fortress Press. 109–17.
28. Cone, J. 1997. *Black Theology and Black Power.* 82.
29. Cone, J. 1997. *Black Theology and Black Power.* 82, 83.
30. Cone, J. 1997. *Black Theology and Black Power.* 89; Cone, J. 2011: 30–34.
31. Cone, J. 2004: 151.
32. Cone, J. 2004: 143.
33. Cone, J. 2004: 151.
34. Cone, J. 2004: 151.
35. Vanhoozer, K. 2005: 308; Thiselton, A. 2007. *The Hermeneutics of Doctrine.* Grand Rapids: W. B. Eerdmans. 38–39.
36. Pederson, D., and B. Owen. 1971. *Jesus People.* Pasadena: Compass Press; Palms, R. 1971. *The Jesus Kids.* Valley Forge: Judson Press.
37. Cone, J. 1984. *For My People.* Maryknoll: Orbis. 11–18.
38. Lee, D. 1971. *Dynamite Voices: Black Poets of the 1960s.* Detroit: Broadside Press. 46.
39. See also Franz Fanon on religion and the colonized. Fanon, F. 2004. *The Wretched of the Earth.* Translated by R. Philcox. New York: Grove Press. 18.
40. Cone, J. 1997. *Black Theology and Black Power.*
41. Washington, J. 1993. "Are American Negro Churches Christian?" In *Black Theology: A Documentary History, Vol. 1.* Edited by J. Cone and G. Wilmore. Maryknoll: Orbis.
42. Cone, J. "Black Theology and Black Liberation." *The Christian Century* (Sept. 16, 1970): 1084–1088; 1972: 54–69.
43. Cone, J. 1997. *God of the Oppressed.* 36–56.
44. Cone, J. 2018. *Said I Wasn't Gonna Tell Nobody.* Maryknoll: Orbis. 97, 103, 104.
45. Cone, J. 2018. *Said I Wasn't Gonna Tell Nobody.* 85–87.
46. Cone, J. 2018. *Said I Wasn't Gonna Tell Nobody.* 90.
47. Cone, J. 1975. "The Content and Method of Black Theology." 90–103.
48. Cone, J. 2018. *Said I Wasn't Gonna Tell Nobody.* 92.
49. Cone, J. 2018. *Said I Wasn't Gonna Tell Nobody.* 92.
50. Cone, J. 1997. *God of the Oppressed.* 134–38.
51. Cone, J. 2018. *A Black Theology of Liberation.* 87–120.
52. Johnson, A. "The Prophetic Persona of James Cone and the Rhetorical Theology of Black Theology." *Black Theology* 8, no. 3 (2010): 266–85.
53. Johnson, A. 2010.

54. Ware, B., and W. Linkugel. "The Rhetorical Persona: Marcus Garvey as a Black Moses." *Communication Monographs* 49, no. 1 (1982): 50–62.

55. Joseph, P. 2009.

56. Stewart, C. "The Method of Correlation in the Theology of James Cone." *Journal of Religious Thought* 40, no. 2 (1983): 27.

57. Lee, D. 1971: 13.

58. Jones, M. 2007.

59. See Cone, J. 1997. *Black Theology and Black Power.* 6–9, 11–14, 18–35, 71, 124; 2018. *A Black Theology of Liberation.* 18, 60, 61, 67, 76–78, 84, 89–90, 105; 1997. *God of the Oppressed.* 139, 162, 199.

60. Camus, A. 1956. *The Rebel.* Translated by A. Bower. New York: Vintage Books.

61. Camus, A. 1956: 9.

62. Cone, J. "Christian Faith and Political Praxis." *Encounter* 43, no. 2 (1982): 129–41.

63. Fanon, F. 2004: 238–39.

64. Cone, J. 2018. *Said I Wasn't Gonna Tell Nobody.* 7.

65. Baraka, A., and L. Neal, eds. 1968. *Black Fire: An Anthology of Afro-American Writing.* Baltimore: Black Classic Press.

66. Cone, J. 2018. *Said I Wasn't Gonna Tell Nobody.* 9.

67. Fanon, F. 2008. *Black Skins, White Masks.* New York: Grove Press.

68. Cone, J. 2018. *A Black Theology of Liberation.* 123.

Chapter 2

Influences on Cone's Body of Work

Cone's work is shaped by his agenda and his rhetorical persona, but it is also shaped in conversation with other intellectuals and intellectual movements. Among these, one must examine his "intellectual trinity," as well as the Black Arts Movement, other Black theologians, and Marxism. The role of White theologians in Cone's work must also be assessed—specifically Karl Barth, Paul Tillich, Jürgen Moltmann, Reinhold Niebuhr, and Dietrich Bonhoeffer— to place Cone's theological work in context.

THE INFLUENCE OF INTELLECTUAL MOVEMENTS

Cone's Intellectual Trinity

Cone uses the term "intellectual trinity" to summarize how Malcolm X, Martin Luther King Jr., and James Baldwin shaped his view of Black theology. He describes the central importance of Malcolm and Martin: "Martin Luther King, Jr. and Malcolm X were like two hot flames burning inside me that would not go out. Malcolm represented the flame of blackness in black theology and Martin the flame of faith in its Christian theological expression."[1]

This chapter considers Cone's use of dialectic later. But Malcolm X and Martin Luther King Jr. represent for Cone a central dialectic whose synthesis is found in Black theology. Malcolm's view of Blackness and Black self-consciousness, coupled with King's justice-seeking Christianity, forms the foundation upon which Black theology is built. The influence of Malcolm and Martin on Cone cannot be underestimated. Nor should it be misappropriated. Evangelical scholars who see Malcolm X as suspect, because he participated in the Nation of Islam, must understand how Malcolm informs Cone's theology. Cone simply chooses to ignore the theological underpinnings in

Malcolm's views on race. Cone insists, rather, that Malcolm's views on blackness can be severed from their theological basis in the Nation of Islam and replaced by King's Christian theology.

Baldwin is the third person of Cone's intellectual trinity. Baldwin inspires the way Cone writes. But Baldwin also factors directly into Cone's work. While Baldwin only receives nine mentions in Cone's major theological writings, five of those appear in Cone's later work. Cone developed his appreciation for Baldwin's theological significance over time. In fact, Cone devotes an entire chapter of his autobiography, *Said I Wasn't Gonna Tell Nobody*, to theological engagement on suffering in conversation with Baldwin.[2] Cone's editor at Orbis confirmed that before his death, Cone was planning a book on Baldwin; but when he realized he could not complete it, he included reflections on Baldwin as the final chapter of his autobiography. This chapter reads like a theological essay, albeit an unfinished one, not an autobiographical account. So Baldwin may have shaped Cone in ways that went beyond the purely literary. Perhaps Baldwin represented a theological model that combined both Black consciousness and Christian thought. Cone suggests this himself: "Baldwin joined my intellectual trinity along with Martin King and Malcolm X. They told the truth about black people, and that's why we still remember them. Baldwin shared Martin King's incredible love of humanity. And he shared his rage, defined by a love of blackness with Malcolm X."[3]

Cone's intellectual trinity grounds his theological work. Both Malcolm and Baldwin are problematic for evangelicals as theological conversation partners—evangelical theologians must carefully assess how these individuals shape Cone's work and how King's Christianity often stands in for the more problematic theology of both Malcolm and Baldwin.

The Black Arts Movement

Cone can also be placed within the general milieu of the Black Arts Movement of the 1960s and 1970s. He saw himself in relation to this movement, clearly stating that he believes "that all aspiring black intellectuals share the task that LeRoi Jones has described for the black artist in America: 'to aid in the destruction of America as we know it.'"[4]

Cone views his theological work as synonymous with the work of the Black artist and cultural revolutionary. In the Black Arts Movement, he found both a calling and a language that directed his theological agenda and informed his theological rhetoric. He connected the movement to the content of his work by quoting and interacting with LeRoi Jones, Don Lee, and the authors of the *Black Fire* anthology. He also drew extensively from antecedents, including Richard Wright and Baldwin. Cone's participation in the broader cultural Black Power revolution, including the Black Arts Movement, enabled him to conceive of the necessity for a separate Black theological space and to insist on a uniquely Black theology.

Evangelicals must consider the ways Black Arts hyperbole plays out in Cone's writing. Jones' phrase "destruction of America as we know it" carries poetic weight beyond its literal application. America, as experienced by Blacks in the 1960s and 1970s, needed tearing down. The destruction of America in Cone's context has more to do with the dismantling of White supremacy than the armed overthrow of an entire nation.

Hyperbolic language is itself a methodology. The image of an America destroyed by Black men and women brings into relief the pain and anger created by racism. The language of the poet and revolutionary creates clarity in ways normal theological discourse does not.

Black Theologians and Historians of Religion

Cone was very involved in conversations and debates with other Black theologians and scholars. Among these were outright detractors, such as Charles H. Long, William Jones, and Major Jones, and those who sympathized but pushed Cone to reconsider directions in his work, including Cecil Cone and J. Deotis Roberts. Later, Black Womanist scholars, including Delores Williams, challenged Cone on gender issues.

Chapter 1 introduced Long's opposition to theology as a discipline. Per Long, the essence of Black religion and its most decisively Black signs, symbols, and images lay in African religion, not Christianity.[5] While Cone does not discount Long's argument, he also largely ignores it. His source material depends primarily on African American Christian culture; he shows little interest in African religions either as a direct source of theological discourse or as a means of uncovering a distinctly non-European theology within Black-American Christianity. Cone admits, "I acknowledged the need to pay careful attention to the African in Black religion, but not to the extent that the God of Jesus would be rendered marginal in Black theological discourse."

Cone had similarly contentious interactions with William Jones and Major Jones. In lengthy footnotes, Cone accuses William Jones of misreading his theology by excluding his Christocentric perspective.[6] He also accuses Major Jones of intentionally misquoting him. Cone does concede their point that theodicy is central to Black Theology but insists that the question of theodicy is unanswerable.

Cone seems more accepting of Roberts' criticism.[7] Roberts opposed Cone's use of Black Power to the point of excluding reconciliation, and he also believed that Cone's view was "too limiting."[8] Cone recognizes that reconciliation is not clear in his work but wants to reserve conversation about reconciliation until liberation is a reality.

Both Roberts and Cecil Cone critiqued James Cone's continued use of White theologians and White methodologies, considering them antithetical to his argument. As a result, Cone's first work focused on "doing" Black Theology as opposed to "defending" it. *The Spirituals and the Blues* is a direct result of this critique.[9]

In the prefaces of his subsequent works—*Black Theology and Black Power*, *A Black Theology of Liberation*, and *God of the Oppressed*—Cone admits that "the most glaring limitation . . . was my failure to be receptive to the problem of sexism in the black community and society as a whole."[10] He also acknowledges the challenges made by womanist theologians such as Williams, particularly her view of the cross and atonement. In the end Cone demurs, "I didn't have the experience or knowledge to really hear what I needed to hear."[11] Yet Cone makes no effort to correct his work in response to feminist and womanist critiques, apart from using gender-inclusive language in subsequent publications. Cone recognizes that gender, class, and race all relate to oppression in unique ways, but he seems to lack the sophisticated understanding of shifting power dynamics that are the hallmark of contemporary theologies employing intersectionality to map power relationships.

Marxism

"Marxist" or "socialist" may seem like apt descriptions of Cone. He demonstrates familiarity with Marxism and uses Marxist analysis to his advantage in his early work, particularly *God of the Oppressed*.[12] However, Marxism holds several challenges for Cone. He is also well-versed in Barth's defense of theology against the formidable attacks on religion made by Feuerbach and Marx. Cone holds up Black Liberation Theology as a positive defense against Marx's view that religion is "the opiate of the people."[13]

Cone acknowledges the need for class analysis but is reluctant to incorporate it into his work. For Cone, class seems to undermine the centrality of race as the primary driver of Black poverty in America. Classism becomes an easy excuse or replacement for racism. So, a Marxist insistence on class as the sole driver of social issues is problematic for Cone.

He does, however, discuss a socialist alternative to monopoly capitalism in an article for the *Christian Century*. Cone comes close to accepting the socialist model: "We must therefore form a social arrangement that is democratic, both economically and politically. No one should control for profit those goods and services needed for human survival."[14] But ultimately, he rejects the model out of hand: "The absence of a historical model that embodies fully my political and theological imagination makes it difficult to speak meaningfully and concretely about the socialist alternative."[15] Instead, he proposes focusing political models on an eschatological vision that champions human flourishing and equality and promotes nonexploitive economic systems.

To connect Cone with either Marxism or socialism is therefore difficult. His critique of capitalism seems intended more to reform the system than to completely tear it down. His defense of Christianity and his economic aspirations for Blacks in America pull him away from outright defense of Marxist systems. He seems inclined more toward a distributed capitalism, where wealth and resources benefit all and are not manipulated for White profit. Cone suggests, then, an altruistic, antiracist form of democratic capitalism— an important point for evangelicals who might mistake Cone's discussion of Marx and his insistence on dismantling the discriminatory aspects of capitalism as affirming some form of Marxism, when the opposite is true.

Given Cone's recognition of the validity of pan-African, womanist, and Marxist critiques, evangelicals can easily mislabel Cone's theology. But Cone's acceptance of a position does not necessarily mean that he incorporates it into his work, as is true for each of these intellectual movements.

THE INFLUENCE OF WHITE EUROPEAN AND NORTH AMERICAN THEOLOGIANS

Understanding Cone's theology and method requires differentiating what Cone borrows from traditional White theology from his unique theological contributions—and most importantly, understanding how the two coalesce in his Black Theology. Understanding White theology in Cone's work also means specifically understanding his use of Karl Barth, Paul Tillich, Jürgen Moltmann, Reinhold Niebuhr, and Dietrich Bonhoeffer. The two most central to Cone's theology are Karl Barth and Paul Tillich. Cone seems averse, however, to engaging with evangelical and conservative theologians. He does mention Jonathan Edwards negatively but never more than briefly.

Scholars disagree on the extent to which Cone is influenced by White Euro-American theology. Keith Bolton asserts, "Cone has merely appropriated aspects of European existentialism to gain 'white' approval for his 'Black' theological stance."[16] Raymond Carr is more generous: "Black theology is both a critical appropriation of European theology and a reconceptualization of American theology at its best."[17] Black and White scholars alike point out Cone's seeming dependence on White theology.

Cone's acceptance of this dependence varies. For example, he self-identifies as a Barthian and even claims to be misunderstood by non-Barthians because he draws on Barth. He claims he merely discusses White theologians to point out either the contradictions in their views or their usefulness to his argument. Cone ultimately cannot fully claim that White theological influence is lacking in his work; but his detractors, with a few exceptions, have also failed to discuss the varying ways he does draw on individual White theologians.

Karl Barth

Karl Barth was the subject of Cone's dissertation and figures prominently throughout Cone's work.[18] Cone's dissertation admittedly lacks any real critical analysis of Barth, beyond a single chapter that superficially engages Barth's Reformed dogmatics. His lack of serious engagement does call into question—at least in his early development as a theologian—the level of sophistication and familiarity with Barth's theology. That said, Cone did use Barth in several ways.

Barth was known as a dialectic theologian, and Cone's theological method is thoroughly Barthian. The central guiding metaphor of Cone's Black theology, and his primary motivation, synthesizes the seemingly disjointed views of Malcolm X's radical blackness and Martin Luther King Jr.'s radical Christianity. This frame brackets and drives all of Cone's theology.[19]

Cone uses Barth's infinite qualitative distinction between God and humanity to nuance his view of God's act of liberation and to distinguish the opinions of oppressed individuals from God's revelation in the oppressed community. "When the oppressed are inclined to use their position as a privilege, as an immunity from error," Cone argues, "they will do well to remember the Scriptures witness to God's righteousness as other than human. On this point, Karl Barth was right."[20] Barth's argument affirms Cone's position that God is revealed through the oppressed community but that the oppressed community errs whenever it speaks or acts apart from this revelation.

Cone also understands God as the ground of freedom, per Barth, to further his argument that God is the God of liberation. In "The Gift of Freedom," Barth asserts, "God's freedom is essentially not freedom from, but freedom to and for. . . . God is free for man."[21] God's freedom for mankind finds articulation in Cone's idea that God is at work granting freedom to the oppressed. God as the foundation of freedom—God's free choice to be for humankind—makes him the liberator of the oppressed. Cone is less interested in Barth's restrictions on the freedom of mankind to be for God, found in that same essay. Barth especially disallows human freedom "to preserve, to justify or to save oneself";[22] Cone's work does not build on the limitations of human freedom.

In addition, Cone appropriates Barth's view that God's revelation is evident and complete only in the person of Jesus Christ, but Cone qualifies his support: "Because Christian theology begins and ends with the Biblical story of God's liberation of the weak, it is also Christological language. On this point Karl Barth was right. Unfortunately, Barth did not explicate this

Christological point with sufficient clarity, because his theology was determined too much by the theological tradition of Augustine and Calvin and too little by scripture."[23] According to Cone, Barth is wrong because he does not share Cone's view that Scripture points to the liberation of the poor. Had Barth focused on the liberating nature of Scripture, Cone argues, he would have proclaimed that God's revelation in Christ points to the liberation of the oppressed. But because Barth does not reach this conclusion, his approach must be unscriptural. Cone's insistence on liberation as the a priori guiding motif of Scripture leads him to view Barth as insufficient.

The degree to which Cone's writings demonstrate Barth's influence remains a matter of debate. Cone's dialogical approach to theology was common in his day and would have been part of his training, apart from any clear understanding of Barth. Cone's work uses Barth's arguments but never in an extended way and often with qualification. Perhaps this distance is explained by Carr's assessment that Cone is reading Barth within Barth's political context—that Cone "read Barmen as precedent" in his view of Barth—ensuring that this unconventionally political Barth lies latent at the heart of Cone's theology.[24] However, this assessment seems unlikely, given that neither Cone's dissertation nor his subsequent writings evidence a delineated thesis on the political nature of Barthian theology,[25] even though Cone's theological mentor, William Herndon, was an early proponent of a political reading of Barth.

Paul Tillich

Examining the influence of Paul Tillich in Cone's work yields similar results. Cone utilizes Tillich's methodology, particularly Tillich's use of symbol and correlation, but never consistently or predictably. Per Bolton's assessment above, Cone seems to fully embrace Tillich's existentialism, but never without qualification. He seems especially drawn to Tillich's notion of being and nonbeing, but he transforms their use. Cone also seems to both embrace and oppose Tillich's notion of culture as the operative element of theology.

Cone's acceptance of Tillichian symbolism is clear. "Black Theology," he says, "takes seriously Paul Tillich's description of the symbolic nature of all theological work."[26] James Robison[27] makes the case that Cone's use of ontological blackness functions as just such a symbol, while the word "God" is a symbol that must contain the liberation of the oppressed; otherwise it must be overturned.[28] But Cone is reluctant to draw a clear line between symbol and reality, preferring an intentional blurring that requires his readers to work out whether his pronouncements are one or the other.

Cone also employs correlation, but his corollaries are different from Tillich's. According to Carlyle Stewart, Tillich's primary corollary is between God and humanity, viewing the latter as a universal whole. But Cone makes clear distinctions between the correlations of God and the oppressed, God and the oppressor, and the oppressor and the oppressed. Stewart also does not see these corollaries as foundational in Cone; he posits that the central work of correlation in Cone connects the liberation of the oppressed in Scripture and in contemporary contexts.[29] If Stewart is right, little relation exists between Tillich's working out of correlation in his theology and the theological conclusions that the same method yields in Cone.

Thus, any connections to Tillich's theology seem secondary in Cone. Even Cone's use of Tillich's corollary between being and nonbeing forms primarily a subpoint or illustration in Cone's overall argument. That the fight for liberation is a fight for being against nonbeing is evident, though not always explicit, in Cone's primary arguments. But his arguments do not rely on Tillich's understanding, nor do they extend beyond the wording to engage extensively with Tillich's theology of being and nonbeing. Cone even leverages the terms toward a different end, applying them to Black consciousness as opposed to the fullness of all humanity as it finds its being in God. In many ways, Tillich's theology functions like a proof text in Cone's work.

Fredrick Herzog provides an important comparison between Cone and Tillich. Tillich's primary method brought the questions of contemporary society into conversation with God's revelation, whereas Cone grounds his theology in a preexistent revelation of God the liberator and asks how that view of God speaks to the contemporary lives of the oppressed and the oppressors. Herzog explains: "It is one thing to predicate theology on the statement, 'I am anxious, what's the answer?' It is another thing to base theology on God's question, 'Your neighbor is oppressed. What is your responsibility?'"[30]

Cone distances himself from Tillich's use of culture in theology. While Cone affirms that the intersection of the two is readily accepted in contemporary society, he challenges culture in opposition to Feuerbach's assumption that God is a manifestation of man's deepest aspirations for himself. Cone asserts, "The question is whether divine revelation in scripture grants us a possibility of saying something about God that is not simply about ourselves." He concludes, "Unless this possibility is given, however small it might be, then there seems to be no point in talking about the distinction between white and black theology or the difference in falsehood and truth."[31] Cone affirms an authoritative, revelational check on culture that he sees lacking in Tillich.

Like his use of Barth, Cone's use of Tillich is primarily methodological and polemical. Tillich serves Cone as an illustration, proof text, negative example, and starting point. Unlike Barth, Tillich appears primarily in Cone's early work; his influence wanes in Cone's later theology.

Dietrich Bonhoeffer, Reinhold Niebuhr, and Jürgen Moltmann

Cone's work features other White theologians, including Dietrich Bonhoeffer, Reinhold Niebuhr, and Jürgen Moltmann. Bonhoeffer primarily serves as an exemplar in Cone's work. Cone finds much of Bonhoeffer's work useful because of the latter's exposure to Black theology in Harlem and his oppression at the hands of the Nazis. Even so, Cone offers no sustained treatment of Bonhoeffer.

The only White theologian to receive more than sporadic treatment is Reinhold Niebuhr. Cone has a lengthy theological engagement with Niebuhr in *The Cross and the Lynching Tree*,[32] chastising Niebuhr's gradualism on issues of race and his lack of significant engagement of race in his theology. Cone does, however, see both Niebuhr's ethical realism and his concept of the transvaluation of values as useful. Niebuhr's ethical realism appeals to Cone because its starting point is justice, not love. Justice as a concept resonates for Cone because it denies the supremacy of love in racial relations and at least opens the door for liberating acts beyond nonviolence. Likewise, Niebuhr's transvaluation of values fits into Cone's understanding of God's privileging of the oppressed. This work engages with this concept in detail later; suffice to say that in Niebuhr's ethics, Cone found actual theological principles to engage, in ways he did not with the work of other White theologians. This is also a later development in Cone's work. No sustained treatment of Niebuhr appears before or after the publication of Cone's *The Cross and the Lynching Tree*. His engagement with Niebuhr in this one instance is substantial, but not enough to view Niebuhr as influential in the full body of Cone's work.

Jürgen Moltmann also had at least a limited influence on parts of Cone's theology. Throughout much of his writing, Cone is reluctant to allow the influence of eschatology. He seems concerned that the "otherworldly" focus inherent in the doctrine would pull Black Liberation Theology away from the actual liberation of the oppressed in this world. But he also struggles with the real eschatological hope evident in the worship of the Black Church. Cone seems to reconcile this tension in Moltmann's view of eschatology as a present hope. Cone's assessment is that "Moltmann's analysis is compatible with the concerns of black theology. Hope must be related to the present, and it must serve as a means of transforming the oppressed community into a liberated-liberating community."[33] While Moltmann does seem to solve Cone's problem with eschatology, the doctrine itself is at best a minor point in Cone's theological system.

Bridging White Theologians and Cone

What then can be said about the influence of White theologians on Cone's theology and about how evangelical theologians should engage with Cone? Cone does engage with the methodologies of both Barth and Tillich and with the theologies of Niebuhr and Moltmann to a lesser degree. Cone's use of Niebuhr and Moltmann does lend itself to constructive engagement. Likewise, his tacit approval of Bonhoeffer seems to present a point of departure for White theologians left unexplored by Cone.

But if most of Cone's uses of these theologians were withdrawn from his work, his theological conclusions would not change. Cone is working within a liberal modernist theological perspective, but his engagement can be viewed as critical of traditional liberal theology. Evangelicals must be careful not to assume that discrediting the theological views of Tillich, Barth, or Niebuhr necessarily discredits Cone's arguments. Conversely, these White theologians, if used cautiously and critically, might serve to bridge White theology and Cone.

If one accepts this view that White theological influence is secondary in Cone's work, then his work is more unique than has otherwise been assumed—even his early work directed primarily at White theologians, whom he frequently references there. White evangelicals must, therefore, view Cone as unique and consider Black theology as reflecting a position that is at times in direct tension with modernist liberal theology, while allowing Cone to view himself as working within the general frame of liberal theology. More common ground might be found in Cone's work than either Cone or evangelicals would acknowledge.

CONE'S THEOLOGICAL METHOD

Understanding Cone's uniqueness requires an examination of his method, to develop a composite picture of his theology and method that can then be accessed in light of White evangelical theology. Cone's method can best be described as fragmentary, contextual-dialectical, foundational, and hermeneutical. Although Cone himself only mentions contextual-dialectical method as his preferred understanding of his methodology, much of his actual discussions can be better explained under the other three methodology categories.

Fragmentary

Referencing David Tracy's work on theological fragments, Ryan Cummings suggests the fragmentary nature of Black theology generally and Cone's work specifically.[34] The term "fragmentary" expresses the particular and unique concerns of Black theology in contrast to the supposedly universalizing and totalizing concerns of White theology. The argument suggests that White theology—in limiting itself to those elements of existence seen as universal to the human condition—misses the equally important theological concerns particular to subsets of humanity. Cone's theology, however, emphasizes the way these concerns (fragments) create a unique theology but also the ways this unique theology intersects with the totality of humanity. Black theology is fragmentary because it begins with the particulars to determine the universals. Cone's theology therefore resists large-scale metanarratives, overarching and controlling dogmatic categories, and systematic schemas.

Both Cummings and Tracy view this approach as positive, and its use raises important questions for White evangelical theology. How, for example, does the totalizing tendency of White theology tend to ignore the particulars of race, gender, class, and other categories that are difficult to assimilate into broader White theological systems? How does this omission render evangelical claims to universal truth lacking or incomplete? Finally, can one conceive of a particularist, fragmentary evangelical theology that can create a legitimately universal theology?

Contextual-Dialectical

Cone describes his theological method as contextual-dialectical. By "contextual" Cone means that truth is found in the lived experience of the Black community.[35] All truth emerges for Cone out of lived contexts, and all truth is evidenced in the concrete actions that those truths elicit. To be true, theology must be contextual and must, as a matter of methodology, be derived from lived experience.

But the theological task is also dialectical, in two senses. First, theology places in dialogue God's revelation in Scripture with God's revelation in the community's lived experience. Theological truth emerges from this dialectic. Second, theology is dialectical because its answers are paradoxical. They are understood and voiced only in light of temporal circumstances. God and God-talk are understood only in light of shifting contemporary experiences. Thus, for Cone, the dialectic between God's past revelation and ongoing work in the contemporary context generates a relevant theology.

The dialectical nature of Cone's theology presents a critical challenge to evangelical theology, which sees theological truth as set. It is a legitimate issue for evangelicals who wish to maintain the authority of scriptural truth. But this issue also raises the question of how evangelicalism can deal with the ongoing work of God in the lives of believers. That is, to what degree does the anemic nature of contemporary experience in evangelical theology relegate

God's work to the historical past and limit God's ability to speak into contemporary reality?

Foundational

Requiring little elaboration, Cone's method is also foundational. His theology rests on authoritative sources, namely Scripture, God's revelation in Christ, and his revelation of God in Black experience. The implications for evangelical theology are clear: at least in the case of Scripture, one finds a starting point to converse with Cone's theology.

Hermeneutical

Cone's theology is also hermeneutical in his focus on form as equal to content, his use of liberation as a hermeneutical lens, and his focus on praxis as theology.

Cone insists that form equals content. This insistence is part of his justification for embedding theology in the Black cultural experience: "The style of Black worship is a constituent to its content, and both elements point to the theme of liberation."[36] He explains the way praise, shouting, call-and-response preaching, and other aspects of Black worship carry specific theological meaning. Cone's central task is to recover theology from the Black community, which involves a deep historical-theological reflection on the spirituals and the blues, sermons, slave testimonies, and other artifacts of Black culture, and a consideration of how the way a story is told affects its meaning as much as its content.[37]

Cone also works within the confines of a hermeneutical lens, viewing everything from the standpoint of liberation. It is an a priori understanding for Cone. He does justify this choice at points by locating the theme in Scripture, but its identification seems clearly to precede the study of Scripture, not follow it. Cone also uses this lens to disallow any discourse that omits liberation.

He insists that theology must also lead to a liberation-focused praxis. He argues for an orthopraxy centered on the realization of truth in action: "Truth therefore is not an idea but a divine event which invades history and bestows freedom in wretched places."[38] The invasion of divine truth is a continuous action in the present. The holistic nature of theology ensures that it cannot be simply an intellectual exercise but must be realized in action toward liberating the oppressed. Thus, theology is understood most fully in its practical applications in life. The proof of theological consistency with the Gospel is its ability to change the world. In this sense, Cone's work is consistent with Thiselton and Vanhoozer, both of whom view theology as a hermeneutical task that moves from orthodoxy to orthopraxy.

Cone challenges evangelicalism with his insistence on liberation as the guiding hermeneutical lens for both biblical interpretation and theological formulation. His view that liberation must be seen in its literal, historical context also challenges evangelicals who spiritualize this theme. What must be resolved is the degree to which Cone's singular use of liberation excludes other important themes in Scripture. Regardless, Cone challenges evangelical theology to think in more nuanced ways about liberation in theological and biblical discourse.

CHALLENGES POSED BY CONE

This chapter points to at least three considerations in relationship to Cone's argument that White theology and exegesis are grounded in biases derived from White power. First, one must explore the question of embedded racisms within the evangelical theological tradition to determine whether additional study is warranted; if the evangelical theological tradition is found to be without racist content, then no additional work is necessary. This exploration is the work of part II.

Then, if racist theological content is indeed found within the evangelical theological tradition, the tradition must be further interrogated, beginning with evangelicalism's denial that liberation is central to Scripture. This interrogation is the work of part III.

Finally, if the study finds that the biblical text prioritizes, or at least affirms, a liberationist stream, then that interpretation must be used to articulate the way Cone and the conclusions of part III intersect with and inform evangelical doctrine and ethics. Such analysis is the work of part IV.

NOTES

1. Cone, J. 2012. *Martin and Malcom and America: A Dream and a Nightmare.* Maryknoll: Orbis. 223.

2. Cone, J. 2018. *Said I Wasn't Gonna Tell Nobody.* 144–69.

3. Cone, J. 2018. *Said I Wasn't Gonna Tell Nobody.* 159.

4. Cone, J. 1997. *God of the Oppressed.* 3.

5. Long, C. 1995. *Signification: Signs, Symbols, and Images in the Interpretation of Religion.* Aurora: The Davies Group. 187–98.

6. Cone, J. 1997. *God of the Oppressed.* 245, 247.

7. Cone, J. 2018. *Said I Wasn't Gonna Tell Nobody.* 90.

8. Roberts, J. 2005. *Liberation and Reconciliation: A Black Theology.* 2nd Edition. Louisville: Westminster John Knox Press. 4–5.

9. Cone, J. 1972. *The Spirituals and the Blues.* New York: Seabury Press.
10. Cone, J. 2018. *A Black Theology of Liberation.* xx.
11. Cone, J. 2018. *A Black Theology of Liberation.* 120.
12. Cone, J. 1997. *God of the Oppressed.* 36–41.
13. Cone, J. 2018. *A Black Theology of Liberation.* 134–35.
14. Cone, J. 1981: 166.
15. Cone, J. 1981: 166.
16. Bolton, K. 1986. "The Theological Method of James Cone." Doctoral Dissertation, Fuller Seminary. 290.
17. Carr, R. 2011. "Barth and Cone in Dialogue on Revelation and Freedom: An Analysis of James Cone's Appropriation of 'Barthian' Theology." Doctoral Dissertation, Graduate Theological Union, 38.
18. Cone, J. 1965. "The Doctrine of Man in the Theology of Karl Barth." Doctoral Dissertation, Northwestern University.
19. Cone, J. 2012.
20. Cone, J. "What Is Theology." *Encounter* 43, no. 2 (1982): 122.
21. Barth, K. 1968. *The Epistle to the Romans.* Translated by K. Hoskyn. Oxford: Oxford University Press. 77–79.
22. Barth, K. 1968: 78.
23. Cone, J. 1982. "What Is Theology." 119.
24. Carr, R. 2011: 30.
25. For a possible exception see Cone, J. 2018. *A Black Theology of Liberation.* 51–52.
26. Cone, J. 2018. *A Black Theology of Liberation.* 7.
27. Robison, J. "A Tillichian Analysis of James Cone's Black Theology." *Perspectives in Religious Studies* 1 (1974): 16–30.
28. Cone, J. 2018. *A Black Theology of Liberation.* 60, 61.
29. Stewart, C. 1983. "The Method of Correlation in the Theology of James Cone." 35.
30. Herzog, W. "Theology at the Crossroads." *Union Seminary Quarterly Review* 31, no. 1 (1975): 61.
31. Cone, J. 1982. "What Is Theology." 120.
32. Cone, J. 2011: 30–64.
33. Cone, J. 2018. *A Black Theology of Liberation.* 148.
34. Cummings, R. "Contrasts and Fragments: An Exploration of James Cone's Theological Methodology." *Anglican Theological Review* 91, no. 3 (2009): 395–416.
35. Cone, J. 1975. "The Content and Method of Black Theology." 100, 101.
36. Cone, J. "Sanctification, Liberation, and Black Worship." *Theology Today* 35, no. 2 (1978): 142.
37. Cone, J. "The Dialectic of Theology and Life or Speaking the Truth." *Union Seminary Quarterly Review* 29, no. 2 (1974): 76–84.
38. Cone, J. 1976. "God Our Father, Christ Our Redeemer, Man Our Brother: A Theological Interpretation of the AME Church." *The Journal of the Interdenominational Theological Center* 4 (1976): 25.

PART II

Evaluating the Evangelical Theological Tradition

Chapter 3

Methodology for Evaluating Evangelical Theology

Having engaged in Movement One, an empathetic-analytical reading of Cone, this study now moves to Movement Two: a historical interrogation of evangelical theology in light of potential issues raised by Cone. Cone asserts that racism is embedded in White theology; the truth of this assumption must be demonstrated before one can engage in a constructive theology of Power that uses Cone as a conversation partner. If Cone's assumptions are not true, then evangelical theology is not racist and therefore needs no further consideration. If Cone is correct, however, then the evangelical theological position may require constructive engagement to mitigate embedded racism. This interrogation is not a straightforward task.

This historical analysis of Cone follows three considerations. The first examines whether Cone makes a strong enough case that racism is deeply embedded in White theology or, if not, where it is lacking. Then, if Cone's work needs clarification, on what methodological grounds would a study of embedded racism proceed? This clarification includes defining "racism." Finally, because this project cannot study the entire evangelical tradition, the discussion must justify which evangelical theologians have been chosen as case studies.

HOW STRONG IS CONE'S ARGUMENT?

Cone makes clear that racism, embedded in White theology, is the central problem he intends to address: "Is racism so deeply embedded in Euro-American history and culture that it is impossible to do theology without being anti-black?" He answers yes.

But to what degree can Cone prove the embeddedness of racism? Cone identifies at least five reasons for arguing that racism permeates White theology.[1] First, sociologists of knowledge have demonstrated how White cultural bias limits White theology. That is, White theologians have no cultural reason to consider race, racism, and White supremacy because their cultural experiences do not suggest its consideration is necessary.[2]

Cone's second argument observes that discourse on racism is largely absent from the work of White theologians. In itself this absence is racist, but it also ensures that White theology never comes to terms with its racist character. Cone states, "As long as religion scholars do not engage racism in their intellectual work, we can be sure that they are as racist as their grandparents, whether they know it or not."[3] The argument from silence is key in Cone's work. All a theologian must do to be accused of racism is to fail to take up the question of race.

Cone's third assertion notes that theology has emerged from a cultural and intellectual environment consumed by White images and ideas, one where the term "universal" is a stand-in for "White." Cone says, "White images and ideas dominate the religious life of Christians and the intellectual life of theologians, reinforcing the 'moral' right of white people to dominate people of color economically and politically."[4] Further, "twentieth-century white theologians are still secure in their assumption that important theological issues emerge, primarily, if not exclusively, out of the white experience."[5] Cone argues that whiteness, being so ingrained in White theology, fails to fully acknowledge the suffering of Blacks.

A fourth reason why White supremacy persists is because White theologians have interpreted the gospel in light of White self-interest.[6] White theologians work for White interests, in opposition to Black interests.

Finally, Cone connects White theology to racial ideologies that emerged from the Enlightenment. "US theology," he asserts, "did not arise from the social existence of black people. On the contrary, its character was shaped by those who, sharing the consciousness of the Enlightenment, failed to question the consequences of the so-called enlightened view as reflected in the colonization and slavery period." He further asserts, "For black and red peoples in North America, the spirit of the Enlightenment was socially and politically demonic, becoming a pseudo-intellectual basis for their enslavement and extermination."[7]

Cone's critique is flawed, however, in at least three ways. He fails to present a complete historical analysis, to recognize the diversity of White theology, and to move beyond a nondiscursive, theoretical sociological analysis.

First, Cone's historical analysis is lacking. His reference to the effects of the "consciousness of the Enlightenment" draws upon theories that trace the emergence of racism to modernist periods that began with the Enlightenment. In this way, Cone seems to be referencing the work of Frank M. Snowden

Jr.[8] But Snowden's assertion that the concept of race and by extension racism did not exist before the modern period has come into question.[9]

In addition, Cone's argument suffers from collapsing White theologies into a single theology. While Cone is aware that various theologies are different, he asserts that "American theologians from Cotton Mather and Jonathan Edwards to Reinhold Niebuhr and Schubert Ogden, including radicals and conservatives, have interpreted the gospel according to the cultural and political interests of their group (whites)." He continues, "White theologians, because of their identity with the dominant power structure, are largely boxed within their own cultural history."[10] This argument fails when mustered to defend Cone's assertions about the totality of embedded racism. He does not account historically for groups of European and American theologians who were by no means connected to power structures when they produced their theologies. As a case in point, radical reformers were themselves persecuted by political powers. But Cone's theory would identify all theologies that emerge from the Euro-American cultural experience as racist because of their connection to White power structures.

Finally, as a nondiscursive analysis, Cone's argument fails to find racist logics and grammar in theology itself. If all Euro-American theology evidences racism, how does it do so within the context of its theological discourse? Cone's analysis focuses on how individuals become racist while omitting a detailed analysis of how theological discourse and doctrine have embedded racism within White theology as a whole. If entire theological systems are impugned, then to prove his thesis Cone must establish some sense of where in theology racism emerges, and how this remains operable at the level of doctrinal formulation across varying doctrinal and theological traditions.

Cone never attempts such analyses, and his historical theological work is lacking. He is particularly uninterested in proving his case in relation to evangelical theology. His assessment of evangelicals is characterized by the remark that "Billy Graham and Norman Vincent Peale . . . are the best examples that religious conservatism and White racism are often two sides of the same reality."[11] Cone does not suggest at the nondiscursive level how Graham and Peale were racist; for Cone, the racism of White evangelicals is self-evident. Cone's critique serves, at best, as a kind of theological intuition, and as such it cannot function as unquestionably valid, rational proof that allows the current study to adopt his argument without question. Therefore, his argument cannot simply be accepted without further examination of racism in evangelical theology.

But Cone's failure at this point does not necessarily forestall the current project. One cannot argue that evangelical theology lacks any element of embedded racism simply because Cone failed to adequately demonstrate its presence. In fact, he never makes the attempt. This study needs further analysis at the nondiscursive and discursive levels, a clear methodology for doing so, and an approach that specifically engages evangelicalism, apart from the larger subgroup of all White theologians. Such a study must consider Cone's argument in light of a clear definition of racism, a clear methodology for uncovering racism, and a clearly defined set of theologians that require interrogation.[12]

Defining Racism

Defining racism may seem simple at first, but the idea is hotly contested within the interdisciplinary study of race. Eliav-Feldon, Isaac, and Ziegler note, "Any study of racism must be based on a clear idea of what it is, what it is not, and what distinguishes it from other forms of inequality and discrimination."[13] However, many scholars discuss race without ever defining either race or racism. Mark Noll's *God and Race in American Politics*, for example, asserts that "race has always been among the most influential elements of American political history"[14] but never defines what he means by race.

Definitions of racism and race are complicated by the uncertain nature of racial definition itself. In the early modern era, race was understood to be synonymous with biology and genetics. This theory is largely denied in contemporary discourse, which calls into question the very existence of racial categories.

Goldberg points out that because biological theories of race have collapsed, race has subsequently been understood as a construct of class, culture, ethnicity, nation, and politics.[15] For Goldberg, race may contain elements of all categories but also must be defined in ways that distinguish it from each. Definitions are further complicated by questions of the distinction between racialization and racism. "Racialization" is understood as placing persons into racial categories with either racist or nonracist motivations. Racialization may be evident when a Black man proclaims that he is "Black and proud" as a form of self-identification. So, definitions of racism must be distinguished in ways that exclude benign racial categorization.

What definition of racism can guide this study? The definitions of Eliav-Feldon, Isaac, and Ziegler are somewhat elusive. They consider racism an "idea, or set of ideas, and an ideology."[16] They further distinguish racism from other forms of prejudice by asserting that racism "claims that the characteristics of the other are determined by nature while the latter attributes them to custom, social forces or education and the like. The former unlike the latter thus claims that human characteristics are unalterable and passed on from one generation to the next."[17] But this definition denies the modern history of racism that ascribed racial difference, in conjunction with racial characteristics, to environmental differences. The scholars' assertion also ignores the continuation of racist logics in contemporary society, even though biological explanations have been largely disputed. Furthermore, their insistence that racism can be "understood as an ideology or an attempt to construct rational, conceptual frameworks for irrational and emotional forms of group hatred" suggests, contra Goldberg, that racism can be both irrational and rational. The scholars claim that racism is irrational and categorize it as ideology, suggesting that racism is a belief structure with no connection to logical, rational systems. This suggestion anchors racism to specific individual or collective emotional responses in specific historical contexts; it does not help determine ongoing embeddedness in theological discourse as a whole.

This study instead relies on both Goldberg's formal definition and his extended supporting argument. Goldberg defines racism as follows:

> promoting exclusions or the actual exclusions of people in virtue of their being deemed members of different racial groups, however, racial groups are taken to be constituted. It follows that in some instances expressions may be racist on grounds of their effects. The mark of racism in these cases will be whether the discriminatory racial exclusion reflects a persistent pattern or could reasonably have been avoided. Racists are those persons who explicitly or implicitly ascribe racial characteristics of others that purportedly differ from their own and others like them. These ascriptions, whether biological or social in character, must not merely propose racial differences; they must also assign racial preferences, or explain racial differences as natural, inevitable, and therefore unchangeable, or express desired, intended, or actual inclusions or exclusions, entitlements or restrictions.[18]

While Goldberg provides a clear definition of racist discourse, his definition does not completely capture the methodological insights he brings to understanding how racism, as a discursive logic, is constructed and operable in various contexts. Therefore, a further examination of his argument is helpful.

GOLDBERG'S FOUR LEVELS OF RACIST DISCOURSE

This study embraces Goldberg's understanding of the inner workings of racist discourse and its subsequent manifestation in various ways, at various times, and in various sociohistorical contexts. His work is complex and not as clearly delineated as the application below. That is, his ideas are central to the method I suggest, but Goldberg might take issue with their simplification.

Goldberg suggests four levels of racist discourse.

1. At the most basic level are racism's primitive concepts: the necessary constructive ideas that lead to the notion of racism but are not explicitly or necessarily racist in themselves.[19]
2. The next level of logical construction systematically brings together the primitive principles toward a racist grammar: "a set of discursive rules (that) emerge from an economy of epistemological production in virtue of which 'truth' may be differentiated from 'falsity.'"[20]
3. A rational and rationalizing logic can be identified in the racial discourse. Goldberg argues against the common perception that racism is irrational; instead, he suggests identifiable ways in which racism constitutes its own rational system, by implication observable in racist discourse.[21]
4. Racist discourse is evident in and shaped by, in varying ways, the deployment of racist logics in different actual cultural and historical contexts. Goldberg states, "The field of racial discourse, then, is a product of socio-discursive praxis in determinate historical circumstances. The power of racist expression conjoins with the power of other discursive expressions—notably, though not only, those of class, gender, nation, and capitalism—to determine the subjectivity of individuals at established times and places."[22]

These four qualifications to Goldberg's definition offer the basic framework that will shape the methodology to be followed throughout the rest of Movement Two. But before moving to that it is also important to outline just how nondiscursive and discursive racist logic will be tracked within the North American Reformed Evangelical tradition.

WHICH BRANCH OF EVANGELICAL THEOLOGY?

The stream of evangelicalism must now be determined in order to delineate the approach to embedded racism pursued below. Understanding what anyone means when speaking of evangelical theology depends on the contemporary vantage point from which they view evangelicalism as a movement or a theological descriptor.

Roger Olson provides seven distinct ways to understand the term "evangelical" historically. The term takes on varying meanings, histories, and theological orientations depending on the ending point of the historian examining it. Likewise, evangelicalism as a contemporary movement represents several denominational groups and theological persuasions, ranging from Calvinism to Pentecostalism. The movement's theological genetics are therefore specific to the groups within the movement; these branches are distinct, and their theologies are diverse. Thus, the current study has less need to focus on the few common unifying theological positions within contemporary evangelicalism, and more need to be very clear about which branch of evangelical theology is under consideration.

Reformed North American Evangelicalism

This study limits analysis to the evangelicalism that emerged in the 1940s in the United States, both out of and as an alternative to separatist fundamentalism. Further, I focus on a stream that is largely Reformed and historically indebted to Calvinism via English Puritanism as it emerged as New England Puritanism. Thus, the study's conclusions, although offering broader possibilities, are limited to this branch of North American evangelicalism. Even with this limited scope, the limited space does not allow full exploration of everyone whose theological work falls within these parameters. So further clarification of the figures under consideration is necessary.

North American evangelicalism within the Reformed stream can be traced by following two mutually interactive but somewhat different branches that come together to shape the movement as a whole: the pietistic and doctrinal branches. One could trace what is called neo-evangelicalism back through Billy Graham to Billy Sunday and Dwight Moody to New England Revivalism and John Wesley. But these evangelists, particularly the more contemporary ones, provide less theological discourse that can be analyzed.

Instead, the approach followed here traces North American evangelical theology through its recognized figures who have produced academic theologies, although not necessarily separate from the Church. Accordingly, four individuals emerge for consideration: John Calvin, Jonathan Edwards, Charles Hodge, and Carl F. H. Henry.

Case Studies: Four Evangelical Theologians

These four theologians sufficiently represent the evangelical tradition to make good candidates for analysis.[23] Each represents a different era in the development of reformed evangelicalism. Calvin, the early reformer most referenced by later reformed evangelical theologians, offers a foundational tradition from which later reformed evangelical theology emerges. Edwards inherited Calvinistic theology through early English Puritanism. He is also the leading theological example of what became known as New England Puritanism and the later strands of North American theological thought that emerged from it. In the mid- to late-nineteenth century, Princeton Seminary inherited the Calvinism of Edwards through the theological work of Hodge. Hodge himself was the early architect of what became under his successors—A. Hodge,

H. Gresham Machen, and B. B. Warfield—the early roots of North American fundamentalism. Later fundamentalism emerged from Hodge to become North American separatist fundamentalism, the movement from which Henry emerged and distinguished himself. Henry sought to preserve the legacies of Hodge, Edwards, and Calvin while suggesting a different path that fundamentalists called neo-evangelicalism but that he and others simply called evangelicalism.

Direct discursive evidence connects the four theologians. Henry interacts directly with Calvin, Edwards, and Hodge in his six-volume Systematics, *God, Revelation, and Authority*. Hodge makes great use of Edwards and Calvin in his systematic theology and other works; Edwards likewise references Calvin in his writings. These discursive and nondiscursive ties allow further connections to be drawn between the theological systems of each representative theologian, and one can highlight instances of theological convergence that suggest different outcomes for the question of embedded racism. Ultimately this approach allows the discourse of theology to be mapped to the discourse of race and racism so that one can determine intersection and divergence.

FINAL METHODOLOGY

Application of Goldberg's Framework

Goldberg's understanding of racist discourse provides a method by which theological discourse can be examined for racist content. However, how the study uses this model and what it specifically examines at each level needs clarification.

To better differentiate the levels of complexity suggested by Goldberg, I employ a literary analogy to govern the discussion of each theologian in this part. At the most basic level, Goldberg's primitive terms form the *vocabulary* of racist discourse. The secondary level brings together the vocabulary by conjoining ideas within various discourses, forming the *grammar* of racist discourse. The third level of racist argumentation deploys both the vocabulary and grammar in a concerted argument: the *narrative* of racist discourse. Finally, the nondiscursive praxis flowing out of an assumed or evident racist discourse constitutes the *performance* of the narrative. If these four levels of complexity are accepted as a framework, how then might they be applied to analyze historical theological discourse?

For each theologian, first I consider the racist vocabulary that is apparent in the theologian's work, from the standpoint of certain basic ideas implied by Goldberg's definition of racism. These terms are not, however, intended to be foundational in any structuralist way. Not all terms need to be present to indicate a tendency toward racist discourse. Their existence also does not require a racist outcome. They are merely a part of the underlying web of ideas out of which racist logics can emerge. Goldberg provides the following vocabulary, which I use in the analysis of each theologian: "classification, order, value and hierarchy, differentiation and identity, discrimination and identification, exclusion, domination, subjection, and subjugation, as well as entitlement and restriction." The historical analyses in chapters 4 through 7 attempt to determine whether any of these terms are operable in the writings and theological discourse of the respective theologians. At this stage, how they function is not important; the analysis will simply ask whether and where they are present in the theological discourse. So, by way of example, if Calvin includes hierarchy both in his discussion of the doctrine of God's sovereignty and in his commentary on Ephesians 6, then the chapter on Calvin will note the presence and location of his discourse on hierarchy.

The analysis of each theologian then moves to the grammatical level, asking specifically how the theologian's discourse extends the vocabulary to form a coherent defense for either latent or inherent racism. To continue the hypothetical example above, if hierarchy is addressed within (or is supported by) Calvin's doctrine of the sovereignty of God, the analysis will consider what discursive elements hold together and define Calvin's use of hierarchy. Further, the discussion will examine how these discursive elements connect the doctrine of God's sovereignty to other doctrinal formulations that might carry these notions of hierarchy beyond the immediate instance. The discussion might also engage apparent doctrinal structures that seem to be suggested independent of vocabulary. In other words, given the scope of the task, the study will use a "surgical" approach to examine elements in the work of each theologian that are suggested either by the secondary literature on racism or by the secondary historical literature on each theologian.

Each chapter in this part continues the analysis by considering the levels of narrative and performance, asking to what degree each theologian deploys racist vocabulary and grammar to make specific arguments for racist outcomes and ends. Are the concepts simply latent in the theological arguments, or does a given theologian marshal them for a specific racist narrative and outcome? So, for example, if Hodge uses racist vocabulary and doctrinal grammar to defend race-based slavery, this defense would be identified as a racist narrative.

Finally, each chapter's analysis moves from the discursive to the nondiscursive to examine any performative evidence of racist sentiment in the lives of its respective theologian. If, say, Hodge opposes slavery in his writings but owned slaves, or if Edwards's writings praised Native Americans but his policies harmed and subjugated them, then in both cases one must look for some connection between the discursive and nondiscursive that explains the disparity. Each theologian will be addressed in turn using this methodology, and then conclusions will be drawn for each.

NOTES

1. Cone, J. 1999. *Risks of Faith: The Emergence of Black Theology, 1968–1998*. Boston: Beacon Press. 131.
2. Cone, J. 1997. *God of the Oppressed*. 48.
3. Cone, J. 1999: 132.
4. Cone, J. 1999: 131.
5. Cone, J. 1997. *God of the Oppressed*. 42, 43.
6. Cone, J. 1997. *God of the Oppressed*. 43.
7. Cone, J. 1997. *God of the Oppressed*. 42.
8. Snowden, F. 1970. *Blacks in Antiquity*. Cambridge: Harvard University Press.
9. See Eliav-Feldon, M., ed., with B. Isaac and J. Ziegler. 2009. *The Origins of Racism in the West*. Cambridge: Cambridge University Press; Kaplan, M. 2019. *Figuring Racism in Medieval Christianity*. Oxford: Oxford University Press.
10. Cone, J. 1997. *God of the Oppressed*. 43.
11. Cone, J. 1997. *God of the Oppressed*. 46.
12. For a full consideration of alternative approaches to embedded racism see Joseph W. Caldwell, *Toward an Evangelical Theology of Power and Privilege in Conversation with James Cone*, unpublished doctoral dissertation, North-West University, 2023.
13. Eliav-Feldon, Isaac, Ziegler. 2009: 5.
14. Noll, M. 2008: 1.
15. Goldberg, D. 1994. *Racist Culture: Philosophy and the Politics of Meaning*. Oxford: Blackwell Publishers. 69–89.
16. Eliav-Feldon, Isaac, Ziegler. 2009: 12.
17. Eliav-Feldon, Isaac, Ziegler. 2009: 12.
18. Goldberg, D. 1994: 98.
19. Goldberg, D. 1994: 48–52.
20. Goldberg, D. 1994: 52.
21. Goldberg, D. 1994: 117–58.
22. Goldberg, D. 1994: 115.
23. For a full discussion of the historiographical method followed in the analysis in part II, see Joseph W. Caldwell, *Toward an Evangelical Theology of Power and Privilege in Conversation with James Cone*, unpublished doctoral dissertation, North-West University, 2023.

Chapter 4

John Calvin and Racist Logics

Before moving directly to an analysis of Calvin's work this chapter first recognizes a few dynamics at play in Calvin scholarship, addresses the intentionally limited scope of the study, and provides some sense of the use of the extensive primary literature. Calvin, as well as the various Calvinist systems derived from his teachings, plays variable roles within particular global contexts. Calvinism and Calvinist ideas came to play some role in the defense of race-based slavery in the United States.

In fact, these teachings were used more to defend slavery than to support abolitionist beliefs.[1] While, in South Africa, Calvin and Calvinism were used both to support apartheid and to advocate for its elimination. Such variable use of Calvin, therefore, points to the possibility of (mis)reading Calvin's theological corpus, and that of his theological successors, in ways that support racist logics, while indicating a paradox in Calvin that allows for variable readings on race. This issue is taken up directly by de Gruchy and Naude.

Both de Gruchy and Naude suggest that Calvin can be read in a multiplicity of ways. De Gruchy discusses the malleability of Calvin's thought as it regards social transformation. "Perhaps," de Gruchy concludes,

> The main problem which the proponents of Calvinism have to overcome is the tendency, which has recurred several times in history, for it to start out as a theology of social critique and transformation and end up as a theology of totalitarian dominance. Gwendolen Carter in her *Politics of Inequality*, it may be recalled, remarked that "from the political point of view it is significant that Calvinism is inherently authoritarian. Where Calvinists have fought for freedom of conscience," she continues, "it was due to circumstances rather than theology."[2]

De Gruchy is not suggesting that nothing in Calvinism can be read as antiracist or antiauthoritarian. Rather, he is suggesting that such readings coexist with more authoritarian and hierarchical readings of both Calvinist theology and social ethics.

Naude offers more hope of finding a transformative social ethic in Calvinist theology but recognizes the possibility of reading the tradition in a way that supports authoritarianism: "Those of us who have been writing and doing theology in South Africa over the last three decades know that the Christian gospel—as interpreted from the Protestant or more specific Reformed tradition—can simultaneously be used as a powerful force against social transformation and as a positive force for justice and the transformation of society."[3]

Uncontested, then, is the argument that Calvinism holds at least the possibility of being (mis)read to support authoritarianism, hierarchy, and racist policies and attitudes. This finding does not affirm subsequent interpretations of Calvin along these lines; I simply suggest that Calvin scholars and Calvinist theologians are aware of this stream within Calvin and Calvinism. The current project, then, needs greater definition and specificity than is provided in the work of either de Gruchy or Naude.

This suggests the need to articulate the limits of the current study. First, by suggesting that this authoritarian, racist stream exists within Calvin's work, I do not claim that all later Calvinist systems reproduce Calvin's reasoning at every point or that all of Calvin's theology is corrupted by this stream. Although, as an aside, Cone would say that the latter is of necessity the case. This study suggests only that the evidence of racist or precursory logics in a particular theologian, including those studied in this part, points to its more likely emergence in subsequent uses of that theology. All that this part ponders is the potential for such use.

Second, this study looks at four influential theologians within the context of a particular strand of Reformed North American evangelicalism. Therefore, I make no claims to identify racist logics amid other strands within the Calvinist tradition as a whole or within specific Calvinist traditions outside this limited North American context.

Third, what I envision here is not a full study of Calvin's theological system, or subsequently those of Edwards, Hodge, and Henry, but rather an attempt to identify potential parts of that system that could subsequently be used to support racist logics. This scope fits my primary focus on embeddedness. An embedded component is by definition a part of a system even if it is not intentional, required, or primary to the system. When each chapter moves from Goldberg's level of vocabulary to his level of grammar, for each respective theologian, I offer specific suggestions about how racist logics affect or are determined by broader categories of theological reasoning. But the discussion should make clear that the components operating at even the vocabulary level suggest on their own the potential for racist use.

As the study of each theologian moves from vocabulary to grammar to narrative and performance, the greater impact the embeddedness has—but the primary reason for Movement Two of this study must be kept in mind.

This part simply purports to ask whether racist logics or elements are embedded in the North American evangelical tradition. An assessment that a particular doctrine is racist (or supports racist logics) does not mean that the doctrine must be removed from evangelical dogmatics. My intent is not to pass judgment, at this point, on the implications of embedded racist logic for contemporary systems of theology, or on the viability of particular doctrines. That work is reserved for part IV. Part II considers only the existence or nonexistence of racist logics within evangelical theological systems that will be necessary to the conclusions of part IV.

Finally, given the work of de Gruchy and Naude, I take as an a priori conclusion that elements within each theologian might be useful in constructing antiracist theologies. Part IV examines this possibility in detail, but part II focuses exclusively on racist logics.

Before proceeding to an analysis of Calvin, one must understand the approach I'm taking to the primary literature. Calvin's corpus is extensive, and this chapter simply lacks the space for a full analysis. What I offer is a specific look at those points in Calvin's work where he suggests a racist or precursory reading. These texts are not chosen randomly; they are drawn from, and suggested by, the secondary literature as well as Calvin's treatment of biblical texts that seem most susceptible to racist or precursory racist interpretation, including Romans 13, Paul's Household Codes (Colossians 3:18–19 and Ephesians 5:22–33), and the patriarchal narratives. Calvin's discussions of these passages appear primarily in his commentaries and sermons, but he also discussed them in his theological reflections in the *Institutes*, especially Book 3 on the Christian life.

As suggested by the secondary literature, this chapter also engages specific texts addressing broader theological issues as they appear in the *Institutes* and Calvin's more polemical works. Because this historical study is offered primarily within the context of a constructive theology, it includes ongoing conversation with secondary literature where it intersects the narrow concerns of this study.

VOCABULARY

Goldberg's definition of racist vocabulary suggests that components of racist thought are evident in discursive texts—perhaps not directly related to racist discourse, but forming the primitive components of racist logic, including "classification, order, value and hierarchy, definition and identity, discrimination and identification, exclusion, domination, subjection, and subjugation, as well as entitlement and restriction."[4] Given these categories, Calvin does appear to evidence primitive racist thought. Although Calvin says little about race specifically, he does apply categories of exclusion, hierarchy, and negative characterization as a form of classification; these components are central in primitive racist speech. This vocabulary will be connected later to larger theological and doctrinal categories.

Exclusion

Calvin's primary means of exclusion are religious. The distinctions between the elect and the non-elect, the believer and the non-believer, are pronounced. Distinguishing between those who are in and those who are outside God's grace is a repeated theme for Calvin.[5] While all humanity shares a common tie in Adam and God, God does not ask that we "altogether despise others," Calvin says; but that does not change the fact that "the more nearly a man approaches to God, he (the man) ought to be more highly esteemed by us."[6]

In addition, given how later racist discourse uses the patriarchal narratives to justify racial exclusion—particularly passages about Abraham and Ishmael, Babel, and the "curse of Ham"—one must examine the degree to which Calvin might interpret these passages similarly. Calvin does not evidence the exclusionary language found in later exegesis on Babel and the "curse of Ham," but he does directly tie election with ancestral descent in his discussion of Abraham and Ishmael. "Ishmael," Calvin exclaims, "shows that the whole progeny of Abraham should flow from one head. He promises also to Ishmael that he shall be a nation, but estranged from the church so that the conditions of the brothers shall, in this respect, be different; the one is constituted the father of a spiritual people, to the other is given a carnal seed."[7]

Calvin frames this distinction in the context of race, ethnicity, or perhaps ancestral origin. Either he claims a direct connection between ethnic heredity and election, or he is offering Abraham's line as spiritually representing the Church/elect and Ishmael's line as representing all unregenerate or non-elect peoples. Within Goldberg's definition, either spiritual or hereditary forms of exclusion fall within primitive racist categories.

Hierarchy

If exclusion is primarily confined to religious exclusion in Calvin, the same cannot be said for hierarchy. Calvin recognizes myriad categories that rank and subject individuals within human society, such as gender, economic status, slave/master relations, and governmental authority.

Calvin's views on hierarchy and social order are well-established in the secondary literature. The authoritarian tendency identified by de Gruchy, Kayayan's exposition of Calvin's support of slavery, and Vorster's and Thompson's view that Calvin so limited women's role that he subordinated

God's image within women to make his point are all examples.[8] Potgieter sums up Calvin's view: "Calvin admitted that within God's providence, there is variety and indeed room for inequality with regard to earthly means, wealth, and potential among people."[9] Calvin's views are expressed in his writings on the Pentateuch, the Gospels, and Paul's letters, particularly Romans 13 and the Household Codes.

As Wallace notes, Calvin affirms that "the subjection of the inferior to the superior in the relationship of ruler to people, master to servant, husband to wife, child to parent, is part of an individual order established by God the Father; unless such order is observed and those under authority submit to those over them, then human society cannot be maintained."[10] For Calvin, this order is sometimes grounded in the created order and sometimes necessitated by the Fall; the latter is true of the relationship between men and women and of some forms of slavery. But what is important here is the degree to which submission and authority, and the attendant hierarchy, become a divine mandate for Calvin.

Calvin argues that God has determined fixed relationships that humanity is bound to both preserve and honor. In his discussion of Miriam and Aaron's uprising against Moses, for example, Calvin states, "Now since Aaron and Miriam were not superior to others, they were thus reminded that they were far behind Moses in rank."[11] He does not limit this judgment to the narrative but extends it through application: "The pride and temerity of Miriam were sufficiently chastised, but God wished it to be a lesson for all, that everyone should confine himself to his own bounds."[12]

Calvin sees stepping out of bounds as violating God's authority and providence and subject to divine punishment. Likewise, in discussing the sins of the people of Babel, Calvin asserts, "It cannot be otherwise than that everyone who transgresses his prescribed bounds, makes a direct attack on God."[13]

Status based on religious standing, wealth, and occupation also informs Calvin's thought. In his exegesis of Peter's stay in the house of a tanner in Joppa, Calvin points out that someone of Peter's status would surely have stayed with a chieftain, had any been present. But the community must have had only "the common sort of men." He also insists that the tanner must have been a merchant, not merely a tanner. Calvin's extratextual speculation is based on his cultural perspective.[14] This passage highlights his sensitivity to class distinctions and class etiquette.

Calvin likewise accepts disparities between the rich and poor as God's providence:

> For although rich and poor are mingled together in this world . . . in saying that the condition of each is divinely appointed, he (Solomon, Prov. 24:13) reminds us that God, who enlightened all, has his own eye always open, and thus exhorts

the poor to patient endurance, seeing that those who are discontented with their lot endeavor to shake off the burden which God has impressed upon them.[15]

For Calvin, any attempt to change a person's position by "shaking off the burden which God has impressed" is outside the will of God.[16]

Calvin recognizes the hierarchy inherent in relationships between husbands and wives, masters and slaves, and parents and children.[17] Thus, hierarchy applies to the micro-relationships of the household as clearly as it applies to larger social roles and relationships. His views of slavery maintain traditional hierarchical relationships while requiring masters a duty of benevolence. Some might see this requirement as indicative of a softening of authoritarianism in Calvin. But as both Kayayan and Sytsma point out, Calvin is employing the Aristotelian notion of distributive justice or analogical right.[18] There exists a duty of benevolence, but it is still determined and limited by a strict understanding of role, place, and order within the established hierarchical relationship of inferiors to superiors. Thus, distributive justice creates an ideal of ethical treatment but leaves undisturbed the hierarchical relationship and grounds of power and authority.

Additionally, Calvin affirms the responsibility of Christians to submit to civil authority. He makes no distinctions among types of government, nor does he allow for revolution. Everyone must recognize the authority of all magistrates because they are given that authority by God.[19]

Some mention should be made of Calvin's highly limited doctrine of contingent submission. Calvin only reluctantly applies it and hesitates to affirm it at all. An individual has the right to refuse submission only when the government asks the person to do something that God forbids, but Calvin remains cautious about this.[20] Regardless, for Calvin a clear hierarchical distinction remains between magistrates and private citizens.

Hierarchy is not only present in society but is both necessary and ordained. "It is God," Calvin says, "who appoints and regulates the arrangements of society."[21] Calvin also provides a reason for social hierarchy: "In the human race God has so arranged our condition, that individuals are only endued with a certain measure of gifts, on which the distribution of offices depends."[22] He asserts that these gifts create a mutual dependency within society, leading to good order and goodwill.[23] When Calvin makes hierarchy both a divine act and part of the natural order, he opens himself fully to Goldberg's assertion that racist categories are "natural, inevitable and therefore unchangeable."[24] Calvin certainly would see hierarchy as natural, inevitable, and unchangeable.

In Calvin, therefore, hierarchy extends God's providence, ensures social order, can be found at all levels of society, and is incumbent on obedient persons to maintain. Hierarchy is also fixed and unchanging, as stated above, all the more so because Calvin has no notion of progress or of attaining higher social status.[25]

Negative Characterization

Another mark of Goldberg's racist vocabulary is the negative characterization of persons based on some innate feature that is not necessarily attributable to individual character traits. Calvin engages in such discourse regarding gender, class, and possibly race. The secondary literature does not treat this aspect of Calvin's discourse, but evidence can be found in his commentaries.

Calvin characterizes women, for example, as weak, ambitious, and high-spirited. The latter term is not intended as a compliment: "For the ambition of the female sex is wonderful," he says, "and often have women more high-spirited than men been the instigators not merely of squabbles, but of mighty wars."[26] Likewise, Calvin at times characterizes slaves negatively. He describes slaves as diseased, addicted to flattery, prone to duplicity, wicked, depraved, useless, and unfaithful.[27]

Calvin's estimation of the poor can easily get lost in his insistence on the charity that they are owed because of Christ's command to care for them. However, a close reading shows that Calvin does occasionally characterize the poor as lazy, afflicted, and despised. He rarely chastises the wealthy for despising the poor and indicates that the poor deserve it. His only admonition is that the wealthy should not let this attitude stop them from caring for the poor—not because the poor have any value themselves, but because God commands their care.[28]

Finally, in at least one instance, Calvin makes, if not a direct characterization, at least an implied negative assessment based on race. In his commentary on Miriam and Aaron's objection to Moses' wife Zipporah, Calvin states that she is "called an Ethiopian" but opines, "I have no doubt but that they maliciously selected the name (Ethiopian), for the purpose of awakening greater odium against Moses."[29] Calvin suggests instead that Zipporah was other than Ethiopian. He moves beyond the literal sense to assert a personal bias that implies that if Zipporah were indeed an Ethiopian, then Aaron and Miriam's complaints against Moses would be reputable. Therefore, Calvin suggests, they must have labeled Zipporah inaccurately to bolster their case. While this example cannot convict Calvin of racial bias alone, it does suggest that he harbors negative feelings for "Ethiopians," a term used in Calvin's day to distinguish Africans of all origins from more Middle Eastern–looking North Africans.

Calvin's discourse, then, evidences those components of thought that Goldberg considers primitive racist categories forming the vocabulary of racist logic—although only two cited instances apply this logic to a racist or hereditary category (that is, Abraham and Ismael, and Moses and Zipporah). But Calvin does provide discursive material that, in its primitive form, could be appropriated for racist discourse. He evidences at least three of Goldberg's categories: exclusion, hierarchy, and negative characterization, a form of negative classification. The question then remains: Does Calvin also employ these categories and contingent ideas in a way that could be described as racist theological grammar?

GRAMMAR

To what extent does Calvin's theological discourse evince racist grammar that may form racist logics? Goldberg's understanding of racist grammar is "a set of discursive rules (that) emerge from an economy of epistemological production in virtue of which 'truth' may be differentiated from 'falsity.'"[30] For Calvin, these truths are formulated by what he views as correct doctrine. So given his doctrinal pronouncements that include the primitive vocabulary of hierarchy, exclusion, and negative characterization, does he advance these concepts as theological truths and thereby form the basis of racist logics?

Several points of doctrine and theological argumentation do seem to have the potentiality, latent or otherwise, to support racist logics in Calvin. Although he does not explicitly employ this discourse toward racist ends—at least not like a modernist discourse on race—Calvin's arguments might be considered supportive of racist logics, even if it is not part of an explicit racist narrative. This finding is true to the extent that they presuppose later racist constructions. Among the theological categories examined in this section analyzing Calvin's grammar are providence; the operation of authority, submission, and obedience; objections to revolution; and the divine ordination of civil government.

Providence

The degree to which many have used providence to justify race-based policies and institutions is well documented in the historical literature.[31] Does Calvin's understanding of providence undergird such racist logics, regardless of his intentions? Michelle Sanchez writes, "One could think of providence (in Calvin) as the leitmotif closing the first movement of a musical. It is the climax of the opening act, but it also establishes a central motif that will repeat throughout the show, enabling layers of semiotic richness and narrative complexity."[32] Sanchez's poetic view expresses a common understanding: that the doctrine of providence plays an important role in Calvin's theology and is a repeating theme in his work.

Thus, providence deserves attention as a primary unifier in Calvin's theological logic. Providence functions as a principal argumentative tool for explaining ethical issues and interpreting biblical texts that run counter to Calvin's own sentiments. Kayayan, for example, demonstrates convincingly that although Calvin had personal distaste for the institution of slavery, he nonetheless defended Paul's support for the institution and its contemporary practice. According to Kayayan, Calvin frames all of this by referring to slavery as an institution within the providence of God: "[Calvin accepted] that (the) condition (of slavery) and the political order that engendered it . . . [fall] under the scope of divine providence."[33] Being particularly concerned with the malleable use of providence to explain and justify contemporary practices, this study considers Calvin's formulation of the doctrine of providence as it appears in his *Institutes*, Commentary on the last four books of Moses, Commentary on Paul's Letters (particularly Philemon), and his Commentary on Ezekiel. These texts may suggest ways in which the doctrine might be (mis)applied to racist discourse.

Calvin's view of providence insists that God has not released his providential acts to an ambiguous set of natural laws. "Those, moreover, who confine the providence of God within narrow limits, as if he allowed all things to be borne along freely according to a perpetual law of nature," Calvin says, "not more dethrone God of his glory than themselves of a most useful doctrine."[34] By this Calvin makes the greater point that God is the "prime agent" who is also fully present and fully engaged in everything that occurs.

Calvin wants his readers to understand that God is not only a creator but "also a governor and preserver, and that not by producing a kind of general motion in the machine of the whole as well as in each of its parts, but by a special providence sustaining, cherishing, superintending, all the things which he has made, to the very minutest."[35] God's involvement in the "minutest" details of human existence undergirds Calvin's understanding of human will, God's means, and God's engagement with evil actors.

To Calvin, the human will is clearly under the influence of divine providence, so much that individuals are "so governed as to move exactly in the course which he has destined."[36] Likewise, he asserts not only that God exerts his will through invisible, passive influence but that God's providence uses means and assumes a visible form.[37] This insistence on God's asserted will and God's use of means requires Calvin to affirm that God also uses evil actors.

Calvin is convinced that God uses, as Augustine says, "the evil wills of bad men" for God's providential plan.[38] Likewise, Calvin asserts that God not only gives permission to bad actors but directs their evil actions.[39] He justifies God's acts by concurring with Augustine that such acts might be evil, were it not for the fact that God is "omnipotent to bring good out of evil."[40] All actions work not merely by the power of God but by God's "election and decree." Calvin is distinguishing between God's allowance for evil, or incidental evil, and God's incorporation of evil actors into God's divine plan. In Calvin's view, God has ordained that evil actors will perform evil deeds according to God's will.[41]

The result of this view of providence—which sees all acts and actors, whether good, evil, or neutral, as guided by God's providential hand to serve as means for God's providential ends—is that it locks all human conditions into the will of God. Thus, Calvin sees everything, including economic disparity, slavery, and tyranny, as within God's providential will. A few specific examples illustrate this point and the connections among ideas inherent within racist logics.

Calvin uses the doctrine of providence as an explanation and defense of inequality. According to Calvin, it is God's will that "some are elevated, while others remain without honor."[42] He insists that success in this world equals God's blessing, and calamity is the result of God's curse.[43] God also afflicts the innocent according to his own good will.[44] As a consequence, humanity must take the position that "the Lord willed it, it must therefore be borne."[45]

Similarly, Calvin seems to recognize the contradiction between a good God and one whose providential will includes suffering. But he refuses to allow human critique to replace God's truth by removing God's providence from human suffering; instead, Calvin prefers to believe that what appears evil is in fact working for good within the "hidden counsel" of God. Slavery is one example: God has ordained that those who are slaves are enslaved according to God's providence. Slavery, therefore, must be borne as a part of that providence. Why God would choose to impose such suffering on those enslaved is unknown; it must be accepted and left to the "hidden counsel of God," in the knowledge that it will all work out for good according to God's plan.

This belief also applies to economic inequality. Regarding disparity of wealth, Calvin states, "God in whose hands are the ends of the earth, to destroy and to overturn at His will its kingdoms, and to change the government of nations, much more (has the right) so to distribute the wealth and possessions of individuals, as to enrich some and to reduce others to want."[46] God has "decreed and elected" the lot of the impoverished. Furthermore, changing the status of the poor would be an extraordinary, not ordinary, act of God. Calvin makes this point in his Commentary on Ezekiel, estimating that God's concern for the mistreatment of the poor arises from extraordinary injustice that requires God's extraordinary intervention on their behalf.[47] If, therefore, God has decreed and elected the poor to poverty, then it is incumbent on the poor to endure their condition with patience, according to Calvin, lest they "endeavor to shake off the burden which God has impressed upon them."[48] Attempts to rise above poverty would be acts of rebellion against God and his providential will.[49]

As for slavery, again, Calvin sees slavery as part of God's providential will, but the degree to which he involves God in the institution is significant. Interpreting Paul's advice in his epistle to Philemon, Calvin states, "It is as if Paul had said, 'do not suppose that by the judgement of men you were thrown into slavery. It is God who has laid upon you the power of your masters.'"[50] Of course, Paul did not say this—Calvin did. Thus, God is, in Calvin's mind, the instigator of slavery. The whole institution exists as a result of the providential will of God, and anyone caught up in the institution is enslaved because God wills it. They must be content with their lot and their place. But Calvin is not interested solely in their contentment; he also requires them to do their duty—not as a duty to the master but as a duty to God.

Calvin's doctrine of providence therefore functions as a specific theological grammar that pulls God's will into conversation with specific ethical conditions that ultimately allow the doctrine to excuse or support inequality, disparity, subservience, and submission. While this approach certainly is not the only use of the doctrine, it is one primary way Calvin used providence to resolve ethical questions. While Calvin does not apply it directly to race, he certainly makes available the logic of fixity, inequality, and divine justification for future applications of the doctrine toward racist ends. Providence upholds concepts of inequality, but it also supports the concepts of authority, obedience, and submission in Calvin's theology.

Authority, Obedience, and Submission

In reflecting on the Pauline household codes, Calvin recognizes six classes of persons in relationships defined by authority and submission:[51] wives in submission to husbands, children in submission to parents, and slaves in submission to masters.

Calvin voices no view of mutual submission; that idea does not emerge within the evangelical tradition studied here until Carl Henry. Calvin focuses instead on the household codes' required submission of subordinates to superiors. This distinction is magnified by Calvin's comparison of husbands to Christ.[52] Calvin ignores the implication of Christ's sacrifice on behalf of the Church and focuses instead on the Church's obligation of submitting to Christ's authority. Likewise, the wife must submit to the husband's authority. Calvin says that wives are not "to refuse the subjection by means of which they might be saved," for to do so "is to choose destruction."[53]

Although Calvin's focus remains on submission, he does invoke the concept of a mutual yoke of duty, described in the chapter's previous discussion of distributive justice and hierarchy. This duty does not erase but must sustain the difference in station and the requirement of obedience and submission on the part of those subjected. At best, the duty they are owed in turn is benevolent treatment. But this duty in no way implies being owed equal treatment.[54]

As regards enslaved persons, God requires this benevolent care because God "is no respecter of persons" and sees the work of both the master and the slave as equal in value.[55] But again, this equality of work in no way changes their worldly statuses. Even if the subject is a "brother in Christ," he is not afforded different treatment as a result of this spiritual connection. Later discussion in this chapter takes up the distinctions Calvin makes between carnal and spiritual realities, but for now, it is enough to recognize that while either a master or a slave may be included among either the redeemed or the reprobate, inclusion among the redeemed does not change God's will for the person's earthly state. Spiritual redemption does not necessitate worldly liberation.

For Calvin, therefore, authority is grounded in the person's fixed position in society and the social obligations and duties required by their station. Authority derives from God's divine decree and therefore requires submission as obedience to God. Submission for Calvin is a universal state. Everyone, even those with the highest earthly authority, has an obligation of submission because even the highest monarch must submit to God. As God decrees earthly submission to earthly authorities, failure to submit also incurs the punishment of God.

Thus, Calvin uses the divine decree and divine revelation found in Scripture to support divinely mandated distinctions of inferiority and superiority, authority and submission, and obedience and power within human relationships. He joins Goldberg's primitive categories of racism to a theological discourse and grants divine sanction to these ideas as bases for racist logics. The result is a grammar of submission and authority, inferiority and superiority, within Calvin's idea of hierarchy, one that carries the weight of theological "truth" for Calvin. While such truth may not exist within a racist narrative in Calvin, it does forward a theology of subjection for future racist applications.

Revolution

If Calvin embeds a grammar of submission in a theological truth supported by the doctrines of divine revelation and decree, would rebellion and revolt ever be allowed within Calvin's theology? The answer is no. Calvin denies the right of revolution and rebellion, and he grounds his defense in the doctrine of the Fall, whereby Adam's original sin was rebellion, and humankind's tendency to rebellion and revolution is part of humanity's sinful nature. In grounding the original sin in revolt against God, Calvin shows strict regard for the need for humanity to keep "in its proper place": "The prohibition to touch the tree of knowledge of good and evil was a trial of obedience, that Adam, by observing it might prove his willing submission to the command of God, for the very term shows the end of the precept to have been to keep him contented with his lot, and not allow him arrogantly to aspire beyond it."[56] Calvin views Adam's disobedience as a revolt against God, the result of Adam's ambition to rise above his station and be more than he was created to be. According to Calvin, this ambition is the pathway to sin. "Infidelity opened the door to ambition," Calvin writes, "and ambition was the parent of rebellion, man casting off fear of God, and giving free vent to his lust."[57] It is, therefore, central to Calvin's view of Adam's sin, and its subsequent imputation to all of humanity, that Adam's discontent with his proper place, his ambition in trying to rise above it, and his refusal to remain subjugated to God's command all lie at the heart of humanity's ongoing sinfulness.

For this primary reason, Calvin opposes political revolution, even against tyrants and brutal monarchs. Because Calvin sees government, even bad government, as ordained by God and empowered by his providential will, Calvin does not allow for political revolution. To rebel against the magistrate is to rebel against God. Again, one can see his ideas of subjection, obedience, and observing one's proper place. "Although the Lord takes vengeance on unbridled domination," Calvin argues, "let us not therefore suppose that that vengeance is committed to us, to whom no command has been given but to obey and suffer. I speak only of private men."[58]

Individuals or groups have no recourse, then, to "throw off the yoke" of a tyrannical king; "all that remains to us," according to Calvin, "is to implore the help of the Lord, in whose hands are the hearts of kings, and inclinations of kingdoms."[59] Those afflicted by government oppression are left with prayer and patient suffering as their only remedies. Rebellion against the king is rebellion against God, even when the king acts in ungodly ways toward his subjects, and even when the king himself is reprobate and without God. Calvin allows only one exception: "We are subject to the men who rule over us, but subject only in the Lord. If they command anything against Him let us pay the least regard to it."[60] But this very narrow exception does not imply rebellion so much as civil disobedience and an understanding that the Christian subject must also accept the consequences. Calvin is not even clearly committed to this exception, given his refusal to support John Knox's proposed rebellion against the Catholic monarchs in Scotland.[61]

Thus, for Calvin rebellion is not an option and does not provide recourse against unjust authorities. Calvin grounds his opposition in a theological concept of sin and firmly embeds it in his notion of the Fall and Adam's original sin. Calvin, therefore, all but forestalls any means of mitigating disparity, inferiority, and inequality; he defines such mitigating efforts as sinful. He again creates a theological grammar that moves submission to the level of theological doctrine and divine "truth."

Civil Government

Bouwsma summarizes Calvin's views on civil authority: "Just as rulers are required to maintain order, subjects are obligated to obey them."[62] Again, Calvin's views on civil authority intersect with his views on divine order and decree. Calvin lays out these views in his Commentary on Romans and the Institutes.

Calvin bases his theological work on civil government primarily on his interpretation of Romans 13:1–7. His primary view is that government is a divine institution ordained by God to keep order by enacting justice for the protection of all. Because God, in God's providence, has duly ordained all forms of government, all forms of government are acceptable—including those that fail in their obligations to God and human society. The government exercises God's will in the world, whether for good or for evil. The magistrate holds a divinely ordained office and is due honor. Private persons have no right to object to, oppose, or rebel against the will of the magistrate. Three aspects of Calvin's doctrine here require special scrutiny: the operability of divine investiture in magistrates and particularly monarchs, the role of private persons in civil government, and the distinct roles of the Church and civil government in God's divine economy.

First, to what degree can the divine mandate of civil government be ascribed directly to rulers? For Calvin, this ascription is direct and absolute. The divine ordination of kings invests them "with a kind of sacred veneration and dignity."[63] He further suggests that those who serve as kings receive from God a special giftedness:

> When he (God) was pleased to set Saul over the kingdom he made him as it were a new man. This is the thing meant by Plato, when alluding to a passage in the Iliad, he says, that the children of kings are distinguished at their birth by some special qualities—God, in kindness to the human race often giving a spirit of heroism to those whom he destines to empire.[64]

Again, this distinction is true whether the king is good or evil, Christian or not, or whether he executes properly the office to which God has raised him.[65] Calvin sees kings in much the same way that he sees nations. Good kings represent God's blessings on the people; bad kings represent God's punishment.[66] Both serve as instruments of God—as instruments of either mercy or wrath. What is certain is that for Calvin, not just the office but the person is sacred and, in an iconographic way, is holy and worthy of reverence.

Thus, their authority is absolute, second only to God's. Here Calvin's thought exhibits some continuity with the medieval idea of the divine right of kings.

Calvin also addresses the role of private persons in civil society, already covered somewhat in this section's previous discussion of revolution. Not only do private individuals owe the magistrate general obedience and submission, but they also must not interfere in public matters: "Under the obedience, I comprehend the restraint which private men ought to impose on themselves in public . . . not interfering in public business, or rashly encroaching on the province of the magistrate or attempting anything at all of a public nature."[67] But what about cases where laws are unjust? Calvin covers that as well: "If it is proper that anything in a public ordinance should be corrected let them not act tumultuously or put their hands to work where they ought to feel that their hands are tied, but let them leave it to the cognizance of the magistrate, whose hand alone is free."[68] Thus, not only are private citizens not allowed to rebel, they are also not to involve themselves in any civil affairs. Calvin affirms both the absolute authority of the magistrate and the absolute subjugation of private persons related to civil matters.

But might the Church have a role to play in checking civil government? Calvin's answer seems to be no, as long as the government does not force Christians to abandon God or engage in idolatry. Calvin holds to a division of roles between the government and the Church. The Church tends to the things of God and the souls of humanity, while the government preserves order and administers justice. In fact, Calvin sees the Catholic Church's usurpation and exercise of civil power as one of its chief failings; he denies that his views of the Church include the right to exercise any powers of government. In a debate with Jacopo Sadoleto, Calvin argues: "The power of the sword and other parts of civil jurisdiction, which bishops and priests under the semblance of immunity had wrested from the magistrate and claimed for themselves, have not we restored to the magistrates?"[69] The Church, therefore, has no right to exercise power over the government, according to Calvin. The Church's only recourse—and it remains a "maybe" in Calvin—is to disobey laws that forbid worship of God or require worship of a false God. Even then, the government still has the right to punish those who violate even these unjust and ungodly laws, and the Church must submit gracefully to punishment and endure persecution. Thus, the state holds absolute power in civil matters, even over the Church.

Calvin's doctrine of civil government, then, affirms authority and submission to the government, doctrines that he centers in his theology of God's divine decree and order. God has decreed submission, and submission is required. Submission moves beyond a mere ethical or moral good; this divine requirement includes and ensures divine punishment for disobedience. Calvin weds social submission to his theological reflection on God and divine authority in a way that elevates it to the level of theological truth. Calvin's doctrine of civil government affirms governmental authority even when that authority includes racial exclusion and prejudice. This affirmation remains true whether Calvin himself applies it to racial logics or not.

Ancillary Matters

Several ancillary matters undergird both Calvin's vocabulary of hierarchy and his grammar of obedience, authority, and submission. These matters offer critical support for these views and require specific attention. They include his exegetical method, the limits he places on charity to the poor, economics, and Calvin's general rhetorical orientation.

Calvin's exegetical method is far more complex than the often-prescribed designation "precritical" suggests. George Stroup, following Hans Frei, says that what Frei "believes to be distinctive and important about Calvin's precritical reading of the Bible is that Calvin was convinced that the grammatical literal sense of the text was indeed the true sense and that Calvin recognized the 'natural coherence between literal and figural reading and the need of supplementation by the other.'"[70] But despite Calvin's insistence on coherence and uniformity of interpretation, Stroup recognizes his tendency to provide interpretative material and theological consistency where neither exists in the biblical text. Stroup highlights this tendency as Calvin's inability to honor "what Auerbach describes as the 'shadows' in the text." Stroup suggests that Calvin adds such material and consistency because "he is unwilling to allow the text to be silent on theological matters that are of overriding significance for him."[71] Calvin, that is, resolves the text's silence and ambiguity by speaking for it. He explains what the text refuses to explain. Stroup believes that Calvin's tendency "impoverishes both his theology and the biblical text he seeks to interpret."[72]

Why is this issue important to the current study? If racial logics depend on both the affirmation of inferiority and the denial or curtailment of basic freedoms or privileges, then such racist logics require a methodology that reconciles the apparent differences between the biblical texts supporting authority and those suggesting liberation and freedom. In his exegesis, Calvin both resolves the disparity and provides the methodological practice for doing so. Unsurprisingly, Karl Barth surmises that for Calvin, "spiritual liberty is truly compatible with political subjugation. Our human status and the national laws under which we live are not the thing that counts, for Christ's kingdom does not consist of such things."[73] With this in mind, just how Calvin employed these exegetical principles must be examined to consider how his exegesis creates openings for both subordination and the suppression of liberation.

Roland Frye goes a long way in identifying Calvin's various strategies in his interpretations of figurative texts. He ascribes Calvin's identification of a figurative text to his understanding of the doctrine of divine accommodation, which holds that God, through his word, has presented his revelation in ways that humanity can understand.[74] Anthropomorphism is the prime example; ascribing human features like arms, hands, or a face to God, who is spirit, represents a specific use of figurative language.

Even when the language is not literal, the figure or sign can be directly attributable to a spiritual truth or reality. Frye suggests that Calvin recognizes three rhetorical devices in Scripture: metaphor, metonymy, and synecdoche. Specifically, Calvin understands metaphor as the use of signs and symbols in the biblical text. Metonymy, Frye says, is "a figure of speech which consists in substituting for the name of a thing the name of an attribute of it or of something closely related."[75] Frye provides the classic example of the White House's switchboard operator answering, "This is the White House"; this figure of speech suggests that the operator represents the White House, not that the operator is the literal White House. Synecdoche, the third rhetorical device Frye recognizes, was identified by Calvin as "when the whole is sometimes taken for a part, sometimes a part for the whole." Calvin commented that "this figure is constantly occurring in Scripture."[76]

The problem with applying Calvin's rules for figurative language to submission and liberation texts is that Calvin does not use either subset of texts as figurative in the sense implied by any rhetorical devices. The only possible exception is Calvin's use of synecdoche to deprioritize charity and to downplay God's preference for the poor in Scripture. However, understanding Calvin's disparate interpretations of submission and liberation texts may require applying Stroup's understanding of Calvin's need to reconcile texts theologically, as opposed to the specific categories suggested by Frye. So how does Calvin utilize synecdoche to interpret texts related to charity and God's preference for the poor? A definitive study requires reviewing substantially more texts, but a look at how Calvin handles the parable of the sheep and the goats in the Gospel of Matthew might be instructive.

This parable is particularly difficult for Calvin because it seems to connect salvation with offering charity to the poor and oppressed. Calvin's commentary casts the parable as exemplifying true virtue. However, Calvin is not willing to allow the text's prioritization of charity to the poor to stand. He employs synecdoche to suggest that the passage has more in view than charity and benevolence toward the poor and oppressed:

> Christ does not here specify everything that belongs to a pious and holy life, but only, by way of example, refers to some of the duties of charity, by which we give evidence that we fear God. For though the worship of God is more

important than Charity towards men, and though, in like manner, faith and supplication are more valuable than alms, yet Christ had good reasons for bringing forward those evidences of true righteousness which are more obvious. . . . Accordingly, Christ does not make the chief part of righteousness to consist in alms, but, by means of what may be called more evident signs, shows what it is to live a holy and righteous life, as unquestionably believers not only profess with the mouth, but prove by actual performances, that they serve God.[77]

Calvin does not, of course, suggest that charity to the poor is unimportant, but he does shift the text's focus to the broader category of virtuous living, thereby decentralizing the charity that a more literal reading suggests. This rhetoric is a prime example of Calvin's interpretation of synecdoche as an exegetical strategy.

This approach has implications for the present study. Biblical texts related to the poor as defenses against racist forms of oppression are standard parts of the debate around liberation theology and biblical exegesis—used by both those who defend racist oppression and those who oppose it. At the very least, Calvin's use of this exegetical strategy weakens liberation theology's use of texts related to the poor and strengthens the case for those opposed to liberationist interpretations.

This exegetical method is also problematic for those offering literal interpretations. The subsumption of liberation texts within a larger theological explanation creates a history of text reception that minimizes liberation themes. Part III takes up the degree to which Calvin and others in the Reformed evangelical tradition (mis)read these texts contrary to the intent of the texts. But here I simply note that these potential uses of Calvin's reading and method do support anti-liberationist readings and potentially racist readings.

But Calvin exhibits a more apparent interpretive move. He is, as Barth says, able to envision the coexistence of both liberty and political servitude. Calvin interprets texts related to authority and liberty differently when he applies them to the temporal world. Specifically, he interprets texts related to submission as decrees from God to be applied literally to the physical world, whereas texts on liberty and freedom reference either an internal spiritual state or an eschatological future reality for the elect in heaven. Calvin notes and resolves this tension in his Institutes:

So why is it that the very same apostle who bids us "stand fast in the liberty wherewith Christ has made us free, and be not again entangled with the yoke of bondage" (Gal. 5:1), in another passage forbids slaves to be solicitous about their state (1 Cor. 7:21) unless it be that spiritual liberty is perfectly compatible with civil servitude.[78]

Calvin's theology, rooted in civil order and the consistency of the biblical text, is unable either to live with "the shadows," as Stroup suggests, or to abandon the literal temporal interpretation of submission in favor of the literal temporal interpretation of liberty and freedom. Calvin's theology makes spiritualization the primary hermeneutical lens for envisioning liberation and interpreting such biblical texts. His intention here, as Frye suggests, is "to make clear the saving meaning of God's word." But in doing so, Calvin may confirm Stroup's insight that "Calvin wants the text to say more than it does. And when the text refuses to do so, Calvin provides the missing material."[79] Stroup's final assessment of Calvin is telling; he asks "whether Calvin's theology is least compelling precisely at those points where his theology leads him to say more than the text does."[80]

Whether this is true is the work of part IV. For now, the key issue is the degree to which Calvin's spiritualization of liberty texts has been crucial to later racist logics that use this process to emphasize submission and deemphasize liberty.[81] This history of text reception presents a primary stumbling block to including liberationist interpretations within the evangelical tradition; a different interpretive history might have forestalled racist logics within the tradition. If spiritual theology can connect liberty and freedom to human interiority and eschatological hope by an exegetical "sleight of hand," then the biblical text cannot support an earthly liberation, and racist logic has at its disposal the tools of subjugation.

Thus, Calvin's exegetical method and conclusions hold real potential to support racist logics. He merges a theology of spiritual liberation with one of earthly submission to limit the text's impact on the question of liberty and strengthen its impact on questions of earthly authority and submission. Likewise, his use of synecdoche minimizes what scholars view as a biblical preference for the poor. So again, Calvin uses both methodology and a theological interpretation to limit liberty and freedom and enforce authority and submission—combining a racist primitive vocabulary with a theological focus that lends truth to the racist primitive vocabulary.

What should be apparent is that Calvin does evidence interpretative rules that bring his primitive racist vocabulary of hierarchy, authority, and submission into direct relationship with theological claims that lend "divine truth" to his understandings of hierarchy, authority, and submission. Among these theological categories, or grammars, are providence, the authority-obedience-submission triad, revolution, and civil government, as well as biblical revelation and interpretation leading to spiritualized readings of liberty and freedom. All of these critical moves create the potential for later racist use of Calvin, even if he does not directly offer racist rhetoric and applications.

RACIST NARRATIVE AND PERFORMANCE

As regards racist narratives and performance, any argument regarding Calvin is largely an argument from silence. Calvin does not engage in direct argumentation that can be identified as racialized or racist. The documentary evidence does not indicate any interest in race in his discourse. This lack of direct racist language seems subordinated to what Lindsey Kaplan describes as the Reformers' preoccupation with "intra-Christian enmity."[82] Calvin seems to have no interest in racial dialogue. Even his discussion of slavery avoids racial distinctions by treating slavery more as a class-based institution, rather than a race-based one, and by engaging it regarding its historical manifestations in ancient Rome.

Calvin did not own African slaves or directly participate in the African slave trade. According to Kayayan, Calvin was aware of the thriving Portuguese and Spanish trade in African bodies, but he makes little use of it in his discussion of slavery and certainly does not engage in what was at the time a prevalent rhetorical debate on the inferiority of Africans compared to other ethnic and racial groups.[83]

But something can be said, even if very tentatively, about Calvin's silence on the issues of racial categorization and trafficking in human bodies. As Cone suggests, Christian theologians should speak on these issues if they are aware of them. Calvin's awareness and his deprioritization (or ignorance) of race as an issue suggest not that he held antiracist views, but rather that racist views, categorization, and the justification of the trade in Africans formed a set of arguments fully reasonable to Calvin and did not require (or were irrelevant to) theological debate. While nothing definitive can be said in this regard, such discussions were certainly not anachronistic; they had been part of the theological debate since the fifteenth century, as Jennings makes clear.[84]

That said, little in Calvin seems to conclusively support a racist narrative, and nothing suggests a nondiscursive practice supportive of racist logics. The argument from silence remains speculative at best. Ultimately a strong case cannot be made for narrative and performative racist acts in Calvin's corpus.

EMBEDDED RACISM IN THE THEOLOGY OF JOHN CALVIN

What these arguments point to are elements of Calvin's thought that could be used later for more clearly racist purposes. Calvin's theology may be seen as in keeping with Goldberg's understanding of racist vocabulary and grammar, but these categories in Calvin do not ultimately generate a racist narrative or defend performance of racist acts.

Calvin's primitive vocabulary supports racist logics per Goldberg's definition, as it includes an understanding of hierarchy, negative characterization, and exclusion. This vocabulary has also been shown to be a part of a larger theological grammar. The combination of primitive vocabulary and theology lends "divine truth" to Calvin's claims about authority and submission. His theological engagement includes providence, the authority-obedience-submission triad, the order of creation and the Fall, revolution and civil government, spiritualization of liberation and freedom, and an exegetical method that supports the latter. But again, Calvin does not use any of these arguments to develop a specifically racist narrative.

At best, what one could say of Calvin is that he evidences what contemporary historians of race consider a "proto-racist" logic.[85] The understanding of proto-racism points to ideas that developed before specifically racist logics in modernity, ideas that are evident in antiquity, even if they are not applied directly to racial categories. Therefore, one can say that Calvin at a very primitive level does evidence at least components of racist thought and does succumb, again tentatively, to Cone's assessment of embedded racism. This assessment becomes more substantiated as the ideas' continuity and divergence are examined with regard to Edwards, Hodge, and Henry.

NOTES

1. Harvey, P. 2016. *Christianity and Race in the American South.* Chicago: University of Chicago Press.

2. de Gruchy, J. 1986. "The Revitalization of Calvinism in South Africa: Some Reflections on Christian Belief, Theology, and Social Formation." *The Journal of Religious Ethics* 14 (1986): 42.

3. Naude, P. "Toward Justice and Social Transformation? Appealing to the Tradition Against the Tradition." *HTS Teologiese Studies/Theological Studies* 73, no. 3 (2017): 1.

4. Goldberg, D. 1994: 50.

5. Loader, J. "Calvin's Election Mix in Small-Scale Theology." *HTS Teologiese Studies/Theological Studies* 65, no. 1 (2009).

6. Calvin, J. 2003. *Commentary on a Harmony of the Evangelists: Matthew, Mark, Luke, Vol. 3.* Translated by W. Pringle. Grand Rapids: Baker. 181; on election see Link, C. 2009. "Election and Predestination." In *John Calvin's Impact on Church and Society.* Edited by M. Hirzel and A. Sullmann. Grand Rapids: W. B. Eerdmans. 105–29.

7. Calvin, J. 2005. *Commentary on the First Book of Moses Called Genesis.* Translated by J. King. Grand Rapids: Baker. 544–45.

8. de Gruchy, 1986: 42; Kayayan, E. "Calvin on Slavery: Providence and Social Ethics in the 16th Century." *Koers Bulletin for Christian Scholarship* 78, no. 2 (2013); Vorster, N. "John Calvin on the Status and Role of Women in the Church and Society." *The Journal of Theological Studies* 68, no. 1 (2017): 178–211; Thompson, J. "Creata Ad Imaginem Dei, Licet Secondo Gradu: Woman as the Image of God According to John Calvin." *Harvard Theological Review* 81, no. 2 (1988): 125–43.

9. Potgieter, P. "John Calvin on Social Challenges." *Acta Theologica Supp* 28 (2019): 81.

10. Wallace, R. 1997. *Calvin's Doctrine of the Christian Life.* Eugene: Wipf and Stock. 158.

11. Calvin, J. 2005. *Commentary on the Four Last Books of Moses Arranged in the Form of a Harmony.* Translated by C. Bingham. Grand Rapids: Baker. 45.

12. Calvin, J. 2005. *Commentary on the Four Last Books of Moses.* 46.

13. Calvin, J. 2005. *Commentary on the Four Last Books of Moses.* 324.

14. Calvin, J. 1993. *Institutes of the Christian Religion.* Translated by H. Beveridge. Grand Rapids: W. B. Eerdmans. 404.

15. Calvin, J. 1993: 178.

16. Freudenberg, M. "Economics and Social Ethics in the Work of John Calvin." *HTS Teologiese/Theological Studies* (2009).

17. Calvin, J. 2005. *Commentary on the Epistles of Paul to the Galatians and Ephesians.* Translated by W. Pringle. Grand Rapids: Baker. 317–33.

18. Kayayan, E. 2013; Sytsma, D. "John Calvin and Virtue Ethics: Augustinian and Aristotelian Themes." *Journal of Religious Ethics* 48, no. 3 (2020): 519–56.

19. Calvin, J. 2005. *Commentaries on the Epistle to the Romans, Vol. 2.* Translated by C. Fetherstone. Grand Rapids: Baker. 477–85.

20. Hall, D. "Exegesis and Resistance: The Calvinistic Political Revolution of 1530–1580." *Puritan Reformed Journal* 8 (2016): 51–83.

21. Calvin, J. 2005. *Commentary on the Epistles of Paul.* 331.

22. Calvin, J. 2005. *Commentary on the Four Last Books of Moses.* 303–4.

23. Hall, D. 2016: 54, 59.

24. Goldberg, D. 1994: 98.

25. See Bouwsma, K. 1986. *John Calvin: A Sixteenth-Century Portrait.* Oxford: Oxford University Press. 181, on social determinism.

26. Calvin, J. 2005. *Commentary on the Last Four Books of Moses.* 46.

27. Calvin, J. 2005. *Commentary on the Epistles of Paul.* 330, 331, 357, 356.

28. Calvin, J. 2005. *Commentaries on the Evangelists.* Translated by C. Fetherstone. Grand Rapids: Baker. 180.

29. Calvin, J. 2005. *Commentary on the Last Four Books of Moses.*

30. Goldberg, D. 1994: 52.

31. Harvey, P. 2016; Noll, M. 2008; Kaplan, M. 2019.

32. Sanchez, M. "Calvin, Difficult Arguments, and Affective Responses: Providence as a Case Study in Method." *The Journal of Religion* 99 (2019): 470.

33. Kayayan, E. 2013: 5.

34. Calvin, J. 1993: 174.

35. Calvin, J. 1993: 172.

36. Calvin, J. 1993: 179.
37. Calvin, J. 1993: 187.
38. Calvin, J. 1993: 203.
39. Calvin, J. 1993: 200.
40. Calvin, J. 1993: 199.
41. Calvin, J. 1993: 177.
42. Calvin, J. 1993: 178.
43. Calvin, J. 1993: 179.
44. Calvin, J. 1993: 183, 184.
45. Calvin, J. 1993: 185.
46. Calvin, J. 2005. *Commentary on the Four Last Books of Moses.* 214.
47. Calvin, J. 1948. *Commentary on the First Twenty Chapters of the Book of the Prophet Ezekiel.* Edited by T. Myers. Grand Rapids: W. B. Eerdmans. 253.
48. Calvin, J. 1993: 178.
49. Potgieter, P. 2019: 72–87.
50. Calvin, J. 2005. *Commentary on the Epistles of Paul.* 330.
51. Calvin, J. 2005. *Commentary on the Epistles of Paul.* 317.
52. Calvin, J. 2005. *Commentary on the Epistles of Paul.* 317–18.
53. Calvin, J. 2005. *Commentary on the Epistles of Paul.* 318.
54. Calvin, J. 2005. *Commentary on the Epistles of Paul.* 329.
55. Calvin, J. 2005. *Commentary on the Epistles of Paul.* 331, 333.
56. Calvin, J. 1993: 212–13.
57. Calvin, J. 1993: 213.
58. Calvin, J. 1993: 674–75.
59. Calvin, J. 1993: 674.
60. Calvin, J. 1993: 674, 675.
61. Knox, J. 1994. *On Rebellion.* Cambridge: Cambridge University Press. 195.
62. Bouwsma, K. 1986. *John Calvin: A Sixteenth-Century Portrait.* Oxford: Oxford University Press. 206.
63. Calvin, J. 1993: 668.
64. Calvin, J. 1993: 252–53.
65. Calvin, J. 1993: 671.
66. Calvin, J. 1993: 670.
67. Calvin, J. 1993: 669.
68. Calvin, J. 1993: 669.
69. Calvin, J. 1966. *Jacopa Sadoleto: Reformation Debate.* Translated by H. Beveridge. Grand Rapids: W. B. Eerdmans. 55–56.
70. Stroup, G. 1990. "Narrative in Calvin's Hermeneutic." In *John Calvin and the Church: A Prism of Reform.* Edited by T. George. Louisville, Westminster John Knox Press. 161.
71. Stroup, G. 1990: 163.
72. Stroup, G. 1990: 168.
73. Barth, K. 1955. *The Theology of John Calvin.* Edited by G. Bromiley. Grand Rapids: W. B. Eerdmans. 208.

74. Frye, R. 1990. *John Calvin and the Church: A Prism of Reform.* Edited by T. George. Louisville: Westminster John Knox Press. 172–94.
75. Frye, R. 1990: 184.
76. Frye, R. 1990: 186.
77. Calvin, J. 2005. *Commentaries on the Evangelists.* 179.
78. Calvin, J. 1993: 651–52.
79. Stroup, G. 1990: 164.
80. Stroup, G. 1990: 165.
81. Harvey, P. 2016.
82. Kaplan, M. 2019: 14.
83. Kayayan, E. 2013.
84. Jennings, W. 2010. *The Christian Imagination: Theology and the Origins of Race.* Ann Arbor: Sheridan Books.
85. Kaplan, M. 2019.

Chapter 5

Jonathan Edwards and Racist Logics

To what degree can Jonathan Edwards be considered an heir to Calvin's sixteenth-century continental European theology? According to George Marsden, "Edwards was loyal to the theology inherited from the seventeenth-century Puritans and their continental 'Reformed,' or Calvinist, counterparts and he was pivotal in the emergence of international evangelicalism in the eighteenth century."[1] Likewise, Minkema says, Edwards "is an exponent of the Reformed, Puritan theological and pietistic framework that prevailed in New England since settlement and owed so much to Calvin."[2]

If Marsden and Minkema are correct, then Edwards perpetuates certain core values held by Calvin while also innovating on those values. Simply stating that Edwards shared values with Calvin is not enough. This project must also affirm the argument that Edwards perpetuates the proto-racist distinctions of Calvin within areas that the two agreed on, and also showed either racist or proto-racist tendencies in areas where Edwards significantly differs or innovates. This study must consider whether the divergences change the assessment of Edwards for better or worse in terms of racist logics.

Edwards' historical context also bears on the discussion, particularly to the degree to which race and racial diversity were intimately part of his life. Unlike Calvin, who was largely isolated from persons of non-European descent, Edwards had direct contact with African slaves, and he spent a substantial part of his ministry as a missionary to Native Americans in Stockbridge, Massachusetts. Race and racial diversity, then, were more directly part of Edwards' experience than Calvin's.

Edwards is also the first theologian considered in this study to work within a modernist Enlightenment frame of reference. This fact is particularly important for this study because this period first about which there is agreement among contemporary scholars that racist ideologies exist in their most readily identifiable form.

All of these facts suggest that any assessment of Edwards should be easier, simply because he had more points of contact with the modern phenomenon of race than did Calvin. Approaching Edwards from a textual basis, however, becomes somewhat more difficult because his literary corpus, though less extensive than Calvin's, is also less systematic. Of the four theologians evaluated here, only Edwards did not produce a work of systematic theology. As with Calvin, then, this study of Edwards will follow the lead of the extensive secondary literature while also favoring primary sources derived from Edwards's time at Stockbridge, including his sermons to his Native American congregation, letters referencing his work among Native Americans, and his theological works from this period, specifically *The Nature of True Virtue* and *Original Sin*. This chapter also refers to Edwards's scant primary text documents related to slavery. The study diverges from these documents where the secondary literature suggests doing so is appropriate or necessary.

As with Calvin, subsequent generations have also viewed Edwards in numerous ways that might suggest an approach different from the one taken by this study. However, these views generally reflect scholars' failure to deal adequately with the materials that focus specifically on race. The reality is that even given all the aforementioned factors and points of intersection between Edwards and the question of race, very little scholarly work has been done in this area. This study aims to fill that void and so remains distinctly focused on Edwards's discursive output and its potential use in furthering racist logics. Elements of Edwards' works might be utilized to undergird anti-racist theology, and that part of Edwards' legacy will be revisited in part IV. With that in mind, this chapter begins the analysis of Edwards by asking whether he evidenced components of racist logics at the level of vocabulary.

VOCABULARY

Edwards shares Calvin's use of language that affirms hierarchy, negative characterization of groups, and exclusion. His vocabulary not only is directed at class, gender, and religion but also at times focuses on race.

Hierarchy

In Edwards, one finds a disposition toward hierarchy and the requirement to maintain one's place or station in life. Marsden places Edwards well within the eighteenth-century British cultural milieu: "Eighteenth-century Britons viewed their world as British-American society depended on patriarchy. One's most significant relationships were likely to be vertical rather than horizontal."[3]

Likewise, Jon Pahl makes a strong case that Edwards takes an understanding of the spontaneity of God at work in the Northampton revivals and replaces it with an ever-increasing hierarchical and ordered society. Pahl insists that this hierarchical bent has political implications within Edwards' theology.[4]

Edwards affirms the idea of inferiority and superiority in human relationships and continues Calvin's idea of a dual bond of duty between superiors and inferiors, governed by the law of love, without denying the deference due to superiors by virtue of their position: "Love will dispose to sustainable carriage between superiors and inferiors . . . it will dispose children to honor their parents, and servants to be obedient to their masters, not with eye-service, but in singleness of heart; and it will dispose masters to exercise gentleness and goodness toward their servants."[5] He says further that humility "leads also to a meek behavior toward men, making us condescending to inferiors, respectful to superiors."[6] While Edwards' language affirms the need for loving relationships, his focus is on the way love sustains the social order, as Marsden suggests; what is in view remains a securely hierarchical society. Edwards' argument also sustains the concepts of superiority and inferiority despite his suggestions for the ethical treatment of inferiors.

Edwards' view of hierarchy was also racialized. In a letter to William Pepperrell regarding the education of Native American children, Edwards considers one benefit to be "that they would learn to respect their superiors"[7]—referring not to adults but to the English and others of higher class and station.

Per Pahl, Edwards sees hierarchy as necessary for order, which, as with Calvin, reflects God's intended order in nature. Edwards insists, "There is a beauty of order in society . . . when the different members of society have all their appointed office, place, and station, according to the several capacities and talents, and everyone keeps his place and continues in his proper business."[8] Thus Edwards perpetuates a hierarchical structure that meets Goldberg's definition of a primitive category. The fact that he does so in direct reference to a racial group is even more critical, although not necessary to satisfy Goldberg's definition at this level. What is important is that Edwards distinguishes between inferior and superior persons and implies an exclusion that, if applied to racial categories, can fuel racist logics of superiority and privilege.

Negative Characterization

Negative characterization, when it functions to classify, also meets Goldberg's definition of a primitive term. In his writings about the Native Americans from his time in Stockbridge, Edwards does engage in negative race-based characterizations, which he sees as inherent in the group and not just incidental among individuals.

Among other things, Edwards refers to Native Americans as savage, unclean, ignorant and stupid, uncivilized, wild, and unhappy. In a letter to Pepperrell, he states that he is educating and evangelizing the Native American children "in view of leading them to renounce the coarseness, and filth and degradation of savage life, for cleanliness, refinement and good morals."[9] He also characterizes the Native American nations as "the dark parts of the continent" in a letter to Joseph Paice.[10] In all fairness, he also describes the Dutch in the New York colony as "exceeding ignorant, stupid and profane." But even here his baseline for comparison is the "savages of our American desert."[11]

The secondary literature does occasionally note Edwards's negative characterizations, but generally only in passing and rarely specifically connected to his racial attitude. The topic usually emerges in articles that characterize Edwards as progressive in his views toward the Native Americans "for his time."[12] These arguments are taken up in greater detail below. For now, regardless of any proof that Edwards was "less" racist than other pastors and theologians of his time, the fact is that his language, directed at Native Americans as a group, constitutes the negative characterization of an entire racial group.

Exclusion

Likewise, Edwards' language is exclusionary. Like Calvin, Edwards distinguishes between the regenerate and the unregenerate, the elect and the reprobate. Facing Native American religions, Edwards does not take an inclusivist position. Instead, he sees them as devoid of real truth and even derived from demonic origins. Any truth or similarity between native religion and Christianity is a remnant of divine revelation from before the Flood but corrupted by the devil.[13] Thus, even the truth in indigenous religions is corrupt, for Edwards, and excludes Native Americans both morally and spiritually from any relationship with God's elect people.

Edwards argues that Native Americans as a people were previously excluded from God's grace and have since lived in darkness, ignorance, and unhappiness. He ascribes many of his negative characterizations directly to the distance at which God's providence placed them from Christ.[14] Edwards' rhetoric also suggests that the English are the elect, being called, in the providence of God, to deliver the Native Americans from this state of ignorance and unhappiness.[15]

Apart from religious exclusion, Edwards also insists on cultural exclusion, or perhaps he equated inclusion within Christianity as requiring or inculcating the adaptation of British cultural norms and abandonment of Native American culture. Thus, exclusion and inclusion become predicated on acculturation. For example, Edwards requires, as a precondition for a true understanding of God, that Native Americans learn to read the Bible in English.[16] He points to the supposed inadequacy of Native languages, "their own barbarous languages being exceeding barren and very unfit to express moral and divine things."[17] Beyond considering Native languages unable to express religious matters, he sees the English language as civilizing. "Being brought to the English language," he argues, "would open their minds, and bring 'em to acquaintance and conversation with the English, and would tend above all things to bring that civility which is to be found among the English."[18]

In this way, Edwards connected inclusion in God's kingdom with civility supposedly evident in English culture but not Native American culture. He associated the negative traits of Indigenous culture with their prior exclusion from the election of God. Notions of religious exclusion thereby merge with cultural superiority in Edwards' estimation of Native Americans as a hereditary group. While religious exclusion remains a religious category for Calvin, Edwards associates it with a history of racial and national redemption that features the English as elect and the Native Americans as reprobate; uses that history to explain deficiencies in Native language, culture, and morality; and ultimately expects acculturation into English culture as at least an outcome of, if not a requirement for, religious inclusion.

Thus, there is good reason to suggest racist vocabulary is found in Edwards' work. The assessment differs, however, between Calvin and Edwards. Calvin's use of hierarchy, negative characterization, and exclusion cannot be directly tied to specific race-related conclusions. Edwards, on the other hand, applies these categories directly to a specific racial group; therefore, one can more easily recognize his categories as supporting racist logics. Edwards' negative characterization of Native Americans, his insistence on categories of superiority and inferiority, his call for individuals to observe their proper place, and his exclusionary language that treats Native Americans as deficient in character because they have not aspired to either Christian religion or to English language, manners, culture, and habits—these all point to a view of Native Americans as racially and culturally inferior and of English Christians as superior spiritually and culturally. Although Edwards offers hope for the elevation of Native Americans as a group if they turn to Christ, this elevation comes only when attached to acculturation. Beck's assessment, following Wilson Kimmich, rings true: "Edwards' attitude toward the Indians was, for the most part, that of a typical eighteenth-century European: paternalistic and superior."[19] Thus, one can reasonably posit that Edwards does exhibit a racist vocabulary tied directly to a racial group.

GRAMMAR

If Edwards exhibits a racially directed vocabulary, the next step is to determine whether theological points—and in Edwards' case, philosophical arguments—undergird his vocabulary and can be viewed as a racist grammar underpinning a racist logic. To show continuity and discontinuity with Calvin, this section first takes up the doctrine of providence; Edwards's theological arguments related to authority, submission, and order; and his views on civil government and revolution. The study then examines grammatical ideas unique to Edwards that pertain directly to the question of race and racism: his theology and philosophy of knowledge; his assertion of an eschatological manifest destiny (millennialism); his views on aesthetics, beauty, and benevolence; and his prioritization of the spiritual over the material. The first three categories are suggested by the preceding chapter's analysis of Calvin. The secondary literature on Edwards suggests examining his theology of knowledge, eschatological manifest destiny, and prioritization of the spiritual; and an examination of his theories of beauty, aesthetics, and benevolence is suggested by Cornel West's study of discursive arguments that fed racist ideology in the Enlightenment.

Providence

This section asks whether Edwards maintains Calvin's view of divine providence that is deterministic of human disparity and hierarchy. The short answer is yes—but within a very different formulation. Both Calvin and Edwards agree that providence is more than a set of natural laws that God has put in place and then left to work on their own. Calvin's view suggests a cosmic chess player moving pieces on both sides of the board at a distance to achieve his desired ends. Why God makes the moves he does, what moves he will make in the future, and how to interpret the moves he made in the past—these are all lost to the hidden counsel of God. But what is certain is that everything that happens does so because of God and should be accepted.

While Edwards would have concurred with Calvin, his theological description of providence differs significantly. Edwards believes that the connection between God and God's creation is relational and undergirds the doctrine of providence. This idea derives from Edwards' understanding of the relational Trinity; his notion of participation, emanation, and remanation; and his idea of continuous creation.

Gerstner summarizes the intimate connection between Edwards' doctrines of providence and creation: "Creation and providence are the same in Edwards' thought. Creation is merely the first time that God brought something out of nothing. Providence is the subsequent times. Continuing creation is his doctrine of creation and we might say that continuing creation is his doctrine of providence."[20] Providence, then, is God's continuing creative act, on which creation totally depends for its continued existence.

Edwards also sees creation and God's continuing creative act as relationally linked. God is no distant chess player in Edwards' thought. As Delattre points out, Edwards builds his ethics and much of his theology on the idea of humanity's participation in God, framed as a relational connection. Edwards goes so far as to suggest that creation is an enlargement of God's self.[21] Thus, an intimate connection exists between creator and created that is preserved in the constant work of continuing creation. This is what Delattre means when he claims that "the process of continuing creation is represented by Edwards in this image of a cosmic flow of divine fullness in emanation and remanation."[22] There is a back-and-forth between creator and created as God extends God's self through God's providential acts and as creation responds in an intimate recognition of God's glory.

This relational notion of God's providence has three important components. First, the purpose of everything within God's providence is to glorify God. Humanity, creation, and human history are all continually created in and for the glory of God. Second, humanity exists as a relational extension of God; God's providential involvement in the world takes place through this relational connection. This involvement is imminent and personal. God is not a chess player moving pieces on the board. God is directly connected to those on whom God's providence acts. Edwards' view of providence is therefore far more personal and intimate than Calvin's. And the third aspect of creation's connection to God is that the emanation and remanations that bind created to creator result in the creation's extreme dependence on the creator. The doctrine of continuing creation heightens this dependence by making the preservation of humanity dependent on God's continuous creative act.

This notion is deeply connected to Edwards' understanding of the relational Trinity. Henry summarizes, "God creates a world that reflects his own perfection. Since God has lived in Trinitarian communion, his creation reflects the divine nature by also living in relational community."[23] Thus, Edwards envisions the connection between God and creation as reflecting the connections within the Godhead.

But what of those whom regeneration does not connect to God in this relational way? This question remains a problem for Edwards, one that he does not resolve. The reprobate are still acted upon according to the providence of God; but this action is God's external action, not God's internal connection and influence with the elect. Edwards describes this relation in terms of infusion and coercion. God's will is infused into the elect, but God's will is coerced in the reprobate. But again, this description sometimes seems out of sync with the rest of Edwards' views on providence.[24]

While Edwards' conception of providence differs from Calvin's, it maintains Calvin's determinism. And while Edwards avoids assigning God culpability for conditions like poverty and slavery, ultimately, he affirms that all human conditions come from God and must be accepted. Minkema agrees that Edwards' doctrine of providence "outdoes Calvin's concerns to preserve absolute divine sovereignty and human dependence."[25] When one adds Edwards' views on hierarchy and order to his emphasis on sovereignty and human dependence, all events that occur within God's providence require submissive acquiescence.

Henry demonstrates this in his study of Edwards' views on property rights.[26] Henry argues that Edwards views personal property and wealth as gifts bestowed on individuals by God's providence. Similarly, a lack of property is also a part of God's providential act. According to Henry, the idea of providence is critical to Edwards' defense of personal property rights. Likewise, Gerstner points out that providence in Edwards is synonymous with God's distributive justice.[27] As is clear from the previous chapter's discussion of this concept in Calvin, "distributive" does not mean "egalitarian." Edwards shared Calvin's view that inequality can exist within the justice of God.

Edwards also differs significantly from Calvin in relation to how he uses history to map God's providential work. Ronald VanderMolen charts the changes in the use of history from Calvin to Anglicanism to early Puritanism. According to VanderMolen, Calvin denies "the validity of human judgements (as regards God's providential will) based on historical obscuration."[28] Calvin sees no credibility in those who use history as a guide to the providence of God; he shrouded historical events in the hidden counsel of God. Early Puritans, however, were not content to allow God's providence to remain hidden but insisted that "God's disposition and intentions in historical events are not limited to what scripture records; instead, the ordinary course of history becomes the revelation of God's judgement."[29]

Edwards shared this belief with the larger Puritan tradition. This approach to providential history allowed him to speculate on the spiritual history of Native Americans. According to Edwards, after Christ's ascension, Satan was forced to flee the known world for less habitable regions of the North, and he took his followers, which included the indigenous peoples who ended up in North America. Likewise, God in his providence led the English to colonize North America in part to evangelize the Native Americans.[30] God, Satan, and other spiritual forces were at work in the events of human history.

What then can one make of the differences between Calvin's and Edwards' views of providence? First, Edwards' relational explanation for providence does not alter the doctrine's deterministic nature—he remains as deterministic as Calvin. Human conditions including poverty, slavery, and other forms of inequality continue to be intimately intertwined with the will of God, and Edwards maintains the requirement for patient endurance. Second, far from exonerating Edwards from racist use, his differing views on history allow him to narrate a history of Native Americans that frames them as demonic and savage and supports British colonization as the providential will of God.

Thus, Edwards' doctrine of providence contains Calvin's same basic language of passive submission and inequality but also uses it to support a racist account of Native American history and British colonialism. Calvin's views allowed for the suppression of individuals according to class, gender, and vocational position, whereas Edwards's doctrine expanded to include hereditary groups described in racist ways. Thus, providence for Edwards functions as a theological truth that supports racial distinction, inferiority, inequality, and passive submission.

Authority, Submission, and Order

As the preceding discussions have made clear, Edwards did not deviate from Calvin's ideas about authority, submission, and order. Marsden, Pahl, and other Edwards scholars would affirm in Edwards' theology the need to submit to authority. But Edwards' view moves beyond that of Calvin.

Edwards sees authority and submission as necessary to maintain proper order. For Edwards, order is paramount. While Calvin's idea of proper social order may be supported by an obligation of obedience to Scripture, Edwards provides a far more metaphysical defense. In *Nature of True Virtue*, Edwards argues that creation participates in God's self. This participation therefore reflects the divine. The beauty of God, and by extension of creation, rests in God's harmony, evidenced in the rational Trinity and God's order. As an extension, through its participation in God, the world should reflect the order and harmony of the Godhead. This social order, realized through relationships of inferiority and superiority, is part of God's natural design.[31] Thus, for Edwards, order is part of God's imprint on human society, providing for humanity's good. Ideas of authority, subordination, place, and station are thereby wedded closely to the person of God. This approach infuses Edwards' ideas of social stratification with far more divine authority than exists in Calvin. For Edwards, order is mandated by the divine person; in Calvin, it is mandated by the divine decree.

Thus, Edwards's theological system codifies order, harmony, authority, inferiority, and superiority as direct attributes of God's person. While Edwards may spend less time on the practical aspects of these ideas, they remain central to station and place within his worldview. He finds a way to make order an aspect of the doctrine of God, and he extends that order to humanity through notions of authority, inferiority, and superiority. He brings together ideas inherent in racist logics and links them with the doctrine of God to create a truth claim that is deeply embedded in and dependent on his theology, creating the opportunity to extend it to racist logics.

Civil Government and Revolution

Pahl best summarizes Edwards' views of civil government: "Calvinists undoubtedly loved order at least as much as they loved freedom, and this logical side of Calvinism, the side inclined to social stability, order and hierarchy, has remained largely unexplored in recent American studies."[32] This gap is a particular shortfall in scholarship on Edwards. Alexis says, "Except for the occasional piece, like a funeral sermon for a magistrate, Edwards writes as though almost totally preoccupied with 'things of religion,' civil matters neither constituting a real problem nor possessing vital interest."[33]

But any suggestion that Edwards has no theory of the social is untrue. Caleb Henry points out that Edwards did develop a theory of human society based on his interactions with John Locke. Henry maintains,

> Edwards' relational ontology gave Edwards a solid foundation for his political thought. Man's instincts drive men toward society and politics, while his relational nature provides (or at least points toward) the natural laws that should guide the society and regime more specifically. Edwards believed that providence could resolve the tension between the communal demands of natural law and the individual's self-interested natural right to property.

But Edwards seems to advance this theory of the social not in the interest of a true social ethic, but more as a theoretical answer to Locke's epistemology. He does seem to address the tension between communal and individual rights but offers little that opposes Calvin's pragmatic and exegetical reflections on civil government.

Edwards' exegesis of Romans 13 in the Blank Bible is instructive. He spends more time discussing his understanding of original revelation and affirming that civil government is a natural law—including the idea that in antiquity God taught this law as part of the original revelation, even to the "heathen" nations. But although Edwards' focus shifts from pragmatic exposition to the conception of civil government within a redemption-historical context, he does not stray from Calvin's pragmatic conclusions. Civil government is still "ordained of God," and the requirement to honor civil government remains intact in Edwards' thought. He does not, however, fully develop his theory of government, so he avoids questions like submission to tyrannical regimes. However, Edwards' exegesis, like Calvin's, supports submission to authority. Thus, it would be difficult to imagine that Edwards' views on the relationship of private persons to civil government diverge significantly from Calvin's.

What Edwards lacks in pragmatics, he makes up in theological innovation. He places his hierarchical view of government into conversation with his view of divine monarchy. Given Edwards' belief that the created order and divinely ordained institutions reflect the nature of God, his views of divine monarchy bring into view the extent of civil authority as a divinely appointed institution. Thus, the sovereignty of God within the divine monarchy becomes conflated with the sovereignty of government in the carnal world, again regarding God's reflected order in creation.

This observation links directly to a secondary topic. Edwards has no theory or ethics of revolution, but most scholars believe he opposes it, based on his views of order outlined above. However, he does develop a theory of passive submission within his concept of the divine monarchy: the sovereign is owed complete submission, and rebellion is a sin. By extension, revolution against God's ordained governmental powers constitutes rebellion against God and God's order. Thus, Edwards was highly unlikely to have supported civil rebellion, certainly not a revolt based on class or race.[34]

What does this say about Edwards' grammar of civil authority when applied directly to racial equality? Edwards so trivializes the question that he risks minimizing the theological significance of any question of political import, including racial, ethnic, or class inequality. Edwards also carries forward Calvin's hierarchical and submissive views of civil society and strengthens them theologically through his understanding of divine monarchy and God's sovereignty. Thus, submission to governmental authority becomes intimately connected to the theology of divine sovereignty and elevated to divine truth. This responsibility of dual submission to God and human superiors further makes it possible to codify submission within race-based systems.

PHILOSOPHY OF KNOWLEDGE

Edwards' chief epistemological conclusion is that no thought exists "without external ideas immediately impressed by God."[35] Knowledge comes from revelation, and without this revelation, humanity would exist in a state of barbarism.[36] In fact, all who lack knowledge of God dwell in a state of barbarism and are inferior to those who have the revelation of God.

From this doctrine, Edwards proposes two imaginative, and highly negative, views about the existence and distinctions of races. His first theory, already mentioned, is that proximity to revelation in place and time determines the barbarism of a people:

> I am of the mind that mankind would have been like a parcel of beasts with respect to their knowledge of all important truths, if there never had been any such thing as revelation in the world, and that they never would have rose out of their brutality. We see that those that live at the greatest distance from revelation as to time and place, are far more the brutish. The heathen in America and in some (of) the utmost parts of Asia and Africa are far more barbarous than those that live at Rome, Greece, Egypt, Syria and Chaldea formerly; their traditions are more worn out, and they are more distant from places enlightened with revelation.[37]

He also saw China as more civilized because they descended from people taught by Noah.

Edwards also has a second imaginative theory of racial diversity: Before the time of Christ in the Roman empire, the devil held power over the people of the known world; but at Christ's ascension, the devil fled the Roman world with his followers and went North, including the northern uninhabitable regions and the Americas. Edwards equates Native Americans with this satanic exodus: "Some of the Americans gave this account when the Europeans first came hither."[38]

Edwards' speculative theories would never be incorporated into contemporary theological discourse, but they do exhibit some basic patterns of racist grammar that have been incorporated and can be continued. Views of the relationship between Christian "civilization" and "heathen" cultural "barbarism" continued in some form throughout early Western missionary movements, which often associated salvation with "civilizing." Edwards' theories also evidence the kind of racial categorization that prevailed well into the modernist period. His belief that Europeans and Chinese are less "barbaric" than Native Americans, Africans, and other Asians echoes the elaborate theories of racial superiority and classification that emerged in the fifteenth century and characterized the nineteenth and early twentieth centuries in the United States and Europe.[39]

The intellectual, cultural, and spiritual privileging of Christian "civilization"—which in Edwards' era was primarily a white Euro-colonial enterprise—and the comparative ethnography of racial inferiority evidenced in his writings, all represent a racist grammar that positions English colonialists in a superior position over Native Americans and Africans. But Edwards embeds these tendencies in his doctrine of revelation, philosophy of knowledge, and doctrine of redemptive history, tying racist logic to theological doctrine and allowing racist grammar to prove the theological doctrine.

Eschatological Manifest Destiny

At the end of his article about Edwards' eschatological millennialism, C. C. Goen speculates,

> At all events, he gained the distinction of being America's first major postmillennial thinker. As such, he may be said to have furnished the religious philosophy for responding to the challenge of 'manifest destiny.' The importance of the religious background of the idea of progress can never be disparaged; and though direct evidence may be lacking, it is difficult to believe that Edwards' historicizing of the millennium did not furnish strong impetus to utopianism in America.[40]

Goen's article firmly establishes Edwards' belief in an imminent, historical millennial reign brought on by the Church, but he fails to examine the racial undertones of Edwards' perceptions. Edwards did see the millennium as heralded by the evangelization of both the Native Americans and the nations abroad. In Edwards, Goen sees an embodiment of manifest destiny, but he fails to comment on the British superiority that undergirds Edwards' claims—even though Goen directly quotes Edwards as saying, "The most barbarous nations shall become as bright and polite as England." Goen is correct that Edwards' vision is ultimately a benevolent one in which "ignorant and heathen lands shall bask in the brightest light of gospel truth, men shall live as brothers in a world of love."[41] But Goen's work lacks a critical analysis of power that underlies Edwards' views about the salvation of Native Americans and other nations.

Edwards views the subduing of nations as part of God's providential will for the English Church in America. "All things are subordinated to the redemption and happiness of the saints," Edwards insists, "that not (only) is their Redeemer set over all things, but they are set over all things and shall reign over all things in and with him. They shall reign over all things as sitting with Christ on his throne."[42]

Edwards' language of subordination and subjection is a central part of his discourse on evangelization. But in the Native American mission, he also sees political advantages that tie the missionary endeavor directly to colonization. Edwards makes this political angle clear in a letter to Paice:

> The English have not only greatly failed of their duty in so neglecting there the instruction of the Indians but we have been extremely impolitic and by our negligence in this matter have brought the whole British America into very difficult and dangerous circumstances. . . . While we have been asleep, our most dangerous and inveterate enemies, the French, have been aware; they have discerned and taken advantages which we have overlooked.[43]

When one considers this overt colonial political agenda alongside an evangelizing program that characterizes those without the gospel as lacking not only spiritual truth but also proper "civilized" behavior and then combines this with triumphal millennialism, one gets a picture of white colonial dominance and the subordination of nations.

Setting aside whether Edwards' views on evangelism are biblically and theologically correct, what emerges is a direct agenda of subjugation, acculturation, and inferiority based on racial categorization that itself deeply depends on Edwards' doctrines of revelation, redemption history, providence, and eschatology. The result is a racialized argument that depends on a theological doctrinal grammar, has the potential to fuel racist logics, and embeds racist objectives in theological truth claims.

Aesthetics, Beauty, and Benevolence

Many studies of Edwards' ethics are based largely on interpretations of *The Nature of True Virtue* and *Charity and Its Fruits*, but all lack the critical analysis of power and racial implications envisioned by this study.[44] Thus, this discussion examines elements of Edwards' philosophy of beauty and virtue that scholars have overlooked while attempting not to stray too far from standard interpretations of the broader issues.

Edwards offers an early example of the emerging Enlightenment focus on aesthetics, which West relates directly to modern racist logics. While Edwards never applies this focus directly to racialized discourse, the implications of his reasoning directly enable racist applications.

His very densely reasoned philosophical treatise, *The Nature of True Virtue*, argues that true virtue consists in the love of God and God's creation—what Edwards calls "benevolence to being in general." Virtue, according to Edwards, consists in a beauty of heart reflected in a benevolent disposition.[45]

What Edwards hopes to achieve might be described as a hierarchy of benevolence. Within this hierarchy, the most virtuous act is benevolence toward God as supreme being and to his created order. Ultimately Edwards' goal is to demonstrate that all virtuous acts begin and end with a benevolent disposition toward God.

The problem, however, is not Edwards' primary thesis but his ancillary arguments. In placing God at the top of a hierarchy of benevolence, he cannot help but create a hierarchy of goodwill within humanity as well. As he turns from benevolence to God and toward benevolence to particular being—by which he means both humanity and the created order—he advocates for benevolence according to superiority and inferiority of being:

One being may have more existence than another, as he may be greater than another. That which is great has more existence and is further from nothing, than that which is little. One being may have everything positive belonging to it, or everything which goes to its positive existence (in opposition to defect) in a higher degree than another: a great capacity and power, greater understanding, every faculty and every positive quality in a higher degree.[46]

Edwards further clarifies that benevolence is owed "particular beings in greater and lesser degree, according to the reason for their existence and beauty which they are possessed of."[47] He establishes a hierarchy of benevolence based not only on degrees of being and virtue but also on beauty.

When Edwards speaks of "degrees of being," he is advancing the idea that a higher degree of being is found among anything that works toward its "appointed ends" or is fit "to answer the design for which it was made." "Therefore," Edwards says, "they are good moral agents, whose temper of mind or propensity of heart is agreeable to the ends of which God made moral agents." Add the degree to which particular beings possess capacity, power, and understanding, and what comes into view is what Edwards means by "according to the degree of its being" and "according to the reason of existence." That is, those beings who serve diligently the purpose for which God created them, with respect to the greatness of their capacity, power, and understanding, are to be accorded more benevolence than those who work contrary to their purpose and place and also those of lesser capacity, power, and understanding. Degrees of virtue, on the other hand, are determined by the degree to which a particular being possesses benevolence to being in general or, put another way, to which a particular being loves God.

Finally, Edwards develops an aesthetic theory to account for what he means by "beauty which they are possessed of." Edwards describes natural beauty as "secondary" or "inferior" in relation to the beauty of being in general, but he sees natural beauty as an important distinguisher in his hierarchy of benevolence. He argues that God created natural law that has embedded in the mind of humanity an appreciation for beautiful things. Conversely, humanity has a distaste for those things that are not beautiful.[48]

Edwards' understanding of beauty lies both in the correct usefulness of the object in question, as above, and in its symmetry, form, and harmony. He applies this understanding to the human body. "So a man," insists Edwards, "may be affected and pleased with a beautiful proportion of the features in a face."[49] Edwards again argues that physical beauty is secondary to spiritual beauty, but he insists that we could not know inward beauty apart from an innate understanding of physical beauty.

How does this argument affect an assessment of Edwards's racist grammar? It delineates a hierarchy of benevolence that further positions those in power, those with intellect, and those with material means over those who lack any of these things. It amplifies Edwards' focus on superiority and inferiority and ascribes a greater degree of goodwill to those in power while perpetuating the value of "knowing one's place." This argument also assigns greater benevolence to believers, and it advances an understanding of aesthetic beauty that makes what humans view as beautiful anything that God's natural law has inscribed on their hearts.

Thus, Edwards opens the door to codifying as sanctioned by God anything that White Euro-Americans accept as standards of beauty, symmetry, and form. What humanity sees as physically ugly and deformed, in other words, God sees in the same way. Ascribing this aesthetic to the human body only expands the potential for its use as a component of racist logic. Thus, Edwards' views on true virtue become a logic with racist implications.

The Priority of the Spiritual

In several instances above, Edwards' views on the priority of the spiritual over the material affect his understanding of particular issues. He summarizes his views on the priority of the spiritual in his notes on natural philosophy: "It follows that those beings which have knowledge and consciousness are the only proper and real and substantial beings, inasmuch as the being of other things is only these, from hence we may see the gross mistake of those who think material things the most substantial beings, and spirits more like shadow; whereas spirits only are properly substance."[50] Edwards likewise insists that those with "true religion have their hearts loosed from things of this world and have their hearts in heaven"; that their time in this world is short; and that the existence of the spiritual world, meaning heaven and hell, is the only just resolution for the suffering of the good and the blessings of evil persons in this world.[51]

Few scholars, if any, deny the degree to which Edwards elevates spiritual concerns over material and worldly concerns. A growing consensus among scholars of Edwards' biblical hermeneutic holds that Edwards favored either the spiritual interpretation of texts or their redemption-historical interpretation.[52] The latter view seems consistent with the former, given the degree to which Edwards's redemption-historical interpretation prioritizes the spiritual over the literal. Edwards consistently applies the spiritual in lieu of the material, in both his exegetical method and his philosophical views.

Edwards also directly maintains a dichotomy in his treatment of racial groups based on disparate views of their temporal and spiritual existences. This chapter has already demonstrated the degree to which Edwards engages in racist categorization of Native Americans' temporal state and the extent to which he affirms English superiority. But in assessing the spiritual state of those Native Americans who embrace Christ, Edwards' rhetoric implies equality before God. This aspect of Edwards' views toward Native Americans allows both Wheeler and Armstrong to assess Edwards as ahead of his time; but both almost totally overlook Edwards' temporal rhetoric and the pragmatic, racist implications of his thought beyond a future or internal state. Edwards does not move beyond Calvin and in fact may have exceeded him by integrating a specific race-based dimension into this spiritual/material split.

Edwards tended to either spiritualize or completely ignore passages of Scripture dealing explicitly with freedom and liberation. The Blank Bible notes on Galatians 5 offer a prime example. Edwards omits any mention of either verse 1 "for freedom Christ has made us free" or verse 13a "you were called to freedom." His exegesis instead comprises a lengthy discussion of the redeemed spirit and "the flesh" as references to the unregenerate nature—suggesting that any conception of freedom and liberty beyond freedom from sin was not a primary concern for Edwards.[53] This concept is absent in his theology.

Thus, one can see that Edwards spiritualized texts to minimize freedom and liberty; that he held to a dichotomy between this world and the next that created pragmatic problems for marginalized groups and suggested a sharp divide between spiritual liberty and worldly subjugation; and that he fully applied these ideas to a racist rhetoric about Native Americans that could sound at once highly offensive yet, when shifted to spiritual matters, liberating. But regarding this world, like Calvin, Edwards is ultimately careful to preserve standards of superiority and inferiority, and unlike Calvin, he does so in relation to race.

The foregoing analysis suggests a racist grammar inherent in Edwards' theology, formed by connecting theological doctrine with racist argumentation. Edwards' views of providence, authority, and civil government, although different from Calvin's views, evidence the same issues and raise their own concerns. Edwards adds two theories of race—grounded in an epistemology focused on the primacy of revelation—that affirm Europeans' religious and cultural superiority and the inferiority of Native Americans, Africans, and non-Chinese Asians. Further, he evidences an eschatological manifest destiny that weds evangelistic effort to colonial political power and undergirds both with eschatological triumphalism. In doing so, he positions White European Americans as the triumphant conquerors and redeemers and Native Americans as the conquered and rescued heathens.

Additionally, Edwards' philosophical reflections on true virtue create a hierarchy of benevolence that defers to those with power and suggests a God-ordained notion of aesthetic beauty that deifies Euro-American ideas of the same. This thinking is all the more problematic because Edwards also inscribes this notion of aesthetic beauty on human bodies.

Finally, Edwards prioritizes the spiritual over the material in ways that favor the passive submission of the oppressed, deemphasize or ignore biblical themes of freedom and liberation, and deprioritize social ethics in favor of personal morality. These arguments suggest that Edwards' theology has elements that easily fit Goldberg's definition of racist grammar. By combining primitive racist logic with theological doctrinal prescription, Edwards elevates racist vocabulary to the level of truth claims in his grammar.

RACIST NARRATIVE AND PERFORMANCE

Edwards' two theories on racial diversity mentioned above seem to meet the definition of racist narrative. To these might be added his correspondence characterizing Native Americans as savage, bloodthirsty, unclean, drunk, stupid, lazy, wild, immoral, and lacking in character. Both of these types of writings either use or are used in racist vocabulary and argumentation, directly as part of theological and philosophical reflection.

Beyond his characterization of Native Americans, one might add Edwards' one extant piece of writing on slavery. The document is labeled as a letter in the WJE Online archive; but who the recipient was, or even whether it was intended as a letter, is uncertain. The writing is also very difficult to decipher in places. But its argument seems to be offered *reductio ad absurdum*. Edwards suggests, specifically, that it is absurd to find it sinful for a pastor to own slaves when those making that argument purchase goods generated by enslaved persons. Portions of the document suggest the negative nature of slave labor, but ultimately Edwards leverages the point to conclude that it is not a problem, moral or otherwise, for ministers to own slaves.[54] Thus, the document offers a specific narrative justification for enslaving people.

Given the race-based nature of slavery in the American colonies during Edwards' lifetime, his defense of the institution—along with other remarks about differences between Europeans and Africans, cited above—suggest that this document forms the basis of a racist narrative and defense by Edwards. But this document need not be accepted as sole evidence of Edwards' explicit support of slavery, because he owned slaves. Among Edwards' documents is a bill of sale for a fourteen-year-old enslaved girl named Venus, sold to Edwards by Richard Perkins in 1731. So, in both the narrative sense and in the performative sense, Edwards demonstrates racist tendencies.

To return to the primary question, this chapter suggests that Edwards does show evidence of at least the early development of a racist logic. He maintains a vocabulary of hierarchy, exclusion, and negative characterization that depends on racial identity and assessment; this vocabulary is totalizing in its application to an entire group and is, in Edwards' mind, derived from hereditary connections.

He also offers logical arguments that seem to advance a racist grammar focused on racial categorization, aesthetics, colonial-political and religious triumphalism, a hierarchy of benevolence, acculturation, and a societal order that includes authority and subjugation. These arguments emerge from and can be directly tied to theological arguments related to redemption, providence, the glory of God, creation, the nature of God, and eschatological millennialism. The direct connections between his theological doctrine and his racist arguments and primitive racist concepts frame the conclusions as theological truth claims. They also demonstrate continuity of thought with Calvin and an expansion of similar discourse.

Finally, Edwards maintains a racially focused narrative that defends his negative characterizations of Native Americans, Africans, and other groups and specifically defends the race-based institution of slavery. All of these assessments are predicated on European-American superiority. Edwards even participated in the institution of slavery as a slaveholder. While this study is preliminary, it does find enough evidence in the primary and secondary literature to see Edwards as exhibiting at least an early racist logic, a conclusion that is certainly on firmer ground than any conclusion related to Calvin. Observably racist ideals are embedded in Edwards' theology, and so he does succumb to Cone's claims of embedded racism.

NOTES

1. Marsden, G. 2003. *Jonathan Edwards: A Life*. New Haven: Yale University Press.
2. Minkema, K. "A 'Dordt Philosophe': Jonathan Edwards, Calvin and Reformed Orthodoxy." *Church History and Religious Culture* 91, no. 1 (2011): 242–43.
3. Marsden, G. 2003: 3.
4. Pahl, J. "Jonathan Edwards and the Aristocracy of Grace." *Fides Et Historia* 25 (1993): 62–71.
5. Edwards, J. 2000. *Charity and Its Fruits*. Carlisle: Banner of Truth Trust. 9.
6. Edwards, J. 2000: 13.
7. Edwards, J. 1751. "Letter 135: *Letters and Personal Writings in Works of Jonathan Edwards Online Vol. 16*. Edited by G. Claghorn. New Haven: Yale University Press.
8. Edwards, J. 1980. *The Nature of True Virtue*. Ann Arbor: The University of Michigan Press. 35.
9. Edwards, J. 1751. "Letter 134."
10. Edwards, J. 1751. "Letter 141."
11. Edwards, J. 1751. "Letter 129."

12. Armstrong, A. "Last Were the Mohicans: Jonathan Edwards, Stockbridge, and Native Americans." *Southwestern Journal of Theology* 48, no. 1 (2005): 19–31; Wheeler, R. "'Friends to Your Soul': Jonathan Edwards' Indian Pastorate and the Doctrine of Original Sin." *Church History* 72, no. 4 (2003): 736–65.

13. See Beck, P. "Edwards and Indians: Inclusion or Evangelism?" *Fides Et Historia* 38, no. 2 (2006): 23–33, on Edwards' "Prisca theology."

14. Edwards, J. 1750/51. "Sermon 1000." *Sermon Series II in the Works of Jonathan Edwards Online Vol. 43.* Edited by the Jonathan Edwards Center. New Haven: Yale University Press.

15. Edwards, J. 1731. "Miscellany 702." *The Miscellanies in the Works of Jonathan Edwards Online Vol. 18.* Edited by A. Chamberlain. New Haven: Yale University Press.

16. Edwards, J. 1750/51. "Sermon 976."

17. Edwards, J. 1751. "Letter 131."

18. Edwards, J. 1751. "Letter 131."

19. Beck, P. 2006: 26.

20. Gerstner, J. 1991. *The Rational Biblical Theology of Jonathan Edwards, Vol. 1.* Powhaton: Berea Publications. 285.

21. Delattre, R. "The Theological Ethics of Jonathan Edwards: An Homage to Paul Ramsey." *The Journal of Religious Ethics* 19, no. 2 (1991): 76.

22. Delattre, R. 1991: 90.

23. Henry, Caleb. "Pride, Property, and Providence: Jonathan Edwards on Property Rights." *Journal of Church and State* 53, no. 3 (2011): 406.

24. Pahl, J. 1993.

25. Minkema, K. 2011: 245.

26. Henry, Caleb. 2011: 401–20.

27. Gerstner, J. 1991.

28. VanderMolen, R. "Providence as Mystery, Providence as Revelation: Puritan and Anglican Modifications of John Calvin's Doctrine of Providence." *Church History* 47 (1978): 30.

29. VanderMolen, R. 1978: 82.

30. Edwards, J. 1750/51. "Sermon 1003."

31. Edwards, J. 1980.

32. Pahl, J. 1993.

33. Alexis, G. "Jonathan Edwards and the Theocratic Ideal." *Church History* 35, no. 3 (1966): 329.

34. Gerstner, J. 1991: 2:44, on Divine monarchy.

35. Edwards, J. 1714. *Outline of a 'Rational Account.' Scientific and Philosophical Writings in the Works of Jonathan Edwards Online Vol. 6.* Edited by W. Anderson. New Haven: Yale University Press.

36. Edwards, J. 1722. "Miscellany 350." *The Miscellanies Entry Nos. a–z, aa–zz, 1–500 in the Works of Jonathan Edwards Online.* Edited by H. Stout. New Haven: Yale University Press.

37. Edwards, J. 1722. "Miscellany 350."

38. Edwards, J. 1731. "Miscellany 815." In *The Works of Jonathan Edwards Online Vol. 18*. Edited by A. Chamberlain. New Haven: Yale University Press.

39. Jennings, W. 2010; Carter, J. 2008. *Race: A Theological Account*. New York: Oxford University Press; West, C. 2022. *Prophesy Deliverance: An Afro-American Revolutionary Christianity*. Louisville: Westminster John Knox Press.

40. Goen, C. "Jonathan Edwards: A New Departure in Eschatology." *Church History* 28 (1959): 38.

41. Goen, C. 1959: 28

42. Edwards, J. 1731. "Miscellany 702."

43. Edwards, J. 1751. "Letter 141."

44. Delattre, R. 1991; Holbrook, C. "Edwards and the Ethical Question." *Harvard Theological Review* 60 (1967); Danaher, W. "Beauty, Benevolence, and Virtue in Jonathan Edwards' *The Nature of True Virtue*." *The Journal of Religion* 87, no. 3 (2007).

45. Edwards, J. 1980: 2–3.

46. Edwards, J. 1980: 9.

47. Edwards, J. 1980: 23.

48. Edwards, J. 1980: 32.

49. Edwards, J. 1980: 33.

50. Edwards, J. 1714.

51. Edwards, 1750/51. "Sermon 976"; 1745. "Sermon 74." *Sermon Series II in the Works of Jonathan Edwards Online Vol. 43*. Edited by The Jonathan Edwards Center. New Haven: Yale University Press; 1750/51. "Sermon 979."

52. Stein, S. "The Quest for the Spiritual Sense: The Biblical Hermeneutics of Jonathan Edwards." *Harvard Theological Review* 70 (1977): 99–113; Barshinger, D. "'The Only Rule of Our Faith and Practice': Jonathan Edwards' Interpretation of the Book of Isaiah as a Case Study of His Exegetical Boundaries." *Journal of the Evangelical Theological* Society 52, no. 4 (2009): 811–29.

53. Edwards, J. 1730. "Luke." In *The Blank Bible (The Works of Jonathan Edwards Online Vol. 24)*. Edited by The Jonathan Edwards Center. New Haven: Yale University Press.

54. Minkema, K. "Jonathan Edwards' Defense of Slavery." *Massachusetts Historical Society* 4 (2002): 24.

Chapter 6

Charles Hodge and Racist Logics

Charles Hodge, in a critique of the progressive theology in J. W. Neander's *History of the Planting of the Christian Church*, expresses his preference for orthodox, Reformed theology: "The system of the Reformers was not only a great advance upon that which it superseded, but was vastly superior to that which would now displace it. The same service which was rendered to Luther and Calvin by Augustine may be rendered to Neander and Twisten by Luther and Calvin." Hodge stands more firmly than Edwards in the Reformed, Calvinist tradition.[1] But like Edwards, he is an Enlightenment theologian shaped in part by the arguments and controversies of his era, particularly the debates on science, slavery, and nineteenth-century American politics. As such, he is the first theologian studied here to deal directly with the question of race.

As a topic of recent academic study, Hodge has been largely confined to Reformed evangelical circles and those interested in the history of North American fundamentalism.[2] These studies tend primarily toward biography and historiography, not historical theological assessment. Sociological studies have focused primarily on Hodge's "moderate defense of slavery."[3] A handful of other works address his eschatology and hermeneutics.

Hodge therefore presents a problem somewhat different than that of Calvin and Edwards, with less secondary literature available to guide the current project. That said, the secondary literature on Hodge is far more instructive on the question of race than the literature on Calvin or Edwards.

Beyond the secondary literature, Hodge's writing directly addresses the questions under consideration here. The primary literature includes Hodge's systematic theology, articles that he wrote on slavery and the unity of the human race, and his commentary on Romans. In these works, Hodge succinctly describes his position on race and White supremacy.

VOCABULARY

Like Calvin and Edwards, Hodge evinces a vocabulary of hierarchy, exclusion, and negative characterization. Like Edwards, he also filters his vocabulary through the lens of racial hereditary inferiority.

Hierarchy

Hodge's hierarchical vocabulary, like that of Edwards and Calvin, depends on categories of superiority and inferiority. Hodge scholars would question any attempt to frame Hodge as an Enlightenment egalitarian. Torbett summarizes the attitude of the Princeton theologians:

> Politically, the Princeton theologians are not radical egalitarians, they were patriotic citizens of the American republic, but their patriotism was the patrician federalist, not the plebeian Democratic variety. They believed that a free republic could only flourish within limits. They balanced a qualified social egalitarianism with a similarly qualified elitism, a high regard for the authority of those who possessed merit, experience, education, and wealth. They balanced a qualified love of personal liberty with a similarly qualified regard for formal authority, the rule of law, strong government institutions, and strong Protestant churches.[4]

Later this chapter challenges Torbett's view that the Princeton theologians believed in "balance," particularly concerning Blacks, both free and enslaved. When it comes to racial distinctions and their impact on social status, Hodge clearly distinguishes between Whites and Blacks:

> It would be folly to deny that the blacks are as a race inferior to whites. This is a fact which the history of the world would place beyond dispute. Whether under a process of culture extending through generations, they might rise to equality with their favored brethren, is a question which we need not discuss. It is probable in their highest development they would retain their distinctive characteristics.[5]

While Hodge affirms, contra Calvin, the ability of racial groups to grow and improve, he does not see in Blacks a real possibility of improvement that would ever make them superior or equal to Whites. Even with much work and time, he says, "they would retain their distinctive characteristics."

In Hodge, hierarchical class distinctions are tied up in discussions on race. He sees a real distinction between wealthy and poor Whites, suggesting that the latter harbor jealousy and, as a result, poor judgment.[6] However, according to Hodge, more class animosity exists between poor Whites and Black slaves, which he ascribes to poor Whites' fear of losing their class status if enslaved Blacks are elevated by freedom. Moreover, he sees Blacks, as both a class and a racial group, as an undesirable burden on society and says that poor Whites are preferable to either slaves or "free blacks."[7]

What these examples demonstrate, as borne out in Hodge's larger body of work, is that Hodge hierarchically conceives of the world in relation to both race and class. Wealthy Whites are superior to poor Whites in his conception; and Black men and women, free or slave, are inferior to all Whites, including poor Whites. Thus, for Hodge, race clearly defines social status by demarcating "superiors" defined by whiteness and "inferiors" defined by blackness.

Exclusion

Hodge's vocabulary of exclusion also has a strong racial component. As part of an early argument echoing the doctrine of "separate but equal," Hodge suggests, "All experience shows that the only chance for any race radically distinct from another to arrive at general prosperity, is that it must be kept separate and placed in circumstances favorable to its development."[8] Hodge also opposed "intermixing" of races:

> The effect of the amalgamation of distinct races is seen in the physically, intellectually and socially degraded mongrel inhabitants of Mexico and South America. In these cases the chief elements were the Spanish and Indians, elements less widely separated than the Anglo Saxon and the Negro. The amalgamation of these races must inevitably lead to the deterioration of both. It would fill the country with a feeble and degraded population, which must ultimately perish. For it is a well ascertained fact that the mulatto is far more frail than either the White or the negro.[9]

Hodge adds that "amalgamation is contrary to the will of God." He also supported the repatriation of Black slaves to Africa, believing that White Americans would be better off without either enslaved or free Blacks.

Hodge's vocabulary of exclusion insists on separating the races while affirming the dangers of amalgamation. Goldberg's definition—that racist behaviors "express desired, intended or actual inclusions and exclusions, entitlements or restrictions" based on race—clearly applies to Hodge's exclusionary language.[10]

Negative Characterization

Recognizing a hereditary continuance of race-based characteristics within "the black race," Hodge engages in race-based negative characterization and classification of persons of African descent. He sees inferior characteristics as inherent in the race, through environmental and social factors. "The Caucasian and the Negro have existed with their present distinguishing characteristics for several thousand years," according to Hodge.[11] In addition to asserting Blacks' general inferiority to Whites, Hodge also asserts that Blacks are "ignorant, generally indolent and content to live in the poorest conditions." Moreover, enslaved Black people are physically, intellectually, and morally "incompetent to exercise the rights of freemen."[12]

Hodge considers African slaves to be the "weaker race" and argues that even adult slaves have the characteristics and legal standing of children. In fact, because they are to be viewed as children, he says they may be "disposed of without consent in any way consistent with benevolence and justice."[13] Ultimately, Hodge ascribes negative characteristics to argue for the inferiority of Blacks as a race and to justify White supremacy.

GRAMMAR

While Hodge's theology is consistent in many ways with those of Calvin and Edwards, he departs primarily in his interactions with social questions that broaden, but rarely fully depart from, the orthodox Reformed tradition. Hodge interacts with racial discourse, or grammar, at the same points Calvin and Edwards do, including providence, authority, civil government, and spiritualization. He differs, however, in his views on revolution. He also expands on the Reformed Calvinist tradition with his doctrines of justice, eschatology, and human unity. All of these theological doctrines intersect with his arguments on race and race-based slavery, forming what can be called a racist grammar.

Providence

Hodge's *Systematic Theology* lays out his views on providence. He also addresses providence specifically in relationship to race and race-based slavery in articles in the *Biblical Repository* and *Princeton Review*.

Hodge differs slightly from Calvin in his views on providence, in that Hodge ascribes more to secondary causes and also defines the operation of natural law with a slightly different focus. He affirms a sharper distinction between *potentia absoluta* and *potentia ordinate*, ascribing acts of God's providence to the latter and acts of God's grace to the former. Acts of God's grace are extraordinary acts likened to "prophecy, inspiration, and miracles"; in these cases God's providence affects something that secondary causes cannot. Yet Hodge asserts that God's providential intervention in the ordinary events of human life, particularly the lives of the wicked, effects "nothing ... that transcends the efficiency of second causes." He also suggests that although God's grace is infused without the actions of human agents, "the ordinary acts of men, and especially their wicked acts, are determined by their own natural inclinations and feelings. God does not awaken or infuse those feelings or dispositions to determine sinners to act wickedly."[14]

Hodge sees the human will operating according to what he calls the law of the mind, which he sees as analogous to the law of nature. Through the law of the mind, God prescribed actions and placed them in motion at creation. These actions operate within these laws, but without the need for God's continued guidance. God has decreed what is possible and necessary and has absolute control over the laws of nature and the laws of the mind; but God designed them to operate according to God's will without direct intervention. So, humanity, especially wicked humanity, functions independently but also remains fully part of God's providence.[15]

Hodge is trying to distance himself from Calvin's views of providence, which makes God culpable as the author of evil acts. Hodge insists:

> We should be equally on our guard against the extreme which merges all efficiency in God, and which in denying all second causes, destroys human liberty and responsibility, and makes God not only the author of sin, but in reality the only Being in the universe; and the opposite extreme which banishes God from the world which He has made, and which, by denying that he governs all his creatures and all their actions, destroys the foundation of all religion and dries up the fountains of piety.[16]

Setting aside the efficacy of Hodge's claims about secondary causes, given his internal logic, Hodge could have postulated that race-based slavery is an evil human invention, operating from evil causes within God's providence but as a result of humanity's evil intent—thereby making slavery an evil secondary cause for which God is not culpable but humanity is fully responsible. But Hodge refuses to see slavery or slaveholding as a sin, much less as a secondary cause. In all cases, he sees the institution of slavery as fully within the providential will of God.[17] Enslaved persons are not born into slavery as an accident of birth; according to Scripture, they are there by God's divine will.[18] Hodge speculates that "the designs of providence are already so far unfolded as to be deciphered with no small confidence. God seems to have brought the Negros to our land that, after sustaining a state of pupillage in the house of bondage they may return as to the promised land."[19]

Hodge does hold to his belief in the potential for human improvement. Individuals and groups can, through effort and time, change their station within God's providence. Torbett summarizes this position:

Flexibility allowed the Princeton theologians to accommodate and excuse a degree of racial discrimination, but it also precluded their absolutizing racial differences. The Princetonians depicted individual human beings and whole peoples as fluid entities, susceptible to change for good or ill. Conceivably a race of people could be so damaged by environmental influences that they could be unfit for freedom or social equality with other races, even for a long time. In such cases, a degree of racial discrimination would be proper. This condition of inferiority need not and should not be permanent.[20]

Torbett is not wrong about Hodge's views, but he incorrectly suggests that Hodge held out some hope of improvement in the case of the "Black race," especially in relationship to Whites. As already noted, Hodge, in reflecting on the final state of the "Black race" even after generations of improvement, remains convinced that they would exhibit the same "inferior" character. Hodge is reluctant to draw any conclusions that suggest a shift, even hypothetically, in the balance of power between Blacks and Whites.

So, although Hodge advances a theory of providence that could have classified race-based slavery among secondary evil causes and not part of God's direct providence, he maintains Calvin's views on slavery as being wholly within providence and divine will, and he does not admit, in the case of the "Black race," any chance of improvement that could shift the balance of power. His arguments maintain White superiority. He uses providence as an explicit defense for discrimination against an entire race of people. His views on race inform his engagement with the doctrine of providence, and he presents them as indisputable truths.

Authority

Hodge holds views similar to those of Calvin and Edwards on the doctrine of authority, as ascertained from his commentary on Romans and his articles on race-based slavery in *The Biblical Repertory* and *Princeton Review*. For Hodge authority rests on divine decree and divine appointment; failure to submit constitutes a violation against God. But Hodge also modifies his position by suggesting that those in authority hold the authority only of their appointed position. So, the husband cannot exercise the authority of a king over his wife, but only that authority given to a husband. However, Hodge does not specify the difference in power; and from a practical standpoint, given the requirements for submission, Hodge's distinction makes little difference in the degree of power wielded by those in authority. The only exception that Hodge makes for submission concerns when someone in authority requires something that God forbids. In that case, "disobedience becomes a duty."[21]

Hodge applies his understanding of authority directly to race-based slavery. Slaves have an absolute requirement to obey and submit to their masters, a requirement ordained by God as part of society's natural order.[22] In this Hodge stays close to Calvin and Edwards. Hodge also affirms Calvin's idea that the master owes the enslaved person a "duty" of benevolence, reciprocated by a "duty" of submission on the part of the slave.[23] In admonishing masters to care for their slaves, Hodge recognizes their power to do as they please; but he suggests, "What men have the power to do, in virtue of the relation which they stand to others, and what they have a right to do in virtue of that relation, are two very different things."[24]

But for Hodge, the master's injustice does not alleviate the slave's obligation to submit. Hodge shares Calvin's views on the absolute requirement for submission to all authority, "whether their authority be legitimate or usurped, whether they are just or unjust."[25] Hodge makes this point clear when he requires enslaved persons to be obedient even in the face of unjust physical injury—asking the slave to consider how Christ patiently endured physical injury on the cross.[26]

Authority functions in Hodge, then, as it does in Calvin. But the question receives Hodge's more focused treatment related to master and slave relationships. Hodge also directly connects the biblical text with the institution of slavery as practiced in the United States during his era. Thus, he embeds his theology in specific discussions of race-based slavery. His intermixing of theology and racial commentary, paired with specific discussions of authority, creates an identifiably racist grammar.

Civil Government

Hodge's views on civil government parallel his treatment of authority, primarily because both derive from his commentary on Romans 13, which closely parallels Calvin's commentary on the same book. According to Hodge, government is ordained by God, but God does not require a particular form of government. If government exists, it must be obeyed. Submission is required whether government is good or bad, and disobedience of civil authorities will be punished by God because it is an act of disobedience against God.[27]

But Hodge's views about the purpose of government and the obligation of obedience differ slightly from Calvin's. For Hodge, government exists to secure civil and religious liberty.[28] Calvin has no perception of the government's role in securing civil liberty. Whereas Calvin emphasizes the government's role in maintaining order, for Hodge it exists to promote the advantages of the ruled.[29] For Calvin, obedience is absolute; for Hodge, obedience is limited in some sense, because governmental power is also limited.[30]

But while the obligations of submission to governmental authority extend to enslaved persons, the duties are not mutual. The government's responsibility to secure liberty and promote the advantages of the ruled extends only to citizens. Slaves are not citizens and cannot become citizens.

While Hodge's view weakens, slightly, the authority of the civil government by making that authority limited and contingent, while presupposing that government exists for the good of the ruled, he does not adjust his views on slavery and racial discrimination. Neither slaves nor free Blacks were citizens, and governmental duties and supposed limitations did not extend to them. Thus, Hodge's doctrine of civil government advances the responsibility of human liberty while simultaneously denying liberty to Blacks, because their inferior status made them ill fitted for citizenship. Again, a direct relationship exists between this doctrine and racialized grammars. But what about Hodge's view of revolution? Might a slave rebel?

Revolution

While neither Calvin nor Edwards allows for revolution, Hodge does. These views on revolution will also play a part in the constructive work of part IV.

Hodge believed, along with Calvin and Edwards, that any current power is wielded by God's will.[31] But the power wielded by government is not unlimited, absolute, or indefinite.[32] In fact, according to Hodge, the Bible repudiates the divine right of kings and the doctrine of absolute power.[33]

As a result, Hodge allows two responses to unjust laws and bad government: individual civil disobedience and the group's right to revolt and overthrow the government. In committing civil disobedience, the individual is free to ignore a bad law but must submit to the consequences of his actions. Hodge allows civil disobedience under one condition: when obedience to civil government requires disobeying God, the individual may ignore the government's commands.[34]

Revolution must be a collective action by a group and should be exceedingly rare because disorder is far worse than bad government. But if government is irreparably failing in its duties to those it rules, then the ruled can rise and replace either the ruler or the system.[35] Hodge does demur, however, that tolerating an evil ruler is often preferable to rebellion that leads to chaos or uncertainty.[36]

Given how Hodge's views both soften governmental authority and open the door to rebellion, does he create an opening for an antiracist theology that offers racial minorities a chance to fight White supremacy and structural racism? When his logic is removed from his context, the answer is "possibly"; part IV will return to Hodge's argument. But how the doctrine operates in Hodge's context is in view here, so one must consider Hodge's doctrine vis-à-vis Hodge's specific use of it.

Hodge was a federalist or classical Republican. He believed in limited democracy and rule by an educated elite.[37] Thus, even within White society, Hodge's thought considers only a small class of elites competent to determine that revolution is the proper course of action. Most Whites are left out of this particular right to revolt, and both slaves and free Blacks are unable to participate. Again, Hodge emphasizes that slaves are not "competent to exercise the privileges of liberty."

Goldberg's definition of racism is met both by affording liberty only to an elite group and by withholding the rights of citizenship based on race. By embedding these notions in his theological discourse in his interpretations of Romans 13 and other theological works, Hodge raises it to the level of racist grammar.

Spiritualization of Liberation

Given Hodge's strong advocacy of verbal inspiration and the inerrancy of the biblical text, one might assume he would see the Scriptures' advocacy of freedom and liberty as justification for freeing slaves.[38] This is not, however, the case. Like Calvin and Edwards, Hodge reads the biblical text as referring to spiritual, not temporal, freedom and liberty.

One example illustrates this point. In Luke 4 Jesus proclaims that he came to "preach deliverance to the captives" and "he must deliver his people from bondage"—claims that Hodge reads as a call not to temporal liberation but to freedom from "condemnation, the law, the devil, sin, or subjection to the influence of man."[39] Hodge interprets the passage as spiritual deliverance and negates the literal, potentially liberationist interpretation of the text.

He does not interpret this passage apart from any direct consideration of slavery; his notion of slavery is spiritualized in direct relationship to the passage. Hodge continues, "So a slave may be truly and perfectly free. He is the Lord's freeman. And this is the reason Paul exhorts slaves to regard their bonds as if of little account."[40]

Thus, for the first time in this study, a theologian applies the spiritualization of liberty and freedom directly to race-based slavery, with the result that slaves are told to be happy in their spiritual freedom yet content with their worldly lot. Spiritualization becomes a theological practice that minimizes temporal liberation; it focuses on spiritual states while enforcing racial discrimination and slavery.

Justice

Hodge's systematic theology explicates God's justice in ways important to the current study. While not directly tied to racial discourse, his views limit using the notion of justice in God as a reason to abolish slavery.

He views justice as judicial (punishment) and distributive. However, he focuses almost entirely on law and punishment. He offers a lengthy discussion of the difference between God's punishment of the wicked and his chastisement of the righteous, drawing a sharp line between the two.[41] Other than a brief etymological note, Hodge says nothing about equality in the concept of justice.

Hodge also makes two points clear. First, humanity's happiness is not the highest end of justice. The highest end is the exercise of God's holiness. Second, justice should never be commingled with benevolence. The discussion of Carl Henry in the next chapter revisits this concept, but for now, the key is that God's mercy and God's justice must be completely differentiated.[42]

In his discussion on God's love, Hodge invokes the same idea: human happiness is not the reason for God's love, but God's love is a matter of God's own delight. Hodge also insists that for God's mercy and love to be manifest, then misery is also required. He offers the latter as his answer to the problem of theodicy.[43]

Although race and slavery are not a direct part of this discourse, one can imagine how Hodge's views on justice and love, as attributes of God, might influence his views on slavery and racial discrimination. The happiness or misery of the slave would never be considered when discussing the justice of God, nor would love and mercy, because God's love and mercy are a product of God's own will and have nothing to do with human happiness. If pushed, one might see the misery of slavery as a counterbalance necessary to understanding God's love and blessing for others.

These tentative connections do at least seem to be logical extensions of Hodge's reasoning. Certainly, Hodge must have had a reason for deemphasizing equality in the justice of God. Given how much slavery was at the forefront of his ethical debates, enslavement seems at least as likely a reason as any other.

Eschatology

Hodge shared Edwards' belief in a postmillennial eschatology.[44] He also shared Edwards' belief that the millennium would bring the salvation of the Jews and the nations and a reign of peace on earth. While Hodge's eschatology lacked the Edwardsean colonial triumphalism, Hodge retained, and perhaps expanded, the idea of human progress. What Hodge also lacked from Edwards' theology was any sense that the millennium is imminent.

This lack might explain Hodge's belief in gradualism, beyond the more commonplace political and denominational theories. His belief in human progress is well documented. However, progress and improvement require time and effort and must be pursued gradually, or calamity may ensue. To Hodge, the emancipation of slaves seems a necessary future occurrence, certainly required by the millennium; it would be a natural step in God's redemptive history. But emancipation, for Hodge, has to be pursued with care and hard labor. Hodge's view of gradualism has no sense of immediate expectation. He certainly does not imply the same urgency about the evangelism and training of slaves that Edwards voices about the evangelism and civilization of Native Americans.

While no certain connection can be drawn between gradualism and a distinct millennial vision in Hodge's work, certainly gradualism would be inconsistent with the immediate expectation of a near millennial reign. Hodge does link, as mentioned, the Christianization and training of slaves and their return to Africa as Christians as part of God's providence. To this extent, perhaps Hodge did, after all, envision gradual emancipation and recolonization as inherent in an eschatological call to bring the good news to the nations. If so, then there is reason to suspect a connection between Hodge's eschatology and his racist views on gradualism.

Human Unity

David Torbett makes much of Hodge's defense of the doctrine of the unity of the human race. Torbett says, "Despite the fact that many conservative protestants have accommodated and even encouraged racial inequalities, evangelical Christianity contains in its essence an idea that militates against racism, the doctrine of human unity. . . . A basic belief in the essential similarity and equality of all people."[45]

But Torbett applies the doctrine in ways that Hodge does not. Torbett is aware of this fact but seriously downplays it. Hodge defines the unity of all humanity against the emerging (pseudo)scientific belief in a polygenetic origin of humanity. This theory posits multiple creations resulting in multiple species to explain the differences evident in the human race. The theory was also used extensively to defend slavery and portray Africans as not human.

Hodge argues that multiple origins are inconsistent with biblical truth. Using a synthesis of (pseudo)science and theology, he maintains a single origin of man in Adam and says that differences in races are not the result of different parental lineages. Torbett believes that this doctrinal realization pushed Hodge and the other Princeton theologians toward a willingness to acknowledge racial equality.

But Torbett's theory about Hodge exhibits several problems. First, Hodge does not argue against racial differences or the inferiority of the Black race; he simply finds the cause in environmental, social, and moral factors. Second, Hodge argues a single origin for humanity not to build a case for human equality but to defend the truth of Scripture against the challenge of polygenetic origins. Finally, as demonstrated above, Hodge consistently believed in the inferiority of Blacks and the superiority of Whites. His work argues for a genetic link, not for a racially unifying theological anthropology. In this essay, Hodge makes it clear that he is not arguing for racial equality:

> There is a marked difference physically, intellectually and socially, between the Caucasian and the Malay. They are indeed one blood. They are the children of the same blood. They are the children of the same parents. They are brethren having the same nature in all its essential attributes, but separation and protracted operation of physical and moral causes, have given each its peculiar and indelible type. While therefore we joyfully admit the negro race to be bone of our bone and flesh of our flesh, to be brethren of the same great family to which we ourselves belong, it would be folly to deny that the blacks are as a race inferior to whites.[46]

Ultimately Torbett's claims cannot be substantiated. Though he may be right about the doctrine's inherent usefulness to forge racial unity, in Hodge's hands it becomes a platform for suggesting divergence and Black inferiority despite common ancestry. Hodge embeds racial logic into his theological grammar of creation and anthropology.

Thus, Hodge exhibits a racial grammar constructed by wedding theological arguments with racial and racist discourse. He marshals the doctrines of providence, authority, civil government and revolution, scriptural interpretation, justice, eschatology, and anthropology toward specific racist purposes.

RACIST NARRATIVE AND PERFORMANCE

Hodge is the first theologian in this study to clearly articulate a racial narrative. His narrative focuses primarily on defending enslavement and slaveholders.

A narrative that supports slavery, as disturbing as contemporary society might find it, is not in itself a racial narrative. As an institution, slavery could be based on class, warfare, or criminal punishment and function purely outside racial considerations.

What this chapter argues is that Hodge's understanding of slavery is race-based and that he expresses opinions of free Blacks similar to those of African slaves. Hodge viewed slavery as a necessary evil, because the ignorance and dependence of Black slaves, in his view, required the institution. Hodge also viewed even adult slaves as equivalent to children and therefore perpetually as minors in the eyes of Whites and under the law. Even free Blacks, for Hodge, were inferior to the lowest class of Whites. Ultimately, he views it as necessary for Whites to train Blacks over several generations to ensure their capacity to care for themselves. Even then, their ability to thrive as a race requires that they be removed to Africa and segregated from White society, whose superiority would stifle their long-term progress.

This chapter's analysis leaves little doubt that for Hodge, any discussion of slaves is also a discussion of the Black race. Therefore, the slave narrative in Hodge is race-based and racist. These are important points for understanding Hodge's racist narrative.

Also, key are his views on gradual emancipation and his assertion that slave owning is not a sin. In describing his views on slavery and that of most Old School Presbyterians, Hodge notes that "emancipation was to be gradual, and attended with the expatriation of slaves." Scholars debate the motivation behind Hodge's support for gradualism.[47] What seems clear is that slaves could not be released from slavery because their inferior state made it impossible for them to function outside bondage.[48] Thus, again, society needed time to educate slaves both intellectually and morally. By time, Hodge means generations, not years.

Hodge's gradualism tries to preserve the possibility of improving "the race" while preserving the inferiority of one racial group, in this case Blacks, and the power of another, in this case Whites. Gradualist arguments have persisted beyond slavery in the United States and underpinned some logic behind segregation in the Southern United States and apartheid in South Africa. As a mechanism for preserving White supremacy, gradualism holds up the promise of liberation and equality—but always at an ambiguous future date controlled by those in power. Gradualism also attempts to disguise racist motives in a paternalistic language of compassion and uplift. Hodge uses this language in defending the institution of slavery in his day while calling for education and gradual emancipation.

Additionally, Hodge argues that the institution of slavery is not morally wrong and therefore cannot be sinful. While he requires greater benevolence in the treatment of slaves and argues vehemently that slavery should not be a perpetual institution, he refuses to call it a sin, and he disagrees with abolitionists who called for excommunicating slaveholders:

It will of course be admitted that what God has at any time sanctioned cannot be evil in its own nature. If therefore it can be shown that God did permit his people under the old dispensation to be slaveholders, slaveholding in itself cannot be a heinous crime. It will further be admitted that anything permitted under the old economy, and which the apostles continued to permit to those whom they received into the church, cannot be a crime justifying exclusion from Christian communion.[49]

Hodge's view of the morality of slavery is based on his view of the authority of Scripture. Because the Bible, as God's revelation, allows and does not condemn slavery, slaveholding is allowed for all time and cannot be condemned. Therefore, God justifies both slavery and slaveholding, with the understanding that God also requires the proper treatment of slaves. Hodge holds that the duty of the slaveholder "is to instruct, to civilize, to evangelize the slaves, to make them as far as can, intelligent, moral and religious, good husbands, good fathers, as well as good servants."[50]

Hodge additionally offers justification for separatist racial unity: "Within this vast brotherhood of man there are more intimate bonds of relations. The people of one race, one nation, of the same tribe, of the same household are bound by peculiar ties and have the general obligation of love modified and strengthened by the special relationship."[51] He implies that this greater love for one's own race is a kind of natural law.

The foregoing analysis makes clear that Hodge engages in an explicitly racist narrative supported by an equally racist vocabulary and doctrinal grammar. Blacks are inferior to Whites, slavery is morally justifiable, and slave owners, because of the inferiority of the slaves, are justified in continuing the institution. This inferiority is hereditary and not merely biological; it includes the perpetuation of character traits. Thus, humanity, although unified through common parentage, exhibits distinct categories of races and economic classes characterized by relationships of superiority and inferiority, with race being the primary category of distinction.

Given that Hodge evidences a racist logic at the level of vocabulary, grammar, and narrative, the question remains: Does he also demonstrate a nondiscursive performance? The answer is yes—because Hodge owned slaves.[52]

Thus, on every level, Hodge's theology shows evidence of racist logic. Hodge's vocabulary supports strong elements of hierarchy, exclusion, and negative characterization with explicit language of racial superiority and inferiority. He maintains a doctrinal grammar that weds race-based argumentation to his theological reflections on providence, civil government and revolution, authority, spiritualization, eschatology, justice, and anthropology. He advances his vocabulary and grammar to defend slavery based on the inferiority of Africans, and he favors a view that says environmental factors shaped African inferiority, even as he holds a view of the unity of the species. For Hodge, these not only are biological distinctives but also encompass intellectual and moral differences that characterize the race. Hodge's narrative introduces a logic of gradualism that remains part of racist logics beyond the slave period in the United States and globally. As a slave owner himself, his nondiscursive practice matched his discursive performance. The conclusion is that Hodge has embedded a decidedly racist logic in his theological discourse. Thus, Cone's theological intuition is correct with regard to Hodge. But what of Carl F. H. Henry?

NOTES

1. Hodge, C. 2011. *Princeton Sermons*. Carlisle: The Banner of Truth Trust. 115.
2. Hoffecker, W. 2011. *Charles Hodge and the Pride of Princeton*. Phillipsburg: P & R Publishing; Noll, M. 2005. *America's God: From Jonathan Edwards to Abraham Lincoln*. Oxford: Oxford University Press; Marsden, G. 2006. *Fundamentalism and American Culture*. Oxford: Oxford University Press.
3. Torbett, D. "Race and Conservative Protestantism: Princeton Theological Seminary and the Unity of the Human Species." *Fides Et Historia* 37, no. 2 (2005); Torbett, D. 2006. *Theology and Slavery: Charles Hodge and Horace Bushnell*. Macon: Mercer University Press; Moorhead, J. "Slavery, Race, and Gender at Princeton Seminary: The Pre-Civil War Era." *Theology Today* 69, no. 3 (2012).
4. Torbett, D. 2005: 127.
5. Hodge, C. 2017. *Commentary on Ephesians*. E4 Group. loc 7675–7677.
6. Hodge, C. 2017: loc 7673.
7. Hodge, C. 2017: loc 7825.
8. Hodge, C. 2017: loc 7804.
9. Hodge, C. 2017: loc 7810.
10. Goldberg, D. 1994: 98.
11. Hodge, C. 1979. *Systematic Theology Vol. 2*. Grand Rapids: W. B. Eerdmans. 80.
12. Hodge, C. 2017: loc 7731, 7737.
13. Hodge, C. 2017 :loc 7837.
14. Hodge, C. 1979. Vol. 1: 615.
15. Hodge, C. 1979. Vol. 1: 615.
16. Hodge, C. 1979. Vol. 1: 616.
17. Moorhead, J. 2012: 280.
18. Hodge, C. "The Integrity of Our National Union vs. Abolitionism." *The Biblical Repertory and Princeton Review* 16, no. 4 (1844): 562.
19. Hodge, C. 2017: loc 7830.
20. Torbett, D. 2005: 129.
21. Hodge, C. 2020. *Commentary on Romans*. Carlisle: Banner of Truth Trust. 405–6.

22. Hodge, C. 2020: 409.
23. Hodge, C. 2017: loc 5204.
24. Hodge, C. 1844: 557.
25. Hodge, C. 2020: 406.
26. Hodge, C. 1844: 568.
27. Hodge, C. 2020: 406; "Conscience and the Constitution." *The Biblical Repertory and Princeton Review* 23, no. 1 (1851): 132; 1851: 133; 2020: 405; 2020: 407, 414 respectively.
28. Hodge, C. 1851: 182.
29. Hodge, C. 2020: 414.
30. Hodge, C. 2020: 407.
31. Hodge, C. 1851: 134.
32. Hodge, C. 1851: 143.
33. Hodge, C. 1851: 135.
34. Hodge, C. 2020: 406.
35. Hodge, C. 2020: 414.
36. Hodge, C. 1844: 580.
37. Torbett, D. 2006: 66–67.
38. White, M. "Charles Hodge, Hermeneutics, and the Struggle with Scripture." *Journal of Theological Interpretation* 3, no. 1 (2009): 64–87; Sandeen, E. "The Princeton Theology: One Source of Biblical Literalism in American Protestantism." *Church History* 31, no. 3 (1962): 307–21.
39. Hodge, C. 2011: 83–84.
40. Hodge, C. 2011: 184.
41. Hodge, C. 1979. Vol. 1: 416–17, 19.
42. Hodge, C. 1979. Vol. 1: 419–20.
43. Hodge, C. 1979. Vol. 1: 420.
44. Coker, J. "Exploring the Roots of the Dispensationalist/Princetonian 'Alliance': Charles Hodge and John Newton Darby on Eschatology and Interpretation of Scripture." *Fides Et Historia* 30 (1998).
45. Torbett, D. 2005: 119–36.
46. Hodge, C. 2017: loc 7676–7677.
47. Torbett, D. 2006: 56–58.
48. Hodge, C. 1844: 579.
49. Hodge, C. 1844: 554–55.
50. Hodge, C. 1844: 580.
51. Hodge, C. 2011: 267.
52. Torbett, C. 2006: 70–71.

Chapter 7

Carl F. H. Henry and Racist Logics

Carl F. H. Henry (1913–2003) is the only theologian in this study whose career was contemporaneous with James Cone's. The height of his writing coincides with the Civil Rights and Black Power movements in the United States and with the emergence of a socially conscious but theologically conservative neo-evangelicalism, of which some consider Henry the principal architect. So unsurprisingly, Henry's language lacks anything approaching the explicitly racist language or even the class distinctions evident in Hodge. In fact, Henry's writings refer to the need for "racial equality," the "Black man as our brother," and the need for racial reconciliation. Yet evidence still points to lingering, perhaps latent, elements of racist logic in Henry's theology and social ethics that might be categorized as, for lack of a better designation, racially insensitive.

If Calvin evidenced a primitive racist development, and Edwards and Hodge evidenced explicit racism, Henry can be characterized as advocating a social ethic that minimizes race and creates barriers to confronting White supremacy and racial segregation. His vocabulary and grammar, in their nondiscursive applications, tend toward the perpetuation of White supremacy and the advancement of racial inequality. So, while Henry's discursive works use language more typical of antiracist dialogue, his theology worked out in practical contexts limits racial advancement, at the levels of vocabulary, grammar, and narrative and performance.

Engaging Henry's work at this level can be daunting. His writings are voluminous, and most deal with social issues, specifically his ethical works and his six-volume magnum opus *God, Revelation, and Authority*. Fortunately, he includes lengthy, consistent, and clear discussions of the topics covered in this chapter, so his primary literature is easy to access. This chapter primarily draws on his systematic treatments in *God, Revelation, and Authority* and his ethical treatments in *Evangelicalism at the Brink*, *The God Who Shows Himself*, and *Social Ethics*, with additional reference to his various addresses, particularly his keynote address to the World Congress on Evangelism in

Berlin. To allow Henry to provide his own assessment on the question of race, this chapter also consults his autobiography.

The secondary literature on Henry is less extensive and limited primarily to confessional, conservative evangelical scholarship; it includes the important work of Russell Moore, James Patterson, Curtis Evans, Augustus Cerillo, and Murray Dempster.

VOCABULARY

Goldberg's definition of vocabulary is not limited to the categories of exclusion, hierarchy, and negative characterization. Goldberg's categories encompass anything that, if not inherently directed at race, operates as subcategories or latent concepts within the idea of race. Henry does not engage explicitly in any of those categories so evident in Calvin, Edwards, and Hodge. In fact, he employs the language of racial equality; but he also uses language that contradicts these statements. Henry's language includes a Western, Euro-American worldview, coded racism, a tendency to limit racial progress, and a redirected latent logic.

Western, Euro-American Worldview

Henry's Western-centric worldview connects primarily with his evangelical missionary spirit. For Henry, this Euro-American, evangelical missionary triumphalism envisioned a White missionary saving the souls of Africans and Asians:

> To the Congo, missionaries came preaching, teaching and healing—as did the early disciples—and as they penetrated the African bush they built churches, schools, and hospitals seeking the redemption of the whole man. In those jungles dark with fear, treachery, and witchcraft, they summoned their new neighbors in need to the high prospect of a redeemed soul, informed mind, and consecrated body—in short to renewal in the image of God.[1]

The image of jungles "dark with fear, treachery, and witchcraft" in a passage meant to emphasize holistic ministry implies a rhetoric reminiscent of Edwards' assessment of Native Americans; at best this is ethnocentric, hyperbolic speech.

Henry also justifies the early missionary practice of a "double conversion"—to Western culture and Christianity. In doing so he advances the idea that Western European and American culture is closer to Christianity than non-Western cultures: "Western culture, unlike that of Asia or Africa, contained many Christian elements; it was therefore easier to identify Christianity with American and European than with Asian and African cultures."[2] By directly identifying Christianity as more inherently Euro-American than African and Asian, he suggests that these cultures lack the ethical, moral, and spiritual connection to New Testament Christianity found in their Western counterparts. Henry never asks, as Cone does, whether experiences inherent in African and Asian cultures come closer to New Testament culture than Western culture does, and whether perhaps this implies a closer connection to the central message of Christianity. Henry also never asks whether Western Christianity distorts the Christian message in ways that make it unfit for transmission to other cultures. Certainly, Henry has the requisite familiarity with hermeneutic theory to correct his assumptions here.

To be fair, Henry's priorities did not focus on missiological method. His primary thrust was to challenge the modernist Western tradition and present Western evangelicalism as a positive alternative. Carillo and Dempster highlight this focus:

> Appalled that the Biblical world-life view no longer shaped modern (Western) cultural, intellectual, and political thought, Henry in 1946 wrote *Remaking the Modern Mind* to confront the naturalistic and humanistic assumptions underlying much of modern life. He incisively and brilliantly laid bare the philosophic and practical inadequacies of modern belief in the ultimate reality of nature, man's inherent goodness and the inevitability of progress.[3]

Henry's total immersion in the Western philosophical and intellectual traditions, and his lifetime of engagement with them, seems to have made him at best insensitive to non-Western traditions or have led him to value Western thought and the Western philosophical tradition as superior, even amid his critique of that position.

Henry's observations and Western bias go beyond his missiological reflections. Henry views Western logic, thought patterns, and rules of argumentation as the "universal" form for reasoned debate. He says they represent a "universal" set "of valid logical rules" that all cultures must learn and follow to "present their own alternatives logically."[4] Henry embeds this argument in a negative assessment of liberation theology.

Henry's views echo Edwards' views on the evangelization of Native Americans and eschatological manifest destiny. White Euro-Americans are characterized both as saviors of Africans and Asians living in ignorance and darkness and as conveyors of universal rules of logic, to which all cultures must submit their own patterns of reasoning to think properly. Henry would likely object to this characterization, but within his reflections lies a latent suggestion of intellectual and moral White Euro-American supremacy, or perhaps an unevaluated White ethnocentrism.

Race Coding

The politics of race in the late-twentieth and early-twenty-first-century United States featured a propensity toward race coding; that is, politicians facing increasing scrutiny for using racist language shifted to offer negative comments about "the poor," welfare, and poverty in the United States, replacing negative comments about Black men and women.[5] US Blacks continued to be the face of poverty in North America, so negative comments about the poor were often by extension disguised references not to class but to race. In this way, race coding was introduced into American political rhetoric.

White theologians of the era, including Henry, were not beyond using race coding. Henry asserts, "The Christian view of life can help lift above perpetual poverty and defeatism those whose surrender to drunkenness, gambling, prostitution, and other weaknesses robs them of the basic necessities of life. Some people tend all too readily to 'hook themselves' on poverty as a way of life."[6] Associating poverty with vice suggests character defects, ignores systemic root causes of poverty, and characterizes the poor as morally flawed.

Henry's stereotyping goes further: "For many of the impoverished, a television set or some other luxury represents the first material necessity after shelter, food and clothing. Others splurge their first savings on expensive additional wardrobes. One may smile at such overreactions; something can be done, however, by way of guidance."[7] Here Henry overlays a negative assessment of the judgment and intelligence of those living in poverty. His analysis also tends toward paternalism, not unlike Hodge's attitude toward slaves, as evident in Henry's suggestion that "one may smile at such overreactions"—oddly like a parent's reaction upon seeing their child "play dress up." But an even clearer paternalistic sentiment lies in his suggestion that the poor need "guidance." Another passage implies a paternalistic dependency of the poor on the wealthy by suggesting that the poor need and desire a "viable prospect of rescue for the whole man."[8]

Thus, Henry characterizes the poor as morally and intellectually deficient and existing in a state of dependency that requires rescue. His negative assessments do not stop there. He also explicitly calls those in poverty who use the welfare system "idle and lazy."[9] One might object that his language is more classist than racist, but the degree to which poverty is synonymous with race in the White American imagination suggests otherwise, as does Gilens' work cited earlier. Thus, Henry's characterization of "the poor" can be viewed as race coding.

If any doubt remains that Henry's categories of race and poverty are synonymous, an early passage more directed at race may be illuminating:

> The problem of racial discrimination can be permanently met only by Christian behavior that faces up to the ugliness of bias, the evils of immorality and delinquency, and the whole social range of problems that surrounds race feelings. The predilection for public issues over personal holiness in liberal social ethics is all the more disconcerting in view of this fact. Although liberal churchmen will throw their energies behind a public health program, they tend to remain silent about many of the personal vices; such concerns are left to the "purity nuts."[10]

This passage describes racial discrimination as the problem of both Whites and Blacks. On one side is "ugliness of bias"; on the other is "immorality and delinquency" and "personal vices." Henry does not imply that White racists are immoral and delinquent or practicing personal vices; this characterization falls on Black Americans. He makes the identical argument regarding "the poor" in his later works.

Limitations on Racial Progress

In addition to Henry's Western ethnocentric bent and race coding, his arguments also limit Black action. Henry accuses those fighting for racial justice of engaging in the "selfish exploitation of constitutional government" and not being interested in the "public good."[11] Evans, analyzing evangelicals and civil rights, includes Henry in his assessment of *Christianity Today*'s views on the civil rights movement:

> *Christianity Today* was commenced under the auspices of men (including Henry) who were not sympathetic to the civil rights movement as it had developed up to that point. From 1956 to 1960, Christianity Today's editorials and articles on race took a "moderate" position. The editors called upon Christians to confront their racial biases and cease discriminating against individual blacks. Voluntary segregation was seen as a middle path between the "extremists" of the segregationist right and the integrationist left. This position placed them in opposition to civil rights legislation and the proposals of militant segregationists. However, the magazine's harsher criticisms were directed more pointedly toward integrationists than toward segregationists. The possibility of interracial marriages was deeply feared and always lurked in the background as the principal reason for the editors' desire to halt rapid social relations between blacks and whites.[12]

This "moderate" position, as Evans points out, worked against the interests of the civil rights movement.

Henry affirms racial justice but negatively assesses efforts by racial groups to affect change, insisting that racial groups should not use legislation to prevent practices deemed racist. He limits race-based legislation to those laws that ensure "equal rights," by which he means equal access. He opposes laws that punish individuals or institutions for specific behaviors that minority groups deem discriminatory: "Minorities should not simply impose legal restrictions governing whatever practice they find ethically objectionable."[13]

Thus, Henry allows equal access but limits both the enforcement and scope of laws to eliminate racial injustice. In this way, he limits racial progress and preserves and protects institutional racism.

Continuation of Latent Racist Logics

Henry removes an important ally in the fight for racial justice when he insists that individual evangelicals must "identify themselves conspicuously and publicly with Negros and others in their struggle for equality before the law" but also asserts that "it is not the task of the institutional church to promote legislation."[14] In this way, he limits the movement toward racial equality by limiting equality of access, curtailing the advocacy of racial groups, and removing the institutional church from direct legislative lobbying.

In the final assessment, Henry's vocabulary of racial justice lives in tension with his Western-centric philosophy, his race coding, his limiting of direct actions for racial justice, and his continuation of latent racist logics. Henry, therefore, advances a primitive racist vocabulary even while avoiding or deprioritizing explicit conversations on hierarchy and exclusion. His vocabulary is far more subtle than that of either Edwards or Hodge. But it is not latent or precursory in the same way as Calvin's. Race exists as an issue for Henry and is evident even when not explicit.

GRAMMAR

Henry perpetuates a theological discourse that has racist potentialities. His grammar is observable in the way his theological battles weaken his vocabulary of racial equality, the way he continues previous theologians' racial logics, and the way his discursive output has the potential to strengthen racist logics.

Theological Battles on Two Fronts

Henry fights two primary theological battles that tend toward a weakened social ethic and a resulting weakened perspective on racial equity. These battles include his fight against Social Gospel utopianism and naturalism.

Social Gospel Movement

Henry's battle against the Social Gospel Movement is directed less at liberal Protestantism per se and more at fundamentalist isolationism that used the Social Gospel as an excuse for social and political isolation.[15] Henry stands at the center of these polar extremes: isolationism and social withdrawal on one end, and the Social Gospel's efforts to impose new social structures on the other. Moore offers a sharper clarification by correctly insisting that Henry does not assume a position between the Social Gospel and isolationist fundamentalism. Henry did not view the Social Gospel as part of an acceptable spectrum; he considered it wholly outside reasonable Christian debate. For that reason, Henry sits far closer to fundamentalism than to the Social Gospel. If a spectrum must be delineated, Henry would sit right of center on this issue.[16]

With both groups in mind, Henry critiques the lack of evangelical social action. "Evangelical Christianity," he says, "reacted against liberal Protestantism's concentration of effort in this area of concern by non-involvement and this withdrawal yielded the field to the speculative theories of liberal churchmen and largely deprived evangelicals of an ethical witness in the mainstream of public life."[17] He suggests the need for social action. But he also argues that

> The stance of non-evangelical Protestantism had now become so anti-metaphysical and anti-intellectual that truth was subordinated to unity, theology was widely viewed as a matter of subjective preference, and in place of an absolute dogma stood an approved program of social action which—as the liberals saw it—was now the real test of genuine Christian commitment. Instead of personal evangelism and the spiritual regeneration of individuals they advocated changing the social structures by the church's direct engagement in political controversy.[18]

Thus, he suggests that both fundamentalist isolationism and liberal Protestantism's Social Gospel are incorrect.

So, Henry suggests an alternative view of social involvement that represents a passive view of social action leading to a weak ecclesiology. Henry's position weakens his stance on racial equity and favors racist logic.

For one thing, if Henry wants to build an evangelical view of social involvement, he believes he must first attack and dismantle the Social Gospel.

Henry's main disagreement lies with the Social Gospel's replacement of personal salvation with social concern. For the proponents of the Social Gospel, he says, "Direct ecclesiastical engagement in political campaigns, in civil rights demonstrations, endorsement of legislation, and advocacy of government welfare programs become preferred means of fulfilling the church's mission in the world."[19] Henry sees this engagement as more insidious than just a shift in focus. Henry is concerned that the Social Gospel "substitutes the notion of corporate salvation for individual salvation."[20]

Dismantling the Social Gospel is important to Henry's theological discourse. His strategy is both rhetorical and theological. Rhetorically, Henry identifies the Social Gospel with socialist politics.[21] Imposing this label at the height of the Cold War, he creates an effective means of "demonizing" Social Gospel theology for many North American Evangelicals. While Europeans might distinguish between socialism and Soviet-style communism, these distinctions are never clear in American popular discourse or its contemporary imagination. This lack of clarity creates several problems, not just for the Social Gospel but also for Christian social action in general. First, for those unfamiliar with the deeper theological underpinnings, it is an easy step to view all faith-based social action as part of the Social Gospel. Thus, any social engagement, including that which Henry proposes, falls subject to the accusation of being nothing more than socialist political rhetoric disguised as theological discourse. Second, this "demonization" not only works at the theory level but extends to method. Henry directly connects the Social Gospel to "ecclesiastical engagement in political campaigns, in civil rights demonstrations, endorsement of legislation, and advocacy of government welfare programs." The methods, despite the motivation or theology driving them, therefore become deeply entrenched in Henry's rhetoric of socialism. "Civil rights demonstrations" are among those methodologies he singles out. Labeling becomes potentially destructive because it is like "dropping a bomb on a house to kill a fly." The fly is dead—but the house becomes uninhabitable. The same holds when contemporary evangelical culture demonizes all theological discussions of race as "woke" and "CRT," no matter how grounded those studies are in biblical and theological orthodoxy.

Henry's discourse on the Social Gospel is not limited to rhetoric; he includes more theological arguments. For example, he blames "the Social Gospel theologians" for deleting "the wrath of God" and "dissolving God's righteousness into benevolence of love."[22] Thus, Henry develops a sharp distinction between justice and love that affects several points in his theology and echoes Hodge. As a result, he limits definitions of justice to equal treatment under the law. He tends to understand "justice" as equal punishment, rather than the pursuit of equal degrees of human flourishing. His treatment of love is frequently negative throughout his works. The discussion of grammar considers justice in detail below. For now, Henry's arguments against the Social Gospel result in a crime-and-punishment view of justice that diminishes the concept in his perception of evangelical social engagement, and his view particularly weakens any positive statements he might make on racial social equity. Thus, he preserves privilege and power and normalizes racial, class, and gender distinctions by making justice a matter of crime and punishment while discounting justice in the creation of opportunities for basic human flourishing.

In relation to ecclesiology, Henry also argues that the Social Gospel's "socio-political platform raises more fundamental doubts about the authenticity and uniqueness of the Church than about the social aberrations against which she protests."[23] The Church, in Henry's view, loses its redemptive distinctiveness when it focuses on social action and becomes less a church and more a political party. The primary problem with Henry's argument is that it depends on degrees. Isolationists could counter Henry's call for social involvement by arguing that any social engagement whatsoever makes the Church a political party or a social service organization.

Moore argues for a clear ecclesiology in Henry's thought. He insists that Henry joins an inaugurated eschatology with redemptive soteriology and discipleship to create an evangelical idea of church. But Moore also admits that this view, grounded in the "plastic" parachurch nature of the North American evangelical movement, still produces a weak theology requiring expression within various confessional denominational traditions.[24]

Finally, Henry insists that the primary role of Christianity in the world is to create "a new race of men, new creatures in Christ."[25] This redemptive work is primary; social involvement is secondary and flows out of the work of redemption. Henry suggests that social and racial justice is incidental to redemption, which limits the impact of social justice in changing oppressive systems. Evans offers a far more pointed assessment of how this belief applies to the question of race:

> Although there is much to be said about evangelical individualism, I am not convinced that it is (by itself) a sufficient explanation of their approach to race. Evangelicals have selectively applied an individualistic ethic primarily to social practices with which they disagreed. A close analysis of evangelical thought in its historical evolution indicates that evangelicals invoked a "spiritual solution" or personal conversion (in general) to social problems when solutions to these were being promoted by interest groups where values differed from their own and when it appeared that government support of such positions would challenge evangelical conceptions of the proper social order. Hence their endless refrain that legislation could not change a person's heart precisely when others were supporting legislation to deal with legal discrimination of African Americans.[26]

Evans' assessment, supported by his larger body of work, seems appropriately applied to Henry.

Thus, both Henry's rhetoric and his theological discourse, as they relate directly to his attack on the Social Gospel, evince racial motivation or at least a reluctance to favor moves toward full equality. By connecting socialism to both the Social Gospel and most forms of social action, he demonizes both. This demonization makes social action untenable and creates a status quo mentality that favors racist systems of power by positing inactivity as preferable. His focus on wrath over love furthers a social critique limited to equal punishment at the expense of equal quality of life, which in turn perpetuates racial and class disparity. His insistence that the Church's mission remains distinct from social justice programs isolates the church from larger partnerships and prevents it from engaging in direct social action. Thus, he minimizes the ability of the Church, as the Church, to effect change in racist structures. Finally, his insistence on the secondary or incidental nature of social action limits confrontation of racist structures, beyond individual redemptive engagement removed largely from social purpose and intention. In each case, Henry pragmatically attacks racial justice efforts and in doing so enforces the existing White system of power.

While Henry's attack on the Social Gospel can be seen as limiting racial advancement and protecting White power, his alternative plan has similar limitations. Its consequences direct Christian social action away from any practical program to alleviate either racial inequality or White supremacy. Henry's plan for the Church's involvement in the "social crisis" can be described as ecclesial, spiritual, moral, individualistic, apologetic, and passive.

The ecclesial role lies at the center of his argument. Henry begins by asking a fundamental question:

> In an hour of widespread revolution, when political forces are reshaping the larger frontiers of modern life, the church's concern with the problem of social justice is especially imperative. But how this social involvement is properly carried out—whether by the institutional church acting in a political way, or by individual Christians conscientiously fulfilling their civic duties—is a very important question.[27]

He answers by affirming individual conscience while limiting the role of the Church. Richard Mouw summarizes Henry's views:

> The institutional church has no mandate, jurisdiction, or competence to endorse political legislation or military tactics or economic specifics in the name of Christ. . . . The Bible limits the proper activity of both government and church for divinely stipulated objectives—the former, for the preservation of justice and order, and the latter, for the moral-spiritual task of evangelizing the earth.[28]

Thus, the Church, as the Church, plays no direct role in social action, and its work is limited by God to moral and spiritual matters.

When Henry speaks of the Church's role in social justice, he speaks in almost Hauerwasian terms: "The church approximates God's kingdom in miniature, mirroring to each generation the power and joy of the appropriated reality of divine revelation" and "its task is not to force new structures upon society at large, but to be the new society, to exemplify in its own ranks the way and will of God."[29] In its fellowship, the Church exhibits the kingdom of God as a witness to or mirror of righteousness to the world. It does so because the world is fallen and can never approximate God's kingdom, and because the Church in its regenerated nature must represent something unique and separated from the world.

The Church, however, is not wholly devoid of responsibility. Henry sees a role for the Church in morally educating its members' social conscience and perhaps excommunicating those without a social conscience. He affirms that individual Christians lack an innate moral social conscience and that "sanctification therein does not come about automatically without pulpit instruction in sound biblical principles."[30] Furthermore, "Christ's church cannot signal hope to those whose destitution and deprivation annul the dignity and meaningfulness of human survival if it uncritically condones as members those who profess devotion to Christ while they consciously support socially oppressive powers, policies and programs."[31] So although the Church must not participate in direct action, its programs may discipline members who disregard social conscience, and it may provide a program of moral training that instills an effective social conscience in its members.

Henry sees individual social action as key to revitalizing Christian involvement in the social order. Christians with a morally developed social consciousness and a sense of civic duty will work for social justice. However, the social action even of individual Christians is limited both in terms of programmatic content and method.

Henry argues, "To the evangelical Christian, the best alternative to the 'welfare' state is the just state, and the best alternative to political demonstration is civil obedience. The evangelical champions and strives for just legislation, and for obedience to law and respect for judicial process rather than for directly coerced action."[32] Henry views government as limited, to the degree that it has no benevolent role to play in its citizens' material lives. The Christian is, therefore, not allowed to advocate for state-sponsored "welfare." Furthermore, Christians are bound by laws in how they can seek social justice; they should avoid both violent and nonviolent demonstrations, as well as direct acts of civil disobedience. They are limited to what the judicial process affords in challenging unjust treatment. Thus, Henry restricts the path to redressing racial inequality to a citizen's right to vote, influence elected officials, and successfully litigate against inequality. He fails to consider the degree to which this is possible if the judicial and legislative processes themselves are corrupt and racially biased.

Henry also encourages individual Christians to participate in government vocations. He hopes that Christians within the government will employ their religiously influenced moral conscience, and the government will then lean toward justice. Henry believes that evangelical Christians "can and ought to use every platform of social involvement to promulgate the revealed moral principles that sustain a healthy society and that indict an unhealthy one. More than this, the evangelical Christian should be represented in his personal convictions on the frontiers of government and in the corporate process of society."[33] Thus, individual Christians embedded within governmental systems will have a positive "leavening" effect on society.

Henry not only makes social transformation an individual task, with limited objectives and limited methods, but he insists that a spiritual agenda lies at the core of social transformation. Social action cannot replace evangelistic effort as the primary witness of the church.[34] Additionally, the battle for social justice, Henry says, is a spiritual battle whereby "the emancipating Redeemer grants new life to them and enlists them as a committed community, as the new society, to his ongoing victorious combat over evil."[35] The battle for social justice is a battle against the prevalence of Satan and sin in the world. Only triumph over sin makes real liberty, life, and love possible. Spiritual reality envelopes the total work of social transformation, and a "good" society is possible only through spiritual regeneration.

Not only is the spiritual the driving motivational factor for social action, but Henry prioritizes spiritual outcomes over material outcomes in social justice work. "The dissatisfactions of unregenerate man lack a spiritual quality, as do his satisfactions," Henry states:

> Complaints against the emptiness of life are often obscure, and easily given false labels. The African protesting the 'white man's domination' may really want material betterment, however he sees it. The wealthy African is not beyond exploiting the poor African and greater differences actually exist within the race than between the races. The Gospel must not be tapered to unscriptural aspirations whereby religion is made a mere instrument of personal or social gratification.[36]

Thus, the gospel for Henry is about spiritual regeneration, not material uplift.

The spiritual principles that underlie social good, and the championing of these principles and values, lie at the heart of social action. For Henry, these efforts are largely an apologetic task. The church's role is to reveal the theological underpinnings of a moral society. Thus, several things lie at the core of Henry's message. First, "the church's theological existence involves an inescapable political dimension." Next, "the church has a joyful good word to speak to the sphere of politics—that God is the true king." Also, "God's faithful and gracious action toward man puts his seal on the dignity of the individual." Then "the coming kingdom is not merely a future possibility but is already in some sense actual." Finally, "even in the political arena God's main concern is not ideology, isms or ideas, but rather persons and their relationship to God and one another."[37] Thus, the Church's role is to remind the government of its role and its dependence on God's providential will, as well as its responsibility to operate within God's parameters. The Church should also work to undergird civil society with "scriptural standards and moral power."[38]

"When evangelicals manifest social concern," Henry clarifies, "they do so first by proclaiming the supernatural revelation of God and the historical resurrection of Jesus Christ." So social concern manifests primarily in a Christian apologetic witness that emphasizes "the transcendent basis of justice and the divine basis of the Gospel. (It) declares both the standard by which almighty God will judge the human race and the redemption from sin unto holiness that is to be found in Jesus Christ. (It) affirms God's institution of civil government to preserve justice and order."[39] The Church's social engagement is meant to speak to the government and society about the spiritual realities that create social unrest and injustice and about the moral and spiritual requirements necessary to correct them. The hope is that secular society will embrace these moral principles.

This all makes for a passive process. The Church is limited to evangelism and moral instruction. Social action is the purview of individual Christians, who are constrained to actions they can take within established judicial and civic processes. Civil disobedience is disallowed. Individual Christians may pursue government careers and work for change within the confines of their duties, but they are further constrained to prioritizing an apologetic witness that both demonstrates the theological principles at work in society and urges civil society to adopt Christian moral principles and standards.

This limiting vision makes substantive impacts on the ability of Henry's theology to address racial injustice and White supremacy. First, it weakens his ecclesiology, leaving the Church, as a corporate body, an indirect role in challenging racist structures. The Church loses the power of numbers and organized response to social change—not only on questions of race but also on all social issues. The Church has no direct voice in racial justice and must trust only in individual conscience and spiritual regeneration to affect racial inequality at the individual and systemic levels. Beyond the theoretical, Henry does not admit that the Church in the past has failed to address racism. His suggestions of church discipline, though moving in the right direction, exhibit a certain naiveté. Identifying racism in mostly homogeneous church bodies seems unlikely except in the most extreme cases.

A second impact on Henry's theology is that, by limiting racial justice work to individuals, Henry overlooks the role of social systems in creating and perpetuating racism. Racism is primarily a failing of individual morality. While he encourages participation in the processes of civil government, he limits government so that its function is almost entirely judicial. Henry frames racism as a moral problem that results from a moral lapse in the racist—but also from moral failings in persons of color as well. He seems to argue that the racist is wrong in making judgments based on race, but that persons of color are in some way responsible for furthering stereotypes. Indeed, Henry insists that racial inequality does not result from environmental or social factors but primarily from individual moral and intellectual failures on the part of poor persons of color.[40] Black poverty, for Henry, is primarily the result of characteristics inherent in Blacks living in poverty—not of systemic societal racism. He both condemns racism and blames the objects of it. Thus, Henry simultaneously opposes and strengthens racist logics.

Third, his insistence on limiting social transformation efforts to existing legal processes fails to address systemic racism adequately. By insisting on change within the bounds of law, he disregards instances when the civil processes are themselves racist or engineered for racist outcomes. Segregation laws in the Southern United States during Henry's lifetime were designed to prevent civil redress by persons of color. As a result, had they followed Henry's advice, Blacks would have had no means of redress because he advocated leaving the process to those who benefited from and established the laws. Even if one assumed a neutral system of redress, Henry's atomization of social change within the established judicial and governmental system minimizes the likelihood of success. He also disregards civil processes that do not allow individual participation but vest power in a small ruling group or single individual, and he denies the rights of participation while engaging in discriminatory practices against minority groups. Later in this section, I show that Henry affirms individual submission to even tyrannical governmental systems. This view strengthens those in power and limits those who are subject to their rules and systems.

As a final theological impact, Henry opposes extrajudicial means even when they seem likely to produce positive social outcomes. He opposes demonstrations, protests, and civil disobedience, violent or nonviolent, limiting opportunities for those with limited civil participation to effect change. This exercise is not theoretical for Henry; he applied it directly to the civil rights movement under Dr. Martin Luther King Jr., whose civil rights protests Henry directly attacked as un-Christian. By directly attacking extrajudicial methods, Henry's theology limits the possibility of redress for persons of color and thus supports, even if latently, White supremacist systems.

Naturalism in Modernist Thought

Henry is not only fighting the Social Gospel but also directly debating against the naturalist tendency in modernist thought. He continues the old modernist-fundamentalist debates over faith and science. But his participation in this discourse aims at recovery and prioritization of the supernatural and the spiritual over the natural; it is not primarily an attempt to discredit scientific reasoning.

Henry objects to the "replacement of interest in supernatural spiritual dynamisms by secular sociological dynamisms" and "the loss of Biblical orientation to the need of personal faith in the redemptive work of Christ as the sole means of deliverance from the wrath of God."[41] He advocates for both a supernatural explanation of civil processes and outcomes and a personal spiritual regeneration as the primary method of social reform.

In an address to the World Congress on Evangelism in 1966, Henry lays out his primary concerns with both secularist and liberal Protestant solutions to world problems:

> For good reason we repudiate the inversion of the New Testament by current emphasis on the revolutionizing of social structures rather than on the regeneration of individuals; we deplore the emphasis on material more than on spiritual betterment; and we renounce speculation about universal salvation that cancels new life in Christ as the precondition of present blessings and eternal blessing.[42]

Why would Henry's concerns with the decline in supernaturalism affect an assessment of his racist grammar? His insistence on the spiritual over the material and individual salvation over social uplift calls to mind earlier racist logics that maintained that spiritual equality before God should be enough for those lacking material and social equality in this world. Henry's logic divides the spiritual from the material and disconnects spiritual uplift from material concerns in ways that are strikingly similar to earlier racist grammars.

Thus, Henry's primary theological battles against racism, and his disagreements with both the Social Gospel and naturalism, have the potential to support racist outcomes. But also crucial are the ways in which Henry perpetuates Calvin's potentially racist grammar and the more explicitly racist grammars of Edwards and Hodge.

Continuation of Previous Theologians' Racist Grammars

Henry promotes and preserves the racist logical grammar of Calvin, Edwards, and Hodge through his views on authority, providence, civil government, revolution, and spiritualization. Thus, there remains latent in Henry's discourse an underlying racist grammar.

Authority

Again, Henry's language differs from that of Calvin, Edwards, and Hodge. When discussing authority, Henry uses the language of "mutual subordination" instead of the mutual but unequal duty. But his phrasing serves as a rhetorical device supporting the maintenance of hierarchical roles. His argument is worth quoting at length:

> In the new society, every human participant holds an important role as a moral agent. Unlike the stoic practice of giving priority to the dominant class in the exposition of social ethics, the New Testament in its "household tables" lists the subordinate person first when speaking of wives and husbands, children and parents, slaves and masters, and thus emphasizes their indispensable ethical role in society. By this pattern the New Testament also calls the dominant partner to subordination in the interest of new and honorable reciprocal relationships. What confers fresh meaning on this mutual subordination is the Christological dimension. Nothing less than the self-humbling of Jesus Christ, whose self-abasement becomes the ground of our redemption and is the larger backdrop for this subordination. In the light of his example the subordination of his followers is fitting and definitive ... by willing and meaningful acceptance, the gospel message of emancipation was not to become an occasion for "insubordination." Even though Christ's liberation has freed him from enslavement to the alienating powers of this world, the Christian is to subordinate himself to the institution of human government.[43]

Henry's view of "mutual submission" seems to advance Calvin's, Edwards', and Hodge's call for "mutual duty." But while he does move one step closer to egalitarianism, what Henry's total argument makes clear is that he is advocating a complementarianism that perpetuates the racist grammar of the "separate but equal" doctrine.

Henry suggests that Paul's Household Codes mention each pairing's subordinate half first to emphasize the important roles they play in society. But this suggestion does little more than advance previous arguments emphasizing the importance of everyone remaining in their place, as well as the value of the work of slaves. He elevates subordination, now in a contemporary context, for praise because subordination is valuable for society. Henry does say that husbands, parents, and masters are called to subordinate themselves in turn to those over whom they have authority—but he makes clear that this subordination does not substantially change the relationship. In the end, authority, power, and hierarchy remain firmly in place, and Henry includes no language of progress or deliverance for the primary subordinates.

Henry also spiritualizes the language of emancipation, implying that emancipation must not be desired and that it was never intended to support "insubordination." But most telling is how Henry's entire argument maintains and elevates a theology of subordination. He grounds this subordination, as do the other theologians considered here, in the doctrine of Christ's kenosis. He thereby provides a divine mandate for submission. The similarities with earlier racist rhetoric, which asked slaves to accept their lot as Christ accepted his suffering on the Cross, are striking.

These arguments' racist potential should be clear. While Henry upholds a call to mutual subordination, he preserves separate roles and power imbalances in human relationships. In emphasizing subordination over social emancipation, he evidences a logic with the potential to preserve systems of White power and subordinate persons of color. His status quo argument renders impotent any attempt at social transformation and preserves the prevailing structures of power inside a doctrine of "separate but equal."

Providence

Henry advances a view of providence that is consistent with Calvin, Edwards, and Hodge but lacks Hodge's discussion of secondary causes. For Henry, providence reaches beyond the purely general notion of God's role in maintaining an ordered cosmos:

> The biblical view of providence is dramatically specific; it unqualifiedly affirms particular divine providence, that is, that God works out his purposes not merely in life's generalities but in the details and minutiae of life as well. The Bible relates to divine providence not only general and universal structures but also personal experiences; nothing falls outside of God's will and concern.[44]

Henry includes the evilest acts as part of God's providence. He goes as far as to argue that the Holocaust was providential because it allowed for the creation of Israel as a nation-state.[45]

His view also lacks any notion of "fixity," so evident in Calvin's thought. Henry argues that a person can rise above his place, but that a person's status and privilege in the world is a direct result of God's providence.[46]

Thus, Henry's theology of providence perpetuates a grammar that has been shown to support racist arguments in Edwards and Hodge. Henry's formulation of the doctrine requires that White supremacy and racism exist within

God's providential will, as assuredly as did Auschwitz and Dachau. All four theologians object to any direct culpability on God's part for evil, but one cannot miss their direct implication that God preserves these evil systems toward God's plans. Thus, their work becomes a powerful tool for those who would use the providence of God to support the continuation of White power and the subjugation of persons of color.

Civil Government

Henry's view of civil government also aligns with Calvin, Edwards, and Hodge. Government is a divinely ordained institution to which citizens owe their committed obedience and subordination. To Henry, "man possesses no rights against government."[47]

His vision of a good government is a limited government. Henry's political stance can best be described as conservative libertarianism. He restricts government to the impartial administration of justice, which he narrowly defines as the maintenance of order and the administration of punishment. While everyone should be treated equally under the law, not everyone should be equal as to wealth and power.[48] He believes that the very existence of government puts a cap on power, but he does not consider that unchecked power can reside in government itself, even if government checks the power of private citizens. Equally problematic is his failure to recognize how government might exercise power on behalf of certain private citizens or groups.[49]

Henry also opposes governmental efforts to create benevolence programs, even when those programs might eliminate racial disparity. "Just as in his (the liberal's) theological view of God the liberal dissolves righteousness into love, so in the political order he dilutes social justice into compassion." Henry elaborates: "This kind of merger not only destroys the Biblical view of God on the one hand but also produces the welfare state on the other." According to Henry, this confounding of justice and love also "confuses what God expects of government with what God expects of the church."[50]

Thus, Henry opposes the role of government in ending racial material disparity. Henry also offers no view of church benevolence that would close the racial economic gap. His view of benevolence means caring for "those we meet on the way," but he offers no specific call to large-scale social concern and action. His view of civil government continues to evidence a rhetoric of equality under the law but a practical application that offers nothing to eliminate racial disparities.

Revolution

Henry agrees with both Calvin and Edwards on the question of revolution. "Evangelical Christians," he asserts, "repudiate this attempt to confer

Christian sanction on secular and often anti-Biblical ends, and they reject revolution as an approved means of achieving social change."[51] He allows for resistance and civil disobedience only when "government requires what God forbids."[52]

He further insists that biblical texts that imply "revolutionary" action should "preserve a Biblical vocabulary and meaning by speaking of regeneration rather than revolution."[53] In this way, he spiritualizes passages whose literal meaning might justify liberation and revolution.

Given that Henry opposes civil disobedience, as already shown, his opposition to revolution is unsurprising. This opposition offers another example of Henry limiting the means to overturn racial disparity and displace White Power.

Spiritualization

Like Calvin, Edwards, and Hodge, as discussed above, Henry spiritualizes passages that support a literal interpretation of liberation and explicitly delineates how this interpretation affects liberation theologies. He also prioritizes spiritual existence over material need. As Evans suggests, Henry applies a strategic spiritual or redemptive solution to avoid supporting direct social action on issues of racial inequality. In this way too, then, Henry advances those theological arguments that the chapters on Edwards and Hodge demonstrated to have the potential for racist use.

Justice

Henry also moves beyond any of the other theologians, with perhaps the exception of Hodge, in advancing a view of justice that strengthens racist logics. He makes a distinction between justice and love: "Justice is concerned with what is man's right and due; Charity goes beyond such claims."[54] He also makes a sharp distinction between justice as impartiality and justice as need, affirming the former and rejecting the latter.

Impartiality is not the only way Henry defines Justice. He distinguishes the love of God—which he says represents the compassion expressed by the Church—from the wrath of God—which he compares to justice exercised by civil authority. "In the Bible," Henry says, "retributive justice is an intrinsic aspect of the wrath of God." He embraces Hodge's definition of justice as "rectoral, or that which is concerned in the imposition of righteous laws and in their impartial execution," and says that justice is "manifest in the righteous distribution of rewards and punishments."[55]

Thus, for Henry justice represents impartiality, wrath, punishment, reward, and law, in opposition to mercy, love, forgiveness, grace, and liberty. He argues for the distinctiveness of love and justice in the Godhead, contra

Barth's claims that the simplicity of God means that there are no divisions of the attributes and, therefore, no distinction between love and justice in the Godhead. Henry argues that Barth's theology subsumes justice into love in a way that loses justice entirely. Henry believes instead that "the unity of the divine being, which Christian theology affirms, must not be made a basis for minimizing the equal ultimacy in God's nature of divine righteousness or justice, and of divine love and mercy."[56] In this way, he preserves justice as distinct from God's love.

Moreover, Henry says, "The source, content, and sanction of justice exist exclusively and uniquely in the nature and will of God."[57] He claims that civil government is the result of God's justice and that any understanding of justice must be modeled on God's justice. Therefore, evangelicals must accept "that not an ethic of grace but rather an ethic of justice should govern social structures."[58]

This sharp separation of love and justice means that any reference Henry makes to social justice must be read as focusing entirely on impartiality and not at all on rectifying racial disparity. Benevolent means fall entirely outside the purview of civil government. Henry departs here from Calvin, Edwards, and Hodge, who saw some benevolent role for government.

In all these ways, then, Henry evidences a theological grammar that acknowledges the need for equality while limiting its practical implementation. He does so in his theological battles, his perpetuation of previous racist grammars, and his sharp separation of love from justice in the context of civil government. The question now is: Does he also evidence a racist narrative and performance?

RACIST NARRATIVE AND PERFORMANCE

Henry focuses on a rhetoric of equality unsupported by his practical social ethic. As stated, he opposes the methodologies of the civil rights movement and the work of King and openly opposes the Black Power Movement not just methodologically but philosophically as well. While Henry maintains antiracist rhetoric, he criticizes movements for racial justice, uses coded racial language to define the "poor" as responsible for their circumstances through poor judgment and immorality, and views the "race problem" as a two-sided issue, holding Blacks equally responsible. These narrative themes are consistent and prevalent throughout Henry's writings.

To assess his performance, I note that Henry lived during the civil rights movement, yet his actions are consistent with his theology. He did not participate in any direct actions related to racial justice. He engaged in few extended discussions of race in his theological works and in his role as editor of *Christianity Today*.

He describes his own treatment of the issue in his 1986 autobiography, recounting his unrealized intention to run a series of articles on "the race problem," which was to include an editorial by Nelson Bell. At the time, Bell summarized his editorial's racist sentiments in a letter to Henry, which he quotes:

> "It [the editorial] represents my own feelings on the matter. It is hard for you men in the North to realize," Nelson wrote me, "that our problem is in many parts of the South, one of ratio, not of race. Also, in many areas of the deep South, Negro children are so filthy, infected with disease and immoral, that white parents will not send their children to school with them. This is not true in the North, generally speaking, or in the West, where the Negros are of much higher economic status and also have much better educational backgrounds . . . the matter will not be solved by a cold recourse to law."[59]

As late as 1986, Henry could recount this story without rebuffing either Bell's blatantly racist narrative or his intentions to publish it. The editorial was not, however, published, and tellingly, Henry indicates why both he and *Christianity Today* were not at the forefront of coverage on racial issues: "We saw the race problem—rightly, I think—as one dimension of a more comprehensive problem, and not the cutting edge of a dramatic social reformation."[60]

The fact that Henry was unapologetic about Bell's language as late as 1986, and his assessment that race was a small part of a larger problem, are both important. Henry's knowledge of the true impact of racial disparity is extremely limited and superficial, which may explain why his calls for racial justice function at a rhetorical level, not a deeper theological level. He discounts both the importance of racial disparity and the need to take any direct action to resolve it. Henry subsumes race under a larger spiritual problem that makes race a tertiary issue. His lack of involvement or concern supports and perhaps undergirds an assessment that his antiracist language functions as rhetorical cover for a social ethic that promoted a passive response to racial disparity.

Henry evidences a logic, then, that consists of a "pragmatically" racist vocabulary, grammar, narrative, and performance. All four levels form a potentially racist logic consistent with that of Calvin, Edwards, and Hodge. Thus, Henry's continuance of a passive racial ethic succumbs to Cone's insistence that racism is embedded in all White theology.

FINAL THOUGHTS ON RACISM IN NORTH AMERICAN EVANGELICAL THEOLOGY

This part, following Movement Two of my methodology, has attempted to ascertain to what degree Cone's claim that racism is embedded in all White theology holds true for a particular strand of North American evangelical theology, extending from Calvin to Edwards to Hodge and finally to Henry. Based on this analysis, I can conclude that racism is indeed evident to some degree in these theologians and by extension in the theological trajectory they represent. However, I must clarify the limits that delineate this conclusion.

I recognize the problem imposed by Western historicism since Kant. Western Kantian history and its relativization of historical interpretation pose a critical issue for any study that suggests a theological coherence that unifies traditions across time and cultures. This study ignores that problem to embrace more recent innovations—including genetic history and actor network theory—that claim that everything, including discursive material, connects forward and backward in time. While this methodology is too complex and lengthy for full application within the current study, the connections made above are substantial enough to warrant their limited use here. A fuller account that builds out all the historical, geographical, and intellectual links awaits an entirely different study.

This study did not need or intend to prove that each of these theologians had specific racist objectives in mind when they composed their theologies. Nor did it intend to prove that each theologian in turn specifically borrowed from those who proceeded them or that their theologies were used for specifically racist purposes. The current work sufficiently demonstrates that components within each theologian's work either can be appropriated for racist logic or specifically evidenced racist logic.

This study attempts to show a connection, but not necessarily collusion, on the part of each theologian that can place their reasoning within a shared theological tradition, and show that each advanced that tradition, specifically regarding race. Moving chronologically from Calvin to Edwards, from Hodge to Henry, offers the advantage of showing development and continuity within the tradition. This part also shows how more explicitly racist theologians—in this case Edwards and Hodge—used their tradition's more precursive theology, in this case Calvin's, to develop explicitly racist theological logics. This part also offers the opportunity to see how contemporary theology, in this case Henry's, retains elements of racist logic even while exhibiting tendencies toward antiracist rhetoric.

This work needs to be considered in light of the following limitation: As a historical study conducted in the interest of constructive theology, the focus on theological continuity and its applications for contemporary theological reflection must be seen as primarily theological, not historical. While the study does not wander from what one would consider reasonable historical interpretations and uses of primary sources—and while the historical secondary text literature supports it as well—I offer these theological conclusions in the interest not of a reworked historiography but of a theological conclusion toward a contemporary theological formulation. This may be problematic for pure historians, but it necessarily advances the use of historical analysis for constructive theological work. The continuity and diversity in traditions must be analyzed so that constructive, contemporary theologians may engage them.

In addition, the study sets a very specific goal and answers a very specific question: Is embedded racism evidenced within the particular strand of White, North American evangelical theology represented by Calvin, Edwards, Hodge, and Henry? The study clearly delineates what it means by "racist components" by using Goldberg's philosophical definition of racism, including his notion that elements of logic and reason constitute primitive forms of racism that suggest potential connections to more explicitly racist grammars and narratives. This study viewed those theologies as precursory to racist logic and as contributing to its use at later stages in the tradition's development.

With that in mind, this study does not suggest that Cone's theory is true for all White theologians—only for the tradition that was considered here. Nor do I suggest that embedded racism is the totality of the tradition or of any theologian considered individually. Elements in the work of each individual theologian and in the tradition may seem contradictory on the surface or may alter the racist or precursory racist components in each theology. Portions of each theologian's work and the broader tradition can indeed be leveraged in constructive ways toward an antiracist theology of power.

Finally, this part carried out a very narrow function: to demonstrate that components within the theological tradition, as Cone said, represent elements of embedded racism. If the study had discovered no elements of racist logic and no demonstrable continuity of racist logic in the tradition, then the research would have ended here, with the conclusion that the tradition has no racist components and needs no further examination toward building an antiracist theology. This study did not, however, require that racism be the tradition's dominant feature or intentional focus. The only finding needed for this study to continue was enough evidence of racist logic within the tradition to warrant further examining it and suggesting corrections.

With those limitations in mind, there is at least enough evidence to suggest the following conclusions. First, a White North American evangelical tradition runs from Calvin to Edwards to Hodge to Henry, each of whose theological system evidenced components that support racist logics. Calvin's theology exhibits precursory argumentation found in later racist discourse. Edwards and Hodge both voice explicit racist logics. Henry, while maintaining an antiracist rhetoric, creates a "pragmatically" racist social ethic. A second conclusion is that the specific racial logic can be connected with the tradition. A retrospective look at the explicitly racist logic of Edwards and Hodge allows one to readily observe Calvin's precursory language and Henry's continuance of its pragmatic implications. Finally, enough evidence suggests that components of contemporary evangelical thought continue these racist logics; these must be evaluated as part of any constructive theological work that applies to race generally and Cone's claims specifically.

Thus, this work can proceed to a constructive examination of those areas of White theology critiqued by Cone and those that this part identifies as connected to racist logics. Before discussing doctrine, though, any evangelical theology must first consider the biblical text and its proper interpretation and theological application as it relates to any subject under consideration. An examination of specific texts suggested as controversial by Cone or these theologians constitutes Movement Three and the work of the next part.

NOTES

1. Henry, Carl. 1966. *The God Who Sends Himself.* Waco: Word Books. 33.
2. Henry, Carl. 1983. *God, Revelation, and Authority* Vol. 5. Waco: Word Books. 395.
3. Cerillo, A., and M. Dempster. "Carl F. H. Henry's Early Apologetic for an Evangelical Social Ethic." *Journal of the Evangelical Theological Society* 34, no. 3 (1991): 367.
4. Henry, Carl. 1984. "Liberation Theology and the Scriptures." In *On Liberation Theology.* Edited by R. Nash. Milford: Mott Media. 198.
5. Gilens, M. "Race Coding and White Opposition to Welfare." *American Political Science Review* 90, no. 3 (1996): 593–604.
6. Henry, Carl. 1983: 5:549.
7. Henry, Carl. 1983: 5:549.
8. Henry, Carl. 1983: 5:545.
9. Henry, Carl. 1983: 5:552.
10. Henry, Carl. 1966: 65.
11. Henry, Carl. 1983: 6:443.
12. Evans, J. "White Evangelical Reponses to the Civil Rights Movement." *Harvard Theological Review* 102, no. 2 (2009): 263.
13. Henry, Carl. 1983: 6:449.
14. Henry, Carl. 1967. *Evangelicals at the Brink.* Waco: Word Books. 71–72.
15. Henry, Carl. 2003.

16. Moore, R. "The Kingdom of God in the Social Ethics of Carl F. H. Henry: A Twenty-First Century Evangelical Reappraisal." *Journal of the Evangelical Theological Society* 55, no. 2 (2012): 378.
17. Henry, Carl. 1966: 55.
18. Henry, Carl. 1967. *Evangelicals at the Brink.* 56, 57.
19. Henry, Carl. 1967. *Evangelicals at the Brink.* 75.
20. Henry, Carl. 1967. *Evangelicals at the Brink.* 74.
21. Henry, Carl. 1967. *Evangelicals at the Brink.* 58.
22. Henry, Carl. 1966: 55.
23. Henry, Carl. 1966: 70.
24. Moore, R. 2012: 389–96.
25. Henry, Carl. 1966: 71.
26. Evans, J. 2009: 205.
27. Henry, Carl. 1964. *Aspects of Christian Social Ethics.* Grand Rapids: Baker Books. 10.
28. Mouw, R. "Carl Henry Was Right." *Christianity Today* (2010), accessed September 11, 2020, www.chistianitytoday.com/january/25.30.html.
29. Henry, Carl. 1983: 5:542; 1984: 191 respectively.
30. Henry, Carl. 1966: 60, 61.
31. Henry, Carl. 1984: 194.
32. Henry, Carl. 1966: 64.
33. Henry, Carl. 1966: 65.
34. Henry, Carl. 1966: 66.
35. Henry, Carl. 1983: 5:542, 543.
36. Henry, Carl. 1966: 27.
37. Henry, Carl. 1984: 191.
38. Henry, Carl. 1964: 9, 10.
39. Henry, Carl. 1966: 67.
40. Henry, Carl. 1966: 69, 70.
41. Henry, Carl. 1967. *Evangelicals at the Brink.* 76.
42. Henry, Carl. 1967. *Facing a New Day in Evangelism: One Race, One Gospel, One Task.* Minneapolis: World Wide Publications. 16.
43. Henry, Carl. 1983: 6:531.
44. Henry, Carl. 1983: 6:459.
45. Henry, Carl. 1983: 6:485–91.
46. Henry, Carl. 1983: 6:459.
47. Henry, Carl. 1967. *Evangelicals at the Brink.* 61.
48. Henry, Carl. 1967. *Evangelicals at the Brink.* 61, 72.
49. Henry, Carl. 1983: 6:436.
50. Henry, Carl. 1966: 55, 60.
51. Henry, Carl. 1967. *Evangelicals at the Brink.* 58.
52. Henry, Carl. 1983: 6:451.
53. Henry, Carl. 1967. *Evangelicals at the Brink.* 59.
54. Henry, Carl. 1983: 6:408.
55. Henry, Carl. 1983: 6:402.

56. Henry, Carl. 1983: 6:411–12.
57. Henry, Carl. 1983: 6:420.
58. Henry, Carl. 1966: 54.
59. Henry, Carl. 1986. *Confessions of a Theologian: An Autobiography.* Waco: Word Books. 158.
60. Henry, Carl. 1986: 159.

PART III

Exploration of the Biblical Text

Chapter 8

Exegetical Methodology and Text Selection

Part III begins the constructive theological work addressing the second point of conversation with Cone, namely, how liberation is to be understood scripturally. Evangelicalism insists that theology be grounded in the biblical text and that the biblical text is central to constructive appraisal of doctrine. Cone is not far from this position in his earlier writings. Therefore, this third part analyzes select texts that are critical to the understanding of questions of race and power, as suggested by the preceding parts' study of Cone and the evangelical tradition.

METHODOLOGY

For a specific breakdown of this part's extensive methodology, see table 0.1 in the prolegomena, corresponding to Movement Three. However, a word regarding the methodology's particular reasoning might be in order.

Movement Three envisions several steps: (1) an analysis of a specific text that is both central to Cone and interpreted differently by the evangelical theological tradition; (2) a critical assessment of that text's theology, (3) the text's theological implications, and (4) the text in relation to other passages that mitigate against Cone's reading. The fourth step is important because Cone himself does not consider texts that oppose his interpretation. The intent here is not a new or novel approach to the text, unless the preliminary exegesis suggests it, but an evaluation of how the existing critical work of biblical scholars understands the text. This part seeks a meaningful interpretation that can then be integrated into the constructive work of doctrinal analysis.

With this in mind, what follows is a broader approach than is common among some theologians who utilize insights from biblical scholarship as proof of their theological conclusions rather than as a source of their theological conclusions. Cone's exegetical insertions are a prime example. He uses the work of Gerhard von Rad and Bernhard W. Anderson almost exclusively without further elaboration or any engagement with opposing interpretations.[1]

Scholars' engagement with this project's central arguments is critical to its success. Therefore, the exegetical reasoning that undergirds the biblical conclusions is central to methodological success. One should be able to follow the coherent logic of the exegetical arguments and their theological applications, even if one disagrees with some exegetical choices. When using Scripture in constructive theology, one also must understand the central debates and conclusions of biblical scholarship as a means to biblically norming theological discussion; but creative engagement with the text is less critical. Of course, the theological work must then be reevaluated as the biblical work on which it is postulated advances and changes. This reevaluation creates a constant dialogue between biblical scholars, theologians, and readers that requires theologians to "show their work" when basing theological conclusions on biblical texts.

Therefore, what I envision here is an interaction with the biblical text and biblical scholarship that is more comprehensive than would otherwise be the norm in many constructive theological works, but that focuses on theological work, not on advancing biblical scholarship—so this discussion may be less comprehensive than would be true of specialist studies in biblical exegesis. With that in mind, what follows describes the methodology outlined in table 0.1, beginning with the question of text selection.

RATIONALE FOR SELECTION OF BIBLICAL TEXTS

Any number of texts could have been selected for consideration. The limited space afforded by this project does not allow for an exhaustive biblical theology of power. Despite that limitation, certain key texts, on which critical doctrinal interpretations have been made, so inform the evangelical tradition that their examination will go a long way in suggesting the acceptability of certain doctrinal formulations and positions within North American evangelicalism. The exegesis offered in this part is limited to questions of race, power, and privilege that seem central to either Cone or the evangelical tradition under consideration and that have implications for contemporary discussions of doctrine.

With this in mind, one text is singled out for detailed analysis: Luke 4:16–30. Given the degree to which the readings of Romans 13 and the household codes by Calvin, Edwards, Hodge, and Henry seem to contradict Cone's liberationist interpretation of Luke 4, this part also examines those passages as alternative perspectives that may challenge literalist interpretations of Luke 4. They are considered here as part of the overall assessment of Luke 4, not as isolated texts, so they are not given as full an exegetical treatment as the primary Lukan text.

Cone points to Luke 4:16–30 as the text that most exemplifies Jesus' mission as a liberator.[2] The text is largely spiritualized or ignored by the four theologians considered in part II. "Spiritualized" here connotes the abandonment of a strictly literal reading of the text in favor of a more typological or metaphorical reading. So, to suggest that "the poor" described in Luke 4 are not actual, literal poor, but rather are those who lack a right understanding of God, would constitute a spiritualization of the text. With that in mind, the importance of the text for Cone's Black liberation theology and the difference in interpretation between Cone and Calvin et al. suggest that Luke 4 is a good starting point for assessing the literal versus spiritual interpretation of liberation texts.

This study prioritizes the Luke passage over Cone's extensive treatment of the Exodus passages for two reasons.[3] First, Cone's extensive dependence on a Barthian Christological priority suggests that his argument would rise or fall on his demonstration of liberation not in the Old Testament canon, but rather as an idea central to the life and work of Jesus. The Luke text allows consideration of this aspect of Cone's theology in a way that the Exodus narratives do not. Second, the degree to which the four evangelical theologians deny or ignore the literal interpretation of this passage in relation to Christ's mission provides an opportunity to engage the ways in which their theology may hinge on specific interpretive choices not supported in the text itself. Linking the text to the work of Christ creates a better point of interrogation for the evangelical tradition than does the Exodus narrative, which the tradition also tends to spiritualize or interpret typologically.

As suggested above, Romans 13 is central to the four evangelical theologians in creating biblical support for theologies of authority (all four), hierarchy (Calvin, Edwards, Hodge), order (all four), governmental power (all four), nonresistance to governmental authority (Calvin, Edwards, and Henry), and understandings of power. Part II has already examined the degree to which interpretations of Romans 13 are central to racist logics within the evangelical tradition. The text is necessary for interrogating or supporting evangelical theology's view of government, providence, authority, power, hierarchy, divine order, and resistance to evil. No study of evangelical theologies of power can ignore it without greatly biasing its conclusions.

The same is true of the household codes in the Pauline corpus. All of the issues arising from Romans 13 are in evidence in the household codes and, because they discussed slavery, have been applied to specific racist logics in parts of the evangelical tradition, especially in the work of Hodge.

This part therefore engages in a full exegesis of Luke 4:14–30 as central to any liberationist understanding that might inform evangelical doctrine. I treat the household codes and Romans 13 as problematic for a liberationist understanding of the text in Luke. The three passages, taken together, then help illuminate questions around authority, power, privilege, and other critical intersections with evangelical doctrine, thus allowing for constructive theological work that engages with, and depends on, the biblical text.

NOTES

1. Cone, J. 1997. *God of the Oppressed*. 69.
2. Cone, J. 1997. *God of the Oppressed*. 69.
3. Cone, J. 1997. *God of the Oppressed*. 57–63.

Chapter 9

Luke 4:14–30
Exegesis and Theology

The Gospel of Luke and the Acts of the Apostles are seen primarily as a unity by scholars such as Green, Marshall, Jeffery, Levine, and Witherington.[1] However, debate among biblical scholars continues to address the primary focus of Luke-Acts. Scholars like Jennings view Acts, and the story of Luke subsumed within it, in primarily political terms. For Jennings, Luke-Acts navigates empire and diaspora, hierarchy and ethnicity, and creates a new political reality for the people of God.[2] Jennings contrasts with Conzelmann, who sees in Luke-Acts a singular focus on salvation history.[3] Coauthors Amy-Jill Levine and Ben Witherington III, throughout their commentary on Luke, highlight the differences in political interpretations of Luke.[4] But most scholars affirm variations on Joel Green's centrist position:

> Throughout, the Lukan narrative focuses attention on a pervasive, coordinating theme: salvation. Salvation is neither ethereal nor merely future, but embraces life in the present, restoring the integrity of human life, revitalizing human communities, setting the cosmos in order, and commissioning the community of God's people to put God's grace into practice among themselves and toward ever-widening circles of others. The Third Evangelist knows nothing of such dichotomies as those sometimes drawn between social and spiritual or individual and communal. Salvation embraces the totality of embodied life, including its social, economic, and political concerns.[5]

This moderated position is also borne out in the more recent work of Rowe, who sees both salvation history and political and social implications in the text of Luke and Acts.[6] This compromising tendency witnesses to the myriad ways in which Luke-Acts might be read and to an extensive reception history that reads the text spiritually, politically, or some combination of the two.

152   *Chapter 9*

With that in mind this chapter's analysis of Luke 4:16–30 focuses on understanding the passage in light of possibilities for reading it from both literalist/sociopolitical and salvation-historical perspectives and also attempts to determine which reading has the most textual support.

TEXTUAL ANALYSIS

This first section examines both the primary points of textual interest and scholars' difficulties interpreting them. I interpret the pericope on its own merits and reserve questions of its place within the narrative for later discussion in the study.

Points of Interest

Luke 4:16–30 forms a pericope that introduces Jesus' Galilean ministry. The text is defined by an inclusio that begins at 4:16a and ends with 30b: "he came," "he went."[7] The passage is also divisible into three parts: Jesus' reading and teaching of Isaiah 68:1, 2 and Isaiah 58:6 in the Nazareth synagogue, found in 4:16–22; Jesus' condemnation of the congregation in 4:23–27; and the congregation's reaction in 4:28–30. Green also makes much of the interaction between Jesus and the congregation as a "structural" element of the text, but more likely it is simply incidental.[8]

Chiastic Structure and Variants

Scholars generally accept the idea that 4:16–20 forms a chiastic structure that centers attention on Jesus' reading of Isaiah in verses 18 and 19.[9] The chiasm is built on mundane elements of the text: "stood up to read," "handed the book," "opened the book" in verses 16 and 17, followed by "closed the book," "gave it back," "sat down," in verse 20. Whether the majority opinion is accepted, scholars agree that the content of verses 18 and 19 is central to the pericope and programmatic for Jesus' ministry in Luke-Acts as a whole.[10]

As Green notes, verses 18 and 19 have a distinct structure. The first three phrases end with "me," and each "me" phrase has a corresponding subordinate infinitive phrase. The parallelism of the word "release" is also key. Green's literal translation of these verses (with his emphasis) is instructive:

> The Spirit of the Lord is upon *me*
> For he has anointed *me*;
> To preach good news to the poor he has sent me
> To proclaim for the captives *release,*

And to the blind sight;
To send forth the oppressed in *release*;
To proclaim the year of the Lord's favor.[11]

The text's emphasis on "me" is echoed in verse 21, where Jesus proclaims that "today this Scripture is fulfilled in your hearing." This echo emphasizes that the claims—the good news preached to the poor, release granted to the captives, recovery of sight to the blind, liberty for the oppressed—are fulfilled in the person of Jesus. Jesus is not simply prophesying that these claims are imminent; he indicates that they have been fulfilled or are being fulfilled in him.[12] Green infers, "The fulfillment of which Jesus speaks must be rooted in his person."[13]

Verses 18 and 19 also contain two notable variants. Some translations include the phrase "to heal the brokenhearted," but both Omanson and Metzger suggest that the manuscript evidence strongly supports not including the phrase.[14] They cite the likelihood that copyists inserted the phrase to make the passage sound less literal. Levine and Witherington note also that the Isaiah text read by Jesus, quoted as verses 18 and 19, ends before the "day of vengeance" pronounced in the Isaiah passage.[15] This omission has important implications for interpreting the passage that I consider below.

Deliverance and Jubilee

Two words are important for an understanding of verses 18 and 19. First, the word ἄφεσις—translated as "deliverance," "freedom," or more literally "release"—holds together Jesus' composite reading of Isaiah 62:1–2 and Isaiah 58:6.[16] Kimball suggests that joining the two passages with this single word points to a first-century midrashic tradition, and therefore the verses should be read as part of Jesus' sermon, not as an actual textual reading.[17] Most scholars have not followed Kimball's midrashic explanation, but many find the use of the word to connect the two Isaiah passages as exegetically significant.[18] Green also highlights the semantic range of "release" within the New Testament, in that release can relate to forgiveness, unbinding from satanic control, or the cancellation of debt that is characteristic of the Jubilee.[19]

Commentators allude to the possible reference to Jubilee found in verses 18 and 19 and Isaiah 61:1–2 and 58:6; but the degree to which they believe it operates in Luke 4:18–19 varies. Ringe gives more credence to Jubilee symbolism, which forms a large part of her liberationist readings of the Gospel; but she does not suggest that Jesus intended to institute an actual Jubilee year.[20] Levine and Witherington admit the connection to Jubilee but say that the "allusion is faint." They prefer to connect "the acceptable year of the Lord" language to the more general call to repentance and its ethical response already evident in John the Baptist's teaching found earlier in Luke.[21] They suggest that Jesus is exhorting the people to be like John, namely to "avoid overcharging, to share food and clothing, and to be satisfied with one's wages." In the end Ringe and Levine and Witherington are not far apart. Neither claims that Jesus intends to initiate a literal Jubilee; they see the statements as referential, signaling an ethical response to Jesus' work. Jubilee will be further considered below.

The Poor

The second term critical to any interpretation of verses 18 and 19 is πτωγός, the poor. This term deserves more attention, given that it has both sociological and religious interpretations. In the context of Luke 4:18, are "the poor" literally the economically disadvantaged, or are they a metaphor for those who humble themselves, similar to what Matthew 5:3 might mean by "the poor in spirit"? Evidence suggests that the "poor" category is primarily sociological, but it does not entirely rule out a religious reading as employed in the Gospel of Luke, specifically Luke 4:18.

First, both the Old and New Testaments employ a broader semantic range for "the poor," but this range tends to focus on sociological uses. Pleins' and Hanks' articles on "Poor, Poverty" in *The Anchor Bible Dictionary* suggest a broad semantic range and many different words and roots for "poor" and "poverty" in both Hebrew and Greek. Of particular interest for interpreting Luke 4:18 is the exclusive use of the Hebrew term *'anî*, which refers to those who suffer the "injustice of oppression" in Isaiah 40–66.[22] Levine and Witherington recognize this distinction, affirming that "the Hebrew of Isa. 61.1 is better translated 'good news to the oppressed' whereas the Greek, which Luke follows, proclaims 'good news to the poor.'"[23] Pleins notes the importance of the writer of Isaiah 40–66 applying the term to those who struggle under exile in Babylon, not just to the economically depressed. The term thus encompasses political and social subjugation. Carried into Luke's Gospel, "the poor" seems unlikely to mean merely the beggarly poor, as the term also carries the sense of "the oppressed." This semantic range means that "the poor" in Luke 4 consists of more than those who are economically disadvantaged and includes those who are social, religious, or political outcasts.

The use of "the poor" in Luke 4:18 must be examined in light of its relationship to Luke 4:26–27. Luke 4:18 must be read as part of the broader pericope that includes Jesus' examples in verses 26–27, where Jesus foreshadows Gentile inclusion by evoking Elijah's ministry to the Sidonian widow instead of the many widows in Israel, and Elisha's care for Naaman the Syrian leper when Israel had many lepers. Although this passage primarily signals why Jesus would not heal in Nazareth, Jesus connects important elements of his mission that become apparent in other parts of Luke-Acts: his care for and inclusion of social and religious outcasts and his inclusion of Gentiles. Thus, connecting the poor, the lame, and the oppressed in verses 18 and 19 with the Gentiles, who were doubly outcast from both the social and religious systems of Israel, expands the poor to include multiple groups of socially and religiously disenfranchised people. This expansion suggests that "the poor" are not a metaphor for sinners but rather refer to a particular sociological group of socially, politically, and religiously disenfranchised individuals, who now become a special object of Jesus' mission. The good news is that Jesus includes them, despite their ongoing exclusion from social, political, and religious power. This trope further expands in Luke 6:20, when Jesus blesses the excluded poor with inclusion in the kingdom of God and excludes the rich, powerful, and privileged. Reversal in Luke is discussed further below.

One must distinguish between the context and use of "poor" in Matthew 5:3 and Luke 4:18. The beatitude in Matthew 5:3—"Blessed are the poor in spirit for theirs is the kingdom of Heaven" (NAS)—is an ethical pronouncement that implies a consequence following from ethical practice. The Beatitudes in Matthew talk about individual virtues. But Luke 4:18 refers not at all to ethical practices, but rather to a particular object of inclusion in Jesus' mission. He does not proclaim the virtue of individuals; instead, Jesus announces his intention to include the poor as a group within his mission. Even the seemingly twin passages of Matthew 5:3 and Luke 6:20 differ in context. Matthew affirms character traits; Luke makes a prophetic pronouncement about who will inherit the kingdom.[24] The distinctions are important: Matthew affirms that the character trait of humility is key for those who will inherit the kingdom, whereas Luke proclaims Jesus' inclusion of the social, political, and religious outcast in the salvific plan of God. Neither Matthew nor Luke intends to say that everyone who is either humble or outcast will be saved—only that humility is a key trait among the saved, that the outcast will be among those saved and included in God's kingdom, and that the rich, powerful, and privileged who assume their place will in fact be excluded. Matthew 5:3 is so different from Luke 4:18 that one cannot be used to interpret the other.

The reception history of "the poor" in Luke plays a role in its interpretation either as a metaphor, or as a reference to a Christian religious sect who adopted poverty as a way of life. Roth outlines the early history of interpretations of the "poor" in Luke, demonstrating that the early source criticism and history of religions movements marginalized discussions of the poor in Luke by subscribing to an outside influence on Luke's text that was peripheral to its theology. Roth recounts the development of the belief, among source critics, that a cultic group committed to poverty at the time of Luke's writing found its way incidentally into Luke's source material and did not constitute an intentional theological focus. Form critics like Bultmann and Dibelius picked up this line of reasoning and posited an unimportant outside influence on Luke's use of the "poor." This argument finds its way into Conzelmann's redaction-critical work and his *Theology of St. Luke*, whose influence on subsequent scholarship should not be underestimated. While contemporary scholars working within literary-critical methodologies are unlikely to engage in such disregard, contemporary ascription to metaphorical interpretations of the poor still could be backgrounded by the early reception history suggested by Roth.[25] This is not to say that textual evidence for metaphor might not exist; I simply suggest that resorting to metaphor against more literal readings owes something to a reception history that sought definitions of "the poor" beyond the text in more speculative source criticism.

Finally, one must understand how first-century social stratification governed the categorization of "the poor." Both Green and scholars Malina and Rohrbaugh point to how honor and shame function in Luke's world to inform an understanding of the term.[26] Green says that Luke defines the world not primarily in economic terms but in terms of "status and social stratification"; specifically, "Luke's social world was defined around power, and is measured by a complex of phenomena—religious purity, family heritage, land ownership, vocation, ethnicity, gender, education and age." Later in his commentary, Green applies this social understanding to Luke's use of the "poor" in Luke 4:18: "Who are the poor? Numerous attempts have been made to find here a referent to the 'spiritually poor' or, more recently, reflecting the concerns of a materialist-oriented interpretative method." Green disagrees: "Both of these definitions of the 'poor' are inadequately grounded in ancient Mediterranean culture and the social world of Luke-Acts. In that culture, one's status in a community was not so much a function of economic realities, but depended on several elements." He then cites the elements listed above. This understanding of the broader exclusion of individuals and groups from political, social, and religious participation advances the argument that "the poor" is not a metaphor for individual spiritual depravity but is rather the focus of greater inclusion within the people of God as central to the mission of Jesus.

Prefiguring of Gentile Inclusion

Beyond Jesus' reading of the Isaiah passage, challenges arise related to the proverbial saying in verse 23, the congregation's turn to anger evidenced between its admiration in verse 22 and its wrath in verse 28, and Jesus' escape in verse 30. The connections between verses 17 and 18 have already been discussed, but one must consider Jesus' exposition on Elijah and Elisha and his prefiguring of Gentile inclusion that Luke and Acts further expand upon. To highlight differences in scholarly opinion on the verse's meaning, Hendricksen and Evans might stand as examples. Hendricksen views the passage as emphasizing God's divine sovereignty in determining the distribution of miracles,[27] whereas Evans insists that Luke is trying to define what election looks like in the new covenant.[28] All interpreters agree that the passage relates to Gentile inclusion. They only disagree on whether Luke merely foreshadows Gentile inclusion or makes it explicit. Siker believes consensus points to the former, but he supports the latter. "I propose," he asserts, "that Luke does more in this passage than just hint at Gentile inclusion in Acts, the position of most interpreters. Rather, Luke uses this inaugural sermon of Jesus exactly to proclaim Gentile inclusion as part of the gospel message."[29] Later discussion examines Gentile inclusion further; the important thing is the connections, muted or otherwise, between the messianic promises of verse 18 and 19 and the partiality shown to Gentiles in the Elijah/Elisha illustrations.

Thus, Jesus' reading and sermon, combined with his rebuke of the congregation in the Elijah/Elisha section, could support a reading that views preaching good news to the poor as including the socially, politically, and religiously marginalized in the providential salvific plan of God; the Elijah and Elisha passages foreshadow the inclusion of Gentiles. Attempts to read the passage in light of individual salvation are inadvisable in this light. The passage refers to God's larger providential plan in creating his new covenant people. I do not suggest that individual salvation, as expressed by Paul, is not in the background; Luke simply has in mind the larger picture of God's mission in the world.

Contested Points of Interpretation

The passage gives rise to three primary points of contention: the misquotation of Isaiah 62:1, 2 to include wording from Isaiah 58:6, the congregation's turn to anger, and Jesus' miraculous escape in verse 30. Each is important to interpreting the passage, although perhaps not for offering a final assessment of the passage's thrust and interpretation.

Misquotation of Isaiah

As already noted, Kimball justifies the misquotation by ascribing the verses not to a textual reading but to Jesus' midrashic sermon on the text.[30] Since scholars have no way to identify a Jewish lectionary as early as the first century AD, Jesus more likely combined both texts in this form following accepted midrashic practices. Ultimately Kimball's explanation cannot be substantiated, and the final-form exegetical process of this project excludes extensive engagement with form or source critical arguments. Actual reconstruction of Jesus' method of reading to create a distinct Lukan theology is not in view here, nor are discussions about how Luke might have drawn on sources and traditions that remembered the reading incorrectly, either intentionally or mistakenly.

Regardless, no provable necessity required Jesus to read only from Isaiah 62:1, 2; his insertion of 58:6 as a natural occurrence of synagogue worship remains possible. Also, in a final-form analysis, how the two texts came to be intermingled is less important than understanding Luke 4:18, 19 and its intermingling of the texts. None of these points of argument advances the interpretation.

The Listeners' Turn to Anger

Another disputed element of the pericope concerns what some have identified as the "turn to anger" in the passage, which begins with the congregation's expression of awe for Jesus in verse 22 and progresses to its homicidal rage in verses 28 and 29. Nolland, Bock, Green, and Siker demonstrate the diversity of opinions on this issue.

Nolland sees the disparity but chooses not to reconcile it, preferring instead to see it as poor source editing by Luke. He suggests, "It seems unlikely that Luke is mainly dependent on a simple unified account. The difficulties in the thought sequence, especially v. 22 to v. 25, v. 23 to v. 24, and v. 24 to vv. 25–26, strongly suggest that various traditions have been welded together here."[31]

Bock locates discontinuity earlier in the text, preferring to identify a disconnect between the congregation's awe in 22a and its contempt for Jesus as "Joseph's son" in 22b. Bock refuses to locate the congregation's anger in Jesus' message but instead locates it in Jesus' person. "The issue," says Bock, "is not what Jesus said, but who Jesus claims to be. How could 'this neighbor' be the fulfillment?"[32]

Green agrees with Bock that the turn occurs with the congregation's statement about Jesus' humble birth, but he believes that Jesus' identity was not the ultimate cause for anger. According to Green, the anger arises from how Jesus clarifies his mission in the Elijah/Elisha section: "Jesus addresses the parochial vision of the townspeople directly, countering their assumptions that, as Joseph's son, he will be especially for them a source of God's favor."[33] For his part, Siker concurs with Green that the anger resulted from Jesus' refusal to make good on his promises by fulfilling them in his hometown of Nazareth.[34]

The one dissenting voice is Jeremias, who sees verse 22a also as an expression of the congregation's anger, not its awe. Jeremias points to the fact that αὐτῷ can be a dative either of advantage or of disadvantage. In the former instance, the phrase would be translated "to bear witness on behalf of"; in the latter case, it would be translated "to bear witness against." Jeremias prefers the latter translation because it resolves the tension in the passage.[35]

The controversy will continue because of the text's ambiguity, but this study relies on Green's and Siker's assessments. Jeremias' contrasting view rests on a translation that he admits could go either way; his preferred translation of "bore witness against" does not reconcile well with the Nazareth congregation's amazement "at his gracious words" (NIV). Bock's suggestion—that the congregation is angry because of who Jesus is, not what he says—does not fit Jesus' reception as a reader or the congregation's amazement in verse 22a. Nolland's suggestion that the text is a poorly edited version of two separate sources is inconsistent with this study's final-form textual methodology, which does not see source critical analysis as compatible. Finally, the passage's chronology must be considered. The text does not suggest that the congregation is angry at Jesus before he introduces the Elijah/Elisha analogies. This chronology suggests—as Green and Siker contend, and this project concurs—that the anger was driven by Jesus' discussions of God's favor offered to the Gentiles over Israel.

Thus, the congregation's turn to anger seems to indicate its objections to Jesus' suggestion that the promise of Luke 4:18, 19 is to be fulfilled among those they see as outside the promised blessings of Isaiah 62:1, 2 and 58:6. This interpretation highlights the aspects of inclusion, particularly Gentile inclusion. That is, the anger is a direct response to Jesus' inclusion of those on the margins of, or wholly outside, Jewish religious society. This notion so offends the congregation at Nazareth that they attempt to kill Jesus. This interpretation emphasizes the literal understanding of Jesus' mission as primarily including the marginalized and those outside the community of God.

Jesus' Escape from the Crowd

The text ends with verse 30, where Jesus simply passes through the murderous crowd. Longenecker summarizes various interpretations as encompassing "(1) the athletic dodge; (2) Jesus the magical mystery man; (3) Jesus gets assistance from sympathizers, and (4) the rewritten ending." But Longenecker's best case surmises that the escape, like those in Acts, is God's miraculous intervention on Jesus' behalf. This divine intervention seems important within the entirety of Luke-Acts; it suggests that the supernatural is never far from view in the theology of Luke-Acts.[36] This interpretation plays an important role in any exegesis of the Lukan texts. Luke attempts to show God's supernatural intervention and active role in advancing his providential plan.

This miraculous rescue illuminates the paradigmatic nature of Luke 4:16–30 for the rest of Luke and Acts. Thus, this chapter must examine larger contexts: the place of Luke 4:16–30 within the entirety of Luke-Acts, followed by the other Gospels and intertextuality with Isaiah.

The Larger Contexts

Luke 4:16–30 within Luke-Acts

As already noted, most biblical scholars see Luke 4:16–30 as programmatic of all of Luke and Acts. Marshall summarizes the prevalent view: "The narrative is placed here, then, for its programmatic significance, and it contains many of the main themes of Lk.-Acts in nuce."[37] Nolland observes that Luke 4:18–19 is directly connected to Jesus' statement in Luke 7:33 that the disciples of John should bear witness to what they have seen and heard of Jesus' ministry: "that the blind see, the lame walk, the lepers are cleansed, the deaf hear, the dead are raised, the poor have the gospel preached to them" (NKJV). What Jesus pronounces in Luke 4:18–19 has literally been fulfilled to mark that Jesus is in fact "the coming one."[38]

While the text's programmatic nature is evident from surface level–narrative connections, Luke 4:16–30 includes no clear connection to the overarching and apparent themes that join Luke and Acts into a single narrative. Understanding the larger context of Luke 4:16–30 requires a constructive analysis that brings together research on the conceptual unity of Luke-Acts, expansion on the underlying theme, and application of this theme to Luke 4:16–30. What follows will explore the importance of covenant as a unifying theme within Luke-Acts—namely, Luke's continuing history of providence that includes Christ's fulfillment of the Old Covenant and his institution of the New Covenant of inclusion. I draw original conclusions from the work of Frank Kovaks et al., Philip La G. Du Toit, Richard Bauckham, and Scott Hahn.[39]

Covenant as an overarching category forming a unified biblical theology is addressed at a later point in this part. Of interest at this juncture is an understanding of the role of covenant as a unifying element in Luke-Acts and its implications for Luke 4:16–30.

Kovaks engages in a highly technical structural-critical analysis of Luke-Acts to find the narrative flow and connectors of the two books. The technical details of Kovaks' work are beyond this study, but his conclusions are valuable.[40] Kovaks points out that as a narrative, Luke-Acts forms a unified story with a unified plot, with certain internal structural markers that signal the overarching unified message. He breaks the narrative into three primary sequences: initial, topical, and final. These sequences, he asserts, point to a primary mandate within the text that guides the whole narrative. Kovaks concludes that Luke-Acts presents an initial disruption, represented by Israel's breaking of its central covenant relationship with God. He places this disruption in Israel's "denial of justice, lack of love for God, and obstruction of proper leadership for the benefit of the people." Throughout the central narrative, Jesus works to restore the covenant relationship by both restoring Israel and expanding the covenant to include Gentiles and others who were previously excluded. Kovaks sees inclusion as the primary act by which the narrative progresses from the initial disruption to its final primary mandate.

Kovaks also insists, "Lukan salvation is inclusive because Luke applies Isaianic passages on eschatological reversal to Jewish society, critiquing accepted norms and then extending the application to include the gentiles . . . The servant's mission, Luke shows from Isaiah, is to proclaim this inclusive salvation." Kovaks notes that the societal changes envisioned in Luke-Acts primarily alter the Jewish religious system and what it meant to be part of the people of God—an important distinction. For Kovaks, the narrative's primary mandate is the establishment of a new covenant that repairs the inherent brokenness of the old covenant relationship and carries a newly imagined, expanded community with the old covenant's same ethical responsibilities to care for one another and to love God.

This new covenant—highlighting fulfillment, restoration, and advance—is central to a coherent reading of Luke-Acts. Kovaks' work is noteworthy because he grounds these conclusions not in tropes or themes but in a structural literary analysis that highlights a central unifying plot and its primary moves and objectives. This approach lends critical assistance to the textual approach envisioned in the current study.

Two other scholars, Richard Bauckham and Philip La G. Du Toit, do not attempt Kovaks' overarching structural analysis, but they echo Kovaks' assertions of the importance of Israel's covenant restoration in Luke-Acts. Both Bauckham and Du Toit offer novel differing views about the restoration of Israel. For Bauckham, the restoration of Israel is a future act "left ambiguous" in the text of Luke-Acts, predicated on Israel's acceptance of the new covenant. Bauckham views the Gentile mission as a tactic: Gentile inclusion was a strategy on behalf of God and Paul "to provoke Israel to jealousy and thereby accomplish Israel's salvation (Rom. 11:11, 14), a notion that has its basis in the Torah's classic prophecy of restoration (Deut. 32:21, quoted in Rom. 10:19)."[41]

Alternatively, Du Toit suggests that Luke-Acts presents the restoration of Israel as a completed act. He bases his argument on both close textual analysis and Second Temple literature that suggests that the term "Israel" was reserved for pre-exilic and exilic Israel, not applied to contemporary first-century descendants. He concludes that Israel's restoration is one part of the Luke-Acts covenant emphasis that envisions the salvation of past Israel through the first advent of Christ and his resurrection, while its descendants fall under the new covenant. Du Toit cautions that his conclusion does not suggest the exclusive salvation of ancient Israel, nor an "over-realized eschatology that excludes future fulfillment or a future resurrection."[42]

The debate regarding how to apply Israel's restoration in Luke-Acts requires further scholarly engagement. Bauckham and Du Toit seem to share the opinion that "Israel's salvation or restoration is a prominent motif in both the Gospel of Luke and the Acts of the Apostles" and that the motif of Israel's salvation or restoration is more prominent in the Gospel of Luke than in any of the other gospels."[43] This opinion highlights and further supports Kovaks' assumptions that the need to restore Israel's covenant relationship with God lay at the center of the problem addressed in the ministry, death, and resurrection of Jesus in Luke, and in the sending of the Holy Spirit and the church's missional work in Acts.

Taking a more traditional biblical-theological approach to the text, Hahn's work assigns a significant primary role to the Davidic Covenant in Luke-Acts and offers extensive textual support to prove this claim. Among more than thirty textual references in Hahn's chapter 8 is his claim that "Gabriel's description of Jesus to Mary in Luke 1:32–33 is taken point-for-point from the key Davidic covenant text, 2 Samuel 7."[44] Hahn also recalls that references to Davidic kingdom restoration refer to covenant; the promises of the Davidic kingdom are covenant promises, and the Davidic covenant as invoked in Luke-Acts also specifically ties to the Abrahamic covenant through the Benedictus of Luke 1:68–79.[45] Hahn draws a conclusion about the restoration of Israel that differs from those of Du Toit and Bauckham, preferring what amounts to a far more secessionist view that reconceives the Ecclesia as the restored Israel. Again, working out this restoration remains debatable. What is important here is that Hahn's work demonstrates the prevalence of covenant restoration in Luke-Acts.

If the work of Kovaks, Du Toit, Bauckham, and Hahn does demonstrate the prevalence of covenant restoration in Luke-Acts—and if the plot structure of Luke-Acts does flow from interest in renewing Israel's broken covenant, as Kovaks claims—then covenant renewal becomes viable as the central organizing principle guiding other aspects of Luke-Acts. It then becomes important to read the programmatic nature of Luke 4:16–30 in light of covenant renewal. Since none of the referenced scholars do so, this discussion draws general conclusions from their work to suggest a constructive way to read Luke 4 in light of this covenantal perspective. Other themes such as reversal, poverty, and mission might suggest different interpretive foci; but for the sake of this work, the research suggesting covenant as a central organizing theme in Luke-Acts seems compelling and inclusive of other identifiable theological themes in Luke-Acts, sufficient to use it as a guide to interpretation.

Luke 4:16–30 can be read in several ways in light of the totality of Luke-Acts. For example, Jesus intends to bring the socially, politically, and religiously marginalized into full participation in the people of God under the new covenant. The poor—understood as the marginalized along with the Gentiles, within the broader semantic range—are not symbolic placeholders but are actual social groups to which God's mission and kingdom extend.

This conclusion must be examined in light of Shellberg's work on the intersection of the physical and spiritual nature of exclusion in the New Testament world. Marginalization based on stigmatization equates with both social ostracization and religious exclusion. Physical infirmity equates to uncleanness and carries both physical and spiritual meaning. Physical deformity connotes God's curse and likewise signifies both physical and spiritual difference; non-Jewish ethnicity also connotes uncleanliness and precipitates exclusion from participation within the elect of God. Thus, the suggestion that the marginalization suggested in Luke-Acts is merely spiritual or merely sociopolitical is inadequate, because such marginalization was both.[46]

What Luke-Acts envisions is the restoration of a broken religious system, not the political overthrow of Rome. The reorganization of God's people under the new covenant and Israel's restoration within it are central to the message of Luke-Acts. But this message has more direct sociopolitical implications than first emerge. The religious hierarchy and system within first-century Judaism exercised great social, political, and legal power over individual lives, well beyond purely religious pronouncements. In the wake of any integration of the religious and social in the first-century world, exclusion from the community's religious life meant exclusion from its social life as well. Such integration had real financial and quality-of-life issues for the excluded. Moreover, the Jewish religious aristocracy, under Roman rule, exercised some policing powers and limited jurisdiction over its own adherents. This reality is directly evident in the stoning of Stephen in Acts and Paul's persecution of Christians before his conversion. It can be seen in the Jewish leaders' influence over Pilate in Jesus' crucifixion. So, Jesus' institution of a new inclusive religious system—one based on the inclusion of the marginalized and Gentiles—had real consequences in limiting the power of the religious establishment by stripping leaders of their ability to direct power through exclusion. This new system also meant including the marginalized in ways that had real power to improve their lives, as evinced in the reversal motif in Luke-Acts.

Any interpretation that leans away from a purely symbolic interpretation of Luke 4:18, 19 as referring broadly to sinners—and toward a recognition of the text's literal sense of the marginalized as a special group singled out for missional engagement with sociopolitical and spiritual implications—does not necessarily suggest the absence of individual salvation in Luke-Acts or the specific text of Luke 4. Bauckham points out that even if unintended by Luke, our canonical traditions read the Pauline doctrines of grace as latent in Luke-Acts.[47] While this point is true, neither the Gospel nor Acts delineate an articulated, detailed soteriology. Put another way, Luke-Acts assumes and therefore does not make explicit a detailed soteriology. Pauline soteriology might be better understood as resting in the background of Luke-Acts (and by implication Luke 4). Most explicit, as stated above, is the Luke-Acts extension of the story of God's providential work; of how the new covenant enacts it through the ministry, death, and resurrection of Jesus; and of how the Church is established in the coming of the Holy Spirit. Luke-Acts can be said to work out the broader sociohistorical implications of God's providential work that emerge from the salvation to be had in Christ. This understanding accounts for singling out groups included by God under the new covenant, rather than offering a clear exposition (with a few notable exceptions) of the means for individuals to embrace the faith. But clearly, underneath the missional call to the marginalized and the Gentiles (as distinct groups, not symbolic representations) lies a Pauline soteriology that makes individual inclusion the result of working out the doctrines of grace, not the mere fact of a particular social, economic, class, or ethnic identity.

Further on this point, Luke 4 does not speak to the universal salvation of all the poor by virtue of their poverty. Luke makes clear that some are excluded from God's eternal blessings and receive eternal punishment by way of God's judgment. In Luke, most of those excluded are the powerful and wealthy, including the rich man in the parable of the rich man and Lazarus, the rich young ruler, and the rich as a class, found both in the beatitudes to the poor and the woes to the rich in the sermon on the plain. Zacchaeus is certainly one person of means who avoids the fate of the rich in Luke's Gospel—but Zacchaeus, a tax collector, would also have been regarded as a social and religious outcast by both the Jewish religious aristocracy and common Judeans. So, he fits the pattern of including the ostracized.

Jesus also said that he came to "preach good news to the poor." But Luke 4 does not say that all those poor, to whom Jesus preaches the good news of inclusion, will receive eternal life. The account of the rich young ruler (Lk 18:18–30) does suggest, however, that the kingdom of God will include more of the marginalized than of the rich and powerful. The account suggests that the requirement to surrender status and power in the interest of the poor and marginalized is too difficult for the rich. But again, universal salvation need not be read into Luke 4 simply because it singles out a socioeconomic grouping for missional activity, any more than this group must be seen as symbolizing all who will be accepted. They merely form an expression of the gospel's broader expansion and the inclusion of new groups within the new covenant community envisioned in Luke-Acts.

Finally, the nature of Luke-Acts as a theological history of God's providential acts in forming a new inclusive covenant community in Christ—as well as Christ's identification and call for the inclusion of the socially, politically, economically, ethnically, and religiously marginalized—together suggest that the providential message of Luke-Acts includes a call to a particular form of ethical living in community. This call requires a unique form of social reversal and contains a social ethic. If the doctrines of grace lay latent or semilatent beneath the surface of Luke-Acts, the ethical demands and implications are slightly more explicit as an ongoing expression of the Church's life in the world. This assessment is particularly true if one accepts the covenantal nature of Luke-Acts, because covenants by definition establish both a new relationship—in this case, one between God and God's new covenant people—and a new way of existing as God's new covenant community. Covenant requires action and relationship. Inclusion in the covenant, understood in light of a broader New Testament soteriology, is the free gift of God; but inclusion in the community brings new ways of acting in relation to the world at large and to the other members. In the context of Luke 4, Jesus is foreshadowing just what that community looks like and the kind of social reversals it requires. The marginalized and the Gentiles will be included; the power to deny inclusion is taken away from the religious elite; and the rich must surrender power, status, and physical possessions to exist as part of a community of commonality with those whom they formerly saw as "less than." The inclusion that Jesus suggests he has come to inaugurate requires real adjustment and presents a real challenge to the status-quo power structures of the first-century Mediterranean world. The ethics of living in diverse communities is a reality of both covenant relationship and of Jesus' and the Church's radical mission of inclusion.

This interpretation of Luke 4 within the context of Luke-Acts is preliminary. I offer it as constructive work following the scholarly literature on the importance of covenant to the narrative structure of Luke-Acts. My suggested interpretation of Luke 4:16–30, within the totality of the narrative of Luke Acts, can be summarized as follows. The text focuses on the providential history of God, understood as being fulfilled in the ministry, death, and resurrection of Jesus and the establishment of the Church through the sending of the Holy Spirit. Framing this providential history is the narrative context of the covenant offenses of ancient Israel and covenant renewal in Jesus, understood to include the marginalized and Gentiles in the new covenant people. Underlying this providential history, a latent or semilatent soteriology assumes the doctrines of grace. From these providential acts emerges a more explicit social ethic, which incorporates inclusion and social reversal within the new covenant community.

In this way, salvation, renewal, and inclusion have real social, political, and religious consequences that cannot be confused with God's free gift of salvation but also cannot be separated from it. Salvation and its social ethical consequences can be said to cohere in much the same way the command to love God and neighbor can be said to cohere in the Mosaic covenant and the two tables of the Decalogue. With this in mind, this chapter can now turn to the relationship between Luke-Acts and the other Gospels.

Luke-Acts among the Other Gospels

Many scholars discuss Luke-Acts in terms of redactional issues and the questions raised by source criticism. Carey says, "Many commentators, assessing the passages (including Luke 4:16–30) individually rather than as a group, regard them not as products of aggressive redaction but as deriving from Luke's access to independent streams of tradition, identifying common redactional dynamics in each of these passages. I maintain that we more plausibly attribute them to Lukan redaction."[48] As this assessment illustrates, the discussion revolves around readings that assume either inadequate editing of diverse traditions or an intentional shaping of the Gospel narratives to present a particular theological perspective. In the latter case, Luke diverges from Mark in presenting his order of the Nazareth sermon and adds material to make a point. Luke also uses varying traditions that fit his theme, and a more extreme interpretation suggests that Luke alters the tradition to make varying or differing theological points. Such debates and reconstruction are outside the final-form analysis envisioned here. More important for the current study is understanding Luke's Gospel in relation to the other Gospels in the canon, specifically how Luke, particularly Luke 4:16–30, is both consistent with and adds to the theological understanding of the other Gospels. Specifically, Luke's Gospel focuses more on the poor and the marginalized and is far more literalistic than the other Gospels in its insistence on Jesus' inclusion of the marginalized and oppressed.

This understanding does not require Luke to be seen as contradictory to the other Gospels. Luke's literal use of "the poor" is different from Matthew's "poor in spirit"; but the extent to which even Matthew spiritualizes the poor is unclear. As Green points out, Luke also does not abandon an understanding of salvation but may simply be seen as shifting the focus on salvation in a different direction.[49] Marshall emphasizes this, suggesting that "Luke's stress is on the blessings of salvation that he brings."[50] Luke can therefore be seen as affirming the liberative and social rewards of God's salvation while highlighting God's intent in bringing those rewards to the poor, as broadly understood.

But because the Gospels include Luke, biblical theologians seem to have difficulty ignoring the importance of a more literal interpretation and a more social application of Christ's mission to the poor and marginalized. This approach suggests that Matthew's spiritualization of the poor cannot take preference over Luke's insistence on Christ's inclusive mission to the poor. Matthew cannot be given hermeneutical priority over Luke if the Gospel's full message is to be understood. Thus, Luke may be said to provide not a contradictory view of salvation, but rather a fuller view that, as Marshall suggests, focuses on the social rewards or "blessings" of salvation here and now. This reading might be ascribed to a distinct eschatological perspective on Luke's part that looked to provide an ethic for Christian living after a delayed Parousia. I explore this perspective in detail below. Regardless, Luke's Gospel must be allowed to speak on its own terms, if its place among the Gospels is to be properly understood.

Intertextuality with Isaiah

As already mentioned, Luke 4:16–30 contains direct quotes from Isaiah 62:1–2 and 58:6, as well as allusions to the stories of Elijah and Elisha in 1 Kings 17:1–7; 18:1; 17:12, 15, 18, 24; and 2 Kings 5:1–14. Luke's use of Isaiah in verses 18 and 19 is illuminating. The texts' selection connects Jesus' mission to Jubilee symbolism and moves that symbolism into Jesus' understanding of his messianic role.[51] Thus, the liberating or restorative nature of "release" and "salvation" in the text is difficult to miss.

Luke's narrative agrees with the Masoretic text of Isaiah in several ways. For one thing, the LXX version says, "Because he has anointed me. He has sent me to proclaim good news to the poor." The Masoretic text has "Because he has anointed me to announce good news to the poor." Luke follows the Masoretic text. The distinction is subtle but important. The LXX text emphasizes being anointed and then sent to complete the task of preaching to the poor. In the Masoretic text and the Lukan text, the implication is that Jesus is anointed for the purpose of proclaiming good news to the poor. The proclamation in the LXX is a consequence of the anointing, whereas the Masoretic proclamation is the purpose of the anointing. Anointing for liberation is more readily apparent in the Masoretic and Lukan texts than in the LXX version. Additionally, Luke's Jesus prefers the Masoretic "to proclaim" over the LXX's "to announce" concerning the "year of the Lord's favor." In at least one instance, Luke omits the text of both the Masoretic and LXX, dropping "to heal the brokenhearted," effectively highlighting the social and political over the emotional and the spiritual.[52]

Likewise, by abruptly ending the Isaiah 61:2 quotation after "to proclaim the acceptable year of the Lord," the Lukan account intentionally omits "and the day of vengeance of our God." Jeremias sees this omission as causing the congregation's anger because Jesus does not recognize God's vengeance on the Gentiles.[53] Whether Jeremias' conclusions are correct, he rightly assumes that the absence of vengeance is significant to the Lukan account. It signals the comprehensiveness and expansion of the grace of God to those outside the established religious order, pointing to the inclusive nature of Jesus' message.

Luke's insertion of Isaiah 58:6 ("to set at liberty those who are oppressed") recalls the rest of Isaiah 58, which makes the point that Israel's primary sin was its oppression of and injustice toward the poor and marginalized. This insertion focuses Jesus' role in restoring and reversing the sins of Israel, as he restores the captive, the poor, the blind, and the oppressed; and it shows the importance of justice for Jesus' mission. Bock concurs: "Jesus will do what Israel was rebuked in Isaiah 58 for not doing: Jesus will meet in love the needs of those who need God. The picture again is of Jesus reaching out to the needy and giving them aid. It is a declaration of injustice reversed."[54] This reading is also consistent with the previous discussion of covenant restoration.

What is apparent is that this Old Testament citation, in the hands of Luke's Jesus, signals the importance of justice, liberation, and inclusion for the poor. Jesus functions as the Messiah who has come to restore the covenant through the inclusion of the poor. This function is signaled through both the Jubilee symbolism and the careful selection and presentation of the Old Testament readings. Jesus' salvation is meant to include the poor, the marginalized, and other excluded groups as a way to undo Israel's past sins. This salvation is literally good news to the poor. Christ's inclusion of the poor, the marginalized, and the oppressed in the new covenant community is not only restorative. It is missional, as the gospel is expanded, and it is social, as the new community embraces restoring the previously marginalized into full membership.

Preliminary Interpretation

The foregoing exegesis now suggests a tentative, preliminary interpretation. I offer this as a starting point which should be evaluated against the work of the biblical scholars and theologians presented below.

First, the Lukan text presents Jesus as literally preaching good news to the poor, granting sight to the blind, setting captives free, and releasing the oppressed. In doing so, the text of Luke 4:16–30 is programmatic of the entirety of Luke-Acts.

In addition, the narrative focuses on the messianic nature of Jesus' mission and uses the Isaianic prophecies as identifiers of Jesus as the Christ. As Messiah, Jesus can be identified through his completion of these tasks. This reading does not suggest that these messianic identifiers must simply be understood as inconsequential; they are intimately connected to what it means for Jesus to be the Messiah. By nature, the Messiah must be one who sets the oppressed at liberty.

A third point is that Jesus—as one who has come to reverse the sins of Israel—focuses on undoing Israel's previous injustices and establishing a new ethic of inclusion and care for the poor, understood broadly as the socially and religiously marginalized. This new ethic is either explicitly or prefiguratively indicated in Jesus' use of the Elijah/Elisha narratives, as well as the covenant restoration structure of Luke-Acts. The poor and marginalized along with the Gentiles form a particular, literal group given a place in the new covenant of Christ. This inclusion has the additional result of reversing the sins of Israel evident in Isaiah 58.

Fourth, Luke-Acts, taken as a whole, provides a unique lens through which salvation can be seen. Lukan salvation focuses more distinctly on liberation than the other Gospels do. Lukan salvation is primarily an exposition of the social and temporal blessings of salvation. This understanding emerges as a result of Luke's move from an imminent to an inaugurated view of eschatology. Additionally, while individual salvation in Luke may be viewed as latent, one must see that Luke intends to capture the broader landscape of salvation or perhaps to address the providential scope of Christ's salvation. Thus, Luke focuses on the expansion of the gospel and the inclusion of specific groups, rather than specifically addressing individual doctrines of grace. In the process, Luke shows how these groups benefit from this salvation, from the status change implied by inclusion in the people of God, and from the community ethic necessitated by their inclusion. Furthermore, including the poor and marginalized and denying the hierarchy's power of marginalization necessitate real change in social systems of power, change that elevates the poor, the marginalized, and the Gentiles within the prevailing religious system.

Fifth and finally, Luke-Acts intentionally positions salvation, liberation, and the Jubilee prophecies in the person of Jesus. In doing so it blurs the boundaries between the spiritual and temporal and privileges Christ's power over political and social entities. This positioning does not set up a contradiction and separation between the spiritual and the temporal; rather it positions the spiritual as a primary actor in social and political systems and as a deeper resource for the formation of communities of justice.

Cone's more literal liberation interpretation of the text therefore seems valid, if understood within a broader and more intimate connection between the temporal and the spiritual. This chapter now turns to demonstrate this validity from the perspective of a broader biblical-theological analysis.

Chapter 9

ALTERNATIVE INTERPRETATIONS

Five scholars' views of Lukan theology should be considered when trying to analyze the theological significance of Luke 4:16–30: those of Hans Conzelmann, Joel Green, I. Howard Marshall, C. Kavin Rowe, and Brian K. Blount.[55] This section treats each in turn, except Green and Marshall, who are discussed together because of their similar views. In light of the identified covenant structure in Luke-Acts, the role of covenant as an overarching motif in Reformed biblical theology also warrants examination.

Lukan Theology

Hans Conzelmann was the first biblical scholar to take seriously the task of identifying a uniquely Lukan theology. Before Conzelmann, most Lukan scholarship focused on Luke as a historian. But in both Luke and Acts Conzelmann saw a clear theological focus and attempted to demonstrate that Luke's narrative choices were intentional support for a theological agenda. Conzelmann's arguments are progressive. He first demonstrates clear patterns in the Gospel, marked by geographical progression from Galilee to the journey narratives to the climax in Jerusalem.[56] Once he demonstrates this pattern beyond chronology, he seeks to identify the issue driving Luke's writing, insisting that this issue is the delayed Parousia.[57] Luke's Church is struggling with Christ's delayed return and how the Church can exist in that light. This is Conzelmann's strongest argument, and it has found the most support in later Lukan scholarship. Luke's theological solution to the delayed Parousia, according to Conzelmann, is redemption history.[58]

How Conzelmann links the delayed Parousia to the need to articulate a redemption history must be rightly understood. Conzelmann believes that while the Church held onto the eschatological hope of an imminent return, it saw the Empire as an institution to be withstood as it awaited the return of Christ, who would make all things right. As these hopes diminished and the Church realized that the return was delayed, it sought to understand its new reality in light of its continued existence under the Empire. The Church began to advance a stance more conciliatory toward governmental authority and emphasized its nonthreatening nature.[59] Luke portrays the Church as those called to live in relationship to God—but in a more mundane way, with a less oppositional and more isolationist posture. The Church becomes the interrogatory step between the centrality of God's redemption in Jesus' death and resurrection and the delayed Parousia.

Conzelmann's influence is undeniable; but as Marshall points out, his redemptive-historical scheme poses problems. Marshall insists that a delayed

Parousia was not that significant in the Church's turn to a redemption-historical account of Christ's work and the Church's place within that account.[60] Marshall affirms that the Church already had a view of salvation history before its understanding of the delayed Parousia. If Marshall is correct—that Conzelmann's progressive view of the development of redemption-historical understanding is not Luke's innovation but rather an articulation of the Church's standing opinion—then one must also question Conzelmann's sharp distinction between the Early Church's view of politics and the relationship between the Church and Empire, and his view that "whereas in the original eschatological perspective it was felt that the State had to be withstood, now the attempt is made to enter into conversation with it, to achieve a permanent settlement."[61] If the Church had always held a steady view of Christ's return and the Church's place in the world, then Conzelmann's view of a sudden move to political quietism seems misplaced. This analysis does not suggest that the delayed Parousia did not affect Lukan theology—merely that it did not play a decisive role.

Ultimately, Conzelmann's primary contribution to any theological interpretation of Luke-Acts is twofold. First, the significance of a delayed Parousia is critical for understanding the importance of an ethic of discipleship and relationship inherent in Luke's Gospel. How one lives in light of Christ's delayed return, in relation to questions of injustice, inequality, and one's neighbor, is important and presents critical interpretive keys to the Lukan texts. Second, Conzelmann's identification of the challenges of living in light of and in relation to empire, as both a theological and political question for the Church, is key to understanding that Luke does include political theology and can be read in light of a particular perspective on political action—whether one believes that this theology is emerging (like Conzelmann) or that it is already fixed in the Early Church (like Marshall). Both perspectives support interpreting Luke 4:15–30 as containing a social ethic that depends on a broader salvation-historical or providential understanding of the Church's work. Conzelmann's actual conclusion that the Church was seeking a way to live in harmony with government and not to express liberationist ideas must be dealt with further, but his underlying assumptions support the interpretation offered above.

Both Marshall and Green prefer a reading of Luke that focuses on the importance of salvation apart from any purely providential notion of salvation history. However, their views differ somewhat. For Marshall, salvation in Luke is spiritual and one-dimensional. Green, however, recognizes a more nuanced understanding of salvation.

While Marshall recognizes the liberationist language in Luke, he sees it as symbolic, not literal, and offers two primary defenses.[62] First, he sees the lack of an actual political insurrection by Jesus as clear evidence that

Luke intended to be symbolic. But this reading assumes the Early Church had already embraced the idea of a delayed Parousia, which, as mentioned, Marshall argues against, supporting his view with extra historical evidence and not interpreting the text in light of its narrative understanding. Within the narrative context, as long as Christ's coming—either imminent or delayed—is kept alive, the overthrow of corrupt and unjust governmental systems remains possible, and the literal language of deliverance and Jubilee remains at least a hope. Thus, literal liberation needs to be liberated from the text only if the text demonstrates no hope for temporal intervention connected with the eschaton. Marshall also concludes that the Early Church, like Christians today, used the symbolic language of war to express purely spiritual ideas. This argument is purely anachronistic.

Green concurs that salvation is the primary theme of Luke's Gospel. But Green sees the message as focusing primarily on ecclesiology and discipleship,[63] described as the benefits of salvation. Luke's Jesus is the Savior whose salvation brings real benefit to all, particularly to the marginalized. The consequence of this radical inclusion is a new requirement for all the people of God to live in light of this new community. This requirement produces a new radical discipleship. Green describes this discipleship as "membership in the people of God":

> The focus is removed from issues of inherited status and a premium is placed on persons whose behaviors manifest their unmitigated embrace of the gracious God. Genuine "children of Abraham" are those who embody in their lives the beneficence of God, and who express openhanded mercy to others, especially toward those in need. Jesus thus calls on people to live as he lives, in contradistinction to the agonistic, competitive form of life marked by conventional notions of honor and status typical of the larger Roman world.[64]

Green, contra Marshall, refocuses Lukan salvation on a broader assessment of ecclesiology and takes seriously the literalness of the text, particularly those parts that treat poverty, oppression, and marginalization. But Green's approach remains primarily Hauerwasian, seeing the calls for justice, reversal, and inclusion as focusing on intercommunal relationships and only secondarily on the Church's relationship to society as a whole. Thus, Green fails to recognize, just as Conzelmann does, the political theology, social reversal, and power dynamics inherent in the text.

C. Kavin Rowe, in his study focusing on Acts, recognizes the importance of the political in Luke-Acts. He points to the fact that any reading of Acts that "argues for the political possibility of the harmonious existence between Rome and the early Christian movement" fails to account for the radical nature of Christianity and its effects on social and political systems. Rowe presents a new way to view the social and political within Acts: "Reading the . . . (the political argument) together with . . . (the spiritual argument) produces a dynamic tension that animates the narrative of Acts and must be thought as whole."[65] He contends that conversion, with subsequent lifestyle changes, had direct implications for Greco-Roman society that are evident in the conflicts in Acts.

The Church did not directly assault the Roman governmental systems. But Rowe argues that Acts does confront Rome with a distinct accusation and that, although the Church did not desire Rome's power, neither did it accept Rome's injustices. The constant argument of Luke-Acts is that Christians are innocent, and Rome is wrong in its condemnation, injustice, and oppression. Jesus died innocent of violating Roman law; Paul ultimately did the same. Luke-Acts condemns the Roman oppression of Christians while attacking the Jewish religious leadership's exclusion of Gentiles and other "outside" groups. Thus, for Rowe, Luke-Acts is not passive in either altering culture or confronting Rome; it simply is uninterested in political power, which it views as subservient to the power of God. Rowe highlights how God's supernatural power is at work in the world: delivering God's people, providing for the poor and marginalized, and engaging in tangible ways. Luke-Acts pulls back the veil between the spiritual and the temporal to reveal the supreme power of God at work in the world and worldly power's inability to match it. The fact that Jesus and Paul do not wish to overthrow the government and assume political power does not mean that God and the Church are not working in the world, transforming it into the image of God. Rowe's view of Acts points toward a social and political theology that shows real promise when combined with Green's ecclesiology.

This discussion must also consider the work of Brian Blount, who follows Sharon Ringe in connecting the Gospel of Luke to the message of justice inherent in the prophets and to the Jubilee symbolism inherent in the Messiah's mission. Directly connecting the Lukan Jesus with this prophetic and messianic tradition results in a thrust within Lukan theology that, according to Blount, means that "Jesus' messianic activity is the work of liberation."[66] Blount adds to Green's understanding a notion of Christian activity in the world that further grounds liberation Christologically and supports Green's notions of discipleship that extend beyond the Church's internal relational dynamics.

Covenant as Holistic Biblical Theology

Given the aforementioned focus on covenant in Luke-Acts, the overarching nature of covenant as a holistic biblical theology must be considered. This consideration includes the primary supports for covenant used in this way and the understanding of covenant followed here.

Biblical theologians—especially evangelical scholars—have offered extensive support for the idea that covenant is a primary, if not the primary, structure of the Scriptures, understood holistically. As Gentry asserts, both covenant theologians and dispensationalists tend to utilize covenant in their theological constructions.[67] Covenant is seen as important by biblical theologians representing a wide array of approaches, including Goldsworthy, Childs, Gentry, Hafemann, and Hahn.[68]

But covenant must be grounded in a clear understanding of how it functions as a biblical theology. Both Gentry and Hafemann are instructive here.[69] They reference two methods of biblical theology that have proven problematic: locating a single theological center in the biblical text and identifying an important theme. Both scholars distance their understanding of covenant from these approaches. Covenant is neither the center of the biblical story nor a theme in it; rather, covenant forms the primary structure that advances the plot. This view is predicated on understanding that the biblical materials, in all their diversity, have in mind a single salvation-historical narrative that illuminates God's interactions with and on behalf of God's creation and for God's glory. The Bible is that unfolding story; in Scripture, that relationship is advanced through the various covenants. Thus, covenant forms the structure or hinge that both unifies and advances a progressive, providential salvation history. Thus, covenant as structure and not theme is in view here.

But what then is meant by "covenant"? Hahn summarizes the primary views about what covenants are and how they must be understood.[70] These views fall primarily into two schools of thought. The first encompasses those who follow the early views of Wellhausen, who sees covenant in a legalistic or judicial light, as a development in Israelite religion that moved away from kinship ties toward ethical and moral contracts. The other school comprises those who follow Eichrodt in seeing covenant as primarily relational, in its capacity to form relationships between persons without biological or tribal affinities. These scholars include Frank Cross, who, according to Hahn, "grounds the concept . . . in the kinship-based social organization of West Semitic tribal groups."[71] Thus, understandings of covenant exist on a spectrum between legal contract and relational bounds.

Many contemporary evangelical scholars lean toward the relational interpretation of covenant. These include both Gentry and Hafemann. Hafemann's definition is especially illuminating; he sees covenant as encompassing the basic ideas of "(1) the essential character of God as King or Sovereign Ruler, (2) the election of a people under his rule who, as his 'adopted' children live in dependence upon him, and (3) the corresponding nature of God's bond with these as their 'Sovereign Father.'" In tying covenant to the salvation-historical plot of Scripture, Hafemann says, "This 'covenant relationship,' in which the basic categories of kingship (Sovereign Ruler) and kinship (Father) are mutually interpretive, is not static, it is the dynamic, historical arena within which God reveals himself. As such, it provides the interpretive lens for understanding who God is, who his people are and how they relate to one another."[72] Thus, for Hafemann, covenant is a relationship with commitments, including humanity's commitments to God, and commitments the people of God make to one another and to humanity. These relational commitments extend to the new covenant and are broadened due to its inclusive and missional nature.[73]

This broader understanding of covenant must be brought into conversation with the foregoing discussion of covenant structure in Luke. Critical to understanding covenant as inclusion in Luke is the idea of covenant as a relationship that brings together, into familial bonds, those who are biologically unrelated. By including the poor, the marginalized, and the Gentiles in God's providential plan for redeeming humanity, Christ brings into relationship and community those who were previously outside; he requires their acceptance and inclusion by those who held places of privilege and power within the older covenant community. Through the passages that focus on reversal, Luke also speaks to a necessary new ethic for the new covenant community, an ethic that requires abandoning old notions of privilege and status in favor of mutuality within the new covenant community. In addition, in the new covenant, God asserts God's sovereign right to election and to a determination of who is in this new community—over and against the religious hierarchy's authority to exclude and marginalize. Only God, in Christ, determines who has a place. So too, the Gentile mission in Acts and its foreshadowing in Luke entails a requirement not only to accept the excluded but to actively seek their participation in the community. Finally, the extent to which Luke unifies the old and new covenants within the theme of Israel's restoration suggests, as mentioned, that the new covenant somehow fulfills the broken obligations of the old covenant. Luke's allusion to Isaiah 58 and the sins of injustice toward the poor and marginalized indicates that including this group in the new community is necessary for the restoration of Israel. Relationality, both vertical and horizontal, is fully in view in a covenant-based reading of Luke-Acts.

These applications of a broader covenant theology to Luke-Acts constitute an attempt at a constructive reading. As a result, they need to be engaged more broadly than is possible given the scope of the current work. But these conclusions are at least logically consistent with both the scholarship on covenant as a structural feature of Luke and the broader scholarship on the covenant's significance and definition in the full canon. They seem important for any attempt to understand the meaning and application of Luke 4:16–30.

Interpretive Assessment of Alternative Views

Where, then, do these varying views of Luke-Acts intersect in a coherent interpretation of Luke 4:16–30? All of these views, except Marshall's, recognize the political within Luke's theology and affirm some place for the literal application of the Gospel's call for both the inclusion and just, ethical treatment of the poor and marginalized within the covenant community, as a requirement of missional engagement.

Conzelmann's focus on a delayed Parousia emphasizes the need for the Church to reimagine life in the world while awaiting Christ's return. In turn, this view suggests vis-à-vis Green that Luke did intend to demonstrate a new way of living in light of both this need and the inclusion of those outside the community in the work of God. Blount grounds this view in a Christology that connects Christ both to the prophetic view of justice and to the messianic mission of Jubilee, which then informs the Church's behavior as a new people of God. Rowe adds an assessment of God's transformative power on society as a whole, through the Church, as well as a focus that sees governmental power as weak in relation to God's supernatural power. Worldly power per Lukan theology is insufficient and undesirable for God's kingdom. But the Church is required to bear witness to the government's injustice, to the "slaughter of the innocents," and to the truth that government cannot clearly see and comprehend apart from the supernatural power of God.

This study also suggests that within Luke one finds an emphasis on covenant that shifts Luke's concerns away from a Pauline focus on the doctrines of grace and individual salvation and toward the broader category of providential history and the new covenant's inclusion of previously excluded groups. This broadened community changes the power dynamic among its members; it requires an ethic of reversal and a different way of viewing social status within the community and in the world, in light of its new missional calling. Taken together these findings move the focus of Luke 4:16–30 toward a more literal understanding—not one that excludes the doctrines of grace, but one that focuses on the implications of those who are already saved and the broader questions of ecclesiology, sanctification, and mission. In short, these views support a more literal reading of Luke 4:16–30 and together suggest that the preliminary interpretation I have offered is accurate.

THEOLOGICAL SIGNIFICANCES

How can the text inform more comprehensive theological assessments, including ultimately the doctrinal work of part IV? This part of Movement Three examines the important theological themes identified above. Per my analysis, at least six overarching theological themes are evident in Luke-Acts generally, and in Luke 4:16–30 specifically: salvation, covenant, Gentile inclusion, Jubilee, the in-breaking of the divine into the temporal, and reversal.

I have already discussed the Lukan view of salvation in recounting Marshall's and Green's understandings of Lukan theology. Green's understanding is preferable, as it takes into consideration what is evident through direct exegesis of the text and the theme of delayed Parousia, so evident in Lukan scholarship since Conzelmann originally proposed it. Green's understanding is that Lukan soteriology includes spiritual salvation but also intentionally extends the notion of salvation to encompass the blessings of salvation and the specific way salvation transforms both the community and the individual toward radical discipleship. As a result, this expanded view looks beyond, while also including individual salvation to suggest its practical and ethical applications.

However, Green's assessment does not move the text toward an interpretation of salvation consistent with modern Latin American liberation theology. The poor are not "saved" by virtue of their poverty. Luke's vision sees salvation as resting in the person of Christ; those who are saved are redeemed through and in Jesus, not by any social or economic classification. Green does not downplay the importance of the poor and marginalized for Christ. Green simply connects the liberation of the poor to their embrace of Jesus, and the salvation of the rich relies on their willingness to surrender a life of power for a life of servanthood and solidarity with the marginalized—a life that flows out of commitment to Christ. Salvation has social implications for those who are saved that are tied up in justice, equality, and mutual service. Ultimately, in Lukan soteriology, salvation happens in service to sanctification, which has a radical social imagination that defies existing ideas of status, honor, power, privilege, and place. This social discipleship is intended to be both a community-building strategy, with a uniquely ecclesiological function, and a transformative spiritual power in the life of the individual believer, as it serves both to identify the "saved" and to guide spiritual growth and practice. The care and solidarity with the poor and marginalized that seems so central to Lukan theology, therefore, becomes both the disciple's core guiding principle and the standard for ecclesiological communal practice.

The latter is true, as suggested above, because of the outgrowth and primary structuring role of covenant in Luke. Christ comes to restore Israel and to inaugurate a new covenant that makes amends for the injustices outlined in Isaiah 58; this covenant does so by including the poor, the marginalized, and the Gentiles in the new covenant community and by restoring what was broken through Christ's death and resurrection. Again, this covenant has real social implications. The power of inclusion and exclusion shifts from the religious hierarchy to God's sovereign will, and the new covenant establishes a community of mutuality contrary to the power and status norms of honor/shame cultures.

The idea of Gentile inclusion is especially central to the theology of Luke-Acts. Gentile inclusion is either stated explicitly or foreshadowed in Luke 4:16–30. The envisioned inclusion shatters not only ethnic distinctions but also distinctions of class, power, gender, and social standing. This vision encompasses even those labeled as impure or those whose social behaviors have placed them outside the community. This inclusion is, however, conditional. It is not a universal salvation. But the conditions shift dramatically. No longer is inclusion based on birth or on compliance with established social, cultural, and religious norms; it is now conditioned on a relationship. Namely, inclusion is offered to all those who embrace Jesus. Salvation rests in the person of Jesus, and inclusion among God's chosen depends on where someone stands in relationship to Christ.

Thus, Gentile inclusion redefines the doctrine of election to envision a more inclusive community determined less by social, ethnic, gender, and class identifications and more by self-identification and acceptance by Christ. The relational nature of covenant also operates here, as the covenantal act of a kinship contract—which binds all parties to one another apart from blood or tribal ties—is central to Luke's understanding of new covenant community and to how this community is shaped by groups who were previously excluded.

Luke also uses the symbolism of Jubilee to articulate the salvation offered in Christ. Luke 4:16–30 invokes Jubilee in its use of Isaiah 61:1–2. Ringe elaborates on the important theological content of the passage's images, which she characterizes as the inauguration of God's sovereign reign and the liberation of the powerless and marginalized.[74] She does not view Luke 4 as calling for a literal Jubilee year, but she recognizes its symbolic significance in asserting God's attempt to establish God's sovereignty and justice. For Luke, the Jubilee symbolism means that Lukan theology focuses not just on the sovereign reign of God but on the inauguration of that reign in Jesus, typified by emphasizing the justice and community that such a reign brings. All power becomes surrendered to the power of God, and all relationships are directed toward the acceptable justice of God. The poor are restored, and the oppressed are released from their oppressors. The power of God in the world becomes available to transform social disorders. It also restores those on the religious margins to the kingdom of God. Luke's Jubilee imagery suggests that God is at work transforming social orders through transforming the people of God. In light of the new covenant of inclusion, God has also directed the inclusion of the poor and marginalized in God's new community, which carries particular social and liberative benefits and becomes "good news" to the poor.

If the theology of salvation, covenant, inclusion, and Jubilee seem primarily directed toward building the community and a common practice of discipleship within God's people, Rowe's emphasis on the power of God breaking into the temporal world, and on the collision of cultures that comes with the practice and witness to the Christian gospel, envisions a God at work in the larger world in activities with real social consequences. This collision takes place as Christian faith is found at odds with, and detrimental to, the prevailing Greco-Roman economic, political, religious, and social systems. The Christian life and inclusive community envisioned in the new covenant cause social unrest between Christians and both pagan and Jewish cultures. Christianity also bears witness—in its teaching and its community—to a social structure that critiques pagan culture and directly acknowledges the injustices of Roman rule and the Jewish hierarchy's administration of justice. Thus, in Rowe's understanding, the Christian community escapes Hauerwasian isolationism and becomes a direct vehicle of God that challenges the prevailing systems of Power.

Finally, most Lukan scholars affirm a theme of reversal that receives very little attention except in the work of Blount.[75] Blount points out that both salvation and inclusion mark reversal, and reversal becomes the ethical principle that governs Christian discipleship in the image of Christ: "In the kingdom, societal insiders who dismiss God's call will find themselves on the margins; those who have been societally marginalized, but who respond to God's call and commands, will find themselves at the center of God's consummate kingdom. God's kingdom, according to the parable, attends to obedience, not status."[76] Likewise, Jesus, the ultimate example of reversal, becomes the basis for Christian interaction. Those with power, status, and position are called to surrender these in the same way that Jesus on the cross surrendered his status and power in obedience to God. Thus, Luke becomes a guide to discipleship for the rich, the powerful, and the privileged—a discipleship that requires unique obedience and surrender. The poor and marginalized have an easier time embracing obedience to Christ because they have less to surrender on that path. This radical reversal in Luke has real implications for ethical practice, discipleship, and relationship within the body of Christ.

SUMMARIZING LUKE'S THEOLOGICAL VISION

How then might one summarize the theological vision of the Gospel of Luke? If anything, it offers a view of the in-breaking of the sovereign reign of God that opens God's kingdom to those formerly outside that kingdom. In doing so, this vision shatters notions of status and honor in society, challenges prevailing systems of power, and reverses status and privilege within God's community. The poor and the marginalized have direct—in many cases easier—access to the kingdom of God than the rich and powerful enjoy. Within the context of this in-breaking, those who receive this new salvation are transformed by it. The poor and marginalized are elevated by virtue of inclusion. The rich and the powerful are called to surrender power in the interest of servanthood and community unity and to embrace as sisters and brothers those whom they formerly viewed as outside God's grace. This newly formed community—as it bears witness to the sovereign reign of God in Christ—also bears witness to the truth, and it challenges the evil that manifests as injustice. It requires new ways to see the world that challenge social, economic, and political systems and illuminate injustice and the persecution of the innocent. Thus, salvation becomes both spiritual and social; sanctification requires reversal and solidarity with the poor; and ecclesiology requires a unity that sets aside power, privilege, and status in the interest of Christ and the Church as it fulfills this sovereign, Jubilee-laden will of God that necessarily challenges society to abandon the lie for God's truth.

If this is Luke's theological message, the Gospel is declaring a more radical message than most evangelical theology recognizes. This message is not one of universal salvation, or salvation predicated on social class or standing, but is rather a radically socially and culturally reorienting gospel that may require reexamining doctrinal and ethical stances. But do other texts challenge or even contradict this reading of Luke? And what might these texts say, alongside Luke-Acts, about issues of status, power, privilege, and the status quo?

NOTES

1. Green, J. 1997. *The Gospel of Luke, NICNT.* Grand Rapids: W. B. Eerdmans. 6–10; Marshall, I. H. 2004. *New Testament Theology: Many Witnesses, One Gospel.* Downers Grove: InterVarsity Academic. 157–76; Jeffery. 2012: 6–8; Levine, A., and B. Witherington. 2019. *The Gospel of Luke, New Cambridge Bible Commentary.* Cambridge: Cambridge University Press.

2. Jennings, W. 2017. *Acts: A Theological Commentary on the Bible.* Grand Rapids: Westminster John Knox Press.

3. Conzelmann, H. 1961. *The Theology of St. Luke.* Translated by G. Boswell. San Francisco: Harper and Row.

4. Levine, A., and B. Witherington, 2019.

5. Green, J. 1997: 24–25.

6. Rowe, K. 2010. *World Upside Down: Reading Acts in the Greco-Roman Age.* Oxford: Oxford University Press.

7. Green, J. 1997: 208.

8. Green, J. 1997: 208.

9. Nolland, J. 1989. *Luke 1–9:20, WBC*. New York: Nelson Reference. 191; Siker, J. "'First to the Gentiles': A Literary Analysis of Luke 4:16–30." *Journal of Biblical Literature* 3 (1992): 77.

10. Marshall, I. H. 1988. *Luke: Historian and Theologian*. Downers Grove: InterVarsity Academic. 177–78; Bock, D. 1994: 394; Green, J. 1997: 207; Nolland, J. 1989: 195.

11. Green, J. 1997: 210.

12. Green, J. 1997: 214; Bock, D. 1994: 412–13, 417, 418.

13. Green, J. 1997: 214.

14. Omanson, R. 2007. *A Textual Guide to the Greek New Testament*. NY: Hendrickson. 114; Metzger, B. 2005. *A Textual Commentary on the Greek New Testament*. Grand Rapids: Tyndale House. 114.

15. Levine, A., and B. Witherington, 2018: 115.

16. Hendricksen, W. 1978. *Exposition of the Gospel according to Luke*. Grand Rapids: Baker Books. 200.

17. Kimball, C. "Jesus' Exposition of Scripture in Luke 4:16–30: An Inquiry in Light of Jewish Hermeneutics." *Perspectives in Religious Studies* 21, no. 3 (1994): 185.

18. Bock, D. 1994: 404; Nolland, J. 1989: 193.

19. Green, J. 1997: 211–12.

20. Ringe, S. 1985. *Jesus, Liberation, and the Biblical Jubilee*. Eugene: Wipf & Stock. 1–16.

21. Levine, A., and B. Witherington, 2018: 117.

22. Pleins, J. 1992. "Poor, Poverty." In *The Anchor Bible Dictionary*. Edited by D. Freedman. New York: Doubleday. 408.

23. Levine, A., and B. Witherington, 2018: 115.

24. Green, J. 1997: 266–67, on the prophetic nature of Luke 6:20.

25. Roth, S. 1997. *The Blind, the Lame, and the Poor: Character Types in Luke-Acts*. Sheffield: Sheffield Academic. 29–33.

26. Green, J. 1997: 59, 211.

27. Hendricksen, W. 1978: 257.

28. Evans, C. "Luke's Use of the Elijah/Elisha Narratives and the Ethic of Election." *Journal of Biblical Literature* 106, no. 1 (1987): 78, 79.

29. Siker, J. 1992: 74.

30. Kimball, C. 1994: 185.

31. Nolland, J. 1989: 192.

32. Bock, D. 1994: 415, 419–20.

33. Green, J. 1997: 216, 217.

34. Siker, J. 1992: 81.

35. Anderson, H. "Broadening Horizons: The Rejection at Nazareth Pericope of Luke 4:16–30 in Light of Recent Critical Trends." *Interpretation* 18, no. 3 (1964), full summary of Jeremias' position.

36. Longenecker, B. 2012. *Hearing the Silence: Jesus on the Edge and God in the Gap: Luke 4 in Narrative Perspective*. Eugene: Cascade Books. 37.

37. Marshall, I. H. 1978. *The Gospel of Luke: A Commentary of the Greek Text.* Grand Rapids: W. B. Eerdmans. 177–78.

38. Nolland, J. 1989: 193.

39. Kovaks, F., F. Viljoen, and J. Gosling. "The Lukan Covenant Concept: The Basis of Israel's Mandate in Luke-Acts: Original Research." *Verbum Et Ecclesia* 34, no. 1 (2013): 1–9; Du Toit, P. "Reconsidering the Salvation of Israel in Luke-Acts." *Journal for the Study of the New Testament* 43, no. 3 (2021): 343–69; Bauckham, R. 2008. *The Jewish World around the New Testament.* Grand Rapids: Baker Academic. 325–70; Hahn, S. 2009. *Kinship in Covenant: A Canonical Approach to the Fulfillment of God's Saving Promises.* New Haven: Yale University Press. 217–39.

40. Kovaks, F. 2013: 1–9.

41. Bauckham, R. 2008: 369, 370.

42. Du Toit, P. 2021: 343–69.

43. Du Toit, P. 2021: 344.

44. Hahn, S. 2009: 218.

45. Hahn, S. 2009: 234–36.

46. Shellberg, P. 2012. "From Cleansed Lepers to Cleansed Hearts: The Developing Meaning of Katharizo in Luke-Acts." Unpublished dissertation. Marquette University.

47. Bauckham, R. 2008: 370.

48. Carey, G. "Moving Things Ahead: A Lukan Redactional Technique and Its Implications for Gospel Origins." *Biblical Interpretation* 21, no. 3 (2013): 303.

49. Green, J. 1997.

50. Marshall, I. H. 1988: 117.

51. Ringe, S. 1985; Blount, B. 2001 *Then the Whisper Put on Flesh: New Testament Ethics in an African American Context.* Nashville: Abingdon Press. 79–91.

52. Hendriksen, W. 1978: 252.

53. Jeremias, 1958: 48–50.

54. Bock, D. 1994: 410.

55. Conzelmann, H. 1961; Green, J. 1997; Marshall, H. 2004; Rowe, K. 2010; Blount, B. 2001.

56. Conzelmann, H. 1961: 18–84.

57. Conzelmann, H. 1961: 95–136.

58. Conzelmann, H. 1961: 137–234.

59. Conzelmann, H. 1961: 137–44.

60. Marshall, I. H. 2004: 14.

61. Conzelmann, H. 1961: 138.

62. Marshall, I. H. 2004: 143–45.

63. Green, J. 1997: 21–25.

64. Green, J. 1997: 23.

65. Rowe, K. 2010: 149–50.

66. Blount, B. 2001: 80.

67. Gentry, P. "The Significance of Covenants in Biblical Theology." *The Southern Baptist Journal of Theology* 20, no. 1 (2016): 24.

68. Gentry, P. 2016; Hafemann, S. 2007. "The Covenant Relationship." In *Central Themes in Biblical Theology: Mapping Unity in Diversity.* Downers Grove: IVP Press. 20–65; Hahn, S. 2009.
69. Gentry, P. 2016: 24–30; Hafemann, S. 2007: 22–25.
70. Hahn, S. 2009: 1–9.
71. Hahn, S. 2009: 3.
72. Hafemann, S. 2007: 22.
73. Hafemann, S. 2007: 49–56.
74. Ringe, K. 1985: 36.
75. Blount, B. 2001: 79–91.
76. Blount, B. 2001: 82.

Chapter 10

Luke 4 in Conversation with Romans 13 and the Household Codes

This study joins Vanhoozer in affirming that "if the canon is to serve as our interpretative framework, it is not enough to make sense of individual texts or even of how they relate to the world; we also have to deal with how the various maps (texts) relate to one another."[1] This mandate is especially true for what Vanhoozer calls "pluriform texts," those that diverge in genre or that suggest a different understanding of theology or ethics. These texts must be considered together, or "coordinated," in any application of the biblical text to doctrine or dogma.

If Luke 4:16–30 primarily concerns inclusion, reversal, and the salvation or liberation of the poor, oppressed, and marginalized, and if it is couched as a narrative, part II has already identified two sets of biblical passages whose interpretation leans instead toward hierarchy, privilege, and exclusion: (1) the duties owed to state authorities, found in Romans 13:1–7; and (2) the Pauline household codes. Traditional interpretation of these texts sets them in direct opposition to the foregoing interpretation of Luke 4:16–30. They also represent a distinctly different genre. Certainly, they must be considered here for this project's final-form, canonical view of Scripture.

For these alternative texts, I focus on the broader hermeneutical issues concerning nuanced exegetical matters primarily when a point of contention in the exegetical literature affects textual interpretation. Therefore, this chapter will assess the competing interpretations of these texts and analyze each in turn, thereby reaching conclusions on their interpretation that can then be "coordinated" with my working interpretation of Luke 4:16–30.

INTERPRETING ROMANS 13:1–7

Given the relative consensus on exegetical matters, biblical scholars tend to give Romans 13:1–7 limited space in their commentaries. The most extensive treatments of the passage, therefore, come from theologians and theological ethicists. John Howard Yoder distinguishes two primary interpretive traditions: traditionalist (or "positivistic") and "normative."[2] Any discussion of the texts' interpretation must also include contemporary insights from postcolonialist biblical scholars and theologians.

Traditionalist Interpretation

Yoder credits the Lutheran tradition, particularly literalist understandings of the two-kingdoms theology, for the traditional view. Calvin and Henry share this view of Romans 13. Yoder summarizes the traditional reading: "One of the ways of understanding the 'institution' of government by God is to claim that whatever government exists, it is by virtue of an act of institution, that is, a specific providential action of God, that it came into being. . . .. Whatever is, is the will of God."[3] Calvin's insistence that God ordains all governments, including evil governments, and that Christians are required to submit to all governments characterizes this type of reading. Henry also affirms the authority of government and the requirement that Christians submit to the "laws of the land." Calvin primarily bases his views on a very high view of God's providence, whereas Henry's views center on the definition of justice as the proper execution of law and order by governmental authorities.

Yoder's primary concern about the traditionalist interpretation, besides his opposition to bearing arms, is that it seems contrary to calls in the Scriptures to oppose evil, particularly human laws that violate the law of God.[4] Yoder wants to decenter Romans 13 as the principal understanding of the Christian relationship to government. While Romans 13 should not stand alone, it also cannot be ignored in any theology focused on submission, resistance to evil, and the maintenance of systems of supremacy.

The more pressing issue related to the traditional interpretation is its application in contemporary settings. Nazi use of the text to support their authority in Germany during World War II, and South Africa's use of it to support apartheid, raise the question of how the text's call to submission can universally apply in all circumstances to all forms of government.[5] Calvin reluctantly suggests that a Christian might have an obligation to disobey a government that forbids worship. Likewise, Henry ponders, without answer, whether a Christian might participate in overthrowing a communist government. The text's application raises many ethical questions in light of actual world events.

Normative Interpretation

Coupled with the instances in Scripture where believers did resist and refuse to obey particular governmental laws, real-world questions have led to the development of the "normative view" of Romans 13. Yoder characterizes this view as running from Zwingli and Knox to Cromwell to Karl Barth and Emil Bruner. This view provides an interpretive framework for both the Barmen Declaration against Nazi attempts to control the Church in Germany and the Kairos Document written to oppose South Africa's apartheid government. Yoder summarizes this view:

> What is ordained is not a particular government but the concept of proper government, the principle of government as such. If, however, a government fails adequately to fulfill the functions divinely assigned to it, it loses its authority. It then becomes the duty of the preacher to teach that this has become an unjust government, worthy of rebellion. It can become the duty of Christian citizens to raise up against it.[6]

The primary textual justification for this interpretation is that the text does present an idealized view of government that assumes that it works for the good of the governed and that its policies maintain order. Thus, Romans 13 seems to offer a clear definition of what a proper government does and a measure by which one can judge whether a government is fulfilling these minimal obligations.

Perhaps the most thorough treatment of Romans 13:1–7, in the normative tradition, appears in Karl Barth's post-WWII theological reflection on the nature of political theology. Barth grounds this theology in Romans 13 and provides a clear understanding of the Church's role in the secular world. Barth works out the larger ramifications of Romans 13 in his series of talks and essays addressing both the horrors of WWII and the rising threats of communism in Eastern Europe. Thus, his later theological reflection diverges somewhat from his earlier commentary on Romans, written and revised between 1918 and 1922.[7]

Barth's Romans commentary maintains a view of the relationship between Christians and the State that joins Barth's larger argument about the qualitative distinction between God and humanity. Using a mathematical formula, Barth maintains that both government and rebellion remain bracketed from God, such that only God's actions outside fallen human institutions can effect real change and bring about positive government or positive revolution.

Humanity should seek the good of God in all things, but all human systems are fallen and broken when compared to God. Barth comments that this "is shown by the unmistakable fact that the passage dealing with human rulers follows after the passage dealing with the enemy and is prefaced by the quite clear statement that men are to overcome evil."[8] Government, when compared to God, can only be seen as imperfect and evil. Its primary value rests in its ability to point to God. But revolution is also never able, on its own, to deliver true order reflected in God. God remains the only equation, positioned as God is outside the bracket, only God can transform what is inside.

Thus, in his *Commentary on Romans*, Barth affirms a traditional reading of Romans 13. But as he turns toward a more immanent understanding of God after WWII, his understanding of Romans 13 expands to include a carefully articulated political theology that expresses a normative interpretation of the text. This understanding is particularly found in an essay he wrote in 1946 titled "The Christian Community and Civil Community." This essay is Barth's enlarged commentary on the fifth thesis of the *Theological Declaration of Barmen* and deserves greater attention than it has received.

Barth begins the essay by insisting on the importance of seeing both the Church and civil society as communities.[9] The Church is a closed community comprising only believers, whereas the State consists of all persons within particular geographic and political boundaries, including believers and nonbelievers. Thus, Barth envisions the Church and State as concentric circles, with the Church being a smaller circle within the larger civil community circle.

Barth does not, however, see the borders as equally porous. The Church is always a member of the civil community and therefore exercises responsibility for the civil community. But the State is not part of the Church community and exercises no such responsibility for the Church, other than to recognize its right to exist. The communities' varying functions are also critical to Barth's analysis. The Church possesses the direct light and revelation of the truth of God, but the State is blind and lacks knowledge of God's truth, even while guided by God's providential will: "One cannot in fact compare the Church with the State without realizing how much weaker, poorer and more exposed to danger the human community is in the State than in the Church."[10]

Barth points out that the Church recognizes in civil community the "operation of a divine ordinance."[11] In this argument, he affirms a traditional view of Romans 13, to the extent that he recognizes that God raises governments to provide order. But Barth goes further by suggesting that God's desire for order is an expression of his patience and grace in giving humanity time to accept his divine salvation. Only in order can the evangelistic work of the Church move forward; thus, God both tarries and provides order to ensure the conditions conducive to the mission of the Church. According to Barth, the State "renders a definite service to the divine providence and plan of salvation."[12] Barth ties the Church's chief concern, salvation in Christ, to the order engendered by good government. He says that because the Church is concerned for the one, it must be concerned for the other. This intimate connection "makes one thing quite impossible, however: a Christian decision to be indifferent, a non-political Christianity."[13]

Because of the deeply political nature of the Christian life in the civil community and the State's role in making possible the mission of the Church, the Church cannot "halt at the boundary where the inner and outer circle meet" but must engage directly in the life of the State. The Church's role is to provide the State with the truth of God, which the State does not possess. The Church also supports the State's primary role of providing order by not withholding itself from full participation in the civil community.

Barth is quick to qualify what submission looks like. He distinguishes subordination from blind obedience. Proper subordination means that Christians assume "responsibility" for the proper maintenance of a proper State that secures order and peace for its citizens. By re-envisioning subordination as responsibility, Barth allows the Church to oppose evil or disordered government as part of the Church's responsibility to support a government that evidences the intended divine order. To submit and do what is best for the civil community, then, the Christian may have to rebel against the State to restore proper order. Rebellion is only supportable when its motivation is the responsible restoration of good order, with a clear plan to reestablish that order.[14]

Barth also insists that the Christian community must not seek special privileges in the civil community or place itself above its laws. Likewise, the Christian realizes that all political theories are fallen and therefore should not Christianize any single political theory. The Church's proclamation of the kingdom of God means that the kingdom is the only truly perfect communal expression, and no temporal government or political system can approximate it. Barth also insists, in agreement with Henry, that God's kingdom will not be realized in this world; therefore, the Church should not be working to set up the kingdom on earth in the form of a temporal government. Although the eschatological kingdom of God cannot be realized on earth through temporal government, both God's model in the Church and the kingdom can serve as exemplars for what the Christian aspires to and advocates in the State. Cone's and Barth's similar eschatology should be noted here.

Working off this idea of the kingdom as exemplar, Barth suggests several ways that the Church's knowledge of the kingdom should affect its responsible citizenship in the civil community. This responsibility includes reminding the State of what true righteousness is. Further, by its understanding of the kingdom, the Church is called to advocate first and foremost for human beings, not for causes. This advocacy flows from the church's call to love one's neighbor. Likewise, the Church demands a rule of law that acknowledges all persons as equal under the law. Because God stands for the poor and marginalized, the Church must especially stand for social justice in the civil community. Finally, the church must stand for freedom of individual conscience. The civil community should benefit as the Church reflects on the truth of its existence and applies those truths to its participation in the civil community.[15]

Several conclusions may be drawn from Barth's view of the relationship of Church and State based on his understanding of Romans 13:1–7 and his later work on political theology. First, God has sovereign authority over the government. Second, the Church is a part of the world and cannot be isolated from it. In addition, the Church's place in the civil community requires its participation in its life, particularly its political life. The Church also possesses a truth to which the civil authority is blind; thus, it is incumbent on the Church, for its own sake, to speak that truth to the powers of this world. But the Church cannot place itself above the law or seek its own ends or privileges. The church instead bases its participation in the political life of the civil community on the Church's own life and God's truth as evident in God's future kingdom. Finally, all of this depends on understanding submission, in Romans 13, as "responsibility."

Barth's later theological reflections on Romans 13 seem to stray from a literal reading of the text. Barth appears to focus instead on the sense of the text. But perhaps Barth's interpretation might be saved by way of appealing to hermeneutical equivalency. While Barth does not employ the concept, he does examine the text through the lens of the modern Western democratic state. A vast distinction exists between citizens in Western democracies who hold some degree of political power and first-century Christians who were doubly marginalized and powerless. Paul and his church had no power within either the Jewish religious hierarchy or the Roman government. He also lived in an era when citizenship was severely restricted and citizens' power was extremely limited vis-à-vis power centered in the ruling elite. The exercise of power was restrained legally, culturally, and practically for Paul and his Christian contemporaries.

In comparison, the power that Christianity has exercised in the West since Constantine, as well as the increasing power of individual citizens in modern Western democracies, is substantial. The ability of contemporary Christian citizens to participate in governmental systems, to influence laws, and to protest and assemble—and the political enthronement of revolution, freedom, and individual rights in the Enlightenment—have created a unique position for at least some citizens in relationship to civil government and processes. Given these realities, maintaining proper order and the common good in

Western society is the responsibility of citizens collectively and individually, not of a ruling elite.

Therefore, Barth does not diverge from the text as much as might otherwise be imagined. In Paul's context, the Church's very survival required it to acquiesce to government rule, and submission necessarily takes the form of quietude. For Christians who hold power within a participatory government, maintaining good order and government may look more like exercising responsibilities as citizens to change laws through the formal and informal means available. Submission might look like using their voices to speak truth, both within and as part of their responsibility for the civil community.

This current study, focused on a theology of power, must see this text as constraining Christians with participatory rights within society to work within the Gospel's confines in exercising those privileges. Christian citizens who occupy this space cannot draw on this passage to justify subjugating fellow citizens. In fact, those who hold positions of power, in the Church and civil society, have a special obligation both to the truth of the gospel—which affirms the dignity of all humanity and the Christian call to love both neighbor and enemy—and to their obligation to use their civil position to build society on the truth of God, which demands equal protection and equal privileges under the law. The Christian citizen within a contemporary participatory democracy stands, therefore, in a unique relationship to Romans 13, one distinctly different from the Early Church.

But what about the marginalized within civil society? Romans 13 does not speak to persons in general or to the government in particular; it is addressed to Christians who believed they could withdraw from participation in civil society and ignore civil authority.[16] Romans 13 in effect calls Christians to stop claiming special privilege for themselves as being above the everyday laws binding them to others in society or above paying taxes required of others. This idea is central to Paul's point. He neither precludes the work of God in elevating the poor and marginalized through revolution nor prevents Christians from standing on the side of neighbors who are treated unjustly or unlawfully. The primary obligation of Christians is a prohibition on self-interested rebellion or withdrawal that places them above the law and outside civil community.

Post-Colonialist Interpretation

Other scholars suggest that Romans 13 might not point to abject submission, as traditionalists propose. This suggestion is the primary contribution of postcolonial biblical and theological scholarship. Using postcolonial theory is difficult within an evangelical interpretive framework. The tendency toward reader-response criticism is problematic. Conclusions with direct connections to reader-response criticism are likely to be rejected by many orthodox, traditionalist evangelicals; so would any further conclusions drawn from them. This section then, delineates how postcolonial observations are used.

This study's narrow framework does not consider the broader interpretative conclusions of postcolonial theory. But some aspects of postcolonial theoretical understanding about the colonial context, and how that context shapes texts, are relevant—particularly for understanding how Paul's text might be shaped by his participation in diaspora Judaism and his status under Roman occupation. This understanding of Paul might suggest a different reading of the text. A postcolonial positioning of Paul might be less anachronistic than views that subscribe political power to Paul. Thus, an analysis of Paul's position under the Roman empire and of how his position might shape his writings is in order.

Postcolonial theory offers two ideas that seem directly applicable to any interpretation of Romans 13: notions of hybridity and the double-voiced text. Hybridity is particularly evident in Paul. He is caught in a space between the role of the occupied and marginalized Jew—as well as the doubly marginalized Christian—and his Roman citizenship. According to Makuka, "Paul is . . . an ethnic hybrid who both affiliates with and challenges the Imperium Romanum at the same time." Makuka sees Paul as occupying a space between the colonizer and the colonized, the Jew and the Gentile, and as suggesting a new, creative way of being that challenges the status quo while avoiding direct confrontation with the colonial powers.[17]

This interpretation directly contravenes much Black exegesis in the United States, where some Black biblical scholars follow the commonly repeated trope of Howard Thurman. Thurman posits that Paul and Jesus occupy distinct social positions: Jesus is marginalized and oppressed, whereas Paul holds a position of privilege as a Roman citizen. Therefore, Paul has little to say to marginalized people, so Jesus' teachings must be the point of departure for the oppressed.[18] This argument prioritizes one part of the canon over another, namely the Gospels over Paul's writings.

But Makuka's view of hybridity rescues Paul from that supposed privileged position. Paul's social position is different from that of Jesus, but he in no way enjoys a place of privilege in relation to the civil authorities. His in-betweenness may in fact isolate and marginalize him more.

Also, understanding Paul's hybridity points to a possible motive for a specific textual strategy. Paul shapes his perspective as a doubly marginalized subject of both Jewish religious authority and Roman civil authority. The conciliatory language of Romans 13 points to Paul's and the Early Church's precarious position to both the Roman government and Jewish antagonism. But Paul also shapes a new reality of the Church, between God and civil authority, and reimagines the world in Christian theological terms.

This reorientation is not without rebellious implications, which become apparent in the second postcolonial insight in view here: double-voicedness, or the hidden text. William Herzog insists, "In a setting where power relations are asymmetrical, it will be much more likely that the political speech of the weak will dissemble, that is, it will feign obedience and loyalty to the colonial overlords while pursuing its own hidden agenda."[19] Sun Uk Lim agrees: "Paul affiliates with the colonial authorities at the public level, he persuades the audience to resist them—especially when it comes to the imperial worship—at the hidden level."[20] Thus, Romans 13 says two things—or better said, the text speaks at two levels.

What does this mean for interpreting Romans 13? This understanding can be grounded more directly in the text itself than either Herzog or Lim suggests. The text's public-facing discourse is not in question. Its call for subordination to governmental authorities and its admonition that government is God-ordained flatters and placates civil authorities. But Paul's theology also has subtle implications.

For one thing, Paul does not place governmental authority under the authority of divinity generally but under the authority of the Christian God, who has a specific plan to elevate and save God's people, deeply embedded in God's providential will and revealed eschatological future. Thus, Paul's proclamation that government is ordained and held within the providential will of God is deeply liberationist. Paul's original readers would receive the text with great hope and confidence that God would deliver them from Roman oppression.[21] The liberationist impact implied in Paul's pronouncement that all government exists under the sovereign will and authority of the Christian God is lost 2,000 years after its writing. Nonetheless, this component of the text likely held great hope for early Christians.

The text also limits the role and power of civil government and subordinates it to the welfare of its citizens and subjects. Government exists for a limited purpose: to preserve an ordered society. The text also distinguishes between good and bad government. The good government gives law-abiding citizens nothing to fear: a criterion by which one may measure the Roman government and its representatives to determine if they are functioning according to God's intended and stated purpose for proper government. Those operating outside God's purpose can expect to incur God's judgment. Paul also demarcates specific limitations of governmental power. Certainly, the idea of such limits, particularly concerning subject peoples and nations, would have been novel in Paul's time.

The text therefore participates in a multilevel discourse that is conscious of its hybrid, in-between space. It calls Christians to take a position within civil society that carefully observes Roman law, but it also signals that God is in control, even of Rome, and is working for the good of God's people.

Romans 13 provides the means, again couched in cautious language, of understanding the boundaries and limits of secular power. It therefore would be hard to suggest, vis-à-vis the traditionalist view, that the text has no subversive meaning.

Dialogue with Luke 4:16–30

How then, in light of all this, is Romans 13:1–7 to be understood? And how can it then be brought into dialogue with Luke 4:16–30?

Understood within its mid-first-century context, Romans 13 has three purposes. First, it forbids Christians from viewing their life in Christ as an excuse for privileging themselves above the law or for withdrawing entirely from civil society. The Christian continues to have civil and political obligations within the larger world. Second, the text subordinates civil government to the providential will and sovereignty of the Christian God, while limiting the scope and sphere of civil authority. Romans limits "what is Caesar's" and extends "what is God's." Finally, Romans 13:1–7 situates Christian civil responsibility within a broader ethic of love for neighbor and particularly of care for the weak. Situated within a fuller ethical parenesis extending from Romans 12:9 to 13:14, which deals with the primacy of Christian love, the passage suggests that any Christian participation in the civil community must be marked by a distinctly Christian love for both enemy and neighbor.[22]

Romans 13 can be read differently, at least slightly, within contemporary Western democratic society, particularly by Christians with access to formal and informal means of full participation within political systems. When political power and responsibility are invested in the citizens, submission takes on the language of responsibility, which may at varying times and places look like either total obedience or rebellion. The people, after all, are the basis for the government and have a responsibility to ensure good government per the dictates of Romans 13. The Christian citizen and the Church have a special obligation to arrange political life under the obligations of Christian love found in the parenesis that includes Romans 13:1–7, as well as the broader ethics of the New Testament canon. This obligation ensures that neither the individual Christian nor churches nor governments can use the call to submission to preserve oppressive systems or maintain personal or privileged group status to others' detriment. This argument, of course, is central to both the Theological Declaration at Barmen and the Kairos Document, concerning Romans 13:1–7.

Romans 13 and Luke 4:16–30 seem to share two important foci. Both passages, particularly given the broader theology of Luke-Acts, seem to emphasize God's sovereign, providential work toward the deliverance of a people from all nations and focus on God's personal liberative/salvific actions on their behalf. Both the Christ of the Jubilee and the God who orders all governmental powers are actively, supernaturally at work creating a people for God's self and securing a place for them in the world.

Additionally, Luke-Acts and Romans 13 suggest ways of living ethically in the world while awaiting the eschatological return of Christ. For Romans 13, this return is imminent, which nonetheless forestalls Christians' withdrawal from secular society and obligations. In Luke-Acts this return is a delayed Parousia, which makes a clear ethic for living in the world even more necessary. The themes of care for the poor and marginalized, the reversed positions of the weak and the powerful, and the focus on inclusion in Luke-Acts provide specificity for the love ethic found in Romans 12:9–13:14, of which Romans 13:1–7 is a part. Thus, both Romans and Luke contain ethical foci that obligate those in the new covenant community to live in love. Brought forward into a Western democratic society, where Christians along with all citizens are responsible for the government, Luke's covenant ethic, centered in the love ethic of Romans, receives greater definition.

This analysis leaves unanswered—and beyond the scope of this project—how to interpret the text in non-Western and non-democratic contexts, where Christians lack direct political agency. But it does suggest that within systems of power, where Christians have this agency, Romans 13 is not at all problematic and may even support, not limit, an ethical reading of Luke 4 and other biblical texts.

What I suggest is that far from supporting Calvin's, Edwards', and Henry's view of submission without the possibility of revolt, Romans 13 may instead suggest a course of action that affirms both Cone's view of God as the God of liberation and Hodge's view of the possibility and necessity of revolt in the interest of good government. In light of the latter, this reading does not seem problematic for a more literal reading of Luke 4:16–30.

If this treatment of Romans 13 is accepted, it sidesteps traditional insistence on the submission of oppressed people to oppressive governments and laws, and it informs a particular Christian political agency that supports a literal reading of Luke 4:16–30. This treatment creates a different way to approach Romans 13 and distances it from traditional readings of this text found in the evangelical tradition presented in part II.

INTERPRETING THE HOUSEHOLD CODES

Submission to government, as found in Romans 13:1–7, is not the only trope used in the evangelical tradition to support or directly formulate racist grammars. The tradition's focus on hierarchy, by all four theologians considered in part II, is also central to racist logics. Their focus on hierarchy found primary support in their interpretations of the household codes found in the writings of Paul. These texts must be considered as a group before returning to a full exposition of Luke 4:16–30.

If the perceived requirement to passively obey government presents a critical problem for liberationist interpretations of Luke 4:16–30, so do literal applications of the household codes in Colossians 3:18–19 and Ephesians 5:22–33. Literal interpretations of the former require adherence to the status quo, even when the system supports White supremacy and centralized power along racial lines. The household codes, interpreted hierarchically, have the potential to reinforce hierarchical systems of gender and class that then become subsumed into racist grammars. These texts then mitigate against the themes of reversal and the elevation of the poor and marginalized envisioned in Luke-Acts. This seemingly contradictory pattern in the New Testament literature warrants attention.

Like Romans 13, the literary exegesis is straightforward. The primary textual disputes rise and fall on interpretations of *hupotassō* (submit) and *kephalē* (head). However, the greatest disagreements relate to the interpretation and application of the text. Therefore, this section first examines the primary hermeneutical debate before placing Luke 4:16–30 in conversation with Colossians 3:18–19 and Ephesians 5:22–33.

The interpretation of the household codes can be classed into four categories. They include first, liberal and post-liberal feminist/womanist/liberationist interpretations. Second, are evangelical interpretive traditions,[23] which are further split between hierarchialists/complementarians (Piper and Grudem) and evangelical feminists/egalitarians (Pierce and Groothius; William Webb's redemptive hermeneutic deserves special mention here). Outside these three positions are scholars best described as "third-way" exegetes, like Michelle Lee-Barnewall and Craig Blomberg, who believe that the standard approach to interpreting these texts is faulty and that the codes include neither hierarchy nor egalitarianism.

Feminist, Womanist, and Liberationist Interpretations

Liberal and post-liberal scholars—including feminist, womanist, and liberationist theologians and biblical scholars—have largely denied the texts' validity. Feminism and womanism have engaged in a cultural critique of the household codes rather than a full exegetical and theological treatment of the texts in their own right. Many feminist exegetes seem to subscribe to Rosemary Ruether's "critical principles of feminist theology," where she encourages "the promotion of the full humanity of women. Whatever denies, diminishes, or distorts the full humanity of women is, therefore, appraised as not redemptive." This principle flows directly into feminist and womanist biblical exegesis, in which the existence of patriarchy necessitates critique and excision of the text from theologies of divine and human relationships.

This principle is evident in the work of Clarice Martin in Cain Felder's *Stony the Road We Trod*:

> The Haustafeln (household codes) and the letters in which they are found are not Pauline. The question of whether the Haustafeln are Pauline is, of course, linked to the question of the authenticity of Colossians, Ephesians, and 1 Peter. I would argue that Colossians and Ephesians are deutero-Pauline, that is, written by circles of Paul's students on the model of the Pauline letters, and that 1 Peter is pseudonymous.[24]

Working off this later dating of the letters, Martin affirms Elisabeth Schüssler Fiorenza's assessment that the authentic view of the Early Church was a "discipleship of equals." Later post-Pauline generations, grappling with infighting, abandoned this authentic egalitarianism in favor of the household codes to restore order. Thus, by this reading, the codes are inauthentic and not helpful for contemporary theological or ethical use.

The problem with this approach for the current study is twofold. First, it suggests a conclusion not in evidence. Authorship and dating of the Pauline corpus constitute a highly subjective field of scholarship and are too suspect to carry the weight of the exclusion Martin suggests, particularly in light of the extensive acceptance of Colossians as part of the uncontested Pauline texts, primarily due to its connection to Philemon. The second problem is that, regardless of the dating or authorship of the text, this study still must object to Martin's insights, no matter how interesting or promising, due primarily to the hermeneutical approach envisioned herein. Dependence on a canonical, final-form approach to the text eliminates questions of textual authorship or date as factors for interpreting the text. This dependence insists on the radical inclusion of texts, even when they seem problematic for the interpretation of other texts or for contemporary readers. Thus, this study cannot adopt a feminist or womanist hermeneutic, because that view of the text is so radically different. The distinction between methodologies of exclusion versus radical inclusion is just too great.

Evangelical Hierarchialists/Complementarians

Instead, this study requires consideration of interpretive approaches that are more serious about the text's authority. The most literalist approach is found among evangelical hierarchialists/complementarians. These two views are closely connected but not necessarily interchangeable, at least not as far as complementarians are concerned. Hierarchialism is the older literalist view, found in the work of Calvin, Edwards, and Hodge, as suggested in part II. This view recognizes and affirms strict social distinctions based on class, gender, education, and (in the case of Edwards and Hodge) race. It preserves cultural views of power that also include distinct value judgments and responsibilities based on social and gender status. Within these systems, nonegalitarian treatment of the "lower classes," women, and racial minorities is often based, as discussed, on Aristotelian notions of distributive justice anchored in a literalist approach to the household codes.

Complementarianism, on the other hand, uses the contemporary language of equality while preserving gender distinctions in roles and authority. Complementarians largely limit their use of the texts to preserve gender distinctions, particularly male leadership and authority within the home and the Church. Their primary logic says that God created men and women for distinct but equally valuable roles and that God gave the leadership role in the home and the Church to men at creation. John Piper and Wayne Grudem clearly define the complementarian approach. The base logic of this view comports with the logic of "separate but equal" that underpinned segregationist laws in the American South and apartheid in South Africa.[25] Regardless of their approach, both hierarchialists and complementarians preserve male authority over women and use the same literal approach to the text.

The most extensive defense of hierarchical/complementarian views is found in *Recovering Biblical Manhood and Womanhood: A Response to Evangelical Feminism* edited by Piper and Grudem. George Knight III's chapter delineates the complementarian position concerning the household codes. He breaks down discussions of submission and headship, extends the husband-wife relationship to include male leadership in church and society, and attempts to avoid affirming slavery by grounding slavery in temporal culture while grounding gender roles in the created order.[26]

As mentioned, the household codes' central textual debate revolves around interpretations of *hupotassō* (submit) and *kephalē* (head). Knight affirms that submission is voluntary and that a wife submits out of love for her husband and out of love and reverence for Christ. This submission is not limited but must be in "every aspect of life."[27] Submission is also not mutual, even though the Ephesians passage calls for submission to "one another." Knight argues:

> It is sometimes urged that mutual submission alone is in view in the section on wives and husbands, and that therefore wives are not being called to a unique or distinct submission to their husbands. Since, however, verse 21 is a transition verse to the entirety of the section on household responsibilities, consistency would demand that the section on children and parents and on servants and masters also speaks only of mutual submissiveness and not of different roles. Since this is self-evidently not so for the section on children and parents, on the one

hand, and masters and slaves, on the other, the implication is that distinguishable roles and specific submission are also taught in the section on husbands and wives.[28]

Thus, submission involves a wife's recognition of her husband's headship and authority. But what does "head" mean in this context? Following Grudem, Knight defines "head" as "leader or authority," not as "source."[29] Thus, assigning the role of "head" to the husband endows him with authority over his wife.

Knight struggles to extend the husband/wife relationship to a generalized understanding of male leadership in church and society:

> Paul does not ask every woman to submit to every man, but rather asks wives to submit to their own husbands. Paul is not insisting that every relationship between a woman and a man is one of submission and headship, but that where leadership is an ingredient of the situation, as in marriage, the woman should submit to that leadership (headship) of a man.[30]

Knight does not clearly articulate how leadership emerges out of the text as a distinct category. Nor does he clarify what societal relationships might be absent in the need for submission.

Finally, Knight argues for the permanence of husband/wife and parent/child relationships, while arguing for the temporality of the master/slave relationship. The parent-child relationship is grounded in Old Testament law, specifically the fifth commandment. Likewise, Knight grounds the husband/wife relationship in creation because of the Ephesians connection to the Genesis account of creation. But according to Knight, "no permanent moral command or any other moral absolute with reference to slavery is used in Paul's instructions to slaves."[31] Knight sidesteps the question of how denial of slavery might affirm the temporality of the entirety of the household codes.

What then is to be made of the complementarian perspective on the household codes? First, the arguments related to submission and headship seem more grounded in the text's original intent than other interpretive perspectives. But later I argue that they may not be pointed in the right direction regarding the application of the texts. Complementarian approaches also apply an understanding of leadership and authority roles that seems more at home in contemporary organizational theory than in New Testament commentary on intercommunity relationships—the latter seeming to have a more organic intent than the former.

In addition, Knight cannot resist doing violence to the text. He insists on its unity when arguing against the mutuality of submission but allows for its discontinuity in relation to the unique temporal, cultural nature of the master-slave relationship, contra the moral/creational eternal imperative of parent/child and husband/wife relationships. Each argument holds inherent logic taken alone, but together they suggest modern interpreters' very real discomfort about the presence of slavery in the texts, presence that did not pose a problem for early hierarchialist exegetes like Calvin, Edwards, and Hodge. Complementarians are forced to stray from the literal interpretation of the text or contrive ways of excising slavery while affirming gender power distinctions.

Another problem lies in the mention of Genesis 2:24 in Ephesians, "the two shall become one flesh," which does not bear the full exegetical weight of the creation complementarianism that Knight suggests is evident. This is true in two senses. First, this quote is embedded not in the section on the submission of wives but in the exhortation of husbands to love their wives as "they love themselves." The clear implication is to convince men of the extent to which they should love and care for their wives. The text itself offers no reference to a larger gendered order in creation. This case might be better built with allusion to other texts, but no clear order of creation is evident in either Colossians or Ephesians. Also—as will be seen in the egalitarian argument below—even direct exegesis of the Genesis account does not clarify whether any authority can be found in the original state of creation or whether division is the result of the fall. Both difficulties create problems for Knight's attempts to predicate gender distinctions and male authority on the created order. Ultimately, complementarian appeals to creation seem more grounded in natural law and general revelation than in specific textual indicators.

Indeed, expanding a text specific to household roles and relationships into broader discussions of male leadership in other spheres seems to stretch the text beyond its intended meaning. The household codes themselves offer no indication that they supported other relationship scenarios outside the home.

Finally, concerning its usefulness for the current study, complementarianism can be viewed as an attempt not to read the text based on its original meaning but rather to defend the text by couching it in the modern language of equal respect but separate roles. The hierarchical approach does less damage to the text's original intent than does complementarianism. In the end, complementarianism uses the language of egalitarianism while espousing a hierarchical praxis that is intellectually disingenuous.

However, complementarianism does take seriously the household codes' emphasis on submission, even if it continues to deny the Ephesian focus on the mutuality of submission. Complementarianism as a system depends on a broader set of arguments and texts to reach its conclusions. Critiquing complementarianism as a holistic system is not in view here. What is under consideration is the complementarian view of the household codes, only secondarily the system as a whole, and only as it connects directly with arguments for male authority. This narrow approach is justified by the focus of this study and the way the codes are used in the evangelical tradition under consideration.

The four theologians considered in part II focus on the household codes to support a more generalized defense of hierarchical roles of both class and gender. Part II concluded that this hierarchical grammar forms the foundation underlying subsequent racist logics. This defense draws less on passages like 1 Corinthians 14:34, which admonishes women to silence. Passages that focus tightly on gender roles to the exclusion of class are rarely extended to more generalized understandings of hierarchy. I do not suggest that sexism and racism do not share a common lexicon and roots in hierarchialism, but only assert that the household codes' inclusion of class (master-slave) distinctions make them far more extendable for racist logics.

Further, this study focuses on power with reference to racism and White supremacy. How these categories intersect with gender is an important question that requires a whole other study and is beyond this study's scope. Gender is engaged here because it is the only section of the codes that contemporary scholars debate and that preserves a literal interpretation of the text. As demonstrated, complementarians prefer to bracket the class distinctions and the text's more generalized hierarchical implications because of their discomfort with the slave-master arguments. They instead maintain a remnant of the generalized hierarchical system found in the full pericope's literal interpretation by Calvin, Edwards, and Hodge. Therefore, the study must engage the whole by virtue of the parts: the hierarchy latent in the complementarian interpretation of the household codes.

Evangelical Feminists/Egalitarians

If the above critique of complementarianism is accepted, does that necessarily require a commitment to evangelical egalitarianism or feminism? Not necessarily. Countering Piper and Grudem's *Recovering Biblical Manhood and Womanhood* is a volume edited by Ronald Pierce and Rebecca Groothius, *Discovering Biblical Equality: Complementarity without Hierarchy*. The chapters by Fee, Gile, Marshall, and Webb are most useful.

Fee's chapter focuses on the hermeneutical issues surrounding the gender debate. He denies the liberal/post-liberal tendency to disallow texts, yet he proposes an evangelical hermeneutic that he believes grounds a thoroughly egalitarian interpretation of the household codes and other passages under consideration. Fee argues that Scripture has a twofold nature: one as the word of God and the other grounded in each author's humanity, historicity, and culture. Certain passages may be so culturally dependent as not to have significance for contemporary theological and ethical considerations.

Additionally, Fee distinguishes between interpretations of implicitly theological texts and texts from which one can derive a theological point only secondarily by inference. In the latter case, any theological maxim must be approached with humility and skepticism. Fee affirms a kind of theological triage that insists that theological propositions, doctrinal beliefs, and ethical applications that must be inferred from the text are always second-order doctrinal statements that cannot carry the same weight as explicit theological statements. Thus, Fee views the household codes as evidencing a strong tendency toward depicting cultural, not theological, norms that are not eternally prescribed on the contemporary Church. "The house codes in Colossians and Ephesians," Fee states, "are not intended to set boundaries but rather to encourage Christian deportment within an existing patriarchal culture."[32]

While Fee's hermeneutic has much to offer—particularly his discussion about explicit and implicit theology in Scripture—his exclusion of propositional statements by means of cultural specificity is problematic for the text-based hermeneutic this project is pursuing. The point where a text's eternal theology is proclaimed and where its temporal cultural implications begin or end is exceedingly difficult to infer; the attempt opens the text to subjective interpretive distinctions that risk excluding the text because of nontextual strategies. In practice, excluding texts based on cultural specificity comes close to the feminist exclusion of texts based on subjective appraisal of their authenticity. The fact that the temporal cultural nature of the text is central to evangelical egalitarianism is also problematic for comparing the household codes to Luke 4:16–30. It would be all too easy for evangelical egalitarians to simply disallow the implications of the household codes in favor of a liberationist reading of Luke 4, or for traditionalists to limit the implications of Luke 4 to Jesus' time and cultural situation. Either approach prevents the canon from speaking as canon and eliminates the possibility that the household codes might speak in harmony with Luke 4 or suggest additional nuances. Thus, exclusion based on culture is antithetical to this study.

Evangelical egalitarians also rebut complementarianism by denying some of its broader theological implications, as evinced in Kevin Giles' chapter on the eternal subordination of Christ to the Father. Giles challenges Grudem's claim that Christ is eternally subordinate to the Father in the Godhead and that, by extension, subordination within male/female relationships can be seen as reflecting the eternal reality of the Father and the Son in the Godhead. Giles challenges Grudem's assertion that the Church held this view "from the Council of Nicaea onward." Giles argues compellingly that the "eternal subordination of the Son (whether ontological or functional) does not have the historical endorsement of the Nicene and Athanasian creeds, the Reformation confessions of faith, or theological luminaries such as Athanasius, Augustine and Calvin."[33] Taking each in turn, Giles shows that the view most prominent in the Church was functional or temporal subordination.

Giles' arguments are germane because they directly assault complementarian views about the eternal subordination of the Son. But this argument remains insufficient to overturn complementarianism and may not be the intellectual coup that Giles imagines. If Grudem's understanding of Christ's eternal subordination were to stand, it would lend more weight to complementarian views by grounding their theology in an ontological distinction in the Godhead. But even without this ontological distinction, complementarians/hierarchialists can still draw on Christ's temporal kenosis to mount Christological arguments for the subordination of women. Giles proves this point by identifying Calvin as supporting a temporal view of Christ's subordination. Calvin, as demonstrated, is a thoroughgoing hierarchialist, particularly in his interpretation of the household codes. Thus, Giles' arguments fail to defeat notions of subordination in favor of egalitarianism in the household codes, although they somewhat weaken the theological basis on which hierarchialism and complementarianism are built.

While the bulk of evangelical egalitarian arguments rely on appeals to the temporality of culture and direct assaults on the theological underpinnings of complementarianism, they also engage in direct exegesis of the household codes. In his chapter, I. Howard Marshall grounds the male/female relationship in the admonition to mutual submission in the Ephesian text and suggests that, despite the cultural dynamics, an egalitarian community is the pragmatic implication of Paul's admonition to the husband-father-master.[34] But Marshall's primary appeal points to the differences between the biblical and contemporary audiences. Modern ideas and institutions of parenting, contemporary gender advances, and the new relationship with work and labor mean that the text must be filtered, and its more antiquarian institutions must be revised, in contemporary applications of the household code. Tellingly, when Marshall returns to the intention and world of the text, he can go only as far as saying that it affirms a kind of "love Patriarchy"—far from the egalitarian interpretation of the text he envisions. In the end, Marshall's interpretation of the text is hard to distinguish from complementarianism when judged primarily by his interpretation of its intent. Marshall, like other evangelical egalitarians, is forced to disregard much of the text as "merely" temporal and cultural and, therefore, not theologically binding.

Evangelical egalitarianism relies on just this view of the distinction between the cultural and theological content of a text. While many contemporary biblical exegetes recognize the validity of culturally bound textual elements and their inapplicability to modern circumstances, the question of when to accept or reject the teaching within a text always seems to be one of degrees. The decisions rise and fall on methodological determinations of whether a propositional text has either temporal or eternal import.

Among evangelical egalitarians, the scholar who has most fully developed a method for distinguishing the temporal from the eternal is William Webb. Webb explores the cultural dynamics of gender roles in his chapter in *Discovering Biblical Equality*, which summarizes his earlier work, *Slaves, Women, & Homosexuals: Exploring the Hermeneutics of Cultural Analysis*. He describes his approach as a "redemptive hermeneutic" that seeks to show redemptive cultural movement both across the canon of Scripture and between the scriptural canon and the larger cultural and sociopolitical context. The result is a reading that can assess the text's redemptive movement. Webb insists, "What we should live out in our modern culture is not the isolated or 'on the page' words of the text but the redemptive spirit that the text reflects when read against its original culture."[35] He views both the slavery and gender portions of the household codes as representing just such a redemptive spirit when compared to the greater culture's treatment of women and slaves. Thus, the application of the text to modern culture would lean toward full egalitarianism for women. Webb is comfortable with a high degree of abstraction in his interpretation of the household codes because they exhibit a degree of redemptive value relative to the culture at large. Webb also asserts a movement within the text itself, with New Testament passages demonstrating a more liberative move from the Old Testament's stance on slaves and women.

Webb's approach has much to commend it. He does at least begin his assessment in the cultural world of the text before subsequently comparing it with the larger cultural milieu. He identifies a methodology that sets parameters for the acceptance or elimination of cultural elements in the text, which makes his assessment less subjective. In this way he merges a diachronic and synchronic view of the text, looking for redemptive movement across both the scriptural canon and the culture at large.

However, Webb's methods still fall outside the text-dependent approach of this study. First, Webb's idea of abstraction offers no clear check other than contemporary culture, which removes the text's interpretive authority and prioritizes culture. This approach differs from the hermeneutical equivalency Barth uses to support his normative view of Romans 13. In the latter case, equivalency asks how the "obedience" required by the text can be realized within modern Western democratic society, whereas Webb abandons submission for the sake of an egalitarian reading of the codes.

Furthermore, while Webb merges diachronic and synchronic approaches to the text, he emphasizes the diachronic. Thus, this study's primarily synchronic approach makes it difficult to apply either Webb's methods or his conclusions. Similarly, to move such a distance from the literary meaning and intention of the text would also diminish its usefulness in conversation with Luke 4:16–30—the primary objective here.

Egalitarian evangelicals are, therefore, somewhat problematic as interpreters of the household codes. They primarily depend on appeals to temporal versus eternal understandings of cultural elements of the text, which leads them to either exclude portions of the text (Fee) in ways similar although not identical to liberal and post-liberal feminists, or to move beyond the text (Webb). Also unclear is how their ultimate textual analysis, when they adhere to the intention of the text itself, differs from that of complementarians (Marshall).

Third-Way Interpretations

If neither feminists, complementarians, nor evangelical egalitarians offer an unproblematic interpretation of the household codes, does any approach suggest a way forward? Yes—Michelle Lee-Barnewall and other scholars who describe their conclusions as a "third-way" approach to the gender debate offer a solution.

Lee-Barnewall suggests that the answer to the evangelical gender debate lies with neither the complementarian nor the egalitarian. She argues that authority, leadership, and power are not central to the household codes; the focus on power is alien to the text and the result of modern ethical applications, not biblical intent:

> The key may be asking not so much whether Scripture promotes equality or authority as how—in a kingdom understanding—gender relates to love and unity between Christ and his bride. We may gain more not from merely asking what rights a person has or who has power but by seeing why unity matters and how it is accomplished by power manifested through weakness (2 Cor. 12:19), such as was exhibited through the cross.[36]

Lee-Barnewall's argument rests on an interpretation of the text based on three ideas central to the current study. First, the codes' underlying context is the need for unity among the people of God. At issue is the need for a growing multiethnic, multiclass, multigendered church to find unity amid preexisting cultural divides that work against the church. The clues come not from a cultural assumption; they are part of the codes themselves. The one-flesh allusion in Ephesians, according to Lee-Barnewall, points to the theme of unity in Genesis 2, and the call to mutual service is an evident appeal to unity in the body.[37]

Lee-Barnewall's second key idea builds on the biblical theme of reversal in both the Old and New Testaments to suggest that Paul has reversal in mind in suggesting mutual submission and requiring that the "head" surrender in sacrificial service to the wife-child-slave. She also draws a direct connection between reversal and the sovereignty of God. "Thus, the concept of reversal," according to Lee-Barnewall,

> speaks to issues of identity found not in oneself, one's position, or personal power but in dependence on God. It refers to a profound willingness to sacrifice what gives people status and meaning in their current context for a value that comes from God alone. As such it causes the credit to be given to God rather than to flawed and sinful humanity. When applied to the community, it results in the deep unity of his people as they consider others before themselves and challenges leaders to be primary examples of this submission of God.[38]

Reversal, therefore, is grounded on God's sovereignty, which explains Paul's insertion of Christ as head of all human relationships.

In her third argument, Lee-Barnewall applies the idea of reversal directly to the idea of headship in the household codes. She recognizes that *kephalē* does have a connection to authority but insists, compellingly, that Paul disrupts the term's definition in the household codes. She shows that in antiquity the idea of the authority of the head held a different meaning and practical outworking altogether. "It was," she says, "the body's responsibility to sacrifice itself for the sake of its head."[39] But by introducing the kenosis of Christ and applying it specifically to the responsibilities of the "head," Paul reverses that expectation so that the head's responsibility is to sacrifice itself for the good of the body. Contrary to complementarianism, which affirms the head's authority, this radical and disruptive view requires the abandonment of power by the husband-father-master in the interest of sacrificial service to the wife-child-slave. In Lee-Barnewall's conception of headship, the head surrenders to God's sovereignty, requiring a total surrender of self. Likewise, the head surrenders power and position in the interest of sacrificial service to the household. While Lee-Barnewall does not say so explicitly, she certainly demonstrates that what Ephesians has in mind is a redefinition of headship that centers on Christ's kenosis.

For advocates of this "third way," neither the complementarian focus on male leadership and authority nor the egalitarian denial of submission in the text helps explain the biblical world of the household codes. These views wrongly insist on a modern obsession with power that the texts themselves seek to eliminate. The child, the wife, and the slave are asked, within the context of society, to serve. This request is not radical when viewed in its own time and culture; it would have been taken for granted. What is radical in Paul's text is his call for mutual submission and his redefinition of headship grounded in the kenosis of Christ. Paul collapses power structures without redirecting them to new systems of shared or redistributed power. He replaces power with radical submission and sacrifice in the interest of radical unity.

This position, considered in light of the others presented above, presents the best way forward for understanding the text. It is grounded in a textual analysis that, contra evangelical egalitarianism, does not preference culture over biblical analysis and does not minimize the centrality of submission within the text. Likewise, contra complementarianism and hierarchialism, this "third way" does not define authority or headship within the context of ancient culture; rather it demonstrates how headship is redefined within the text itself, by way of Christ's kenosis. Finally, it extracts interpretation from the debate around authority and equality and asks the text to speak without taking sides on a superimposed, contemporary problem.

Dialogue with Luke 4:16–30

The present study enjoys three points of intersection with this "third-way" interpretation of the household codes concerning Luke 4:16–30. First, as Ringe points out about Luke 4, and Lee-Barnewall discussed in relation to the household codes, the sovereignty of God is a central component of both. The intent of both Luke's Jubilee imagery and Paul's image of Christ as the preeminent head of the household seems to be twofold: God is sovereign and can demand and bring about the liberation of the poor and marginalized, and God is sovereign over the household and can demand that the husband-father-master sacrifice themselves in service to their wife-child-slave. No less important is the idea that power rests with God alone, and human-to-human exercise of power within the Christian community must defer to God's call to surrender power, place, and position to honor God—just as God can demand the freeing of slaves, the clearing of debt, and the returning of ancestral lands in the Jubilee.

Second, both Luke 4 and the household codes seem to require embracing reversal, particularly when Luke 4 is viewed as paradigmatic of the larger reversal motif throughout Luke-Acts. Lee-Barnewall suggests this requirement implies a new community praxis that redefines headship as surrender and sacrifice; the body that must sacrifice itself for the head is replaced by a head that must sacrifice itself for the body. The general emphasis on reversal in the Lukan narrative finds propositional force in Ephesians 5. The "third-way" understanding of reversal also ties back to sovereignty. God is elevated when human power is surrendered, and through God, the poor and the marginalized are lifted up.

Finally, reversal requires a particular way of being in the world for those believers who hold positions of power. Sovereignty and reversal point to an ethic of self-denial and of solidarity with the poor and marginalized, as well as wives-children-slaves. This self-denial is predicated on Christ's kenosis and exists on a practical level to promote the Church's unity.

Given the less-than-authentic use of kenosis to subject the oppressed, one must make a clear distinction when applying this principle. The household codes apply kenosis not to subject wives-children-slaves but rather to redefine headship toward sacrificial self-giving for the body. And while the admonition to submission remains, one must recall Marshall's assessment that submission, as used in the codes, is a voluntary giving of oneself on behalf of the other. Submission in this light is less a command to obey; it is more an admonishment to cultivate right relationships and an empowerment to take personal responsibility for them.

The requirements of surrender of status and reversal so evident in Luke, plus the household codes' requirement of Christlike kenosis on the part of the husband-parent-master, places a higher ethical burden on the rich, the powerful, and persons of status. This burden requires them to ascribe to an ethical norm not already prescribed by law or custom, whereas Luke's message to the poor and marginalized is the good news of inclusion. The prescriptions to honor husband-master-parent do not require anything that is not already a prescribed social norm. The highest ethical burden placed on Christian converts, therefore, is placed not on the marginalized or oppressed but on the rich and powerful. The latter group, in light of Luke-Acts and the household codes, is required to give up the most in response to the Lordship of Christ.

If one accepts this "third-way" reading of the household codes over the traditionalist reading, many contradictions with a liberationist reading of Luke 4:16–30 resolve themselves. This interpretation removes much of the rhetoric that undergirds traditionalist hierarchy and that subsequently leads to a spiritualized reading of Luke 4. If the work of Lee-Barnewall and others is accepted, there may be no need to look beyond a more literal interpretation of the Luke 4 text.

Thus, both a "normative" interpretation of Romans 13 vis-à-vis Barth and a "third-way" interpretation of the household codes eliminate the need for purely spiritualized interpretations of Luke 4. These interpretations support and further clarify the interpretations of Luke 4 offered in the preceding chapter. It is now, therefore, possible to consider the theological implications of these interpretations.

NOTES

1. Vanhoozer, K. 2005: 299, 273.
2. Yoder, J. 1994. *The Royal Priesthood: Essays Ecclesiological and Ecumenical.* Grand Rapids: Eerdmans. 199–200.

3. Yoder, J. 1994: 199.
4. Yoder, J. 1994: 252–62.
5. See Joachim Hossenfelder in Solberg, M. 2015. *A Church Undone: Documents from the German Christian Faith Movement, 1932–1940.* Minneapolis: Fortress Press. 45–54, on Nazi Germany; Mukuka, T. "Reading/Hearing Romans 13:1–7 under the African Tree: Towards a Lectio Postcolonica Contexta Africana." *Neotestamentica* 46, no. 1 (2012): 105–38, on South Africa.
6. Yoder, J. 1994: 199.
7. Barth, K. 1954. *Against the Stream: Shorter Post-War Writings 1946–52.* Translated by E. Delacour. London: SCM Press.
8. Barth, K. 1968: 484.
9. Barth, K. 1954: 17–50.
10. Barth, K. 1954: 17.
11. Barth, K. 1954: 21–23.
12. Barth, K. 1954: 21.
13. Barth, K. 1954: 22.
14. Barth, K. 1954: 24–28.
15. Barth, K. 1954: 33–37.
16. Dunn, J. 1998. *The Theology of Paul the Apostle.* Grand Rapids: W. B. Eerdmans. 674–80.
17. Makuka, T. 2012: 105–38.
18. Bowens, L. 2020. *African American Readings of Paul: Reception, Resistance, Transformation.* Grand Rapids: W. B. Eerdmans. 232–33.
19. Herzog, W. "Dissembling, a Weapon of the Weak: The Case of Christ and Caesar in Mark 12:13–17 and Romans 13:1–7." *Perspectives in Religious Studies* 21, no. 4 (1994): 341.
20. Lim, S. "A Double-Voiced Reading of Romans 13:1–7 in Light of the Imperial Cult." *Herwormde Teologiese Studies* 71 (2015): 1.
21. Hanc, O. "Paul and Empire: A Reframing of Romans 13:1–7 in the Context of New Exodus." *The Tyndale Bulletin* 65, no. 2 (2014): 315–16.
22. Dunn, J. 1998: 674–80.
23. For the former see Bowens, L. 2020; Crowder, B. 2007. "Luke." In *True to Our Native Land.* Edited by B. Blount. Minneapolis: Fortress Press. 158–85; Martin, C. 1991. "The Haustafeln (Household Codes) in African American Biblical Interpretation: 'Free Slaves' and 'Subordinate Women.'" In *Stony the Road We Trod: African American Biblical Interpretation.* Edited by C. Felder. Minneapolis: Fortress Press. 206–31.
24. Martin, C. 1991: 206–31.
25. Piper, J., and W. Grudem. 2021. *Recovering Biblical Manhood and Womanhood: A Response to Evangelical Feminism.* Downers Grove: InterVarsity Academic. 13–16.
26. Knight, G. 2021. "Husbands and Wives as Analogues of Christ and the Church: Ephesians 5:21–33." In *Recovering Biblical Manhood and Womanhood: A Response to Evangelical Feminism.* Wheaton: Crossway. 215–32.
27. Knight, G. 2021: 222.

28. Knight, G. 2021: 221–22.
29. Knight, G. 2021: 221–22; Piper, J., and W. Grudem. 2021: 449–568.
30. Knight, G. 2021: 221.
31. Knight, G. 2021: 231.
32. Fee, G. 2005. "Hermeneutics and the Gender Debate." In *Discovering Biblical Equality*. Edited by R. Pierce and R. Groothuis. Downers Grove: IVP Academic. 370–80.
33. Giles, K. 2005. "The Subordination of Christ and the Subordination of Women." In *Discovering Biblical Equality*. Downers Grove: IVP Academic. 339.
34. Marshall, I. H. 2005. "Mutual Love and Submission in Marriage." In *Discovering Biblical Equality*. Downers Grove: IVP Academic. 188–91.
35. Webb, W. 2005. "A Redemptive Movement Hermeneutic: The Slavery Analogy." In *Discovering Biblical Equality*. Downers Grove: IVP Academic. 384.
36. Lee-Barnewall, M. 2016. *Neither Complementarian nor Egalitarian: A Kingdom Corrective to the Evangelical Gender Debate*. Grand Rapids: Baker Academic. 7.
37. Lee-Barnewall, M. 2016: 159–64.
38. Lee-Barnewall, M. 2016: 81.
39. Lee-Barnewall, M. 2016: 156–57.

Chapter 11

The Theological Use of Luke 4:16–30

The final step of Movement Three is to examine the way theologians understand and apply Luke 4:16–30. Within the study framework, that assessment primarily means examining how Calvin, Edwards, Hodge, Henry, Cone, and other Black theologians use the text. This chapter then summarizes preferred interpretations in light of Romans 13 and the household codes, the role of Luke 4 in Lukan theology, and the theological significances of all the passages, toward a final interpretation of Luke 4:16–30.

COMPARING THEOLOGICAL USES OF LUKE 4:16–30

Use by Calvin, Edwards, Hodge, and Henry

How does the North American evangelical tradition identified in part II view the implications of Luke 4:16–30? Calvin does not deal with the text in the *Institutes* but does address it in his *Harmony of the Evangelists*. Little in Calvin's treatment suggests a liberationist interpretation of Luke 4. He tends to generalize the text's redemptive aspects beyond the immediate literal context of the poor and marginalized. Calvin's commentary on "to the poor" in Luke 4:18 emphasizes:

> The prophet shows what would be the state of the church before the manifestation of the Gospel and what is the condition of all of us without Christ. The persons to whom God promises restoration are called *poor* [emphasis Calvin], and broken, and captives, and blind and bruised. The body of people was oppressed by so many miseries, that these descriptions applied to every one of its members.[1]

Calvin does not say that those who are saved are poor, broken, captives, blind, and bruised—rather, they are "called" those things, and he generalizes these conditions to all members of the Early Church. Calvin's view of these conditions is highly spiritualized and psychologized:

> We see who are invited by Christ, and made partakers of promised grace. They are persons, who are every way miserable, and destitute of all hope of salvation. But we are reminded, on the other hand, that we cannot enjoy those benefits which Christ bestows, in any other manner, than by being humbled under deep conviction of our distresses, and by coming, as hungry souls, to seek him as our deliverer.[2]

Under Calvin's interpretive gaze, poverty becomes a condition of the psyche, not the body. The poor are those with hungry souls, convicted of spiritual and emotional distress, who take on humility.

Calvin cannot deny that God's sovereignty may lead God to embrace the outcast. "Hence, also, may be collected the general doctrine," he says, "that we have no right to prescribe any rule to God in disposing his benefits, so as to prevent him from rejecting those who hold the highest rank, and conferring honour on the lowest and most contemptible." Furthermore, "we are not at liberty to oppose him, when he entirely subverts that order, which would have approved itself to our judgement."[3] Tellingly, this comment occurs under Calvin's discussion of Gentile inclusion, not the poor, and Calvin never goes so far as to suggest God's preference for the poor. In the final estimation, Calvin seems unlikely to approve of a more liberationist/literalist interpretation of the text.

Edwards' perspective on Luke 4:16–30 takes some constructive work, as no sermons on the text are extant. He does make a short reference to Luke 4:18 in the *Blank Bible* that does not offer a literalist conclusion but does make some literalistic references to what the text means by "captives" and "blind," tying both to the "eastern" custom of blinding prisoners. Three other sermons illustrate Edwards' views on elevating the marginalized, concerning Luke 14:16 (Jesus' rebuke of those who covet the seats of honor), Luke 16:24 (the parable of the rich man and Lazarus), and Luke 6:24 (the Sermon on the Plain).

In his sermon on Luke 14:16, Edwards focuses on both the guests' lack of humility and the lack of inclusion of the poor—but not on their elevation. The sermon concentrates on the need for spiritual humility but does refer to the importance of including the poor. The latter in no way suggests that the poor are to be elevated or that the positions of rich and poor should be reversed.[4]

Edwards' exposition on the rich man and Lazarus focuses almost exclusively on the rich man and the need for rich people not to be secure in their earthly blessings. He does juxtapose Lazarus' elevation, but he refers to Lazarus' character, not his social status. Also telling is that most of the sermon focuses on the torments of hell.[5] Thus, Edwards seems either not to recognize, or to prefer to downplay, the passage's theme of reversal.

Finally, interpreting the Sermon on the Plain, Edwards makes a slight concession to understanding God's concern for the poor but insists on interpreting "blessed are the poor" in light of Matthew's "blessed are the poor in spirit." The focus is spiritual and psychological and shifts the discussion from the blessedness of the poor to the spiritual condition of the rich, who believe themselves to be blessed but are poor and naked in God's eyes. That Edwards acknowledges God's preference for the poor but focuses his sermon on the souls of the rich may indicate his discomfort with the former.[6]

Edwards seems slightly more open to literal interpretation than Calvin, but he cannot bring himself to work out the full implications of God's preference for the poor. He prefers to focus on the spiritual needs of the rich and to expound upon the consequences of favoring wealth over God.

As for Hodge, no primary sources include any comments on Luke 4:16–30, which itself may be telling. But his sermon on the parable of the rich man and Lazarus leaves little doubt as to how he views God's preference for the poor and any liberationist interpretation of New Testament texts. For Hodge, the parable is not about reversal. He uses the text's class distinction to emphasize that the poor must be content in their poverty. "The parable should lead us to be content with our lot," Hodge says; "we may be rich and yet perish, we may be poor and yet be saved. It is a small matter to Lazarus because he had suffered so much while on earth."[7]

He also insists that the poor be seen as "poor in spirit," ignoring the physical, bodily nature of Lazarus' poverty. Hodge suggests, "The great question when Christ was on the earth was to whom did the kingdom of God belong?" Regarding the poor, he answered, "Not the poor as poor and because poor; poverty is not the condition of membership in this kingdom. Its blessings are not bestowed as a recompense for the evil of poverty."[8] He concludes with complete acquiescence to a spiritual interpretation of poverty in the Gospels. "But the poverty intended," he says, "is a poverty as to the spirit.... The poor in spirit are those who are conscious of their spiritual poverty."[9] Hodge leaves no room for a liberationist approach to the text.

Finally, Henry offers an approach to Luke 4:16–30 that is more nuanced than those of Calvin, Edwards, or Hodge but is nonetheless spiritualized. Henry's view of the literalness of the Jubilee references in Luke 4:18–19 makes clear his approach:

> In view of the silence about the Jubilee theme in the teaching of the evangelist, it hardly seems credible that it held such a central and literal place in Jesus'

message. The term aphesis occurs numerous times in the New Testament for God's forgiveness and remission of sin, and the thought of forgiveness is in view even when it means liberation.[10]

Henry decentralizes this text which many scholars view as paradigmatic of the entire Gospel of Luke and deemphasizes the temporal importance of Jubilee symbolism in the life of Christ. Henry also insists that Jesus did not promise political liberation in Luke 4:16–30: "In contrast to one-sided political and nationalistic expectations, he (Jesus) restored centrality to neglected aspects of divine liberation by the messianic deliverer."[11] Henry means spiritual salvation when he refers to the "neglected aspects of divine liberation."

Although Henry minimizes the text's liberation aspects, he does affirm the social concern of liberation theology while attempting to discredit it as a viable theological position. He embraces an understanding of liberation that is supernatural. Christ is the liberator because he spiritually "unshackles the chains that enslave the human race."[12] For Henry, liberation is effective to the degree that a redeemed church forms a new community that challenges evil in the world: "Christ is active in history, leading his followers in resistance against sin and Satan which the wicked serve."[13]

Henry's approach cannot be said to be merely spiritualized. He instead advocates supernaturalism with real second-order consequences for human society within redemption history. But he also is reluctant to accept liberationist interpretations because he sees them as replacing the "truth of the gospel" with Marxist social solutions. "Liberation theologians," he asserts, "accept Marxian analysis of class struggle and proposed Marxian solutions as gospel."[14] According to Henry, Marxist solutions ensure that "liberation theology proceeds on the basis of a distorted Christian gospel." Despite his social focus, Henry cannot be said to support a liberationist interpretation of Luke 4:16–30. He could, however, be seen as supporting a more limited, incidental notion of temporal liberation as a secondary consequence of Christ's salvific mission.

Thus, to varying degrees, Calvin, Edwards, Hodge, and Henry work to mitigate the political implications of Luke 4 and subsume its interpretation in a redemption-historical message. How does their approach differ from Cone's interpretation?

Use by Cone

Cone makes Luke 4:16–30 the centerpiece of a Christological extension of Old Testament liberation themes in the Exodus. In this way, he defines Jesus' mission and, by extension, the Church's mission in temporal, political terms:

> In the New Testament the theme of liberation is reaffirmed by Jesus himself. The conflict with Satan and the powers of this world, the condemnation of the rich, the insistence that the kingdom of God is for the poor, and locating of his ministry among the poor—these and other features of the career of Jesus show that his work was directed to the oppressed for the purpose of their liberation. To suggest that he was speaking of a 'spiritual' liberation fails to take seriously Jesus' thoroughly Hebrew view of human nature.[15]

Cone does not deny the supernatural in God's liberating work. The Christian battle on behalf of the oppressed is a spiritual battle against "Satan and the powers of this world." But the battle has temporal consequences and makes political and social demands on the Church.

Cone also does not succumb to Hodge's accusation of salvation for "the poor as poor and because poor." This is far truer of later liberationist theology, particularly Latin American. Cone's grounding in the Black Church, as shown in part I, does not allow him to deny the revivalist understanding of salvation that is part of that church's life and teaching. He does work, however, to counterbalance an overinterpretation of spiritual salvation to the exclusion of temporal political and social liberation; he grounds that insistence specifically in his reading of Luke 4:16–30 and the larger liberationist stream in Lukan theology, and he does so through literal reading.

Cone also has a radically Christocentric hermeneutic that further elevates Luke 4:16–30 for understanding God as the God of liberation. Cone insists, "As Christians we know God only as he has been revealed in and through Jesus."[16] Thus, Jesus' life and mission become God's life and mission and, by extension, the Church's life and mission. Cone defines Jesus' mission as breaking down those barriers to a relationship between God and humans that resulted from satanic power in the world, including slavery, oppression, hunger, poverty, and racism. Christ's role in restoring humanity to its God-intended order included eliminating these social and political problems. Cone suggests that Jesus "is God himself coming into the very depths of human existence for the sole purpose of striking off the chains of slavery, thereby freeing man from ungodly principalities and powers that hinder his relations to his God."[17]

Further, Cone believes that this mission, when embraced by the Church, shifts the believer from a focus on self to a focus on others that is central to the Gospels: "Indeed, the message of the kingdom strikes the very center of man's desire to define his existence in the light of his own interests at the price of his brother's enslavement."[18] Ignoring the oppressed becomes impossible for a Church that understands Luke 4:16–30 as paradigmatic of not just Jesus' mission but also the Church's mission.

Cone's view of Luke 4:16–30, then, holds that it should be read literally and emphasized as the New Testament's central text, which affirms the liberating mission of Christ and Christ's Church. But while the text has a purely temporal, political meaning for Cone, he should not therefore be read as saying that temporal liberation is God's only work in view throughout Scripture, even though Cone comes very close to this conclusion. Rather, he suggests that liberation is the most important work of Christ and the Church while the Church exists in its temporal state.[19]

Nor should Cone be seen as separating liberation from supernaturalism. While he does downplay supernatural intervention, he sees oppression, poverty, and hunger as manifestations of satanic power; the Christian struggle against oppression, poverty, and hunger is a battle against these supernatural powers. However, Cone's work does not clearly delineate a role for either God or Christ, except as exemplars for human action. The battle against supernatural powers is a human battle in this present world.[20]

Use by Other Black Theologians

Cone often lays the foundations for arguments that are realized more fully in the work of other Black theologians and biblical scholars, including those outside the United States. At least three individuals advance Cone's literalist view of Luke 4:16–30: Stephanie Buckhanon Crowder in *True to Our Native Land*, Paul John Isaak in the *African Bible Commentary*, and Brian Blount's *Then the Whisper Put on Flesh*.

In the Lukan focus on the poor and marginalized, Crowder recognizes a conscious effort to "forefront" the oppressed. This forefronting represents an effort on the part of Luke to show "Jesus as a savior accessible to all people."[21] But according to Crowder, the poor are not Luke's only focus. "Lukan theology," per Crowder, "is grounded in a Jesus who comes not just to offer compassion to those who are wounded but to speak to the evil of those who wound."[22] This nuance is important. A gospel that calls both the oppressed and the oppressor to God and insists on abandoning oppressive power points to a God active in both temporal and eternal liberation.

Crowder also recognized, along with the aforementioned postcolonial scholars, that Luke's text functioned as a coded narrative. Crowder grounds this not in colonialism but, like Cone, in the practices of American slaves. Luke's "imagery" according to Crowder is "reminiscent of the coded nature of the spirituals and other slave songs. While these songs speak of a people's love and belief in the God of heaven, they are also replete with messages of a God who rules over the earth and who can do something about earth's sorrows and pains."[23] Crowder's interpretations advance a literal/liberationist view of Luke 4:16–30 while grounding it in a textual rather than thematic strategy.

Isaak extends the political reading of Luke: "At the outset it should be noted that the political language of Luke 4:14–44 is unmistakable."[24] But he sees Luke as combining the spiritual and ethical into a single message that requires a particular way of being in the world. Isaak notes that Luke gives real priority to Jesus' love for the poor and marginalized while emphasizing the power of the Holy Spirit to transform and reorient humanity to God: "For Luke these two approaches are one. The same Holy Spirit who transforms people's lives also seeks to transform societies and nations to social justice."[25]

Isaak also recontextualizes Luke's emphasis on the importance of living in community and caring for neighbors. Suggesting that what Luke had in mind was akin to the African concept of Ubuntu, Isaak removes the interpretation of Luke from the constraints of Western individualism:

> The concept of Ubuntu is derived from the Xhosa (South African) proverb *Ubuntu ungamnta ngabany e abantur*, which, translated roughly, means 'each individual's humanity is best expressed in relationship to others' or 'a person depends on other people to be a person.' ... People with Ubuntu will be empowered by the Holy Spirit to carry out courageous acts of good works, especially towards the poor and oppressed.[26]

Thus, Isaak expands Cone's understanding of the connections between spiritual and temporal liberation while suggesting that Western individualistic interpretations of the text miss the "communality" embedded in its cultural context. Isaak draws on a cultural (non-Christian) concept that speaks to the importance of community and further enriches notions of the new covenant community Luke envisions. But he also emphasizes the importance of the spiritual, "empowered by the Holy Spirit" aspect of this community's work on behalf of the poor and marginalized. Isaak summarizes Luke's purpose: "The Holy Spirit who transforms people's lives also seeks to transform societies and nations to social justice."[27] The spiritual has real temporal consequence, in which the liberation of the poor and marginalized does not contradict Christ's salvific power and the working of the Holy Spirit. In this view, the one (liberation of the oppressed) depends on the other (the working of the Holy Spirit).

Blount grounds the text of Luke in a clearer argument characterizing Luke as an ethical text. Blount sees Luke's theology of reversal as anchoring this ethical teaching: "Reversal is in the air. It is a part of the fabric of kingdom life; it becomes the modeling mandate for the kind of life expected of kingdom followers."[28] He also recognizes that reversal probably focuses on the community's unity. He suggests that this focus might "strike one as more a message of ethical maintenance than liberation." But for Blount, the mechanism of unity that calls the rich and powerful to surrender their power and status creates an environment that points directly toward liberation for the poor and oppressed. The reality of reversal in Luke is that,

> In the Kingdom, societal insiders who dismiss God's call will find themselves on the margins; those who have been societally marginalized, but who respond to God's call and commands, will find themselves at the center of God's consummate kingdom, God's kingdom, which, according to the parable (rich man and Lazarus), attends to obedience not status."[29]

One must understand how Blount connects the importance of obedience and the abandonment of status. Blount insists that the poor are not saved because they are poor and that obedience is necessary for the poor and the rich. But the difference lies in requiring oppressors to abandon power as their first act of obedience to God and life in God's community.

Blount affirms that Luke 4 recognizes Christ as both Messiah and prophet. This aspect only strengthens the political interpretation of the text. "Thus for Luke," he argues, "Jesus' messianic activity is the work of liberation, and the direct link of the gospel to the message of the prophets is to be found in the prophetic call to justice."[30]

PREFERRED INTERPRETATIONS IN LIGHT OF ROMANS 13 AND THE HOUSEHOLD CODES

What theological significance do Luke 4:16–30, and subsequently Romans 13 and the household codes, have for the preferred interpretations? First, I find only limited reason to spiritualize Luke 4:16–30. As Crowder, Isaak, Blount, and Rowe suggest, the text's spiritual implications do not negate, but perhaps rather strengthen, its social ethic, which is far more evident in the literal interpretation of the language of Luke 4.

Also, while Hodge is right that the kingdom is not for the poor simply because they are poor, a clear call to reversal qualifies what it means for the powerful to obey God. For the powerful, obedience requires a specific commitment to abandon and surrender power and status as part of their role within God's community. This reading is suggested by Blount but also by the "third-way" interpretation of the household codes.

In addition, although traditional readings of Romans 13 and hierarchical readings of the household codes seem to contradict the view of reversal and the insistence on the abandonment of Power, some have suggested that these texts have been read incorrectly. If the normative interpretation of Romans 13 is taken seriously, then the Church is forbidden from withdrawing from the public square, and the Church—at least in a modern Western democracy—has a responsibility to speak God's truth into society and work toward Christian ideals, especially those suggested by the ethic of reversal and mutuality of service to the poor and marginalized. Therefore, one can read Luke 4:16–30 as a divine truth that the Church has the responsibility to model. The liberation of the poor and the oppressed might be seen as something that the Church should support, as a broader social ethic centered in Christ.

Likewise, the "third-way" interpretation of the household codes suggests that the texts do not preserve structures of power but rather call for its radical surrender on the part of the head in sacrificial giving to the body. This surrender ensures mutual submission within the body of Christ. This reading requires the embrace of the ethic of reversal suggested by Lukan theology and is predicated on the kenosis of Christ as applied to not the powerless but the powerful within households. It also requires a covenantal relationality in which the poor, the marginalized, and the Gentiles achieve inclusion into the community and are accepted into the bonds of kinship.

These interpretations of the household codes and Romans 13 go a long way in overturning any perception that these texts require a spiritual instead of a liberationist reading of Luke 4. Read in conjunction with Luke 4, they strengthen the theology of reversal, surrender, and a responsibly engaged social ethic within a new covenant community.

LUKE 4:16–30 WITHIN LUKAN THEOLOGY

Within Lukan theology, Luke 4 might be read as paradigmatic of a theology of social engagement that Luke makes central to the mission of Christ and by extension Christ's Church. A temporal political reading of the text does not necessarily exclude a supernaturalism that also is evident within Lukan theology. As Rowe suggests, both elements are mutually present and never mutually exclusive. God's supernatural intervention has both temporal effects with eternal consequences and also eternal consequences with temporal effects.

The dual objectives of inclusion and unity lay in the background of reversal and God's providential will in broadening the new covenant community. These objectives become necessary components, even strategies, within God's providence for the expansion of God's kingdom. The kingdom expands as it diversifies and opens up to the poor, marginalized, and previously excluded. This new diversity in turn requires the elimination of social status and privilege to ensure the unity of the new community.

Inclusion ensures expansion, while reversal ensures unity. This central idea also creates a new obligation within a community for whom the new marker of inclusion was obedience, not status. The powerful and the privileged had the special obligation to abandon power for the sake of God and the community. This arrangement disentangled power from the blessings of God as signs of inclusion in the kingdom.

Underlying all of these texts is the sovereignty of God. Ringe recognizes this sovereignty in the Jubilee symbolism of Luke 4. The element is central in Romans 13, which elevates the Christian God above Caesar, and in the household codes, which insist that God is the head of all, including the husband-master-father. The presence of sovereignty in Luke suggests both God's prerogative to include the poor and the marginalized and also God's requirement that people execute God's understanding of justice with specific reference to the Jubilee symbolism of Luke 4. Thus, sovereignty in Luke requires both acceptance of those God accepts and active participation in God's justice in the world.

God's sovereignty over the government and the household points to the active supernatural work of God on behalf of humanity. While Cone downplays both sovereignty and the supernatural, both better support his suggestion that God's primary work is the work of liberation.

SUMMARIZING THE PASSAGES' THEOLOGICAL SIGNIFICANCE

How does this understanding of these texts guide, enliven, or constrain the constructive doctrinal work envisioned for part IV? For one thing, the focus on God's sovereignty suggests that the sovereignty God exercises in God's providence is key to understanding the place of the marginalized, the exercise of power by the powerful, and the Church's relationship and responsibility within society. According to Scripture, God's providence does have a specific application that incorporates the inclusion of, and seeming preference for, the marginalized, worked out and signaled in the covenants. Therefore, doctrinal considerations concerning power with specific reference to race must recognize that God's exercise of sovereignty within God's providential will includes a social justice thrust consistent with Luke 4 and with the prophetic tradition that envisions justice as covenant renewal and an outgrowth of the new, inclusive, covenantal community.

Also, within God's providence rests a preference for inclusion, evident in God's determination to expand his covenant community. This understanding of inclusion must foreground any theology of power. The Gospels do not suggest inclusion without obligation or, better put, universal inclusion. The constraints placed on inclusion, however, are not social, political, racial, gendered, or moral; they rest instead on God's call to obedience. The removal of politics, race, gender, and morality as factors for inclusion in God's community certainly has implications for dogmatic reflection on power.

Finally, these texts suggest that inclusion manifests in social and political reversal and that reversal is at least a component of obedience for those who hold power. An ethic of kenotic surrender is required of the rich and powerful, one that forms the pragmatic basis for unity within a diverse community, with implications for ecclesiology and the doctrine of sanctification. Cone may be right when he insists that the gospel makes different claims on different groups within God's community. Thus, kenosis, and its implications for the Church, warrant exploration in light of the prominence of reversal in the texts examined here.

What emerge as the prominent theological concerns in Luke are sovereignty, covenant renewal, inclusion, and reversal as ethical stances and unifying necessities. These are the central biblical themes that have to intersect with the doctrinal work of part IV.

With these biblical concerns in view, at least one particular doctrine needs to be examined with reference to power. One could start with Cone's focus on Christology, but Cone's insistence that all we know of God terminates in Christ presents Christology as a terminus that ends debate. Part II, however, suggested that racist grammars seem to center on providence, revelation, and foundational issues of hierarchy, submission, and obedience. These themes seem grounded in the doctrine of God, just as debates about justice rely on understandings of God's attributes. The biblical material considered in this part also focuses on God's sovereignty and plan, human authority and submission, covenant relationships, and obedience. All of these themes suggest the need to consider them within the doctrine of God. Thus, to extend the logic of this work, part IV focuses its dogmatic work on the doctrine of God.

NOTES

1. Calvin, J. 2005. *Commentary on the Epistles of Paul.* 229.
2. Calvin, J. 2005. *Commentary on the Epistles of Paul.* 229.
3. Calvin, J. 2005. *Commentary on the Epistles of Paul.* 234.
4. Edwards, J. 1745. "Sermon 86." *Sermon Series II in Works of Jonathan Edwards Online Vol. 43*. Edited by The Jonathan Edwards Center. New Haven: Yale University Press.
5. Edwards, J. 1745. "Sermon 87."
6. Edwards, J. 1745. "Sermon 179."
7. Hodge, C. 2011: 165.
8. Hodge, C. 2011: 168.
9. Hodge, C. 2011: 168–69.

10. Henry, Carl. 1983: 6:526.
11. Henry, Carl. 1983: 3:68.
12. Henry, Carl. 1984: 193.
13. Henry, Carl. 1984: 193.
14. Henry, Carl. 1984: 197.
15. Cone, J. 2018. *A Black Theology of Liberation.* 203.
16. Cone, J. 1997. *God of the Oppressed.* 35.
17. Cone, J. 1997. *God of the Oppressed.* 35.
18. Cone, J. 1997. *God of the Oppressed.* 35.
19. Cone, J. 1997. *God of the Oppressed.* 34–43.
20. Cone, J. 1997. *God of the Oppressed.* 61–71.
21. Crowder, B. 2007: 158.
22. Crowder, B. 2007: 158.
23. Crowder, B. 2007: 158–59.
24. Isaak, P. 2006. "Luke." In *African Bible Commentary.* Edited by A. Tokunboh. Grand Rapids: Zondervan. 1231.
25. Isaak, P. 2006: 1229.
26. Isaak, P. 2006: 1230.
27. Isaak, P. 2006: 1229.
28. Blount, B. 2001: 87.
29. Blount, B. 2001: 82.
30. Blount, B. 2001: 80.

PART IV

Doctrinal and Ethical Construction

Chapter 12

Constructive Theological Methodology

Having completed an empathetic analysis of Cone; tested and concurred with Cone's assessment that White theology, based on the data analyzed here, contains racist logics; and directly analyzed biblical material connected to liberation and submission, this study can finally proceed to a constructive engagement with doctrine and with Cone's third question related to the viability of an antiracist theology. The doctrine most connected to racist grammars and most directly suggested by the biblical analyses is the doctrine of God.

This brief chapter advances the methodology to conclude Movement Four of this project. Part IV begins this constructive work of envisioning a theology of power by bringing into conversation the work of the five theologians discussed with regard to specific themes before concluding with suggestions about the ethical appropriation of the doctrinal position affirmed here.

A few limitations to this Movement's work should be acknowledged. First, the work deals with aspects of the doctrine of God that are deemed most relevant for a theology of power, so some aspects will not be emphasized in this study. I am prioritizing particular doctrines based on their relevance to the debate among the five theologians under consideration. The goal is logical consistency given the theologians and traditions under review.

Second, the constructive work is mostly limited to engagement specifically with the five theologians, with a few exceptions. Cone's Barthianism suggests Barth as a reasonable conversation partner in advancing the project's constructive work. The discussion also engages Reinhold Niebuhr, primarily because he is critiqued in Cone's work and advances discussions on kenosis. Bernard Ramm's analysis of Barth and ethics also enters the discussion on appropriation because Ramm ties Barth to the evangelical tradition and bridges evangelical doctrine and ethics. Beyond these, however, the study derives theological conclusions primarily from the work of the five main theologians.

Finally, at this stage, constructive decisions must be made. These decisions represent my best efforts to form logical conclusions from the analysis. I aim to present the material in a way that is logically consistent within the bounded and limited data set, that remains consistent with reformed evangelical orthodoxy, and that addresses racism as identified by Cone and within the evangelical tradition. The conclusions will be presented clearly, perhaps emphatically, but the realization behind any conclusion is the limited scope of its application. I make every effort to ensure accuracy given the materials explored.

With those caveats in mind, it is now possible to proceed to the work of part IV. This final movement discusses the evangelical theologians and Cone simultaneously regarding various parts of the doctrine and offers constructive conclusions and decisions at those points. The doctrines to be so considered, under the umbrella of the doctrine of God, include revelation and Scripture, providence, the attributes and essence of God, and the person of God.

Chapter 13

Revelation

To assess the impact of the evangelical tradition on questions of power with reference to race and racism, one must understand the doctrine of revelation underpinning both the doctrine of God and prolegomena. Calvin, Edwards, Hodge, and Henry use their understandings of Scripture and divine revelation to support a biblical hermeneutic that views both the household codes and Romans 13 literally, while interpreting Luke 4 in light of a broader salvation narrative that makes "the poor" a metaphor referring to those who come humbly to God. This dichotomy affords a biblical support for potentially racist logics by providing a racist vocabulary for personal power and hierarchy (the household codes), structural power and dominance (Romans 13), and the downgrading of God's mandates related to the poor and marginalized (Luke 4).

Three questions must therefore be considered in a more detailed analysis of revelation in Calvin, Edwards, Hodge, and Henry and an assessment of their views in conversation with Cone. First, what view(s) of revelation within evangelicalism are typified by these theologians? Second, are their views consistent with the way they handle the texts under consideration? And third, do Cone's views on revelation and Scripture challenge evangelical views of the same in any way that might alter an evangelical approach to Scripture and, just as importantly, not create a theology so compromised that it fully abandons evangelical identity? These questions are answered in turn during the broader analysis. Because their respective views feature slight nuances, the following section looks separately at Calvin, Edwards, Hodge, and Henry.

EVANGELICAL THEOLOGIANS

Calvin

Calvin organized his theological schema in the *Institutes* under two headings: the knowledge of God and the knowledge of man. In Book 1, chapter 1, he argues that the two topics are so interdependent that where to begin the theological conversation is hard to discern. Calvin in no way implies an interdependence between God and man: he would categorically deny this.

For Calvin, this question centers on schema, not doctrinal content. It is ultimately a question of organization. Calvin settles on the primacy of the doctrine of God: "Man never attains to a true self-knowledge until he has previously contemplated the face of God and come down after such contemplation to look into himself."[1]

Thus, the knowledge of God is central to Calvin's theology. He moves on to define, first, what the knowledge of God is and, second, in what ways this knowledge is made visible in nature and Scripture.

His exposition in Book 1, chapter 2 centers on what knowledge of God one should seek. He outlines certain a priori understandings of God. Whoever God is, according to Calvin, God is both perfectly good and supremely authoritative. God's authority is evidenced in the majesty of creation and in God's place as creator, with the creature owing existence and allegiance to the creator's authority. God's goodness is evident in God's work in sustaining creation. For Calvin, therefore, the knowledge of God to be sought centers on who God is, not in God's essence but in God's nature (authoritative and good). Seeking to understand God's essence is, for Calvin, an attempt to "delude us with frigid speculation."[2] In his discussion of scriptural revelation, Calvin asserts "that in enumeration of his (God's) perfections, he is described not as he is in himself, but in relation to us, in order that our acknowledgement of him may be more a vivid actual impression than empty visionary speculation."[3] Calvin also insists that the reason for pursuing knowledge of God is to gain proper "fear and reverence," to ask God for good things, and to ascribe to God's goodness the good things that humanity possesses.

This way of viewing the knowledge of God has important implications. Calvin's preference for "nature" over "essence" and for God in relation to humanity shifts the focus from theoretical knowledge to God's actions, with specific reference to humanity's response and relationship with God. The practical knowledge advanced thereby is critical to Calvin. God is only understood within the divine-human relationship through which God has chosen to reveal God's self.

Calvin moves from discussing what knowledge to seek to discuss avenues from which knowledge of God is obtainable. He divides the knowledge of God into two types of revelation: general/natural and specific/scriptural.

First, Calvin identifies two kinds of natural revelation: the knowledge of God that is "implanted in the Human Mind" and the knowledge of God discoverable from both creation and God's providential maintenance of that creation. As regards the former, Calvin affirms that God placed in the minds of humanity "some idea of His Godhead," an understanding described as both a "natural instinct" and a "memory of deity."[4] For Calvin, natural revelation makes all persons culpable for rejecting God and forestalls any defense for humanity's ignorance of God. Humanity was created with the "express purpose of learning to know God" but also seeks every opportunity to "throw off the knowledge," and in so doing humankind fails "to fulfill the law of their being."[5] Humanity by its nature attempts to deny knowledge of God either through "ignorance" or "malicious" means. Calvin claims that both result from human pride and vanity that either elevates self or creates God in humanity's own distorted image. Thus, the impression of God in the human heart fails to serve as knowledge adequate for salvation.

Calvin also finds knowledge of God in creation and in God's maintenance of that creation. He is convinced that creation serves "as a kind of mirror" projecting "the invisible" in the "visible." The right study of "astronomy, medicine, and all the natural sciences" makes clear that creation has a creator. Not the least of these "mirrors" of creation is humankind, which serves as a microcosm of all creation.[6]

He believes that God actively maintains the operations of creation through providential intervention in every aspect of the world, including the maintenance of its natural laws. For Calvin, all things hold together in God. Far from a deity who creates and then leaves creation to operate by its own governing rules, God is evident because God continues to be fully and actively engaged in those processes. The next chapter's discussion of providence considers this idea further; for now, the key idea is that God is visible in the natural laws and the sustainment of creation.

Human depravity is central in Calvin's limiting of the salvific possibility of the knowledge of God in the mind or creation. Humanity's sinful nature makes access to salvific knowledge impossible. "(N)o sooner do we, from the survey of the world, obtain some slight knowledge of Deity," Calvin insists, "than we pass by the true God, and set up in his stead the dream and phantom of our own brain, drawing away the praise of justice, wisdom and goodness from the fountain-head, and transferring it to some other quarter." This inability to see God in creation can only be overcome through faith, made possible only through specific knowledge of God, which Calvin calls a "distinct, solid, or certain knowledge." He bypasses the idea of general revelation, making this specific knowledge the only true access to knowledge of God.[7]

For Calvin, specific knowledge rests in Scripture. For this reason, he devotes Book 1, chapters 6 to 10, to discussing his understanding of Scripture and its relationship to God. Calvin makes several distinct claims about Scripture. First, Scripture expands on the general knowledge of God as creator, providing specific revelation of God's relationship to humanity as both creator and redeemer. Also, Scripture expounds on God's true character, understood in relation to Calvin's distinction between the essence and nature of God. In addition, Scripture is written by humans, but they "knew that the things which they learnt came from God, who invariably accompanied his word with sure testimony, infinitely superior to mere opinion."[8] Thus, Scripture bears God's testimony and is the Word of God. Scripture also speaks to creation, announces redemption, and distinguishes the true God from false gods. Calvin affirms that all "right and sound doctrine" must be drawn from Scripture, which bears God's testimony to God's self. He views God as incomprehensible without Scripture as a guide to God's nature, comparing God to a labyrinth and Scripture to a string laid out as a guide through it. In addition, the authority of Scripture rests not in its authorization by the Church but in the Spirit's witness to its authority "through an inward testimony." Scripture's authority and credibility are attested by its inherent unity, rationality, and beauty: "For the truth is indicated in opposition to every doubt, when unsupported by foreign aid, it has its sole sufficiency in itself."[9] Finally, Scripture is superior in every way to notions of contemporary revelation that appeal to the Spirit's inspiration apart from Scripture.

Therefore, Calvin sees Scripture as containing the authoritative revelation (testimony) of God and recognizes its ability to reveal God in God's nature and to attest to this authority through the Holy Spirit's inner testimony in the life of the elect. Calvin's reference to the Holy Spirit's inner testimony answers Roman Catholicism's assault on Protestant views of the individual's ability to interpret Scripture without instruction from the Church. Calvin also makes Scripture the basis of authority for all doctrinal truth.

But Calvin does not cling to an unyielding literalism in understanding and using Scripture. He also ties scriptural revelation more to the acts of Scripture than to set biblical propositions. Calvin lacks the narrow defense of plenary, verbal inspiration that characterizes both Hodge's and Henry's views. Two distinctions may be understood. First, Calvin's precritical view of Scripture means that he had a different relationship to foundational truth than do modern theologians. Therefore, a doctrine of plenary, verbal inspiration may have been either unnecessary or assumed in Calvin's approach to Scripture. Second, perhaps Calvin's emphasis on the unity of the Scripture subsumes any discussion of the specific parts under a general unifying narrative. God works through inspiration to ensure a unified message; that overarching message, not individual parts, is critical to the knowledge of God. The parts are secondary to the whole. Calvin syncretizes individual Scriptures, one to another, to make them consistent with his understanding of redemptive history. Thus, Calvin is less concerned with the literality of any verse and more concerned with the broader unity of the salvation story in the canon.

This analysis explains Calvin's views of revelation and Scripture. But are Calvin's views consistent with his treatment of Romans 13, the household codes, and Luke 4? The short answer is yes. Calvin ignores the literal treatment of the poor in the interest of relating Luke 4:16–30 to a broader redemptive history that includes individuals beyond the poor. He assumes a literal interpretation of Romans 13 and the household codes and relates them to God's desire to maintain order in creation as part of God's overarching providential plan. In both cases, providence and redemption history play decisive roles in the interpretation of individual texts, consistent with Calvin's view of revelation and Scripture.

Edwards

Edwards' lack of a systematic theology makes it harder to fully assess his doctrine of revelation and Scripture. His theology must be pieced together using his theological notes found in his "Miscellanies" and *The Religious Affections*. But both offer enough to enable tentative observations.

Edwards' views of general revelation differ slightly from Calvin's. He engages in greater detail with the workings of the Holy Spirit in granting spiritual knowledge, but he shares Calvin's view of Scripture.

Edwards does not hold to Calvin's strict understanding that general revelation is inaccessible. He concurs that "sin blinds the mind"[10] and that the unregenerate "can see no manner of excellency or beauty in the things of God,"[11] but he states that unregenerate humanity can understand "faintly" good from evil.[12] The latter claim refers to the mechanism whereby humanity is convicted of sin, not a nod to the affective nature of general revelation. Edwards' tone, however, seems more generally disposed to accept natural theology as clearly evident in the minds of the unregenerate. He sees general revelation in nature, even to the point of allegorizing natural objects. Edwards extends his analogy to natural human attributes. He sees general revelation as evident in humanity's inclination toward order, in the human conscience and longing for justice, and in humanity's rational instinct to seek a cause for every effect.[13] While Edwards does see the influence of natural revelation on humanity, he does not view this influence as salvific knowledge that is available absent the Holy Spirit and Scripture.

His understanding of the work of the Spirit in spiritual knowledge is one area where Edwards adds detail to Calvin's understanding of revelation. Edwards sees the practice of holiness, the Spirit's work in conversion, and the enlightenment obtained through the Spirit as paramount for humanity's ability to understand spiritual truth. Thus, the Spirit's work is preliminary to accessing knowledge of God and is central to understanding specific revelation.

Edwards suggests, "'Tis doubtless true that holiness of heart doth from any immediate guidance of the Holy Spirit, keep men from errors in judgement about religion and directs them to truth."[14] He also believes that through "holiness," people "try doctrine" and are led in degrees to long for God. What Edwards means by "holiness of heart" is unclear; this passage serves as a note for a later work and lacks context. But it might suggest that right living leads to a desire for the things of God. This interpretation puts Edwards at odds with Calvin, Hodge, and Henry, as it gives some place to works. At the least, preexistent holiness seems to have a place in Edwards' understanding of conversion, if not directly in his soteriology. But again, this mention appears in a single isolated reference and lacks context, making it difficult to offer anything definitive in this regard except that holiness has some place in Edwards' view of spiritual knowledge and the attainment of spiritual truth.

In both "The Miscellanies" and *The Religious Affections*, he suggests that access to spiritual knowledge results from the Holy Spirit's transforming work that guides the human will toward "religious affections." This argument requires knowing what Edwards means by "affections": "The affections are no other than the more vigorous and sensible exercise of the inclination and will of the soul."[15] Edwards views the soul as mind or heart and, more importantly, as that place where rationality, decision-making, and action abide. For him, it is "the soul only that thinks."[16] Within the soul, the will and inclinations work together to determine both human desire and human action.[17] Thus, the Spirit's work in transforming the soul creates religious affections that alter the will and inclinations of the converted person toward God. God and godly actions become "the practice and business of his life."[18] In this way, Edwards makes inward "conversion" the mark of "true religion" that has a secondary but required relationship to the outward practice of holiness.

In "The Miscellanies" Edwards expands on the spiritual knowledge accessible to those who, through the work of the Spirit, have had their souls transformed and who evidence religious affections. He clarifies:

> We learn that the prime alteration that is made in conversion, that which is first and the foundation of all, is the alteration of the temper and disposition and spirit of the mind: for what is done in conversion is nothing but conferring the Spirit of God, which dwells in the soul and becomes there a principle of life and

action. This is the new nature and the divine nature; and the nature of the soul being thus changed, it admits divine light. Divine things now appear excellent, beautiful, glorious, which did not when the soul was another spirit.[19]

For Edwards this spiritual process alone allows individuals to "distinguish truth from falsehood." Spiritual knowledge allows those who possess it to see the harmony and order of God's revelation in the world, while the mind that is "not spiritually enlightened beholds spiritual things faintly, like fainting, fading shadows."[20] This spiritual knowledge, to Edwards, is not "notional" but experiential. Knowing right doctrine or even imitating religious practice does not provide true spiritual knowledge, which is only available to those who experience the Spirit's work on their affections. Edwards illustrates this point by emphasizing the difference between someone who has read a description of how honey tastes and someone who has actually tasted honey.[21]

Spiritual knowledge is also practical knowledge, "accompanied with the practice of what is known."[22] Edwards distinguishes spiritual from general knowledge. The former focuses on God and makes the converted humble, while the latter, because of its focus on self, makes the unregenerate proud.[23] Spiritual knowledge also opens the mind to reason.

Edwards makes little distinction, then, between spirituality and intellect or, put another way, between mind and soul. The soul is the mind and the seat of the will and inclinations. Therefore, access to truth and real knowledge depends on the Spirit's work in sanctifying the mind.

In his theology of conversion and its consequences, Edwards expands his understanding of the knowledge of God with a view that is more detailed than, but not necessarily discordant with, Calvin's. For Calvin the unregenerate cannot see God, and God can only truly be seen through the Scriptures as specific revelation. Edwards demonstrates the role of the Spirit, through conversion, in giving access to both general and specific revelation.

Edwards' views on Scripture are also evident, though not fully realized, in the "Miscellanies." He suggests that to reveal God's self, God had to use human language and in doing so condescended to humanity's limitations in revealing God's self through the Scriptures.[24] Through the power of the Spirit, God both inspires the writing of Scripture and illumines the readers of Scripture toward God's intended revelation.[25] God has, according to Edwards, infused meaning into the text beyond the plain words: "God had a design and meaning which the penmen never thought of, which he makes appear these ways: by his own interpretation, and by his directing the penman to such a phrase and manner of speaking, that was a much more exact agreement and consonancy with the thing remotely pointed to, than with the thing meant by the penmen."[26] While Edwards preserves God's work in determining the "phrases" and "manner of speech" as intentional and inspired, he emphasizes the broader spiritual meaning.

In this way, Scripture has a unified message that points directly to God, and this divine self-revelation both lends authority to Scripture and gives it harmony, beauty, and unity. Edwards argues that since God is perfect, God's view of God's self is perfection and the basis of all truth. God's revelation of God's self in Scripture must in turn be a perfect revelation. This perfect revelation is demonstrated by way of God's unified work across the canon of Scripture, which shows the work of a unified divine mind.[27] Unity and consistency are found in the Bible's covenantal theology.[28]

Thus, for Edwards, Scripture is both authoritative and inspired while also functioning as God's self-revelation. Edwards also believes that Scripture, when it agrees "with plain reason," does reveal doctrinal truth. But he insists that we know some things about God apart from Scripture, although certainly not in contradiction to it, and that not all doctrinal truth may be made explicit in Scripture.[29]

Perhaps more than Calvin, Hodge, or Henry, Edwards utilizes typology and allegory and draws spiritual insight directly from nature. He is less cautious about natural theology and places more emphasis on the illumining work of the Holy Spirit. But he is also a literalist when interpreting moral and ethical matters from Scripture. His views of revelation and Scripture are characterized by a deeper focus on the work of the Holy Spirit and an expanded account of the development of spiritual knowledge, both general and specific. The rational mind illumined by the Spirit is central to Edwards' thought.

While Edwards writes a great deal about broad unifying themes like covenant, the lack of any treatment of Luke 4 in his work makes it difficult to assess whether he would move beyond the literal toward a more allegorical interpretation. Certainly, his literal interpretations of Romans 13 and the household codes are consistent with his tendency to interpret moral and ethical texts literally. They also evince his focus on common rationality where the literal truth of the text would be affirmed. Thus, one could not say that Edwards is inconsistent.

Hodge

Hodge formulates the specifics of the doctrine of revelation that become typical of many North American fundamentalists and evangelicals up to the current era. He understands theology, in its parts and its totality, to equate with spiritual knowledge.[30] He admits the existence of both general revelation and specific revelation, but like Calvin, he denies any general knowledge of God that leads to salvation. Unlike Calvin, he finds very little use for general revelation, believing that because God cannot contradict God's self, general revelation and Scriptural revelation must agree.[31] He also insists that every truth evinced through nature or religious experience is "recognized and authenticated in Scripture." He recognizes the truth of natural revelation but subjugates, and subsumes, it under Scriptural revelation.[32] For Hodge, "Scriptural theology" is the only means to saving truth.

He both claims an important role for the Spirit and subordinates the Spirit's inward teaching to Scripture. According to Hodge, the Spirit may guide the believer to inward truth. But this truth will always be truth revealed in Scripture and not new truth.[33] Furthermore, this truth must be shown to agree with Scripture. But he does make some concession to the working of the Spirit and "religious experience": "The true method in theology requires that the facts of religious experience should be accepted as facts, and when duly authenticated by Scripture, be allowed to interpret the doctrinal statements of the Word of God."[34] Again, religious experience must be shown to agree with Scriptural teaching.

Hodge also affirms a dual role for the Spirit concerning the Scriptures. The Spirit both inspires the original authors and illumines the contemporary reader. The former ensures the text's authority and the latter ensures that all persons can understand and interpret Scripture without an intermediary.[35] He also draws a sharp distinction not just between inspiration and illumination but between inspiration and revelation. Inspiration, according to Hodge, is the "method of controlling against error," while revelation is "the imparted knowledge."[36] The Spirit is central to both the authority and infallibility of Scripture, but Scripture, itself inspired and authoritative, is the central conveyer of God's revelation. The Spirit plays a supporting role, whereas Scripture is the supreme source of God's revelation.

Three principles summarize Hodge's understanding of the doctrine of Scripture. I quote these in full because his word choices offer important distinctions for subsequent evangelical theology:

> The Scriptures are the Word of God, written under the inspiration of the Holy Spirit, and therefore infallible, and of divine authority in all things pertaining to faith and practice, and consequently free from all error whether of doctrine, fact, or percept. (2) That they contain all the extant supernatural revelations of God designed to be a rule of faith and practice to his church. (3) That they are sufficiently perspicuous to be understood by the people, in the use of ordinary means and by the Holy Spirit, in all things necessary to faith and practice, without the need of any infallible interpreter.[37]

Hodge is affirming the full authority, total inerrancy, and verbal plenary inspiration of Scripture. Each word is inspired and without error, because the words and thoughts of Scripture are "inseparable."[38] His view of Scripture places greater emphasis on the authority of the parts and percepts than is found in either Calvin or Edwards; their concern with the parts served the interest of a unified whole, whereas Hodge's interest lies with the inerrancy of each word, which then ensures right thought and doctrine. From Hodge's modernist perspective, what is critical is defending against secular assaults on various parts of the Christian Scriptures. This focus on the inerrancy of the parts as a defense for the inerrancy of the whole also finds prominence in Henry's theology.

The lack of any full exposition on Luke 4 makes an assessment of Hodge difficult. His literal interpretations of Romans 13 and the household codes seem consistent in light of the first of his principles of biblical interpretation: "the words of Scripture are to be taken in their plain historical sense" and "must be taken in the sense attached to them in the age and by the people to whom they were addressed."[39] But this same principle, if Hodge had considered Luke 4, would require him to justify understanding "the poor" as a metaphor for believers universally. The tighter the focus on inerrancy in the interpreter, the higher the burden of proof to move beyond the literal meaning. All that can be said is that Hodge is consistent in his interpretations of Romans 13 and the household codes. Speculation on his avoidance of Luke 4 would constitute an inconclusive argument from silence.

Henry

Henry builds upon Hodge's fundamentalist understanding of revelation. In his monumental six-volume work, *God, Revelation, and Authority*, Henry outlines fifteen theses related to divine revelation that encompass volumes 2 through 4, more than half of Henry's total work. For this chapter, I consider theses 4 and 10–12. (Thesis 8 on Christ as revelation and thesis 14 on the Church as approximating God's revelation in the world are taken up later in conversation with Cone.)

Henry's fourth thesis posits the unity of divine revelation while affirming both general and specific revelation and allowing for revelation in the person of Christ and God's future disclosure in eschatological completion. Henry bases the unity of God's revelation in God's monotheism. As a single unity, God cannot contradict God's self.[40] Henry also distinguishes between the unified content of revelation and its various forms. All forms or means of revelation are "interdependent," as is the progressive nature of revelation in Scripture, which according to Henry "is in no way destructive of unity." Henry sees the unified content of Scripture as focused on "the electing God and his covenant people." Henry also sees this focus as "central to the whole Bible."[41]

Thesis 10 concerns the nature of revelation as "rational-verbal communication."[42] Specifically, he demonstrates the propositional nature of divine revelation and asserts that the specific truth claim of divine revelation connects directly to the words of revelation. He sees "a proposition as a verbal statement that is either true or false: it is a rational declaration capable of being either believed, doubted or denied."[43] In affirming propositionalism, Henry is fighting the tendency of higher criticism, neo-orthodoxy, and modernist liberalism to view revelation as attached more to an idea or concept that exists beyond the truth claims of the text.[44] Henry wants to establish, contra Pannenberg and others, that God literally speaks, that in speaking God necessarily speaks intelligibly, and that as the author of truth, God necessarily speaks truthfully.[45]

Henry also affirms that God's revelation contains one meaning, referring back to the unity of God's revelation, and not multiple meanings: "If the Word of divine revelation carries an infinite variety of meanings, then none can be normative, and no meaningful hermeneutic is possible."[46] Divine language has a single meaning and is without error. Even though Henry concurs with Calvin's understanding of God's condescension to the limits of human language, he emphasizes that God does not thereby accommodate the divine revelation to untruth. Bringing into conversation his understanding of propositional truth and revelational unity, Henry insists, "Revelation in the Biblical understanding involves not isolated concepts or words but units of thought."[47] He also recalls that not all forms of revelation are propositional. A good example, per Henry, is a command, which makes no truth claim but leans on the authority of the one making it.

Henry's back-and-forth between the unity of the whole and the truthfulness of the parts mitigate against the tendency to emphasize the parts over the whole. For Henry, a single propositional truth is evident in the parts of Scripture and the totality of divine revelation. But Henry's understanding of truth is, like Hodge's, based primarily and necessarily on the plain, intelligible truth claims of the actual word-laden propositions of the biblical text.

The biblical text is central to Henry's understanding of divine revelation. So, understanding how he views the text is also critical to understanding Henry's theology. His understanding forms the bulk of thesis 11, "the Bible as the authoritative norm," and thesis 12, "the Spirit as communicator and interpreter." In these sections he affirms Scripture as authoritative, inspired, illuminated, and inerrant. Henry also insists on the literal interpretation of Scripture and makes room for the fallibility of the exegete.

Henry affirms that "Scripture is authoritative, because divinely inspired, and as such is divine truth."[48] By inspiring the biblical authors, God presents God's revelation, so the teachings of Scripture bear the weight of God's authority. But Henry clarifies that God is the authority and that Scripture's authority is "derivative and contingent."[49] He concedes that Scripture's authoritative teaching is limited, because the authors do not deal with every category of knowledge and because the knowledge they do address, albeit without error, may not be complete. But ultimately Henry insists on the total authority of Scripture.

He also affirms the role of the Holy Spirit in inspiring and illuminating Scripture. No statement or word in Scripture was not intentional; all function as inspired and authoritative. In agreement with Hodge, Henry holds to the "plenary inspiration of the Scripture" and insists that "inspiration extends to the writings in their totality, in the whole and the parts."[50] The caveat is Henry's affirmation that revelation is "not to be sought in isolated words but rather in truths."[51]

The Holy Spirit also illuminates the believer, leading to a proper understanding of Scripture. Henry shares this idea with Calvin, Edwards, and Hodge. But he also clarified, contra Barth, that the Scriptures hold meaning and truth apart from the faith community. Truth, embedded in the text through divine inspiration, precedes and is independent of illumination. This point distinguishes Henry's view from Barth's assertion that the Bible has meaning only within the context of faith.[52]

Like Hodge, Henry is a biblical inerrantist. He quotes affirmatively the Chicago Statement on Biblical Inerrancy.[53] He leaves the statement without comment, barring one mention of the article that limits inerrancy to the original autographs. This clarification of the Chicago statement has little practical effect on Henry's views of Scripture because he believes in its comprehensiveness and infallibility even in the received text.

The Scriptures are not only authoritative, inspired, illuminated, and inerrant; they also are to be interpreted literally. Henry insists, "The evangelical rule has been to opt for the literal sense of the Bible where the language does not preclude it."[54] By "literal" Henry appeals to Ramm's definition that a literal interpretation is "the basic, customary social designation of the word" and concurs with Barr that it "is the historical sense of the text."[55] He wants to eliminate, in opposition to Bultmannian mythologizing, any attempt to find "cryptic" meaning outside the text's literal sense.

Henry is the only evangelical theologian considered here to emphasize the "fallibility of the exegete," devoting an entire chapter to it in his discussion of thesis 12. While God cannot err, and Scripture does not err, the exegete can fail to properly interpret Scripture. The individual interpreter and interpretation bear truth only to the degree that they properly transmit the truth God intended.

Therefore, Henry envisions revelation and Scripture in much the same way Hodge does. He affirms various forms or means of revelation but insists on its unity and the primacy of scriptural revelation. He advocates for the authority, plenary inspiration, illumination, inerrancy, and literality of Scripture while maintaining the potential fallibility of the interpreter. He further insists on the truthfulness of both the parts and the totality of the Bible and maintains its unified, singular theological voice and single possible meaning. Finally, Henry affirms the intentionality of the words of Scripture but insists that truth is found in the larger logical units.

Henry's treatment of Romans 13 is consistent with his understanding of the plain meaning and literal interpretation of the biblical text. Henry would also see his treatment of the household codes as consistent with these principles. Henry does address contemporary concerns for gender equality and downplays the text's explicit hierarchy by asserting an early form of complementarianism.

His reading of Luke 4 is complex. He seems to affirm a literal reading while focusing on a metaphorical or spiritual interpretation. Nowhere is this tension more apparent than in Henry's engagement with Yoder regarding the prominence of the Jubilee motif in the Gospels, particularly Luke 4. Henry denies that such an ethic exists, insisting that "in view of the silence about the Jubilee theme in the teaching of the evangelists, it hardly seems it held such a central place in Jesus' message."[56] He points to those places in the New Testament where aphesis clearly means forgiveness, and he suggests that "even where it means liberation (Luke 4:18 quoting Isa. 61 and 56:1)" it has in mind the forgiveness of sin. But Henry seems uneasy with this assessment. Just one paragraph below this argument he affirms Yoder's instincts that Jesus' message has "sociopolitical" implications.[57]

Henry's attempts to hold on to the literality of Luke 4 are consistent with his understanding of literal interpretation, but he gravitates toward a broader redemption-historical reading of the text. Henry believes that Jesus in Luke is engaging in "liberation" that is both "a reality and a sign," but it is a sign and symbol as opposed to any real politically liberative act. Henry also references Christ's victory over oppression but ties oppression closely to moral failings and the bondage of sin.

Henry's reluctance to fully embrace a literal reading seems to stem from his apologetic against Marxism, revolution theology, and liberation theology. He argues that these "ideologies" abandon the supernatural to pursue a social solution to a spiritual problem (sin) with social symptoms (oppression).

Not wishing to run afoul of his own criticism, Henry tends toward a more spiritual explanation of Luke 4 while not completely disallowing a literal, plain meaning of the text. Thus, Henry deals consistently with the text concerning his principle of the unity of the canon, but he appears less consistent in applying his understanding of literality.

CONSTRUCTIVE ENGAGEMENT WITH CONE

Having illuminated the views of Calvin, Edwards, Hodge, and Henry regarding revelation and Scripture, I can now place their views in conversation with one another and with Cone toward constructive conclusions related to revelation. Cone's views will be critiqued alongside those of the evangelical tradition. The critique focuses not on Black theology as an alternative system, but on the degree to which it can be integrated into evangelicalism to produce a subsequent theology that can be called evangelical. I do not ask whether Black theology or evangelical theology is superior. Instead, I propose to determine how Black theology, specifically Cone's, might shape evangelical theology on questions of power.

Any assessment, therefore, that Cone's views are so diametrically opposed to evangelicalism as to be unhelpful is not a judgment that evangelicalism is correct and Cone is incorrect. It is instead a judgment on the core identity of evangelical theology. My intention here is not to revisit long-standing differences between liberal/neoliberal and conservative theology but rather to ask what one can use from Cone's theology that challenges errors or absences in evangelical theology. With all this in mind, the discussion now places Cone in conversation with Calvin, Edwards, Hodge, and Henry.

The Challenges of Examining Cone

Cone's view(s) on revelation and Scripture are difficult to articulate because, by his own admission, they changed throughout his career. He addresses these issues directly in *A Black Theology of Liberation* and *God of the Oppressed*. As explained in part I, these books, along with *Black Theology and Black Power*, featured Cone's earliest attempts to define a separatist Black theology while speaking directly to the White Church and White liberal theologians about the racist nature of White theology and culture. Cone is attempting to remain faithful to the importance of the biblical narrative in the Black Church while addressing liberal and neoliberal biblical criticism. He does not intend to address conservative biblical scholarship at all. At times Cone, as demonstrated below, speaks at cross purposes when he attempts to build a case for liberation in Scripture while conceding points about its historical accuracy to accommodate more liberal exegetical expectations.

Another problem arises when attempting to understand Cone on revelation and Scripture. In the prefaces to the rereleased editions of *A Black Theology of Liberation* and *God of the Oppressed*, Cone challenges his own views on revelation and Scripture. In the new preface to the 1986 release of *A Black Liberation Theology*, Cone questions his use of a theological schema that depended on Western doctrinal categories and began with an a priori understanding of revelation as theology's natural starting point. By 1986, he assessed that "there is no 'abstract' revelation, independent of human experience, to which theologians can appeal for evidence of what they say about the gospel. God meets us in the human situation, not as an idea or concept that is self-evidently true."[58]

Likewise, in Cone's 1997 preface to the rereleased *God of the Oppressed*, he criticizes his own use and understanding of Scripture. He is responding to the ongoing criticism of feminist and womanist theologians and their insistence on the difficulties posed by the Bible, particularly the "texts of terror," which these scholars believed was ignored by Cone's liberation theology in its appeal to Scripture. Cone insists that he had "never believed that the Bible is above criticism or that it serves as an absolute judge in faith and practice."[59]

Cone adapts his theology of revelation and Scripture to the times. His original views of Scripture move between the Black Church tradition and the biblical criticism of the liberal theological tradition. By the late 1980s, he adapted his view of revelation to accommodate other emerging Black theologians who have attacked his work for adopting White theological categories. In the 1990s, Cone affirms the further distrust of Scripture that emerges from feminist and specifically womanist critiques of the biblical narrative. But even when affirming these changes in his own views, Cone leaves unchanged his original arguments and does not produce later work that contradicts them.

When engaging constructively with Cone on these issues, the theologian is left with a dilemma. Does one access and apply Cone's views according to the later prefaces or according to his original works? For the current project, the latter choice appears logical, primarily because the opinions in Cone's prefaces are unsupported by clear application to his own theology and are left unrealized in his theological agenda. Additionally, even if one could imagine some speculative means of extending these views to Cone's work, his later views are so diametrically opposed to the evangelical tradition that they eliminate any hope of engagement with Cone consistent with evangelical identity. His original views, as will be seen below, at least present a limited intersection that keeps open a degree of conversation between Cone and evangelicalism. Given the constructive, as opposed to historical-theological, nature of this fourth part and movement, Cone's original work appears best suited to advance the current project.

Cone in Dialogue with Evangelical Theology

What then can be said about Cone's understanding of revelation and Scripture as evident in his original work? And how does this understanding inform, rebuke, or enlighten evangelical theology? These questions are addressed simultaneously.

Like each of the four White theologians, Cone recognizes the traditional division between general and specific revelation, although Cone approaches these divisions differently. General revelation, according to Cone, is bifurcated. General revelation "is primarily applicable to oppressed peoples," while the sin that impairs access to the divine through general revelation is "especially applicable to oppressors."[60] Cone holds in dialectic tension, first, the view shared by Calvin, Hodge, and Henry that sin distorts humanity's understanding of general revelation and, second, a desire to make liberation, freedom, and justice aspects of general revelation understood by the oppressed. Cone does so in direct opposition to the views of Barth and Brunner. He disallows Barth's total rejection of natural theology and affirms Brunner's imposition of sin on general revelation only in relation to oppressors while adding his own assessment of the accessibility of general revelation to the oppressed.[61]

Given that Brunner, as presented by Cone, primarily affirms the basic understanding of Calvin, Cone's bifurcated approach could seem wholly antithetical to evangelical theology—were it not for Edwards' direct engagement with the idea that justice and injustice are inherently embedded and understood within the human soul by way of a "memory of divinity." If Edwards' work is applied to the oppressed, then what Cone describes as the natural instinct to freedom in the oppressed coalesces with what Edwards understands as the natural human offense at injustice, making the pursuit of justice a sign of divinity imprinted on the human soul. That is not to say that Edwards would take this to the extreme that Cone does. Cone also comes close to affirming a possible salvation for the poor by means of general revelation for the oppressed.

The critical issue of bifurcation needs to be addressed. Is it fair to say that the oppressed have access to knowledge that is denied to the oppressor? One might consider the imprinted nature of justice on humanity as obscured by the specific sin of oppression in the oppressor, while the oppressed, unburdened by this particular sin, have access to the general revelation of freedom, justice, and liberty.

What then of the sin of the oppressed? If Cone's assessment of Brunner is taken seriously, sin is a universal state. But Cone does not believe that the oppressed are exempt from sin, although he plays loosely with the concept. He does limit the discussion of what constitutes Black sin to the Black community, but he does provide his own definition of Black sin: "The sin of the oppressed . . . is that of trying to 'understand' enslavers, to 'love' them on their terms. As the oppressed now recognize their situation in the light of God's revelation, they know they should have killed their oppressor instead of trying to 'love them.'"[62] Beyond the rhetorical aspects of this definition of sin in the oppressed, one finds the idea that although the oppressed clearly see freedom inherent in general revelation, they are unable to bring about justice and freedom. This inability or unwillingness constitutes the sin of the oppressed.

Perhaps one finds room for Edwards' understanding of a general knowledge of injustice while affirming that this knowledge is missing in the oppressor because of the specific nature of the sin of oppression. But Cone's bifurcation of sin comes too close to making the oppressed immune from total depravity and weakening the entire doctrine of original sin so that it is not useful for evangelical theology. What is useful for evangelical theology in Cone's understanding, apart from any discussion of sin, is the idea that justice and freedom are elements of general revelation—whether one agrees with Edwards and Cone that they are generally understood, or with Calvin, Hodge, and Henry that they cannot be understood by anyone other than the elect. Freedom, justice, and liberty can still be seen as inherent in God's revelation.

But what about Cone's understanding of specific revelation? He sees specific revelation as resting in the historical Jesus: "There has been a self-revelation of God in biblical history and decisively in Jesus Christ. . . . God has been fully revealed in the man Jesus so that the norm of all existence is determined exclusively in him. He is the revelation of God."[63] Cone also goes as far as affirming Christ as the truth. "Jesus Christ," he believes, "is the Truth and thus stands in judgement over all statements of truth." For Cone, this truth is different from the truth found in either Scripture or even the Black Church tradition. While both possess truth, Jesus is Truth.[64] While Scripture and the Black Church tradition serve as sources pointing to revelation, Jesus is revelation.

But who Cone's Jesus is remains unclear. Even in his preface to *The God of the Oppressed*, Cone affirms Christ as the "starting point" of his understanding of God. However, he also clarifies that this Jesus is not the Jesus of Western theology, nor even the Jesus of "Nicaea and Chalcedon." Cone's Jesus is the Jesus of "Matthew, Mark, Luke, and John"—Jesus as he has been understood within the Black Church and cultural tradition.[65] Cone denies much of Scripture's historical witness to Christ. He is skeptical about the virgin birth and allegorizes the miracles. He downplays the specific witness of Christ's life found in Scripture. "We cannot use Jesus' behavior in the first century," he says, "as a literal guide for our actions in the twentieth century. To do so is to fall into the same trap that fundamentalists fall into. It destroys . . . the freedom to make decisions patterned on, but not dictated by, the example of Jesus."[66]

Cone insists that revelation rests in the historical Jesus—the one to whom the Scriptures point but err in describing—and that human interpreters make their best determination about which parts of the biblical witness apply to a description of Jesus. Besides the obvious problem of having no clear means of determining what part of the witness to keep and what to reject—the failed search for the historical Jesus being the prime example—Cone also provides no clear methodology to construct his own understanding of Christ.

The other problem is that his liberationist interpretations of Christ depend on a literal, historical interpretation of Scripture. Cone's assertions that Jesus was born poor, that his crucifixion was a political lynching, and that Christ's ministry focused on the poor all require an actual historical account of Christ found in the Gospels. But by questioning parts of the Christ narrative, Cone diminishes and questions the whole historicity of those same narratives and weakens his argument. His argument that the parts of Scripture that affirm Christ's solidarity with the poor and his liberating mission are the true, authentic witness to Christ derives from a circular argument in which liberation is a predetermined conclusion. Despite his protest that a literal, inerrant understanding of the Christ narratives is problematic, his affirmation of the truth of the liberationist texts would be strengthened by just such a view.

Evangelical theology does not deny God's revelation in the person of Jesus. Henry's thesis 8 in *God, Revelation and Authority* makes clear that "the climax of God's special revelation is Jesus of Nazareth, the personal incarnation of God in the flesh; in Jesus Christ the source and content of revelation converge and coincide."[67] Henry insists that the Christ of Scripture is a historical figure, truthfully portrayed and only knowable in his particularity in Scripture itself, which does not err in what it says about Jesus. Henry also affirms that Jesus does not just reveal God: as God, he is revelation.[68]

Henry's attack on Brunner also illustrates difficulties with Cone's position. Henry criticizes Brunner for dialectically opposing faith and history in favor of the faith that he and other neo-orthodox scholars "overtly or covertly subscribe[s] to the faith and mysticism or idealism with its downgrading of Christianity to 'religion in general.'"[69] Cone can be said to also engage in this dialectical use of faith and history. But Cone spends less time correlating the two and more time utilizing what best fits whatever argument he is currently making. The historical political situation of Christ's crucifixion becomes the basis of liberation theology, whereas the Black Church experience is allowed to redefine original sin apart from the narratives of Scripture as an appeal to faith. The crucifixion texts are treated historically; the creation texts are discounted as myth, valuable only in terms of the faith community's use of the texts, not as historically accurate events. Cone does at least make room for grounding some portion of theology in historical events, but he does not sustain this view of the historicity of the biblical account across the canon.

The obvious problem in Cone's denial of some portions of the biblical narrative might be reason enough for evangelicalism to move past his theological conclusions. But to do so would ignore the challenge that his insistence on the theological significance of Jesus' historical context offers evangelicalism, if it insists on moving quickly past the sociopolitical context of Jesus' incarnational particularity and toward the soteriological mission of Christ. Evangelical theologians cannot ignore the significance and even priority of the latter, but the former also requires consideration, particularly given Henry's and Hodge's insistence on the plain, literal reading of the text in relation to the historical context of the original audience. The intentionality of the incarnation—including where Jesus was born, to whom, and the sociopolitical context that he was caught up in—offers critical considerations in any Christology, even if they do not form the totality of that Christology, as Cone prefers. Cone's critique can be taken seriously for that portion of his argument that is significant to evangelicalism.

Henry seems almost forced to admit this point in his analysis of the revelation of Christ in thesis 8. Taking seriously the biblical witness, he characterizes Christ as "taking up in himself the cause of the oppressed and aggrieved" and applying "to himself the Isaiah prophecy of liberation by the messianic liberator," so that, as stated above, this "liberation is becoming a reality in fact and sign."[70] Henry does not stop by describing Christ as the liberator; he also ascribes ethical consequences to this characterization. He believes that Jesus "is even now active in the rise and fall of nations" and that "Christians bear a special duty in relation to civil government as a divinely purposed instrument for justice in fallen society." In fact, Henry exclaims, "it is an intrinsic aspect of Christian obedience." Further, "Christ anticipatively overcomes not only the sin and death but also the injustice and incoherence that deluge the fallen life of man."[71]

But as has been demonstrated, Henry couches his acquiescence to liberation in language favoring its more metaphorical or symbolic use. He contends that Jesus challenges the political understanding of the liberator in favor of a broader definition. He also transforms the recipients of Christ's liberative work from the literal poor and oppressed into those suffering from "moral poverty and spiritual death." Henry does not deny Christ a liberative work but creates a back-and-forth between social and spiritual implications, creating a tone that elevates the latter over the former.

Neither Henry nor Cone presents a fully satisfactory view of Christ the liberator. Cone's arguments read, despite limited equivocation, as "either/or" arguments: Christ is either the temporal liberator of the literal oppressed or God is nothing at all. Henry's arguments, on the other hand, read as "yes, but" arguments: social implications arise from Christ the liberator, but always in the background of the spiritual implications, which are universal and do not consider social situations. For evangelicals, the primacy of the spiritual or, as Henry would say the supernatural, must always be in view. But one might also argue that God's revelation in Jesus is a "both, and." That is, when evangelical theology considers the historical manifestation of Christ in his birth, ministry, death, and resurrection, it should consider both the literal, sociopolitical, historical events and the spiritual significance as cohering realities in God's revelation in Christ. Of course, this approach does not change any of Henry's conclusions; it simply changes the tone. To deal with the coherence between the sociopolitical realities and the spiritual is to recognize the role of the supernatural in the temporal and to provide ethical significance for the Christ event beyond the eternal destiny of souls. Scriptural interpretation would in this way see the supernatural in the natural and temporal consequences of spiritual reality.

While Cone affirms Christ as the revelation of God, he also sees the Black experience and Scripture as sources of God's revelation. Understanding Cone's view of revelation in the Black experience is a necessary first step to understanding his views on Scripture. One must therefore consider his views on the nature of Black experience, God's acts, history, and truth.

A good starting point is Cone's 1986 preface to *A Black Theology of Liberation*. For Cone, "there is no 'abstract' revelation, independent of human experiences, to which theologians can appeal for evidence of what they say about the gospel"; he insists that "God meets us in the human condition."[72] Because human perceptions of God are caught up in human culture and history, God's revelation is intimately interdependent on the human experience for intelligibility. Humanity cannot perceive of God beyond the limitations of human experience. For Cone, experience must be distinguished from inwardness and instead connected to transcendence. The former is seen in relation to a Schleiermacherian inwardness, where God can be understood only through direct, individual, inward encounter with the divine. Cone does not see the Black experience as an individual experience of encounter with God; he affirms instead the community's encounter with God, a transcendent encounter across time in which God is made known in the community's worship and life. The importance of the communal experience cannot be overemphasized when considering Cone's understanding of the Black experience. Experience is an actual transcendent encounter with God, conveyed and understood by the community as it has existed across time and place, to form a coherent understanding of God's revelation for the experiencing, encountering community.

How does Cone defend this activity as a necessary source of God's revelation? Cone grounds his main argument in a hermeneutics relating the Black Church experience to the sociology of knowledge and his understanding of the axiological distance of the Black community and the biblical witness—the latter of which is central to Cone's understanding of truth in theological discourse.[73] For Cone, revelation is not possible apart from human language and human experience. But, as emphasized above, Cone is careful to make this not about individuals' language and experience, but rather about communal revelation verified by the community.[74] Humanity's "finite existence" means that humanity is incapable of "postulat(ing)" absolute value judgments. Thus, the best that can be achieved is a process whereby the community of faith determines the validity of revelation within the context of faith: "Revelation, then, is the epistemological justification of the claims of a community about ontological reality."[75] Thus, Cone brackets truth within the particular context and experience of each unique community, asserting that Black truth and Black understanding of God are distinct because they arise out of the particularity of the Black experience: "There is no truth for or about Black people that does not emerge out of the context of their experience."[76]

This line of reasoning seems contradictory to Cone's assertion that the Black community has the truth of God and that the White community represents a wrong or heretical perspective on God. How can truth be specific to the community's understanding of it without succumbing to a relativism that makes it impossible to prioritize Black truth over White truth?

Cone attempts to resolve this difficulty by claiming that the oppressed community's truth is closer to God's true revelation because the oppressed community is axiologically closer to that truth than the oppressor. First, Cone asserts that revelation itself is intended for the oppressed, and thus only the oppressed can rightly understand it.[77] Second, he makes a distinction between ideology and subjective interpretation, on the one hand, and revelation and truth, on the other. Ideology is an interpretation that distorts the truth toward the interpreter's political and economic self-interest. Cone equates this truth with the theology of oppressors who do not affirm the entirety of the biblical witness to liberation, especially those who deny the importance of Exodus and covenant as "God's liberating deeds in history."[78] Cone's views, consistent with the views of the oppressed Black community, are socially determined but not ideological.

To prove his point, Cone uses definitions inherent in the sociology of knowledge, which does not view a social a priori as any impediment to truth. Social determinism simply assumes that communities use a particular axiological grid to filter and formulate thought. The starting point is value-neutral. Thought becomes ideological when distorted by self-interest. Thus, the closer a community's axiological grid comes to the truth of revelation, the freer it becomes from distortion. For Cone, the oppressed community is axiologically closer than the oppressor to God's revelation. While Black reflection on God's revelation is not exempt from error, its relationship to truth is closer than oppressors can be. Cone can, therefore, speak of Black truth and White heresy in a way normally prevented by appeals to relativity.

As already demonstrated, Cone affirms neo-orthodox and liberal theology's move away from the propositional nature of revelation, following Barth, Brunner, and Tillich in placing revelation in the person and event of Jesus Christ as God's manifestation in human history. Cone says, "Black theology agrees with contemporary theology," and elaborates further "that God's self-disclosure is the distinctive characteristic of divine revelation which is not the rational discovery of God's attributes, or the assent to infallible biblical propositions, or an aspect of human self-consciousness. Rather, revelation has to do with God, as God is in personal relationship with humankind effecting the divine will in history."[79]

This argument is important for understanding Cone's views of revelation and his use of Scripture. Words about God, or even spoken by God, do not form the revelational content of Scripture; rather, the revelational content consists of the actions of God in the Exodus, the covenant, concern for the oppressed, and Christ's incarnational solidarity with the poor, in both his ministry and his political death. The Bible is a revelation of God in that it records God's actions in history. The God who acted in history, according to Cone, is still acting and revealing God's self in the historical and contemporary experiences of the Black community.

These twin ideas—the revelation of God in his historical encounters with humanity, as recorded in Scripture, and God's ongoing participation in history in solidarity with the Black community—allow Cone to link the biblical witness to the Black community's experience. The God who revealed God's self to the slaves in Egypt as liberator is the God who reveals God's self to the Black community as liberator.

Black Experience as Divine Revelation

Most evangelical theology would not entirely eliminate experience from theological reflection, but evangelical theologians seem likely to reject Cone's emphasis on Black experience in revelation. This does not mean, however, that Cone, in defending his point, raises no important questions to be considered by evangelicals. This section elaborates upon five such questions: whether thought about God begins by reflecting on God or humanity, the importance of transcendence in connecting experience to biblical revelation, the definition of truth, the importance of axiological distance, and God's acts as opposed to God's speech as revelation.

God in God's Self or in History?

Does reflection on God's revelation begin with reference to God in God's self, or instead with reference to God as God has shown God's self in human history? Cone affirms the latter. God is only visible through God's interaction with humanity and only relatable in culturally governed human language. Because humanity cannot escape its finite condition, its understanding of God is bound within itself. Abstractions about God qua God's own self are impossible. Humanity can only see God in relation to how God has interacted with humanity in history.

Henry, as demonstrated, would disavow any idea that God cannot be known as God in God's self. God's existence is not defined in any way by human (mis)perceptions. Further, God is knowable in God's self through Scripture's propositional truths and statements about God. Henry recognizes the limitations of human speech but believes God was not limited in expressing all of God's self that God wished to convey in human language.

However, even if Calvin would concur with Henry about the knowability of God (given that Cone's understanding of cultural determinism would be alien to him), Calvin affirms the interconnection and difficulty in knowing whether theology begins with God or humanity. Calvin begins with God, of course, believing that humanity cannot know itself apart from seeing itself in relation to God. His views do not, however, amount to a discussion of revelation as necessarily determined by the human condition; they are primarily a determination of theological schema. Therefore, Calvin's discussion is unhelpful in resolving the differences between Henry and Cone in either direction. Ultimately the difference cannot be decided without considering the debate over truth and axiological difference.

Transcendence

Cone's poorly developed understanding of transcendent encounter must be considered with Edwards' fuller development in his *Religious Affections* and "Miscellanies." Cone makes room for transcendent encounter as a check on, and connection between, the Black community's experience and biblical revelation. But his brief reference is so poorly developed that it offers only limited value in advancing his argument. Cone articulates no clear understanding of how the work of the Spirit reveals God through the transcendent encounters of the Black community. Cone's entire theology lacks a developed pneumatology and avoids any mention of illumination. One might explain these omissions as part of Cone's insistence on avoiding abstract Western doctrinal categories. But Cone does use these categories in *A Black Theology of Liberation*, and the Holy Spirit is conspicuously absent from the list of doctrines he treats. Cone also makes no distinction between illumination and revelation. Illumination is simply not a category Cone uses. Contemporary encounters that evangelical theology would characterize as the illumination of the Holy Spirit are characterized by Cone instead as God's revelation within the experience and encounter of the Black community. Thus, illumination must carry the full weight of the revelation of God: of equal importance, particularly in Cone's latter thought, with God's revelation in Scripture.

This approach is problematic for evangelical theology on two levels. First, evangelical theology insists on a sharp distinction between revelation and illumination and makes illumination subservient to God's revelation in Scripture. Second, an appeal to transcendence without some clear pneumatological scheme is inadequate. How the Spirit brings meaning and encounter in the context of human experience is necessary for understanding how God continues to work in contemporary contexts. For Cone's understanding of God's revelation in the Black experience to have any resonance within evangelical theology, it needs to articulate a clearer view of the Spirit's work, similar to Edwards' work on the religious affections, and Cone needs to concede the distinction between illumination and revelation absent in his work.

The comparison with Edwards is instructive at another level. In a more detailed way than Calvin, Hodge, and Henry, Edwards demonstrates the necessary work of the Spirit in sanctifying the minds of the elect. Although Edwards takes a higher view of natural theology, he concurs that divine knowledge is possible only through the Spirit's illuminating power. Not only does Cone not develop this idea in relation to the Spirit, but he limits the interpretation of God's revelation to the community in total, and his concept of Black community includes the Black community beyond the Black Church. Given this study's understanding, expressed early on, that one of the two central tenets of evangelicalism is the necessity of the "born again" experience, evident in the pietistic arm of the movement, Cone's belief that God's revelation is evident in the fullness of the Black experience—apart from any requirement of faith or conversion—is antithetical to evangelical theology. But such conclusions also require an examination of Cone's understanding of axiological difference.

The Definition of Truth

Cone draws on modern understandings of the sociology of knowledge and literary hermeneutics to claim that all human understanding and, therefore, the articulation of truth claims are culturally bound. To suggest Cone recognizes no absolute truth would misread him. He does believe that finite humanity cannot access truth and that truth will always be filtered through human culture, which makes human understanding of truth derivative; but Cone does see truth as resting in the person of God in Jesus Christ. Therefore, humanity's understanding of truth, while flawed, could either come to resemble actual truth or might totally distort it. This approach allows Cone to speak of Black truth and White heresy while maintaining cultural boundedness.

Henry, recognizing the limitations of human speech and the fallibility of the contemporary interpreter, does not give as much power to the cultural boundedness of the human understanding of divine revelation. For Henry, absolute truth exists beyond human thought or language; it rests in God's self and is accessible through divine revelation. God has communicated truth through biblical revelation in such a way as to be intelligible to humanity through the illumination of the Holy Spirit. By inspiring the original authors toward writing that presents God in ways sufficient for human understanding, and by guiding the believer to understand the text, the Holy Spirit makes truth fully accessible to the believer. While Henry does not deny contemporary hermeneutical challenges in the interpretation of the text, he downplays these issues in his final analysis. Through the Spirit, humanity has access to the truth of God. This truth is a single unchanging truth and therefore is universal and has no distinct or different cultural manifestations.

So, for Henry, any statement of truth is universal, and the process to recover truth is superintended by the Spirit's guidance so that truth is fully knowable without distortion. Of course, the distinction between Cone and Henry lies in focus. Cone focuses on human fallibility, while Henry insists on God's supernatural work through the Holy Spirit. Also, Cone's work takes more seriously the cultural claims of modern hermeneutics, whereas Henry diminishes these claims.

What must be emphasized is that Cone's approach places so little focus on the work of God as to almost deny or certainly diminish revelation as God's self-disclosure. While Cone's definition of revelation recognizes self-disclosure as central, his actual work does not emphasize this self-disclosure as comprehensible outside human experience. For Cone, God has spoken, and humanity is left to its ability to understand this revelation. Henry, on the other hand, has so articulated his understanding of the movement of God in human understanding as to make truth and its attainment an abstract process operating outside of human intellection. Henry fails to adequately account for the varying and sometimes contradictory interpretations of God's revelation and Scripture, even among believers. Where does Henry's understanding of revelation recognize that the believer can be guided more by self-interest than by the Spirit of God, notwithstanding the degree to which he both affirms and downplays the human interpreter's fallibility? While Cone, as shown below, rests an understanding of revelation upon communal subjectivity, Henry grounds his understanding of revelation in the text of Scripture. Cone therefore lacks a firm authoritative grounding, whereas Henry, despite his supernatural "guardrail," subjects revelation to the strictures of literary hermeneutics. But Henry offers no clearly articulated hermeneutical theory that supports his text-laden understanding of truth, apart from his theology of inspiration and illumination.

To be useful for evangelical theology, Cone needs an expanded understanding of the divine role in moving from divine self-disclosure to the human articulation of truth. At the same time, Henry needs to offer a clearer understanding of the hermeneutical issues between the Spirit's guidance and the human tendency, even in believers, to interpret texts in light of culturally grounded self-interest.

Axiological Difference

Cone's discussion of axiological difference is critical in this regard and can now be considered in light of his understanding of truth, transcendence, and human finitude. Cone's claim, about the truth of God revealed in the Black experience, is that although the Black community is finite and prone to error, it is axiologically closer to the truth of God's revelation than are the dominant White oppressors. Cone is of course referencing Gadamer's understanding of the interpretive horizon between the reader and the original author.[80] Gadamer's work focuses on a Western philosophical tradition that emphasizes the distance in time, in the interest of distinguishing between the horizons of the biblical author and the contemporary interpreter. In this way, Gadamer suggests that historical and chronological distances make the biggest difference in understanding the text—not cultural distinctions, which are absent in Gadamer.

What this approach does not address is exactly what Cone insists on—the differences among the cultural, ethnic, and class horizons of various contemporary interpreters. While all contemporary readers stand at the same chronological distance from the biblical text, sometimes the class, political, or cultural experience of the contemporary interpreter may be closer to that of the biblical author than other contemporary interpreters. If so, the better-positioned contemporary reader and their interpretation would be positioned closer to the truth of the text than are those who are at a greater socioeconomic distance.

This distinction is critical, and it grounds Cone's primary assertion that the Black community possesses a truth closer to the biblical horizon than Whites possess, who by and large read the text from their own position of power and in ways that reflect their own self-interest. Cone particularly argues this about White scholars who have historically emphasized literal interpretations of texts that advanced the oppression of the Black community while deemphasizing the literalness of texts that favored liberation of the oppressed—an approach found, for example, in the theology of Hodge outlined above.

What Cone's work highlights for White evangelicalism is a gap in its hermeneutical self-assessment. He emphasizes the degree to which not only chronological differences but also power, privilege, cultural, and political distances from the text may affect the ability of White evangelical theology to bridge its own horizon and the biblical text. This argument also means that it is important to makesome allowance within evangelical theology for privileging textual interpretations by those positioned closer to the sociocultural and political realities of the text and its original audience. Certainly, Cone highlights the degree to which power can motivate self-interested interpretation.

This finding suggests a need to expand discussions within evangelical theology to consider power's effects on the accessibility of the truth of God's revelation, particularly when grounded, as most evangelical theology is, in the primacy and authority of Scripture, which requires interpretation. Henry's acquiescence to interpretative fallibility notwithstanding, evangelical theology needs a firmer grounding in interpretive fallibility. One suggestion might include a deeper integration of Reformed spirituality,[81] which insists that even believers remain subject to their fallen natures and that the work of sanctification is progressive. This suggests that even believers can interpret in light of self-interest as opposed to divine illumination. This connection between illumination and progressive sanctification identifies a clear spiritual, pragmatic concern regarding an otherwise theoretical idea of the interpreter's fallibility and heightens the concern for the effects of self-interest in believers' interpretation.

Cone's understanding of experience as a source of Black theology and as a location of divine revelation, while occasionally problematic, suggests a necessary refocusing of evangelical theology in some areas. Cone's views of transcendence and divine truth become problematically enmeshed in understandings of relativity that are only partially rescued by his discussion of axiological distance. He also lacks a clear pneumatology and any distinction between illumination and revelation, making any connection between God's self-disclosure and human interpretation tenuous at best. On the positive side, Cone's work on axiological difference speaks to a deficiency in Henry's doctrine of revelation and illumination, which challenges evangelical theology to propose a caveat to the Spirit's work of illumination. The proposal is that evangelical theology intentionally emphasize the Reformed tradition of progressive sanctification—as a caveat against evangelical appeals to spiritual illumination, and as a reminder that even the believer may be guided by power, privilege, or political standing toward a self-interested interpretation or distortion of the text.

Ultimately, experience cannot be integrated as a source equal to biblical revelation in evangelical theology. That said, some aspects of Cone's discussion of revelation in the Black experience do address gaps or missing emphasis in the evangelical understanding of revelation.

God's Acts vs. God's Speech

Apart from revelation in Black experience, Cone also forces a conversation about revelation as act or speech. Cone insists on act over speech. He affirms revelation in the acts of God in Scripture, over the propositional words of Scripture, in determining how God reveals God's self. This approach allows Cone to focus on God's liberating acts in the Exodus and to insist that liberation is central to what God reveals about God's self. Cone also can draw selectively on those acts of God that most clearly make God a liberator—excluding those passages of Scripture that might portray God differently. Cone signals this approach in his doctrine of revelation found in his preface to *God of the Oppressed*. He notes that womanist and feminist theologians have drawn his attention to texts that harm rather than liberate women. Native Americans have pointed out that the Israelites' occupation of the promised land could be read, from the Canaanite perspective, as an occupation by a colonial power.[82] The evangelical tradition represented by Hodge and Henry, however, would object to elevating some texts above others, insisting instead that the Bible be accepted as authoritative in all its parts.

Henry's entire six-volume *God, Revelation, and Authority* expands the overall premise that God both shows and speaks. So, while Henry affirms revelation in God's acts, he emphasizes revelation in the way God speaks through the totality of Scripture. Henry's work constitutes an attack on the Barthian focus on act. As stated above, Henry insists that the truth, revelation, and words of Scripture are not separable from its acts. But in a sense, in attempting to defend the truth of the words, he diminishes the historical acts of God in favor of the literary pronouncements of those acts. This approach poses the very problem that Cone tries to avoid, insisting on the reality of God's literal engagement in liberating acts in the past that are mirrored in acts of liberation in the present, which together reveal God as the God of liberation.

Both approaches lack a balanced assessment of the content of Scripture, although Henry gives more credence to act than Cone gives to speech. Evangelical theology's doctrine of inspiration means that Scripture in its totality is the Word of God—so God speaks even in the less direct meaning of God's actions in Scripture because the Spirit of God has inspired and superintended the original authors to relate these actions. The actions themselves have meaning, as do their historical, social, economic, and political contexts. Thus, evangelicalism, in defending the propositional truths of Scripture, cannot neglect the historical, literal nature of God's acts. The historical fact of God's liberation of slaves from Egypt, of Jesus' life among the poor and marginalized, and the political significance of Jesus' death on the cross—these all must factor into how God is understood. God's specific acts in specific historical circumstances cannot be seen as incidental to God's revelation, particularly in propositional evangelical theology. If the meaning is only identifiable in the words, as Henry suggests, those words conveying historical, social, and political realities also embed sociopolitical meanings in the historical, literal understanding of the textual truth.

Ironically, Cone, who argues against a literal interpretation of the text, argues for a literal interpretation of the context, whereas some evangelicals who insist on the primacy of the text's literal meaning, like Henry and Hodge, make the historical context secondary. Logically, evangelical theology is strengthened by reference to the meanings found in the historical, literal context. Unless it provides clear textual evidence for doing so, evangelical theology weakens its understanding of the clear meaning when it resorts to metaphorical or spiritual interpretations or claims that circumstances and context are insignificant.

God Revealed in the Contemporary Context

The difficulty with using Cone rests not only in his selective use of text and contexts but in his theological assumption that the God who is revealed in Israel's political liberation from slavery is the God who is revealed in every contemporary act of political liberation of the oppressed. This diminishes the uniqueness of biblical revelation and suggests a purely sociological revelation of God evident in the act of political liberation. Both would be inconsistent with an evangelical view of revelation, but not necessarily with an evangelical view of providence that emphasizes the ongoing immanence of God's work in the world, apart from any suggestion of contemporary revelation. The next chapter, on providence, deals with this in more detail.

Cone's view of revelation includes God's revelation in Christ, in Black experience, in God's ongoing liberating acts in history, and in Scripture. For Cone, at least early on, God in Christ represents the norm for theological reflection, while God's revelation in the Black experience, history, and Scripture constitutes important sources but not the norm. Cone's later reflection elevates Black experience to the level of a norm and makes sources out of Christ, history, and Scripture. Because Scripture itself is a critical point of contention between Cone and evangelical theology, this chapter deals with it separately before the study moves to a discussion of Providence.

Cone's View of Scripture

As already suggested, Cone's views on Scripture shift between his original writing of *A Black Theology of Liberation* and *God of the Oppressed* and his 1997 republication of the new preface to *God of the Oppressed*, wherein he voices concern about the work's original understanding of the doctrine of Scripture. But while Cone expresses some concern for the importance of Scripture in his early work, he never demonstrates the same kind of concern for its authority that Calvin, Edwards, Hodge, and Henry demonstrate. What then is Cone's view of Scripture?

First, Scripture is fallible. Cone affirms its fallibility while denying verbal inspiration.[83] He offers no alternative view of inspiration to counter evangelical understandings. How Cone views the Spirit's role in relation to the original authors is unclear. But Cone offers clear reasons for setting aside both verbal inspiration and literal interpretation. He believes that biblical infallibility and literalism allow racists to point to the authority of Scripture and to advance oppressive views of Scripture that they then claim to be the authoritative Word of God. He also appeals to Black Church tradition: "Blacks show little concern about the abstract status of the Bible, whether fallible or infallible; their concern is with Scripture as a living reality in the concreteness of their existence."[84] Black Church apathy notwithstanding, the authority of Scripture is central to evangelical theology, one of its two defining features. Cone's weakening of its authority makes his views of Scripture incompatible with evangelicalism. Further, while part II included examples where Cone is correct in arguing that evangelicals have leveraged literal interpretation and infallibility to support racist views, this argument is not a foregone conclusion. An infallible text can be read literally to affirm a more liberated stance toward the oppressed. In fact, interpretations that deemphasize verses that speak directly about injustice toward the poor are equally problematic for liberation interpretations; a position on their literal interpretation would defend against their omission. Cone's view of Scripture, unsupported by any other theory of inspiration or authority, has limited ability to present a cogent critique of the evangelical doctrine of Scripture.

In addition, Cone does see Scripture, if not as authoritative, then at least as an important source of theology—but with the equivocation that it is not the words of Scripture, but the Word in the words, that matter. Cone makes clear that Scripture itself is not revelation but rather points beyond itself to God's revelation, which is exterior to the text. The extent to which Cone moves meaning outside the text is apparent in his discussion of Black preaching. "The Word and its proclamation in the Black church," Cone affirms, "is more than the conceptualization of theological doctrine. The word is more than words about God. God's word is a poetic happening, an evocation of an indescribable reality in the lives of the people. . ... Here the preacher is not only affirming his freedom in relation to the text, he is also making a sharp distinction between the words of the text and the Word disclosed in the text."[85] Cone emphasizes freedom concerning the text, maintaining that the Bible is neither a "blueprint" nor a "guide"; instead, it points to the ambiguous transcendence mentioned above. The reader exercises full freedom in decision-making concerning the text.

This view is completely antithetical to the evangelical tradition. While both Calvin and Edwards, and even Henry to an extent, would see meanings as lying beyond the individual words of the text, Calvin and Edwards would not affirm any meaning independent of the text, and certainly Hodge and Henry would agree. Within the evangelical tradition, the reader does not exercise freedom concerning the text of Scripture. Scripture exercises authority over the reader; its meaning, centered in the authority of the text and not the interpreter, constrains the reader to seek meaning constrained by the text itself. That approach also means that evangelical readers do not have the right to take liberties with the text. They are constrained to begin with the literal meaning and context and to provide clear textual reasons for moving away from literal interpretation. This constraint is no less true for liberation-focused texts than for those texts that have been used to support racist positions. Further, Cone's appeal to freedom in interpretation has an unintended opposite effect. Abandoning biblical infallibility and literalism in favor of interpretive freedom leaves racist interpreters unbound by those texts that oppose racist views. Thus, evangelical views, properly understood and enforced, provide a better vehicle for challenging racist and self-interested interpretations.

If Cone's views are so antithetical to evangelical views, can evangelicals set aside Cone's arguments altogether? The short answer is no, primarily because a sharp distinction separates what Cone says about Scripture and how Cone uses it. Cone's doctrine of Scripture is wholly inadequate—but when Cone leverages biblical witness in defense of liberationist interpretation, he almost always refers to the historical literal interpretation of the text. This approach, while wholly contradictory to his own system, fully challenges evangelical theologians to, at the very least, defend why they do not share Cone's interpretations. In turn, his interpretations are responsive to their own insistence that this historical, literal meaning be given priority in interpretation. Thus, evangelical theologians cannot ignore Cone's interpretations. They must evaluate the extent to which their interpretations pull the text away from historical, literal meanings and how their interpretive movements might result from their own power, privilege, and self-interest. The text itself might affirm a broader interpretive meaning different from Cone's, but evangelical theologians have the higher burden of textual proof by virtue of their own understanding of Scripture.

That said, Cone's views of Scripture and revelation do point him to a singular doctrine of God's work: liberation, which he describes in much the same way Calvin, Edwards, Hodge, and Henry express their understanding of providence—although they do so by appealing to a salvation-historical view of providence. Part II of this study also identified how the doctrine of providence itself has been used to advance racist ideas. With that, this study turns to consider the providence of God.

NOTES

1. Calvin, J. 1993: 38.
2. Calvin, J. 1993: 41.
3. Calvin, J. 1993: 89.
4. Calvin, J. 1993: 43.
5. Calvin, J. 1993: 45.
6. Calvin, J. 1993: 51.
7. Calvin, J. 1993: 60–61.
8. Calvin, J. 1993: 65.
9. Calvin, J. 1993: 75.
10. Edwards, J. 1722. "Miscellany 248."
11. Edwards, J. 1723–1729. *Sermons and Discourses in the Works of Jonathan Edwards Online*. Edited by The Jonathan Edwards Center. New Haven: Yale University Press.
12. Edwards, J. 1731. "Miscellany 754."
13. Edwards, J. 1722. "Miscellany 119."
14. Edwards, J. 1722. "Miscellany 141."
15. Edwards, J. 2000: 24.
16. Edwards, J. 2000: 26.
17. Edwards, J. 2000: 27.
18. Edwards, J. 2000: 308.
19. Edwards, J. 1722. "Miscellany 408."
20. Edwards, J. 1722. "Miscellany 408."
21. Edwards, J. 1723–1729.
22. Edwards, J. 1723–1729.
23. Edwards, J. 1723–1729.
24. Edwards, J. 1722. "Miscellany 229."
25. Edwards, J. 1731. "Miscellany 68."
26. Edwards, J. 1722. "Miscellany 229."
27. Edwards, J. 1722. "Miscellany 333."
28. Edwards, J. 1731. "Miscellany 754."
29. Edwards, J. 1722. "Miscellany 426."
30. Hodge, C. 1979: 1:15.
31. Hodge, C. 1979: 1:15.
32. Hodge, C. 1979: 1:24–26.
33. Hodge, C. 1979: 1:15.
34. Hodge, C. 1979: 1:16.
35. Hodge, C. 1979: 1:154.
36. Hodge, C. 1979: 1:154.

37. Hodge, C. 1979: 1:152.
38. Hodge, C. 1979: 1:164–65.
39. Hodge, C. 1979: 1:155.
40. Henry, Carl. 1983: 2:70.
41. Henry, Carl. 1983: 2:74,75.
42. Henry, Carl. 1983: 3:455,456.
43. Henry, Carl. 1983: 3:456.
44. Henry, Carl. 1983: 1:44–70.
45. Henry, Carl. 1983: 3:407.
46. Henry, Carl. 1983: 3:408.
47. Henry, Carl. 1983: 3:429–30.
48. Henry, Carl. 1983: 4:68.
49. Henry, Carl. 1983: 4:42.
50. Henry, Carl. 1983: 4:162.
51. Henry, Carl. 1983: 4:46.
52. Henry, Carl. 1983: 4:259.
53. Henry, Carl. 1983: 4:211–19.
54. Henry, Carl. 1983: 4:120.
55. Henry, Carl. 1983: 4:104.
56. Henry, Carl. 1983: 4:526.
57. Henry, 1983: 4:526.
58. Cone, J. 2018. *A Black Theology of Liberation.* xxiii.
59. Cone, J. 1997. *God of the Oppressed.* xii.
60. Cone, J. 2018. *A Black Theology of Liberation.* 52–53.
61. Cone, J. 2018. *A Black Theology of Liberation.* 52–53.
62. Cone, J. 2018. *A Black Theology of Liberation.* 54.
63. Cone, J. 2018. *A Black Theology of Liberation.* 54.
64. Cone, J. 1997. *God of the Oppressed.* 31.
65. Cone, J. 1997. *God of the Oppressed.* xiii.
66. Cone, J. 1986: 34.
67. Henry, Carl. 1983: 3:9.
68. Henry, Carl. 1983: 3:48–62, 75–98.
69. Henry, Carl. 1983: 3:48–49.
70. Henry, Carl. 1983: 3:65, 66.
71. Henry, Carl. 1983: 3:66, 69.
72. Cone, J. 2018. *A Black Theology of Liberation.* xxiii.
73. Cone, J. 1997. *God of the Oppressed.* 36–56.
74. Cone, J. 2018. *A Black Theology of Liberation.* 43.
75. Cone, J. 2018. *A Black Theology of Liberation.* 43.
76. Cone, J. 1997. *God of the Oppressed.* 16.
77. Cone, J. 2018. *A Black Theology of Liberation.* 48.
78. Cone, J. 1997. *God of the Oppressed.* 84–86.
79. Cone, J. 2018. *A Black Theology of Liberation.* 47.
80. Gadamer, H. 2004. *Truth and Method. 2nd ed.* New York: Continuum. 435–92.

81. Ferguson, S. 1989. "On the Reformed View of Sanctification." In *Five Views of Sanctification*. Downers Grove: IVP Academic. 54–78.
82. Cone, J. 1997. *God of the Oppressed.* xi–xii.
83. Cone, J. 2018. *A Black Theology of Liberation.* 33.
84. Cone, J. 1997. *God of the Oppressed.* 53.
85. Cone, J. 1997. *God of the Oppressed.* 18.

Chapter 14

Providence

Unlike revelation, the doctrine of Providence was considered in detail in part II. So, a lengthy discussion of Calvin, Edwards, Hodge, and Henry is unnecessary. A summary of their distinctions here will suffice, followed by an examination of their views in conversation with Cone.

WHITE EVANGELICAL THEOLOGIANS ON PROVIDENCE

For Calvin providence encompasses more than God's initiating, eternal laws that hold together the universe. God is in no way absent, for God guides fully the ongoing work of creation, all the affairs and fortunes of humanity—including the evil acts of evil actors—and all time, past, present, and future. No causes cannot be ascribed to God. Calvin also holds to the idea of the fixity of the human condition and believes in the idea of distributive justice. The poor are poor because God wills it, and the will of God is not to be questioned. Therefore, the poor should be content, and although the poor should expect to be treated with benevolence, they have no right to be treated like the wealthy.

Edwards builds his innovative understanding of providence on Calvin's doctrine. Although Edwards denies God's culpability for the evil actions of evil actors, his inability to tie these actions to a cause outside God means his efforts are ultimately unsuccessful. If anything, Edwards's notion of providence as God's continual creation, emanating from the relational Trinity, makes God's engagement with the minutiae of daily affairs clearer. He advances Calvin's notion of distributive justice and social hierarchy and considers both as existing within God's providence. But Edwards is distinct from Calvin in another way. Edwards' understanding of the knowability of God's providence in human history, including contemporary history, became a prime way to leverage providence to support racist views. The history of conquest, colonization, White supremacy, and even genocide can be explained within a story of God's providential intervention in the world as acts of either judgment or missional expansion. These narratives propel racist logics in both Edwards and Hodge. Edwards also sees ordered society—defined by adherence to authority, particularly governmental authority—as part of God's temporal providential provision. His views of providence as creation, governmental authority as part of God's providential plan, distributive justice, and the knowability of God all need to be placed in conversation with Cone.

Hodge, unlike Edwards, does challenge the idea that God is the cause of all human action. Hodge makes room for secondary actors and causes in events and actions unrelated to salvation and thereby relieves God of direct culpability for the evil actions of evil actors. He also leaves room for human rebellion, under limited circumstances, to overthrow and replace human government, but he maintains that God gives government, in God's providence, to maintain proper order. Hodge inherits from Edwards the knowability of God's providence and maintains distributive justice and hierarchy as inherent features within this providence.

Finally, Henry reverts to denying secondary causes and believes that God moves and is involved in every aspect of personal human experience and action. While Henry uses the language of equality, his attacks on Marxism and communism elevate his support for capitalist systems that allow class distinction and inequality of property and wealth. Henry affirms distributive justice, with qualifications, but opposes the idea of fixity. Through God's power and providence, individuals can rise above their station. Also, contra Hodge, Henry prohibits rebellion against governmental authority, vesting the government, as Calvin and Edwards do, securely within God's divine providential will. In line with Calvin, Edwards, and Hodge, Henry affirms that God can and does bring judgment upon immoral nations as part of God's ongoing providential plans.

CONE IN DIALOGUE

What then can be said of Cone's views, and all five views in dialogue? Cone offers very little regarding the doctrine of providence. He insists, "It is difficult to talk about providence when men and women are dying and children are tortured."[1] Cone's statement has a double meaning. He sees any notion of providence as problematic, and he sees time spent on abstract reflections on providence as wasted while "men and women are dying and children are tortured."

He recognizes that the primary issue with providence lies in the question of theodicy or, more specifically, "the difficulty of recognizing human suffering and divine participation in history."[2] Cone disallows any solution to the question of theodicy that points to a progressive providence that shifts God's responsibility for action into an eschatological future or that, like Hodge, shifts culpability for evil actions from God onto secondary evil actors. Cone points out that God's permissive will creates the same culpability that God's participative acts do, but he offers no answer for these problems.

Cone's views of God's action create additional problems. His vision of divine involvement in history lacks the progressive understanding of redemption-historical views of providence. God is engaged in the singular act of liberating the oppressed, and little practical distinction exists between the Exodus and Jesus. He also denies the full liberation inherent in eschatological culmination as an explanation of the certainty of freedom in Christ's completed work on the cross.[3] The problem is that Cone's reasoning cannot account for the overarching historical reality of oppression. Cone's arguments aim to defeat how White theologians like Edwards and Hodge use providence to claim not only that God allows slavery and the conquest of Native Americans but that these events are part of God's providential will, but in the process, he weakens his own argument for liberation.

Cone cannot reconcile the theodicy question, so he must relegate providence to an existential ideal that also substantially weakens his doctrine of God. He begins by accepting Tillich's understanding that providence is the availability of the divine "under any circumstance, under any set of conditions." God's providence is the potentiality of God to be present in any circumstance. "Black theology interprets this to mean that in spite of whiteness a way is open to blackness and we do not have to accept white definitions."[4] So providential will is God's existential potentiality to point the Black community toward an embrace of blackness that results in Black liberation. But this perception limits God's divine actions to an existential encounter in individual lives, not to direct actions in human history. However, Cone offers little logical difference from the evangelical missiological argument that sees the only means of social transformation as the salvation of individual souls and the transformation of society through the cumulative effect of transforming each life. Both make God's action a matter of internal, individualistic response and human interiority. But this approach weakens Cone's argument related to God's direct, ongoing participation in human history toward liberation.

Cone is not content to make providence an existential event; he also directly attacks God's omnipotence. "Omnipotence," according to Cone, "does not refer to God's absolute power to accomplish what God wants. As John Macquarrie says, omnipotence is 'the power to let something stand out from nothing and to be.'"[5] Thus, God's power is seriously diminished and made operable only as a condition of Black consciousness. God's power has no agency independent of the Black experience, no will of its own, and no end beyond what the Black community makes of it. Besides contradicting Cone's remarks about God's sovereignty, this argument also makes God a product of the Black consciousness without clearly perceiving God's omnipotence as part of who God is in God's self.

Cone expends these efforts to bracket both God's providence and omnipotence, within the experience of the oppressed, such that they become inaccessible to White theologians. Abstractly, if one can make God's providential acts into existential encounters within the consciousness only of Black individuals, and see God's omnipotence as God's power used only to awaken Black consciousness, the definitions become too narrow for White theological use in other areas. Cone redefines these traditional categories in ways that support his singular focus on liberation. But he also weakens his arguments, making God's power and will more potentialities than ongoing realities. He replaces or renders impotent a theology of immanence necessary to carry his overarching argument and replaces it with a transcendent God only awakened in and through the emerging consciousness of the Black community. Traditional views of providence and omnipotence do a better job of emphasizing God's immanence and regard for human reality than Cone's existential redefinition.

CORRECTIVES TO THE EVANGELICAL UNDERSTANDING OF PROVIDENCE

While Cone's definitions may work within the internal logic of Black liberation theology, they are problematic for Reformed evangelical theology. They do not simply challenge evangelical theology but seek to replace it altogether. But part II, exploring Cone's critique that racism is embedded in White theology, suggests that the evangelical tradition's views on providence have been used for racist ends. Since Cone's reformulation of these doctrines is unavailable as a corrective, one must examine where the evangelical tradition goes wrong and whether the tradition's theology can be accessed to eliminate or forestall its use for racist ends. Thus, causality, knowability, relationality, and fixity—as well as the realization of the divine will in societal patterns of government, hierarchy, and authority with reference to distributive justice—must be closely examined in light of the evangelical tradition independent of, or with slight reference to, Cone.

Causality

Causality—whether God is directly responsible for the evil actions of evil actors—is critical to any understanding of God's role in acquiescing to oppression. Calvin, Edwards, and Henry answer this question in the affirmative: God superintends all human actions and all human actors toward God's divine will and plan for humanity. Thus, Henry concludes that even the Holocaust was part of God's plan to restore the nation of Israel. Besides the degree to which the three views ascribe evil actions and oppression within God's will, more importantly, they characterize the state of the oppressed as God's explicit will; at least for Calvin and Edwards, this state must be endured and accepted without complaint. This deterministic perspective becomes an intellectual tool used by persons in power both to maintain power and to justify the subjugation of others.[6]

Besides ascribing culpability for evil to God, this understanding of poverty also blurs the distinction between God and the evil operating in the world in a way that makes evil so impotent that it functions only as a puppet of divine action. Evil, like all creation, must be seen as subordinated to God and under God's judgment. But by including the evil actions of evil actors in God's will, Calvin, Edwards, and Henry ascribe evil actions to God's will in their understanding of providence, even if unintentionally. Thus, this view sees evil as a burden to bear, not an adversary to overcome. It also nullifies the full force of the doctrines of fall and original sin, discussed later.

Hodge offers an alternative. His understanding of the distinction between potentia absoluta and potentia ordinate, of God's absolute control in the acts of grace inherent in salvation and sanctification, and the efficacy of secondary causes in the ordinary events of life all provide distinct means to preserve God's providence—but the causality for the evil acts of evil actors is more directly ascribed to the evil actors, not to God. This Reformed understanding of providence does not diminish evil's temporal power but preserves the view that evil is ultimately subjugated under God's providence, with no power of its own to subvert God's will or redemptive-historical plan for humanity. Hodge's views on secondary causes naturally conclude that those in positions of power cannot necessarily ascribe their subordinates' positions and circumstances to a divine ordering of society; they must submit to a critique of evil's secondary role in producing those conditions. They also cannot view their own position as an act of divine fiat but must assess any role that evil plays in their status, as well as any personal culpability for evil acts. This assessment must include the role of structural as well as personal evil, to be addressed alongside the doctrine of creation below. This possible explanation for suffering lies outside any consideration of divine involvement. Evil becomes an adversary to seek and root out.

With this view of causality, Hodge could have identified race-based slavery and White supremacy as results of evil secondary causes. But he categorizes the subjugation of African slaves within potentia absoluta instead. According to Hodge, the enslavement of Africans was part of God's plan for the salvation of the African continent. This view raises another critical problem within the evangelical understanding of providence. Hodge, Edwards, and Henry all believe that one can identify God's providence in contemporary and historical events. Thus, for Edwards, Hodge, and Henry, God's providential activities in the world are knowable.

Knowability

Knowability—the exposition of God's providence within historical and contemporary events—is not part of Calvin's doctrine of providence, which sees the outworking of God's providence as a mystery. Why some are poor and some wealthy, some sick and some healthy, and even some elect and others unregenerate, is not knowable and must be ascribed to God's hidden counsels. Calvin combines the idea of mystery with absolute divine causality to argue that all that is is of God. So, for Calvin, the only thing accomplished by mystery is to absolve him from addressing why God allows suffering and inequality. It is not for humanity to ask why but rather to accept that God has God's reasons.

For Edwards, Hodge, and Henry, knowability creates the opportunity to define suffering in relation to providence. Providential explanations take two forms in Edwards' and Hodge's theologies. Subordination and inequality are either God's way of working out a specific plan for the salvation of the oppressed or God's judgment for some moral depravity or particular iniquity in a people or nation. Henry is more likely to preserve the latter without reference to the former. While Henry does admit that even nations who succumb to immorality suffer God's judgment, given his more individualistic perspective, Henry is apt to ascribe poverty and suffering more to individual moral failures than to systemic problems with evil. Even God's judgments on the nations tend more to result from the cumulative effect of individual immorality than from any inherent systemic evil.

As already suggested, secondary causality requires distinguishing between the effects of evil and divinity in any given circumstance, particularly in relation to subjugation, inequality, and human suffering. Absent from Hodge and Edwards is any full analysis of the relationship between what they ascribe to God and their full understanding of God's attributes. Is the race-based enslavement of Africans, the displacement and acculturation of Native Americans, or the genocide of millions of Jews in Germany consistent with God's nature? The fault in these historical commentaries lies not in their attempt to understand historical and contemporary events in light of God's providential will, but in their conclusions posited without fuller proof grounded in clear exposition of God's nature and attributes.

Here Cone can be heard more clearly. His suggestion that one must understand the social before ascribing any explanation of God's involvement directly applies here.[7] But Cone also moves so far from traditional definitions of God's nature that his work can read more as sociology than as theology. For evangelical theology to reflect on social situations, envisioned within conversations of divine providence, it requires both a clear understanding of the social condition and a clear exposition of God's nature that moves beyond a simple expression of God's providence. The social must be understood in relation to its historical manifestation, economic and political motivations, individual and collective self-interests, and sociocultural components. Evangelical theology must also consider physical, psychological, and spiritual trauma. It should leverage this understanding and place it in conversation with a clear understanding of God's nature and attributes, to ask whether a condition of suffering or oppression is consistent with that nature. The final chapter discusses this further in its section on ethical appropriation, but Bernard Ramm, following Barth, envisions this approach when he argues that neither command theory nor Kantian rationalism creates an appropriate basis for Christian ethics. Ethics, per Ramm, must be reintegrated into theology proper, with direct reference to the doctrine of God.[8]

Thus, providential knowability is only adequate as part of a broader theological ethical analysis embedded first in a discussion of God's attributes, not God's providence. Of course this is not the case with Calvin's, Edwards', and Henry's notions of causality. If God is responsible for all actions, then any action lies within God's providential will. Then why do Edwards and Henry not adopt Calvin's notions of mystery? Regardless, for the reasons cited above, Hodge's view of causality is preferable. A differentiation between absolute and ordinary providence or between evil, good, and neutral acts within ordinary events is necessary and possible. This differentiation requires that acts within God's ordinary providence be viewed using a particular method of ethical analysis—examining the secondary actions of evil, good, or neutral actors to determine to what degree they align with God's nature and revelation.

Cone's refusal to engage—beyond his brief discussion of God's wrath in his analysis of God's nature—makes his analysis social, not theological. An entire lack of any method to analyze the social in direct conversation with the theological leaves Hodge with the subjective ascription of social events to God, without any clear distinctions that warrant these ascriptions. What Ramm offers is both a way to think about God's role in the social and an ethical-theological method that offers some basis for ascription. Specific ethical analysis is taken up below, but for now one can recognize that evangelical ascription of historical and contemporary events to God lacks any safeguards against self-interested analysis and, as such, has become available for racist use by those in power.

Relationality

If causality and knowability complicate evangelical notions of providence, Edwards' insistence on relationship may create an opening. If, as Edwards believes, God's providence is the act of re-creation, and that within this process God maintains an intimate connection to humanity paradigmatic of God's relationship within the Trinity, then God's providential act is deeply unifying and equalizing. This point is particularly true of divine-human and human-human relationships within the new covenant community. Unity and equality must be seen as motivating factors within God's providence, as God creates a community that personifies God's intimate relationship within God's self. Some may argue that Edwards goes too far in equating providence with re-creation, but that does not negate the implications. God, one could argue, would not pursue a providential cause that operates at cross purposes with God's nature and person. When one accepts relationality as a component of providence, the degree to which any event or act coheres to God's interest in relationship is directly proportionate to the ability to ascribe it to God. I consider this further during discussions of God's nature and person, below. However, questions arise regarding how Calvin, Edwards, Hodge, and Henry specifically ascribe fixity, authority, hierarchy, and governmental order to the providence of God.

Distributive Justice

All of these points are predicated, to some degree, on an understanding of distributive justice. Tied up in distributive justice is the idea that society is necessarily unequal and hierarchical, that every member of society has value, and that all are entitled to certain expectations related to their treatment. These expectations are defined in terms not of universal human rights but of what is due relative to each person's situation and position. This idea can be tied directly to Plato's *Republic* and Aristotle's *Nicomachean Ethics* and *Politics*.

Edwards advances the same understanding of distributive justice Calvin advances. I have already discussed Hodge's views on distributive justice; Henry directly affirms and ties distributive justice, within the evangelical tradition, to Aristotle.[9] These theologians all reference the household codes and Romans 13, and these references serve as proof texts for this broader social philosophy, with a few differences. Calvin and Edwards believe class, position, and status are fixed within God's providence and that any change is an exception to the rule. Both Hodge and Henry deny fixity but allow for necessary inequality within social structures. None of these men hold political positions that approach a socialist vision of the communal that Cone sporadically mentions. Calvin and Edwards espouse a hierarchical understanding of the sovereignty of rulers or the law under God's divine mandate. Hodge is a federalist republican elitist, whereas Henry is a capitalist individualist with libertarian tendencies. All four believe that governmental authority and the rule of law constitute a divinely ordered structure and that any subsequent inequality also lies within God's divine order; total human equality of wealth, position, and status is not in view.

The ways Calvin, Edwards, Hodge, and Henry apply distributive justice affirm equality of value but not of social order, possession, or social standing. Slaves are to be valued for their work, but they do not enjoy the same standing that their masters enjoy or the same reward for their efforts. All are treated fairly according to their station, place, and position.

This argument is central to the logic of oppression. The problem is that literal interpretations of Romans 13 and the household codes do not require the defense of free market systems over more communitarian forms of social order. Per the evangelical tradition above, Romans 13 has no specific political system in view. Perpetuation of distributive justice means the perpetuation of a political philosophy, not the exposition of a biblical theology, and therefore one need not logically embed it in evangelical political theologies or explanations related to God's providential will. Evangelical theology has no biblical mandate to perpetuate systems of social inequality and certainly no clear biblical mandate to ascribe social inequality to the providence of God.

Both Calvin and Henry affirm this argument when they apply Romans 13 to government without regard to structure or political orientation. Hodge affirms it when he says citizens have the right to rebel and reform the government if it is not working for the governed. If no structure or objective order prescribed for government requires social equality, there is also nothing that forbids it. Thus, the perpetuation of inequality under distributive justice cannot be directly attributed to God's divine plan for humanity, not without considerable ethical reflection.

SALVATION AND COVENANT IN PROVIDENCE

Beyond theoretical and philosophical understandings of providence, what is God's plan, and how does God relate that plan through his revelation? Cone and the other evangelical theologians offer vastlydifferent understandings of God's providential will. For Cone, God's purpose is the liberation of the oppressed and the overthrow of the oppressor. For Calvin, Edwards, Hodge, and Henry, God's purpose is the salvation of the elect; they identify a progressive redemptive history within the structure of covenant (all four) and between creation and re-creation (Edwards). It is important to understand these competing, but not necessarily mutually exclusive, views of providence and the doctrinal implications of salvation, covenant, creation, and liberation.

Federalist Covenantal View

All four evangelical theologians in this study see God's providence as pointing toward a redemption-historical work that culminates in the salvation of the elect through the work of Christ, executed within a divine covenant. Hodge and Edwards particularly hold to a federalist covenantal view of providence.

Burger sees federalist theology as a constructive theology of the covenant with three primary covenantal movements. First, the covenant of redemption between father and son focuses on the salvation of the elect and Christ's reward in receiving the elect as his own, as a condition of the covenant. Second is the covenant of works, made with and broken by Adam; third is the covenant of grace, in which the elect are saved by the free gift of faith through the mediation of Christ.[10] Burger summarizes several deficiencies in these Federalist understandings of covenant. He believes that the Federalists' overfocus on election in the covenant of redemption creates an imbalance that uses covenant as a defense of election rather than a vehicle for identifying God and God's plan. He also points out that federalist views of the covenant of works make work, merit, and obedience central to the divine-human equation, as seen in the examples of the covenant with Adam and the necessity of Christ's fulfillment of the covenant of works as the mediator of the covenant of grace. Thus, Burger asks whether work, obedience, or merit "is so important in the relationship between God and humanity."[11] He points out that the three-covenant scheme is highly susceptible to supercessionism, since none of these primary covenants is made with Israel, and the scheme ignores or minimizes the biblical covenants with Abraham, with Israel at Sinai, and with David. Finally, federalist theology creates an ontology where "the optic distance between creator and creation has to be bridged by a covenant."[12] This distance eliminates relationship as a critical component of God's providence in favor of a legal contract.

Burger's critique offers both difficulty and opportunity. Examining the biblical covenants with Abraham, Israel, and David, despite Burger's attempts to move federalist theology away from works, does force a reckoning with work, obedience, and merit in God's covenantal providence. But while these additional covenants entail clear moral and ethical requirements that demand work, obedience, and merit-related consequences, they also contain relational aspects that suggest that relationality is the covenant's primary motivation. This dual aspect focuses on relationality beyond a purely judicial contract. Federalist theology, however, has tended to affirm the judicial nature of covenant while disallowing works, obedience, and merit within the doctrines of grace, leading to a hyperfocus on election.

Election and Eschatology

While election cannot be denied, Burger aptly observes that election plays a disproportionate role in defining God's providential actions, especially concerning Edwards and Hodge. Edwards couches his discussions of the covenant of grace in overly judicial language to the exclusion of relationality.[13] Hodge deals with covenant in an argument against merit-based salvation and defines faith as a gift, not a condition of salvation; as such faith is not a work, because Christ has already fulfilled the conditions of the covenant of redemption. The obligations of work, obedience, and merit are magnified when covenant is considered in isolation from the rest of Edwards' and Hodge's theological systems. Edwards, for example, embeds a highly relational structure in his ideas regarding the relationality of the elect with the divine and God's ongoing act of re-creation.

But Burger correctly states that the context privileges the doctrine of election over ideas of inclusion evident in both the Abrahamic covenant and the new covenant. Thus, federalist constructions minimize ideas of relationality that depend more on God's love and mercy than on God's judicial justice.

Burger's assessments imply that covenant changes, by way of federalist theology, from a biblical covenantal framework holding together the doctrine of providence into an overarching theological construction that diminishes the actual biblical and historical event of covenant—obscuring salvation history in the interest of dogmatic construction. The federalist threefold structure of covenant moves beyond the biblical sequence to posit a prelapsarian contractual agreement between the father and the son. This proposition simultaneously emphasizes the judicial over the relational while ironically downgrading the conditions of the covenants with Abraham, Israel, and David to strip providence of any primary social and ethical concern. Providence becomes so transcendent that any providential action within the imminent historical divine-human relationship has a substantially decreased meaning. The federalist system minimizes every encounter with God, apart from Adam's fall and Christ's atonement, to the point that the only pivotal event of salvation history is the covenant of redemption and eschatological completion. This assessment explains the Reformed evangelical tendency toward spiritual interpretation. Both theology and biblical exegesis that begin within this federalist framework include a logical tendency to emphasize and hyperfocus on a future eschatology as God's plan and to downgrade the importance of God's historical engagement with God's people between the fall and the new creation.

This tendency manifests in either minimization or typology. Edwards is a prime example of the former, in making a distinction between the new covenant in Christ, with whom the covenant was made, and the old covenant "which promised Canaan." Only the covenant of redemption promises life, while the other covenants promise only Canaan. This reading of course makes Edwards susceptible to Burger's claim of supercessionism, identified by Jennings as a form of racist logic. As an example of the typological tendency, Hodge makes Moses a type of Christ as the mediator of the Sinai covenant, which derives directly from Hodge's defense of the covenant of redemption between the Father and the Son.[14]

Exclusion vs. Inclusion

Burger is also correct in believing that federal theology's focus on election over relationship minimizes inclusion and hyperfocuses covenant on exclusion. This focus also makes relationship, both within the Godhead and between God and humanity, primarily transactional.

Inclusion needs more attention. One finds it in God's promise to make Abraham the father of nations (Gen. 17:1–11) and in Christ's inclusion of the poor, the marginalized, and the Gentiles in the new covenant community (Luke 4:16–30). This inclusion, however, does not ignore God's election. The poor are saved not because they are poor but through the free gift of faith. Likewise, the idea of universal salvation is countered by referring to election, which makes room in turn for God's wrath and judgment on oppressors. Cone directly recognizes this and reframes election in opposition to oppression. God has elected the poor and the oppressed and made reprobate the oppressors—but Cone's almost nonexistent soteriology means he leaves, perhaps unintentionally, a categorical universal salvation. That is, all the oppressed are saved because they are oppressed.

Accordingly, the doctrines of grace so essential to evangelical Christianity are set aside in the interest of social liberation. Evangelical theology, however, in the interest of denying any merit in relation to salvation, tends to so randomize God's election as to make election seem either a supreme mystery or even a cosmic lottery. Evangelicalism needs to consider whom God chooses to elect, recognize how God's innate goodness mitigates against the arbitrary nature of God's election, and focus on the pattern of inclusion, particularly of the powerless and marginalized in God's election.

Transactional vs. Relational

Burger suggests that covenantal theology needs to shift its focus from the transactional nature of covenant toward the relationality of God's covenant of works. The idea of a transaction between the father and the son—embedded in federalist theology's overfocus on the covenant of redemption—creates issues for relationality within the Trinity. The transactional analysis of the covenant of works also ignores the relationality between God and humanity. The covenant of works implies a relationship through the law and personifies it in the two tables of the decalogue that make relationship with God and neighbor central conditions of the covenant (Deut. 5:6–21). Jesus reinforces this interpretation in Matthew 26:36–40 when he insists that the greatest commands are to love God and neighbor, and in Matthew 28:18–20, where he calls the disciples to teach the nations to do all that he has commanded.

Abandoning relationship for transaction leads covenant theology to deemphasize social relational responsibility in favor of individual moral behavior. Transaction and conditionality—whether the conditions placed on Israel in the covenant of works or the responsibility believers owe Christ, who elected them by fulfilling the conditions of the covenant of redemption—turn mutual love into contractual agreements.

The opposite could also be true. Relationality can be so overemphasized that it constrains God to love, regardless of human action. This argument is Cone's contention concerning White theology's insistence that the oppressed should love the oppressor and endure oppression with grace. Divine-human and human-human relationships entail some level of conditionality on love; relationships within the new covenant community bear some continued responsibility to both God and humanity. This responsibility is not a merited condition for inclusion but an outgrowth of an organic relationship in Christ.

Toward a Biblical Theology of Covenant

Thus, covenant theology needs to elevate inclusion while maintaining a role for election—to elevate relationality alongside responsibility to connect the doctrines of grace to their necessary social implications, while not losing sight of their application to individual lives. This view emphasizes God's work from creation to the new covenant, with a focus on God's immanent presence and engagement with humankind, moving from federalist theology's dogmatic construction to a biblical theology of covenant that highlights the divine-human relationship. Taken together, these views preclude using providence and election to support notions of election in providence as explanations for the conditions of the oppressed, as justification for oppression, or as excuses for racial, class, or gender superiority. These views also open the opportunity to think theologically about a Reformed evangelicalism that emphasizes the doctrinal and social implications of relationship and inclusion within Reformed ideas of providence and election.

Creation

Redemption history, understood within covenant, is central to outlining God's providence within the evangelical theological tradition. One must also understand the role played by creation. Space does not permit full treatment of the doctrine of creation, but this study need only emphasize aspects that are particularly important for understanding power, including Cone's views on creation, Edwards' views on creation and re-creation, Cone's and Edwards' views on original sin, and Hodge's view of a single humanity deriving from a single creation.

Cone's View of Creation

Cone's view of creation, like his view of providence, is more existential and philosophical than biblical. He begins his discussion with a documentary, diachronic analysis of the creation story and God's aseity. Cone offers a primarily negative assertion: "The biblical view of God as creator is not a paleontological statement about the nature and origin of the universe, but a theological assertion about God and God's relationship to the oppressed of the land."[15] He reads the text, following his documentary diachronic process, as deriving from the Priestly tradition, which originated in the Babylonian captivity. The creation story is, therefore, the story of liberation written by an oppressed people. Of course, Cone is at odds with the current study's synchronic approach to the biblical text, as Cone places the interpretation of the text outside the text itself. How Cone's exegesis carries his interpretation also remains unclear. Other than a statement about authorial origins, he does not engage the text itself and draws none of his conclusions directly from the text. The problem with this approach becomes apparent in my discussion of Hodge's view, below.

Proceeding from understanding the creation story as a liberating text, Cone moves directly into an existentialist theological application of the text. He draws on the theological concept of aseity to reach two conclusions about the importance of creation to Black theology. First, because God creates ex nihilo, he does not depend on any other thing and therefore exists beyond and untouched by Whiteness. Second, because God is the creator, creation owes all allegiance to God alone, not to oppressors or oppressive systems. These views, drawn from Reformed views of divine sovereignty, would be difficult for White theologians to argue—particularly Cone's views on the allegiance owed only to God. However, his limited treatment of the biblical narrative of creation and the fall impoverishes Cone's work. The work of Edwards and Hodge, however, might extend Cone's thought into a direct critique of power that is absent from Cone's own account of creation.

Edwards's Views on Re-Creation

Edwards' view of creation, which is central to his doctrine of providence, is an important consideration for a theology of power. Edwards sees creation before the fall as the ultimate state of perfection to which the new creation points. God's work between the fall and the new creation is a sustaining re-creative work, in which God moves creation toward ultimate perfection. But until completion in the new creation, work remains to be done within God's providential plan. "The scheme," Edwards says of providence, "will not be finished, nor the design fully accomplished, the great event, fully brought to pass, till the end of the world and the last revolution is brought about."[16]

This dynamic view of creation and providence suggests two things in relation to a theology of power: that God remains at work, and work remains to be done. The nature of the work rests in restoring that perfect state of the prelapsarian created order, in which all were created in the image of God and stood equally before God. If the aim of God's providence is a new creation in which all stand equally before God, then perhaps the ongoing work of providence means that believers must create communities that honor this priority in God's re-creative act. It is illogical to suggest, for example, that God either would not use the elect for these plans or else would desire the Church to preserve structures of power that are not evident in either the original or the coming creation. The implications are that the elect, caught up in the work of providence, are called to abandon ideas of power in favor of principles evident in the eschatological realities of a new creation. This is Cone's view of eschatology as exemplar. Of course, Edwards fails to realize this application and how it contradicts his understanding of distributive justice.

Cone and Edwards on Original Sin

Edwards advances ideas of original sin in the fall that also benefit a theology of power.[17] Cone is reluctant to deal with sin in the context of the fall, particularly total depravity. He offers no clear definition of sin, no view of the fall. Cone's theology leaves undiscussed critical questions of the nature of evil and the human propensity to evil acts. Evil and sin have no origin stories in Cone's theology. Evil and oppression simply are and should not be. While this treatment may work within the internal logic of Black liberation theology, it entails a critical omission for evangelical theology. The fall and original sin are central to the nature of redemption and constitute a prime factor in a redemption-historical understanding of providence. Edwards, however, creates a bridge that allows the conversation of sin to both sustain its universal state and also provide a specific definition that gets directly to the heart of power, particularly related to racism.

Edwards gives evil, and the human inclination to evil, an origin story in the biblical narrative of the fall and the resulting Pauline theology of original sin. Because Adam sinned as the federal head of humanity, Adam's sin is imputed to all humanity. Humanity by nature inclines toward evil. But more important is Edwards' definition of original sin: "The best philosophy that I have met with of original sin and all sinful inclinations, habits and principles, is . . . that it is self-love in conjunction with the absence of the image and love of God . . . that natural and necessary inclination that man has to his own benefit together with the absence of original righteousness."[18] While Edwards would not have understood the full implications of this definition for issues of power, it offers implications nonetheless. The definition directly connects the self-interest inherent in racism and White supremacy to human depravity, because both are rooted in the self-interest and self-love of the White community. This connection identifies the evil that Christians are called to fight in the world and grounds Cone's call for direct Christian opposition to evil in a definition that connects evil to racism and White supremacy and roots both in human depravity.

Additionally, Edwards' definition provides a means to test the presence of the Spirit of God in the life of the believer. Believers who are governed by the power of the Spirit, according to Edwards, have their self-love and self-interest checked by the love of God. Racism and White supremacy become impossibilities for those who claim to possess the Spirit of God. This assertion holds true whether, like Cone, one argues that the Spirit is absent in those who maintain racist and supremacist views or whether one argues only that believers have failed to achieve the full sanctifying power of the Spirit in their lives. Either way racism, White supremacy, and self-interested power are alien to the Christian life and are connected directly to human depravity. Further, when one combines Edwards' understanding of the ongoing work of re-creation with his distinction between self-interest in the fall and God-tempered love in the original righteousness, eliminating self-interested structures of power becomes crucial for the believer's fight against evil.

What Edwards does and Cone fails to do is to give place to the spiritual aspect of the fight to overcome racism. Racism, defined as self-interest originating in human depravity, requires a spiritual "fix" possible only through the supernatural, superintending power of the Holy Spirit. But the implications are not merely supernatural. Understanding self-interest as the root of human depravity requires responding to its social manifestations in political, economic, and social structures. The social manifestation of racism rooted in human depravity requires an ethical response on the part of the church, which is called to challenge evil. That response has both natural and supernatural components, which is Henry's primary argument.[19]

Cone's theological intuition that racism is evil and that God calls humanity to fight evil is correct—but it lacks the necessary definitions of sin and evil to place racism and White supremacy in intimate proximity with human depravity. Thus, Cone's intuition is more easily minimized. But when evangelical theology takes seriously Edwards' understanding that self-love and self-interest are original features of human depravity, then racism and White supremacy become more intrinsically related to original sin working in social structures.

While the theological corpus offers no uncontested definition of original sin, Edwards' definition is consistent with the other evangelical theologians under review here, and its use is justified given the study parameters. Calvin sees "pride as the beginning of all evil." He delineates a series of actions by which Adam pursues his own interests: "Infidelity opened the door to ambition, and ambition was the parent of rebellion, man casting off the fear of God, and giving vent to his lust."[20] So for Calvin, infidelity and ambition, not rebellion, are the root cause of sin from which rebellion arises. This reading seems at least consistent with Edwards' definition. Hodge shares Edwards' view that original sin is the total absence of original righteousness that disconnects humanity from God and one another and results in the selfish acts of sin.[21] Henry's reading, though brief, describes original sin as "the story of self-willed man who by seeking independence from God loses his divinely intended life."[22] Each of these definitions is consistent with Edwards' understanding, or at least is not contradictory.

Edwards, of course, never realizes this special aspect of his definition. Individualistic notions of morality predominated in New England Puritanism. But taken to its natural conclusions in contemporary theological construction, Edwards' definition and Henry's discussions of the interactions between social action and supernatural transformation support an antiracist theology in ways that are deficient in Cone.

Cone's discussion of original righteousness, minus original sin, works against his antiracist agenda if appliedto evangelical theology in a discussion of human freedom. Cone insists, "Whatever we say about sin and the human inability to know God because of the fall, it must not in any way diminish the human freedom to revolt against oppression."[23] The problem is that Cone grounds this argument in Von Rad's belief that the image of God is best understood in terms of its function, which Von Rad defines as dominion over the world.[24] Cone equates dominion with liberation through rebellion, but this same principle, isolated within White evangelical theology, might just as easily affirm dominion as the right of the majority to impose order on the minority, even when doing so is not in the minority's best interest. This concept of God's image, devoid of any understanding of universal human depravity, supports the exercise of self-interested power. What one might gain in a theological defense of revolt is lost in the potential approval of racist and supremacist domination. The latter, of course, is defeated by Calvin's understanding of the diminished benefits of the imago Dei in the fall. Cone's desire to champion action against racism and White supremacy is upheld in Edwards' definition of original sin without needing to reach for a theology of dominion. Ultimately, Cone's desire to challenge White theology seems better served by way of Edwards, Henry, and Calvin.

Hodge's View: Single Humanity Deriving from Single Creation

Hodge adds something that moves the discussion of power in Cone's direction. While attacking now antiquated theories of the distinct origin of various races, Hodge insists on a common parentage of the human race and therefore on the unity of the human race. Very little in Hodge's analysis focuses on its direct theological implications.[25] Instead, he defends the literality and inerrancy of the Genesis account against scientific arguments that propagate a theory of multiple origins.

But despite Hodge's neglect, direct implications arise. His arguments affirm that all races are equal as the creation of God. Supremacy of any race cannot be maintained, even though Hodge himself tries to do so, because the idea of multiple races must be abandoned on the grounds of singular origin. The unity of humanity in God requires the restoration of this unity, which was lost in the fall, and directly contravenes separation, injustice, and supremacy.[26] Of course, Cone's denial of the historicity and literality of creation makes this argument unavailable to him, and as a proponent of Black nationalism, he likely would ignore this principle because it fights against any separation based on race.

Liberation

Creation is a category of God's work within God's providence. It adds to evangelical understandings of redemptive history and covenantal structures within God's providence. But Cone insists that liberation, not spiritual salvation, is central to God's providence. What then can one make of Cone's views of liberation?

Cone's View of Liberation

Cone makes the liberation of the oppressed central to God's providential plan: "Jesus Christ in his past, present, and future, reveals that the God of scripture and tradition is the God whose will is disclosed in the liberation of oppressed people from bondage."[27] While Cone's exact theology of liberation must be pieced together across various parts of his corpus, careful work suggests that Cone sees several operative principles in God's plan that point to God's intent to liberate the poor.

First, as already noted, Cone sees the oppressed as having license for rebellion, because God created humanity in God's image and that image for Cone is freedom: "Human freedom in this sense must now be seen as the very heart of the theological concept of the image of God."[28] In this way, the very image of God in humanity is oriented to fight against oppression. Servitude according to Cone runs counter to God's creative order.

In addition, liberation is central to the very nature of Christ. Jesus came to achieve salvation, which Cone defines as political liberation, for the oppressed. This nature is evident in Jesus' past incarnational mission; in his presence in the contemporary Black Church, moving it toward its own liberation, and in the new heaven and new earth yet to be realized in Christ. But for Cone, what defines Christ in the present and future is who Christ was in the past. The Jesus who healed the sick, ate with sinners, and ministered to the poor and marginalized in his earthly incarnation is performing the same acts of liberation in the present and the future. Christ evinces God's preference for the poor and marginalized in his life, death, resurrection, and second coming. Thus, God's work in Christ is revealed to be the liberation of the poor.[29]

Finally, Cone's understanding of liberation includes an eschatological element. He is skeptical about the overemphasis of eschatology in contemporary theological discourse, particularly when it focuses on eschatological culmination to the exclusion of temporal social justice. However, Cone insists on two roles for eschatology as part of any understanding of God's providential will. First, eschatology is a source of hope for the oppressed—that God is working for their liberation. Seen this way, eschatology functions as a secondary dogmatic consideration serving Cone's doctrine of freedom. He describes this eschatological hope as "freedom's transcendence, the soul's recognition that what is ain't supposed to be," and he characterizes history as "freedom's eminence, the recognition that what is, is the place where we have been called to bear witness to the future, the not yet of human creation."[30] Cone's central hope is that God's liberating providential intent makes possible what is not yet but should be.

The second aspect of Cone's use of eschatology is understood in the first. Eschatology serves as a model and example for the social relationships that must be realized in the present world: "Viewed from the perspective of oppressed peoples' struggle for freedom, the holy becomes a radical challenge to the legitimacy of the secular structures of power by creating eschatological images about a realm of experiences that are not confined to the values of this world."[31] Thus, Christians have no excuse once they understand the fallen, inequitable social structures of this age. They have an obligation, in light of the eschatological vision of equality and justice, to pursue that vision in the present. Engagement with liberation struggles in the present is made nonnegotiable by the eschatological vision available to all Christians.

Evangelical Analysis of Providence-as-Liberation

How might Cone's view of providence as liberation be brought into conversation with the evangelical tradition? Cone's construction of providence as liberation is deficient as a source for evangelicalism in several ways. First, Cone focuses on election as exclusion in ways similar to the federalist theologians. Cone of course excludes the possibility that Christianity can in any way be identified with oppressors. He also emphasizes that the biblical record shows God's preference for the poor and marginalized. But as suggested above, he leaves no role for divine intervention to transform oppressors on behalf of the oppressed.

Also, Cone's view of providence as liberation, except for two incidences mentioned below, depends greatly on theological abstraction, in the form of existentialism, and less on the biblical structures of covenant and redemption history. Liberation in Cone's thought is found in the image of God in humanity at creation, in dominion and freedom, in the person of Christ, and in the end times—but again Cone ignores the remaining covenantal material in Scripture or employs it as examples of God's preference for the poor, without critical connection to the ongoing work of providence.

This point leads to a third observation: providence in Cone is flat and lacks connection to a progressive plan. God's intention, from creation to eschatological completion, is the liberation of the oppressed. In Cone's analysis of providence, the pivotal event is the Exodus, despite his insistence on the Christological event as determinative. But Cone's view of liberation interprets Christ in light of the Exodus—the Exodus is not interpreted in light of Christ. The Christ event for Cone takes on no new significance that the Exodus event has not already attained. Every event in the biblical narrative and God's providential acts recorded there exemplify God's ongoing work of liberation and preference for the oppressed. While Cone does not rule out a salvific role unique to Christ's death and resurrection, he offers no clear doctrine of atonement and only an insubstantial soteriology. Cone's Christ becomes more exemplar than savior.

Finally, the lack of a sustained doctrine of the fall or original sin in Cone's understanding of God's work leaves the presence of oppression without a clear explanation of how God works to defeat it. This lack also creates the impression that the imago Dei remains fully functioning in the lives of the elect, which in Cone's case means the oppressed, apart from any necessary work of atonement, justification, or sanctification through the Spirit. This disconnection creates a dualism in humanity to be worked out by humanity—not as a result of God's supernatural work but out of a moral obligation and obedience to God. Humanity must overcome evil that God has made evident in God's solidarity with the poor. God's actual place in liberation is minimized by Cone's theological conclusions. God's role is primarily to actualize an existential consciousness for freedom in the oppressed and to offer a moral judgment on the oppressor.

All four of Cone's views described here are problematic for creating a constructive evangelical theology of power. But two insights may be gleaned from Cone's exposition on providence if taken seriously by evangelical theologians.

First, as already suggested in the discussion of revelation, Cone's insistence on the theological implications of Christ's historical, biblical connections to the poor and marginalized challenges evangelical theology at the point of its high view of Scripture. Evangelicals are exposed to the criticism that they do not take seriously all aspects of the biblical narrative if they dismiss Christ's relationship to, and teaching about, marginalized communities in his incarnation. This criticism challenges the primarily soteriological aspect of Christ's work. Christ's life has theological significance that—even if it does not take precedence over his death and resurrection—is not diminished by them. Christ's incarnation cannot exist without a degree of divine intentionality and therefore is part of God's providential plan and will. Cone's statement that "Christ is who he was, who he is, and who he will be" clearly challenges evangelicals to take seriously the historical reality of the incarnate Christ.[32]

Second, Cone's understanding of eschatology offers an enlarged view that could revolutionize evangelical social-ethical theology. Evangelical theology tends to push the significance of the eschatological vision to a future spiritual reality, with limited impact on the present. This tendency creates a theological fatalism that says "This cannot be that." But Cone embraces the eschatological vision so "that critiques this and pushes towards correction in the present period." That persons in power use eschatology to demand patience on the part of the poor and marginalized is documented throughout this study. Cone's approach provides a way to address this abuse of doctrine. If God has revealed the perfection of the new creation, it stands as God's critique of the present. What God has critiqued, God desires to see changed. For Christianity to ignore possible present change in the interest of a perfected future change is an act of nihilism. The new heaven and earth, where there is "neither male nor female, slave nor free, Jew nor Greek," is a vision that affects a temporal social ethic just as important for the "now" as it is for the "one day."

THE SIGNIFICANCE OF PROVIDENCE

How then does one summarize the significance of providence in light of a conversation among Cone, Calvin, Edwards, Hodge, and Henry? First, by way of theological understandings of providence, evangelical theology must strongly consider issues around causality, specifically Hodge's understanding of secondary causes concerning the evil actions of evil actors. Second, for evangelical theology to remain evangelical, its focus on a covenantal redemptive history remains critical to the system. But evangelicalism needs to think critically about its understanding of covenant, particularly as it drifts toward federalist theology. Its overemphasis on election as exclusion and on covenant as contract rather than relationship are critical theological faults, evident in both Edwards and Hodge. Cone's understanding of providence as liberation is also not useful, because it draws on many problems identified with federalist theology, even if it applies them toward different ends. What Cone's thought does offer evangelical theology is a need to understand Christ's incarnational reality as a component of God's providential will, as well as an expanded eschatology that offers the eschatological future, both its hope and its exemplary nature, as a critical source for temporal ethical reflection and behavior.

For its part, evangelical theology has much to offer doctrinal applications that exclude racist theological understandings that intersect with the doctrine of providence. These include applying the doctrines of fall and original sin to provide an origin story for evil, especially when original sin is defined as self-interested power devoid of God's image and guidance. This approach provides a prime place for the evangelical tradition to critique power and exclude racist logics. Further, election—viewed primarily in light of a bounded inclusion—holds promise for reclaiming evangelical theology as central to the inclusion of the poor, marginalized, and oppressed as part of the elect, with the caveat that these groups are not universally elected merely as a result of their condition.

With this understanding of providence and the previous chapter's discussion of revelation, what emerges is a clearer understanding of the work of God as it applies to questions of power. What remains is an exploration of how the doctrine of the person of God speaks directly to the question of power.

NOTES

1. Cone, J. 2018. *A Black Theology of Liberation*. 83.
2. Cone, J. 2018. *A Black Theology of Liberation*. 84.
3. Cone, J. 2018. *A Black Theology of Liberation*. 86.

4. Cone, J. 2018. *A Black Theology of Liberation.* 86.
5. Cone, J. 2018. *A Black Theology of Liberation.* 86.
6. Harvey, P. 2016: 67–92.
7. Cone, J. 1997. *God of the Oppressed.* 15.
8. Ramm, B. 1983. *After Fundamentalism: The Future of Evangelical Theology.* NY: Harper and Row. 144–50.
9. Henry, Carl. 1986: 45.
10. Burger, J. "The Story of God's Covenants: A Biblical-Theological Investigation with Systematic Consequences." *Calvin Theological Journal* 54, no. 2 (2019): 267.
11. Burger, J. 2019: 272.
12. Burger, J. 2019: 272.
13. Edwards, J. 1722. "Miscellany 235."
14. Hodge, C. 1979: 2:864.
15. Cone, J. 2018. *A Black Theology of Liberation.* 79.
16. Edwards, J. 1731. "Miscellany 557."
17. Edwards, J. 1722. "Miscellany 301."
18. Edwards, J. 1722. "Miscellany 301."
19. Henry, Carl. 1967: 53–79.
20. Calvin, J. 1993: 213.
21. Hodge, C. 1983: 2:230–37.
22. Henry, Carl. 1983: 6:249.
23. Cone, J. 2018. *A Black Theology of Liberation.* 99.
24. Von Rad, G. 1961. *Genesis.* Translated by J. Martis. Philadelphia: Westminster Press. 57.
25. Hodge, C. 1983: 2:77–91.
26. Hodge, C. 1983: 2:77–91.
27. Cone, J. 1997. *God of the Oppressed.* 127.
28. Cone, J. 1975. "Back Theology on Revolution, Violence, and Reconciliation." 5–7.
29. Cone, J. 1997. *God of the Oppressed.* 99–126.
30. Cone, J. 1982. "Christian Faith and Political Praxis." 128.
31. Cone, J. 1982. "Christian Faith and Political Praxis." 129.
32. Cone, J. 1997. *God of the Oppressed.* 106–22.

Chapter 15

The Person of God

Like the work of God, specifically revelation and providence, the person of God has direct significance for a theology of power. A full engagement with the doctrine is not intended or possible here. Instead, this chapter focuses on aspects of the doctrine relevant to questions of power and its specific use in the theology of Cone, Calvin, Edwards, Hodge, and Henry, as well as its specific misuse in the evangelical tradition to support racist logics. With that in mind, this discussion deals first with the nature of the Godhead and then with the triune economy of the persons of the Godhead, mainly the person of Christ.

All five theologians under consideration here would affirm a Nicaean trinitarianism as the basis of their understanding. How this functions in their respective doctrines of the essence and attributes of God is a matter of individual emphasis. Cone, for example, limits his discussion to those aspects of the doctrine of God that present problems for a unique Black liberationist perspective, while Hodge provides a fuller, more systematic treatment of the doctrine. The varying emphases lead to unique foci with unique opportunities for dialogue and constructive engagement.

THE NATURE OF GOD

Cone

Cone's doctrine of God begins with a discussion of language or God-talk. He affirms that there is nothing special about the English word "God." What is important is the dimension of reality to which it points. The word "God" is a symbol that opens depths of reality in the world. If the symbol loses its power to point to the meaning of Black liberation, it must be destroyed.[1]

Cone offers this assertion primarily to deny that White theological perceptions of God, governed by racist understandings, proclaim the reality of God.

Instead, they distort ideas, which in turn are antithetical to the truth of God's nature. While Cone describes "God" as symbolic, he makes room for the substantive reality of God beyond the symbolic nature of language. Cone's view, however, problematically supports Tillich, who, according to Cone, "describes God as being itself, which provides the only answer to human estrangement from self and neighbor. . . . Therefore, God is a symbolic word pointing to the dimension of reality which is the answer to the human condition."[2] God is understood in relation to the way God provides the answer to human being and nonbeing. This understanding weakens, but perhaps does not entirely discredit, Cone's assertion that God is actually a substantive reality.

This perception supports Cone's larger objective of equating God with the liberation of the oppressed. But while God is revealed in God's acts toward humanity, the latter is a cause, not a determinant, of God's essence and attributes. Cone makes God an answer to the existential question of being and nonbeing and thereby jeopardizes God's fullness and independence from humanity, going so far as to state that "the sole purpose of God in Black theology is to illuminate the Black condition so that Blacks can see that their liberation is the manifestation of God's activity."[3] God becomes bound up in humanity in a way that weakens God's distinctness, a view that is at odds with the evangelical doctrine of God.

Further, Cone fails to develop a complete account of God's essence and attributes sufficient to sustain his Tillichian definition. Apart from discussions of the relationship between God's love and wrath, Cone stays out of more detailed debates on the divine nature and attributes that are characteristic of evangelical theologies. Cone would of course fall back on his assertion that Black theology is not interested in theoretical discussions. While this approach might be consistent within his own logic, it is not consistent with White evangelical theology. If, as Cone argues, the racist distortions of White theology exist within theological systems, their reorientation requires engaging with traditional constructions. Black theology might avoid discussing God's nature and attributes as a particularist theological alternative, but it cannot affect reconsideration of evangelical theology apart from theological discussions on the nature of God. What Cone does not supply, therefore, must be sought in conversation with the tradition itself, beginning again with Calvin.

Calvin

Calvin's treatment of the doctrine of God is entirely trinitarian. He carefully avoids speculating on the essence and persons of God, preferring a Nicaean definition. He sees the unity of the persons in the Godhead as the essence of

God and views this unity as marked by God's simplicity, which is a mark of the Godhead proper, not a distinction in the economy of the Father: "For the essence of God being simple and undivided, and contained in himself entire . . . full perfection, without partition or diminution, it is improper, nay ridiculous to call it his (the father's) express image."[4] Most of Calvin's discussions of the Trinity defend the broad trinitarian question of the unity of God in three persons, giving more attention to the three persons than to the divine essence. Thus, Calvin spends proportionately less time on the various attributes of the Godhead and more time on the distinctions of the persons in the divine economy.

Hodge

Hodge has a far more detailed account of the attributes: "God is *ens perfectissimum*, the word *ens* designates him as a being, not an idea, but is that which has real, objective existence; and absolute perfection distinguishes him from all other beings."[5] This definition highlights two components of the doctrine of God that are central in evangelical theology: that God has substance and is not simply an idea, and that God is distinct and differentiated from God's creation. This definition makes Cone's understanding of God problematic for evangelical theology. Cone's quasi-existentialism and his defining of God in direct relationship to humanity would weaken this more substantive definition of God.

Hodge, therefore, insists that being must be understood as essence or substance, not what is "thought, and . . . a mere power or force." This "real essence" for Hodge is "the common subject of all divine perfections, and the common agent of all divine acts."[6] He is building the case that the divine attributes are indistinguishable from the divine essence.

From this definition of God, Hodge examines the divine attributes. He argues that any view of the attributes must avoid two extremes: "First, we must represent God as a composite being composed of different elements; And, secondly, we must not confound the attributes; making them all mean the same thing, which is equivalent to denying them altogether."[7] The best analysis avoids both realism that divides the attributes and nominalism that contracts them into one. Hodge also warns against making the attributes mere causalities, whereby God's justice, for example, is only God's acts of retribution for sin but is not a clearly necessary characteristic of God's self. That is, God is said to be just only because God has been just, not as a result of his eternal state.[8] Hodge ultimately defines the attributes as "different modes with which God reveals himself to his creatures."[9] He leaves unresolved the connections between attributes and essence, making the attributes dependent on God's interactions with humanity, which minimizes Hodge's assertion that they are independent distinctions in God's self. Without at least a theory of connection, Hodge's appeal to modality differentiates the attributes, to the degree that they fall back into a realist understanding. Avoiding the two extremes outlined by Hodge requires some prescription, speculative as it may be, of the means of connection between God's essence and attributes. Hodge's insistence that they simply must be connected without offering a theory of how they are connected is problematic.

Hodge deals with several attributes in succession and individually. In his treatment of God's justice, for example, he sees justice as retributive and distributive: God's righteous response to law and legal infraction. Justice has a purely punitive nature. Thus, Hodge argues at length that justice and benevolence are not connected concepts in God; in this way Hodge divides the divine attributes of justice and love to such a degree that he loses the unity and simplicity of God. Such sharp distinctions necessarily arise from Hodge's approach. His treatment of the attributes is purely categorical and descriptive; it lacks any theory of connection capable of holding them together within the unity of God.[10]

Henry

Henry begins his discussion of justice as an attribute of God by referring to Hodge's definition, quoted above. Henry literally highlights the words "rectoral" and "distributive" in Hodge's definition. He also brings out the retributive and punitive nature of God's justice.[11] He grounds his understanding of distributive justice directly in Aristotelian philosophy and bases it on the fact that God "grants each person his due." He also argues against ideas of social justice that "replace the principle of distribution according to works and merit by that of distribution according to need."[12] Henry rebuffs any attempt to equate or even correlate God's mercy with God's justice. The latter gets merged into Henry's penal substitutionary view of justification, which emphasizes Christ's imputed righteousness as covering just condemnation under the law, satisfied only in Christ's atoning act. These arguments are leveraged toward a view that God's justice is constitutive of God's law. Justice in God is God's righteousness, defined by law and order. Henry then employs this to make an additional argument to reground ethics in the moral, propositionally revealed laws of God in Scripture.[13]

Henry's discussion of the attributes, like that of Hodge, is merely descriptive and lacks any examination of essence. Henry offers no theory of how God's attributes hold together in the Godhead and in fact errs even more on the side of a realist explanation than Hodge does. Henry's discussion of justice and mercy is disconnected from his broader discussions of the attributes. Thus, considering Henry's conclusions is an important step toward a constructive approach to understanding love, justice, wrath, and righteousness within the doctrine of God.

Henry believes justice and love must be held as distinct attributes. Henry defines justice as distributive justice, which he draws directly from Aristotle. In Henry's perception, everyone receives not what they need but what they are due: "Justice consists in treating equals equally, and unequals unequally in proportion to relevant differences, that is, impartially."[14] Justice, therefore, becomes God's partial judgment based on merit and works, not need or compassion. For Henry, justice is God's righteous judgment of humanity for violating God's laws. In its exercise, justice is evident when action is based on "rightful claims, that is, justifying one's claims by standards or rules that apply to all persons": "Justice is therefore to be distinguished both from personal experience or group interest on the one hand, and from charity or benevolence on the other." Henry again tries to distinguish between God's love, which is partial, and God's justice, which is impartial.

Henry's primary point applies God's justice to social settings. He recognizes a relative justice in God's establishment of civil government and views the importance of God's laws, not God's mercy, as underpinning the relationship between God and the temporal social order. Henry is concerned that secular and liberal Christian perceptions of justice have abandoned a biblical ethic. "Modern philosophy, anthropology and sociology," he says, "have isolated the concept of moral right from its biblical connection with divine law, a connection integral to the Judeo-Christian ethic."[15]

Henry's sharp distinction between God's love and justice violates the unity of the Godhead and Henry's own understanding of the attributes. Henry rejects "the realistic view that being is a substratum in which attributes inhere, an underlying substance that supports its qualities or predicates."[16] He believes that God is "the living unity of His attributes."[17] Thus, God's attributes and God's essence or being are the same thing. God is what God does. Further, "if God is noncomposite, and his essence and attributes are mutually inclusive, each attribute in the nature of God interpenetrates every other attribute and no conflict or contrast among them is possible."[18] But given Henry's own affirmation that the attributes feature no "contrast," one cannot see how he maintains such a sharp distinction between love and justice, insisting that law, not mercy, must define justice.[19] Henry attempts to resurrect Hodge's "modified realism" but can provide no clear examples from his or Hodge's work to demonstrate how their largely descriptive and categorical approach to the attributes constitutes any underlying theory of unity.

Given that retributive justice creates critical issues for any theology of power offered by these evangelical theologians, this discussion questionswhether any approach within the tradition both places the attributes within God's essence, as Henry and Hodge would insist, but also provides a theory of unity within the attributes that addresses the importance of God's love for understanding God's justice. Edwards is discussed last in this section because he offers such an approach.

Edwards

In his writings on the Trinity, Grace, and Faith, Edwards articulates a clear theory of the divine essence grounded in God's triunity. He affirms that God is real, not simply an abstraction or inconceivable mystery. He carefully distinguishes between the persons of the Godhead and the Godhead itself, so as not to lose the former in the latter:

> This I suppose to be that blessed Trinity that we read in the Holy Scriptures. The Father is the deity subsisting in the prime, unoriginated and most absolute manner, or the deity in its direct existence. The Son is the deity generated by God's understanding, or having an idea of himself, and subsisting in that idea. The Holy Ghost is the deity subsisting in act or the divine essence flowing out and breathed forth, in God's infinite love to and delight in himself. And I believe the whole divine essence does truly and distinctly subsist both in the divine idea and the divine love, and therefore each of them are properly and distinct persons.[20]

Edwards means that God as absolute being subsists eternally through God's idea of God's self and through God's love for God's self within the Trinity. God's idea of God's self eternally self-generates God. Edwards ties his perception of God's freedom to be more closely a theory of God's being, defining God's idea of God's self as God's means of external self-generation.

Edwards connects God's love to the Trinity and to the unity of the Godhead. The essence of love in the Godhead is a clear indication and proof of the Trinity. One individual's love for oneself equates to egotism; but the transcendent mutual love of three persons for one another, and all for the whole, is a self-giving love on behalf of the other. A God who is love apart from Trinity is a self-serving, narcissistic God. The triune God who is both three and one, with God's unity held together by God's love, both honors God's own perfections and exists for the other.

Edwards' understanding of love is also grounded in a literal reading of Scripture. Edwards draws primarily from I John but also recognizes the connections between Christ's teaching on the love for God and neighbor in Matthew and the two tables of the law in the Ten Commandments—making love central to the law, contra Henry. Edwards' use of I John provides a biblical basis for claiming love as God's essence. John's explanation that God is love and its further elaborations ground Edwards' understanding of the Triunity.

Edwards' trinitarian theology does exhibit a few problems. For example, Edwards subscribes to a type of seminominalism that sees the attributes beyond love and God's idea of God's self as lacking reality. Love and self-ideation are the only realities in God, with all other so-called attributes being "mere modes and relations of existence"; beyond love and self-ideation, "there are no real distinctions in God that can be thought of." Edwards seems to go beyond even suggesting that the other attributes are derivatives of love to indicate that they have no reality in themselves.

As another example, in describing the relationship of love in the Trinity, Edwards makes the Holy Spirit the Trinity's aspect of pure love. The love of the Godhead equates to the person of the Spirit. Even Edwards recognizes that this equation wholly diminishes the place of the Spirit as a person. He attempts unsuccessfully to resolve this by explicating the Spirit's participation in the self-understanding and life of the Father and Son. But this argument simply makes the personhood of the Spirit a derivative of the personhood of the Father and the Son.

Finally, and perhaps related to this weakened view of the Spirit's personhood, Edwards maintains an over realized relationality to the exclusion of substance in the Godhead. Edwards perhaps recognizes and tries to correct this by making love a substantive person of the Trinity in the Holy Spirit. But he thereby diminishes the Spirit to the category of substance while elevating the Spirit to the essence of the Godhead. But Edwards seems more concerned generally with elevating love as essence, understood relationally, than with using the Spirit to establish any idea of substance. Edwards' views of the Trinity are decidedly relational and ideational.

As a whole, though, Edwards' views are helpful, with certain caveats and constructive revisions. He bases his work wholly on an understanding of scriptural revelation not subject to attack by Henry. Edwards provides a clear, albeit somewhat flawed, theory of Triunity that is absent from both Henry's and Hodge's descriptive approaches. Edwards ultimately recovers for evangelicalism the idea that all that God is is grounded in God's love.

Theologians in Dialogue

How can these views be constructively synthesized to speak directly to a theology of power? Given the inability of Hodge and Henry's descriptive approach to create real connections among attributes in the Godhead, this study adapts Edwards' view: that love is that essence in the Godhead out of which all other attributes stand in relation. Critical in Edwards' understanding is the argument that God's love is for God's self, as evinced in the transcendent mutuality of the love that each person of the Godhead has for the other and that each share for the whole. This love forms a real, substantive unity within the Godhead. God's love is not self-interested or narcissistic; it always focuses on the other. By integrating, rather than bifurcating, God's attributes and person, understanding God's essence as love inherits a theory of being that both strengthens it and gives it more provenance in discussions of justice, love, and wrath that are critical to a theology of power.

This study follows Edwards' understanding that all other attributes flow from God's love. While Edwards connects love and God's idea of God's self, he ascribes the attributes to the former, not the latter—although all that God is derives from God's idea of God's self. But unlike Edwards, who loses the attributes by embracing love as essence, I suggest God's subsequent attributes are emanations of God's love, not mere modalities. This strengthens both the individual attributes and also the idea of love as God's unifying essence. Each of God's perfections emanates out of God's essence of love; they remain wholly connected to God's love and, through it, to one another while also being distinctive in their own right. Love creates simplicity in the Godhead in the same way it creates unity in the Trinity, while suggesting that the attributes are also distinct from one another.

But Edwards is not followed in equating love with the Holy Spirit. This study views love, as God's essence, as a constituency of the whole, not a specific economy or substance of any particular person within the Trinity.[21] While this approach eliminates any direct connection of love as substantive in any of the persons individually and grounds it directly in relationality, this study assumes that the Godhead's relationality in its love must be seen as substantive. This assumption is a qualification, not a sustained argument. Ultimately the relational element in God's essence may need to stand on its own, because the metaphysics of God's substance is beyond knowing.

With this view of love as God's essence and of the attributes as emanations of love, it is now possible to explore more directly the divine attributes of justice, power, and omnipotence as they relate directly to a theology of power. A view of love as the essence that holds everything together and governs understandings of each part undergirds the constructive work that follows.

God's Love

One must examine justice, as an attribute of God, in relation to how it arises out of God in God's self. Because justice is only necessary as an expression of God's relation to creation, it must also be viewed as an attribute originating primarily in God's relationship to humanity. God's love is expressed within the Godhead as mutuality, equality, and a focus on the other. Thus, justice must be seen as emanating from God's love—as having within itself, or being answerable to, these qualities.

The other-focused nature of the Godhead refers to that condition of God's love in which each of person of the Godhead loves the others and the whole. And the whole is loved not for the sake of the self but for the sake of the other. The implications are important. God whose love is other-focused exists beyond self-interest and self-love. When God loves God's self, one must see, as Edwards does, that God's triune nature challenges the idea that God's love can be a merited narcissistic appreciation for God's own perfections. Trinity means that love in the Godhead exists beyond self-interest and is innately other-focused.

This eternal focus on love for the other creates a mutuality whereby each exists in relation to their love for the other and in relationship to their shared love of the whole. God's love becomes constitutive of God's unity, and God's unity becomes constitutive of God's love. To the degree that each participates fully in the whole, then each participates mutually in the whole. This mutuality and union of love also indicates the equality of the persons in the Godhead through equal participation in its fullness and their equal share in love for one another and the whole. The equality of the Godhead is central to preserving the Triunity of God.

God's righteousness—part of Hodge's, Henry's, and Edwards' views of justice—should also be understood as emanating from God's love, defined by God's focus on the other, mutuality, and equality. God's righteousness as it exists within God's self reflects God's perfect affirmation of God's self as what is completely correct and right. What is righteous in relation to God's self, without reference to humanity, is God's perfect love: again, understood as other-focus, mutuality, and equality. God is love; so, God's love is righteous, and righteousness is God's love.

God's Justice and Law

How is justice understood in view of God's relationship with humanity? Particularly viewed as an overflow of God's righteousness, justice requires considering several factors mentioned by Henry, Hodge, Edwards, and even Cone: law, wrath, impartiality, and compassion, and mercy. These must be considered in light of their connections to divine justice as it emanates from God's love.

With regard to law, Henry's focus has already been considered. Henry sharply divides God's love manifested in mercy and God's punishment for nonadherence to law, evidenced in God's justice/righteousness. Making law the primary determinant of justice posits who God is in God's self on the basis of God's condescension to humanity. Law as condescension in the divine-human relationship says more about humanity than about God. A sharp distinction between law and mercy does divide the unity of God. Law then must be considered in a way that correlates with a clearer understanding of love as God's essence and of the conditions of love in the Godhead.

Edwards provides a way to look at both the positive and negative aspects of law. From a negative perspective, law highlights and condemns sin in humanity. Understood fully, it condemns sin. Edwards' definition of sin as self-interested pursuit apart from God's guidance and control is instructive. What the law does negatively, seen this way, is condemn humanity for pursuing destructive self-interest separate from God's interests and the compelling interests of neighbors. Since selfishness lies at the heart of definitions of power, particularly related to racism and White supremacy, the law identifies racist abuses of power. If so, then Cone's insistence that racism, and White neglect in seeing racism as original sin, shows merit. His conclusions provide theological significance not just for Black theology but also for evangelical theology,[22] whether one sees racism simply as a sin or instead as original sin. Following Edwards and Cone in this would connect Adam's sin more directly to the sin of racism.

Regardless, the law condemns any system or individual that seeks self-interest over the interest of others and apart from God's direction. Law also subjects unredeemed secular governmental structures to a critique of self-interest in the abuse of power, as they stand apart from direct dependence on God. This understanding also makes impossible the acceptance of any form of Christianity that insists one can pursue self-interest at the expense of others. It particularly condemns as non-Christian any group or individual who maintains that racism, White supremacy, and oppressive systems can exist alongside Christian faith. The law becomes a magnifying glass for viewing the sin of power as the pursuit of selfish self-interest. Thus, Cone's view that White Christianity is heretical when it embraces racism for its own self-interested benefit has merit. As Henry notes, the law remains, even if satisfied fully for the elect in Christ's atoning death, and it continues to define morality, ethics, and notions of justice.[23]

Edwards' understanding of original sin as self-interest is highlighted by the fact that self-interest completely contradicts the mutuality, equality, and other-focus of God's essence. God, whose love is other-focused, mutual, and equal, entirely opposes the pursuit of self-interested power. Individuals and organizations, even the church, that pursue or ignore self-interested power and the propagation of racism and racist systems contradict the very essence of God and, as Cone affirms, have nothing to do with God. The law, understood within the context of justice, serves negatively to condemn self-interested power and self-interest's contradiction of God's own essence. Law is not an attribute of God but rather is an aid to understanding human sin as contradiction of God's nature.

Viewed positively, however, the law affirms the practice of divine love as central to God's justice. Edwards points to Christ's proclamation of the essence of the law found in the commandment that humanity should love God and love neighbors and that the two should cohere. Edwards also notes that the decalogue itself has two tables: the first focused on love of God, and the second focused on love of neighbor. Even Henry seems unlikely to deny this connection between law and love in Scripture. Given Henry's acquiescence that justice ultimately concerns one's relationship to one's neighbor, the law viewed in this way amplifies the positive pursuit of loving relationships with God and neighbor that should be central to concepts of justice as they relate to law.

Following this perspective on justice and law, theology will refer back to love as God's essence and—by logical extension in the current study—God's other-focus, mutuality, and equality. This extension grounds justice not in systems of personal morality—although not excluding them either—but in a broader, more relational understanding of justice derived directly from God's essence as God is in God's self.

Thus, law, contra Henry, must be seen as directly connected to love as God's essence. If one follows Henry's inclusion of law in the concept of justice, then law must be seen as providing a negative focus condemning self-interested power and affirming a positive focus on the other, mutuality, and equality reflecting God's love in God's self. Thus, justice must consist both in condemning and eliminating oppressive systems of self-interested power and also in performing acts of love toward God and neighbor that reflect God's other-focus, mutuality, and equality.

That brings the discussion to wrath, as both Henry and Hodge focus on the punitive or retributive nature of God's justice, distinct from God's love and mercy. One cannot deny retributive justice as an aspect of God's justice. Henry is correct: without it the cross of Christ has no substance. How can God's retribution, or emotively God's wrath, be said to emanate from God's love? At this point Cone is helpful.[24] Cone suggests that denying God's righteousness in the interests of the singularity of love resurrects Marcionism. By denying God's wrath and retribution, one disconnects the God of the Old Testament from the God of the New Testament and affirms a view of God that ignores the fullness of the biblical revelation. Cone does not deny that love is the essence of God but rather he suggests that love is not love apart from God's wrath. According to Cone, if God is for everything and against nothing, then God cannot be said to stand for anything. God's love means that God stands against the oppressor and for the oppressed. Without wrath there is no condemnation and therefore no ability to identify and call evil what it is. Love without wrath is not love at all. Cone rightly points out that without God's judgment and punishment, the problem of theodicy becomes acute.

Contrary to most liberal theological systems, Cone insists on the literality of God's wrath and punishment.

This view of course aligns with Henry's and Hodge's views of retributive justice. The difference arises only in the fact that Henry and Hodge focus on God's wrath toward sin, understood generally and primarily in relation to individual morality, while Cone applies God's wrath directly to God's punishment of oppressors as a result of God's love for the oppressed. Evangelicals can easily react against Cone's language of oppression and oppressed and miss his affirmation of a foundational view of evil and God's punishment of evil.

Indeed, Cone can be brought close to evangelicalism by way of the analysis above. If sin is the exercise of self-interested power, then oppression is sin. Further, God opposes all that contradicts God's essence of love, realized in equality, mutuality, and other-focus. Oppression, by definition, opposes equality, mutuality, and focus on the other. Therefore, oppression and the oppressor exist in a sinful state, in opposition to God, and under God's condemnation and punishment. God does choose sides; God is partial in declaring oppression sin and oppressors sinners. God exerts wrath on the oppressor and therefore can be said to favor the oppressed. This point of course must be seen to operate at the level of common or residual grace, when the oppressed are made a universal class inclusive of regenerate and unregenerate persons. But God's love existent in God's mutuality, other-focus, and equality must condemn that which opposes God's own nature and affirm that which, even in its imperfections, draws closest to it. God's love includes God's wrath. So, justice exercises wrath on that which runs counter to God's essence of love to ensure compliance with mutuality, other-focus, and equality in God.

Closely related to law and retribution (or wrath), particularly in relation to justice, is a third idea: God's impartiality. Henry notes that justice is impartial, whereas love is partial, and this clearly distinguishes between God's justice and God's love.[25] But this distinction does not itself sever the connection. Impartiality can be seen as an emanation of God's love.

Henry equates impartiality with the fact "that God is no respecter of persons," making the point that God sees and rightfully judges all for their sin, following the same laws and applying the same judgment to all. But this point extracts the New Testament reference to divine impartiality from its intended contexts. When Galatians says there is "neither Jew nor Greek, slave nor free, male nor female" (Gal. 3:28, NIV), the intention is inclusion in the new covenant community, not equal punishment under the law. This observation does not deny either the universality of human depravity or God's punishment of the unregenerate. It simply makes the point that the scriptural understanding of God's impartiality—when tied to the idea that God is no respecter of persons—realizes that in the new covenant God is making way for the Gentile, the slave, the poor, the oppressed, and the marginalized. What people have differentiated and excluded God has chosen to include. God ignores humanity's categories of exclusion and inclusion. Given this interpretation, Henry's use of impartiality to sever love from justice seems totally out of place.

The concept of divine justice must consider the idea of need. Henry distinguishes between "each according to their need" and "each according to their due." By the latter he means "each according to their work or merit." He affirms work and merit over need and even insists that need is not a consideration of justice. Henry refers to justice as law and its impartial execution—both concepts that this discussion has already challenged as pertaining more to God's love than Henry allows. If law intends to point to God's love and, within it, God's concern both for loving God and loving neighbor—and if law highlights the sin of self-interest as contradicting God's own essence—then law focuses primarily on restoring mutuality, other-focus, and equality. This neighbor-focus and other-focus means that justice gives of itself on behalf of the other. Even work and merit, in this understanding, become subordinated to the requirement to abandon self-interest in the interest of the other, both God and humanity. It becomes difficult to see how this does not require justice to include the meeting of needs.

Ultimately, justice then, as an emanation of divine love, condemns and eliminates the sin of self-interest in favor of a restored relationship between God and humanity and in humanity toward itself. This understanding must not result in universal salvation; there remains condemnation of sin. But those who are redeemed are returned to the image of God, who is said to be in essence love distinguished by mutuality, equality, and focus on the other. Justice means the pursuit of these qualities in recognition of God's perfection and as an expression of love for God.

This book's theological construction of the justice of God is dependent on Edwards. But Edwards never realizes the specific implications of his own doctrine of love in the person of God in relation to African slavery and Native American colonization. He never extends the doctrine to a full understanding of its implications for justice in his own context. His understanding of distributive justice limits in humanity what is evident in God. Edwards suggests no required mutuality and certainly no true equality, and he defines any other-focus not as love but as obligatory charity. He directs his own definition of original sin to advocate personal humility and obedience to God. While neither is incorrect, his focus is incomplete without a universal *social* application of a universal condition of sin. Thus, Edwards cannot critique slavery or European abuse of power in its treatment of Native Americans as injustice, nor as sin on the part of colonists. Edwards no doubt sees both as allowable because, under distributive justice, African slaves and Native Americans at the time were given their "due" when treated with charity—and because as a

Christian nation, Britain had the right under God to exercise dominion over both groups for their own good and evangelization.

God's Power and Human Power

Edwards allows power to be exercised within accepted cultural norms to impose necessary social order. The idea that evangelization can occur apart from colonization would never occur to Edwards, who sees Christianization and "civilization" as inseparable. Thus, power, in this case colonial power, is necessary for the common good within God's providence. But Edwards offers no sustained engagement with God's power and humanity's exercise of power.

Given this study's central focus on human power, it must attempt to define the power of God and its extension to the human condition. Barth provides just such a definition in *Church Dogmatics* 2.1. Using Barth is justified both because Barth's high view of God's sovereignty is consistent with Reformed evangelicalism, and because Barth's description of God's power suggests implications for the exercise of power—implications not directly available in the evangelical tradition, although not contradictory either. This work cannot provide a full exposition of Barth's theology of the sovereignty of God; the discussion limits treatment to his arguments specifically in *Church Dogmatics* 2.1:490–607. The specificity of Barth's definition of power is what helps the constructive work of this project.

Barth categorizes God's omnipotence under the category of God's freedom. For Barth, God's love and God's freedom are both paradoxically distinct and the same. The essence of God is love in freedom, captured in the way Barth pairs God's constancy and omnipotence. God remains free to be who God wills God's self to be. But God is always also who God is in God's constancy—both determined by God's own morality, but free in the power and ability to do anything to exercise the divine will.

This power of God, according to Barth, requires definition to be rightly understood. Barth defines God's omnipotence. First, he insists that God cannot be defined as power in itself. "Power in itself is not merely neutral," Barth says; "power in itself is evil." God is all-powerful, but power is not God. In an aside, Barth contrasts God with the devil, who manifests power for power's sake; this comment serves to illustrate Barth's argument, but he does not work out the implication for a full theology of evil or of evil power as evidenced in the satanic. He remains focused on distinguishing between power as a manifestation of God and the deification of power itself. The second, related part of Barth's definition is that "God's might never at any place precedes right, but is always and everywhere associated with it." Barth distinguishes between power as "physical possibility" and as "moral and legal possibility."

Might is always guided by moral rightness: "God's moral and legal potentiality is also his physical." Here Barth distinguishes God's power from the pure, unrestrained exercise of power that manifests in tyranny. The third part of Barth's definition distinguishes among the power that God reveals through God's self-revelation, the power God will reveal in the future, and the sum of God's power. That is, the power God exercises is not God's full power in the divine essence. God's power does not "exhaust itself in his omnicausality." Fourth, God's power is the power to "be himself and to live of and by himself"; God's self-sustaining power within God's triunity is the source of all of God's exercise of power. God's power is contained within God's self and is not derivative. Finally, Barth's definition says, "God's power is power over everything." God exercises power over all power, so God's power is sovereign and supreme. Again, Barth emphasizes that God is not the sum of all power making any exercise of power divine; rather, God assumes power over any other power.

One might object that any conclusions drawn from accepting Barth's definition would equally apply to the oppressed. Barth does consider "revolt" also to be an unrestrained exercise of power that he defines as evil. Barth would likely characterize Cone's Black liberation theology, and its call to exercise Black power in revolutionary ways, as a violation of his own understanding of power. For his part, Cone would likely point out that any discussion that minimizes the Black community's use of power diverts attention from the White community's misuse of power. He would also likely deny the applicability of Barth's work to oppressed Blacks, even though Cone was a self-professed Barthian.

This study focuses primarily on power as it speaks directly and generally to the powerful and the privileged. Therefore, I leave to Black theologians the work of applying the following conclusions to the oppressed and to Black liberation theology.

Barth's definition has direct applications to a theology of power. From the outset, one must distinguish between God's power and that of humanity. Omnipotence as an incommunicable attribute is central to any understanding of this distinction. That said, a direct relationship to power in God exists within both the limitation and exercise of human power. This reading excludes human exercise of power for power's sake; this power is not derived from God. If God is not power in itself, and if the power of God is distinguished from neutral power, then neutral power in humanity is necessarily not of God. Barth's insistence that neutral power is evil and results in tyranny is instructive. God cannot be said to be a tyrant and, by extension, cannot be said to be the God of tyrants. Unrestrained power cannot derive from God or be condoned by God.

Related to this point, God's power is exercised in coherence with God's "rightness" and morality. God cannot be said to be connected to human exercises of power that violate God's righteousness, morality, justice, and love. Power that lacks coherence to these attributes revealed by God cannot be described as God working through those who exercise this power. Hitler was not infused with the power of God. God was not present in apartheid's exercise of power in South Africa. The power of masters over slaves in antebellum America, or of White supremacists over Black Americans during US segregation, was not God's power. God's power is not exercised apart from God's morality and love. Power, if allowed at all, requires a moral determinant that guides its acquisition and exercise. It exists under the critical gaze of covenant and biblical revelation and in relation to God's moral constraints on God's free power.

Further, if God's revealed power is not the sum or fullness of God's power, and if God's power is "not exhausted in his omnicausality," then tyrants, oppressors, and others in positions of power should understand that they are subject to divine retribution, even in temporal circumstances, as God exercises God's power on behalf of the poor and the marginalized. If humanity does not know the fullness of God's power, then it can never rest easy in believing that just because God has not yet acted, God will not act. In fact, the idea that God has not exhausted God's power is both a token of hope for the oppressed and a cautionary tale for the powerful and privileged.

The facts that God's power is contained in God's self and that God's power is never derivative apply equally to a theology of power. The incommunicability of God's power to humanity brings into question whether the human exercise of power ever connects to divinity. If God's power is in no way derivative, can humans ever exercise power in relation to God? God's ultimate sovereignty brings into question any notion of political or social power that derives authority from the divine right of kings or divine manifest destiny. I do not suggest that God does not use human agency in God's providence. But God's use of the redeemed for God's purposes manifests in service to neighbor, not in the unrestrained exercise of power.

This analysis brings into view Barth's insistence that God exercises power over everything but that not every exercise of power is divine. Not everything done in pursuit of power can be said, without qualification and critique, to be God working through humanity.

God's exercise of power informs humanity's exercise of power. Human power may in fact be an abuse, not a divine right. Certainly, any exercise of power is subject to evaluation under God's standards of rightness, justice, and love. Humanity must meet a high measure to equate the divine to any human act of power.

Before moving on, it should be noted that the previous definition of original sin as self-interested action seems to typify the human exercise of power. The question then becomes to what degree the human will to power is in fact inherent in humanity's fallen state.

A Theology of Power That Relies on Divine Love

The argument above suggests a direct connection between a doctrine of God's attributes and a theology of power—a connection that intersects with the work of Edwards, Barth, and sometimes Cone. Any theological understanding of power must center on Edwards' consideration of the connections between (1) love as God's essence and (2) understandings of justice and power that move away from distributive justice and toward love as mutuality, equality, and other-focus. Understandings of justice have room to emphasize God's wrath and the exercise of retribution on tyrants and oppressors. Power, in the analysis above, becomes highly regulated if not totally prohibited. Its practice requires strict moral and ethical standards and total acquiescence to God. Humanity's ability to claim that its exercise of power derives from God is sorely curtailed. Connecting the will to power with the original sin of self-interest further weakens power's use in contexts beyond God's own transcendent divine activity.

THE PERSON OF CHRIST

Thus far, this part has demonstrated that the doctrine of the work of God—as seen in the doctrines of revelation and providence as well as the attributes of the Godhead—offers specific utility for understanding power, particularly with reference to racism. These doctrines can be understood at times in agreement with Cone and at times through a new focus on arguments that are already part of the evangelical tradition but are either underused or ignored.

What remains in this constructive section of the study is a consideration of the economy of the persons of the Godhead. While discussing the Holy Spirit might have some benefit in regard to power, the following discussion focuses exclusively on the person of Christ. In considering Christ, I pay specific attention to Cone's notion of the ontological Blackness of Christ, Christ's kenosis, and the meaning of the cross. While many possibilities arise for engaging with a fuller Christology, the specific topics in this section are most critical to a theology of power.

Cone's clearest Christological innovation is his understanding of the ontological Blackness of Christ,[26] which deserves consideration and constructive application. The notion of a Black Jesus has been an ongoing and prevalent image within the American theological imagination for most of the twentieth and twenty-first centuries. As Edward Blum and Paul Harvey have clearly pointed out in *The Color of Christ: The Son of God and the Saga of Race in America*, the racialized Jesus has a very long and complex history in the United States.

While not denying the theological and historical complexity of racialization, this section suggests that a Black Jesus has potential for informing a more nuanced White evangelical Christology. To that end, this discussion first delineates the images of Christ in modern American Christianity, followed by a definition of just what a Black Jesus means, and finally some constructive theological observations for how thinking about Christ as Black might shape evangelical Christology from a White evangelical viewpoint.

White American Images of Christ

American Christianity includes at least four primary images of Christ, excluding the Black Christ: the iconoclastic/faceless Jesus, the Hellenized Jesus, the Christ of American democracy, and the White Christ. I examine each in turn.

Blum and Harvey suggest that, under the influence of New England Puritanism, the early colonial period in the United States avoided any image of Jesus. Consistent with Puritan iconoclasm, Jesus was primarily a spiritual not bodily presence:

> A variety of factors account for the relative absence, unimportance, and even annihilation of Christ's physical body in the British colonies. Few of the groups involved had any inclination to create an image of the divine, and few had the manufacturing or distributing abilities to create a prevailing representation. The newness of Native American encounters with Jesus, the lack of freedom and diverse associations between color and divinity among West African slaves, and the radical iconoclasm of the English settlers created an eastern North America where no physical representation of Jesus dominated.[27]

Blum and Harvey see this iconoclasm as continuing to run through American history up to, and even beyond, the Civil Rights Movement.

Although this image of Jesus, per Blum and Harvey, had ongoing popular appeal, it creates some real theological problems. A faceless Jesus is devoid of historical and social context. This lack of spatial groundedness means Jesus is easily unmoored from biblical narratives in ways that make his person and ongoing work malleable. The faceless Christ can easily be made to fit subjective needs. At its worst, a spiritualized Christ can dissolve into a contemporary form of Gnosticism. It minimizes Christ's earthly, bodily, incarnational ministry and spiritualizes his work to a degree that Jesus lacks significance beyond personal spiritual salvation.

The second prevalent image of Jesus is the Hellenized Christ: Jesus stripped of Jewish ethnicity and even faith. Countless studies have examined how the early church fathers, Martin Luther, and Calvin attempted to distance Jesus from his Jewishness. These reformers lacked any robust definition of Jesus as a first-century Jew or any clear statement of what this would mean in terms of Christology. Jesus' Jewishness seems incidental to who Christ is. Theologically this image has the same effect as the faceless, raceless Christ. It unmoors Jesus from the social, political, and ethnic implications of his historical existence. The Hellenized Christ risks becoming the receptacle for Platonic and Aristotelian philosophies, which often take the message of his life beyond the horizon of the biblical texts. Also, by lacking any significant suggestion about how Christ's spatial, geopolitical position as a first-century Jew matters to evangelical Christology, any arguments that Christ was not Black but Jewish become hollow, devoid of theological consequence.

The third prominent image of Christ is the Jesus of American nationalism. Both Nathan Hatch and Mark Noll note how American democracy has shaped the American Church in its own image. The Constantinianism of American Christianity, so evident in America through the 1950s, saw Christianity as the center of American democratic values and the capitalist work ethic. Henry's earliest editorials in *Christianity Today* defend democracy against communism on the grounds that democracy best represents Christian values and Jesus' teachings. This Christianized American exceptionalism is still evident within at least some streams of popular evangelicalism. What seems to drive this impulse is the prevalence of supercessionism. The predominant New England Puritan ideal that sees America as the promised land, and the Puritan colonies as the new Jerusalem, runs deep in the American evangelical imagination. But supercessionism in all its manifestations—including the divine rights of kings and the doctrine of discovery—removes Christ and Israel from their historical realities and hermeneutically re-creates Christ in the image of contemporary society. Certainly, evangelicalism aspires to the opposite. If one considers that more Gospel parallels exist between America and Rome than between America and Christ, then the hermeneutical and theological damage of associating Christ and Christian values too closely with American democracy becomes evident.

The final image of Christ prevalent within American society is the White Jesus. Again, Blum and Harvey describe the long career of the White Christ and equate its rise with American White supremacists' reactions to the freeing of slaves and civil rights legislation. But in both Black and White churches across America, the most prominent image of Jesus is a Nordic Christ with long flowing hair and distinctively European features. Most academic White theologians would deny that this image of Christ is realistic, but they are also at a loss to present a compelling argument against its continued use. The White Jesus lies latent in the back of every White American's notion of who Jesus is. But to make Christ part of the dominant culture, and of the dominant racial majority within that culture, again brings contemporary meaning to the biblical text that in no way offers hermeneutical equivalency. It also suggests very real theological problems. As Major Jones has argued, if everyone's image of Jesus is White, and if Blacks take seriously the inequalities between Whites and Blacks in America, then the question of theodicy looms large. Blacks have a very real opportunity to ask Jones' question: "Is God a White racist?" The whiteness of Christ carries real theological weight.

If these are the dominant images of Christ within American popular evangelicalism and, at times, the defaults within academic evangelical theology, then the discussion lacks any distinct starting point for talking theologically about Jesus. To ignore or minimize the real cultural, social, political, and ethnic contexts in which Jesus carried out God's mission is to ignore whole portions of the biblical message. But given the difficulty of bridging contemporary notions of Jesus' Jewishness and first-century realities of what it meant to be Jewish, then this study has a responsibility to speak of Christ in terms of hermeneutical equivalencies. Cone's location of just such an equivalency in the Black Jesus carries some weight.

Cone's Black Christ

Historically two ways of viewing the Black Christ have dominated. The first sees Christ as historically Black. This view often postulates a racial dualism in which Jesus must be either White or Black, a position represented most prominently by Albert Cleage, the pastor of the Church of the Black Madonna and a radical Black nationalist preacher:

> When I say Jesus was black, that Jesus was the black Messiah, I'm not saying, wouldn't it be nice if Jesus was black? or let's pretend that Jesus was black, or it's necessary psychologically for us to believe that Jesus was black. I'm saying that Jesus WAS black. There never was a white Jesus. Now if you're white, you can accept him if you want to, and you can go through psychological gymnastics and pretend that he was white, but he was black. If you're such a white racist that you've got to believe he was white, then you're going to distort history to preserve his whiteness.[28]

Cone does not follow this literalism and instead posits an ontological blackness of Christ, by which he means that the best contemporary hermeneutical equivalent of a first-century Jew in Palestine is oppressed Black people.[29] He believes that understanding Christ's political, ethnic, and class distinctions means looking to Blacks within the American context and to other oppressed peoples around the world. Thus, Jesus' suffering and oppression within his historical context finds its equivalent in contemporary American culture, where Christ is best identified with the suffering Black community.

Cone's ontologically Black Christ has very real potential for informing evangelical Christology. What would White evangelical theology look like if it were to take seriously a Black Jesus? For one thing, if White evangelicals seriously accept a Black Jesus, they will need to see Christ's social position as central, not merely incidental, to who Christ was. The previous chapters on revelation and providence have already argued this point.

In addition, the Black Christ requires White evangelical theology (and White evangelicals) to see Whites reflected less in Christ. It would require them to position themselves differently within the biblical narrative. A Black Christ on the cross, observed by White evangelicalism, must be viewed differently. A Black Christ can position White theologians in the biblical narratives more clearly as oppressors and can hermeneutically demonstrate the real distance between Christ and White humanity. A Christ who is different racially, culturally, and politically becomes more difficult to appropriate into contemporary defenses of power and more difficult to make complicit in racist logics.

Finally, an ontologically Black Christ would require White Evangelical theology to reorient its ecclesiology. Cone describes the White Church as antichrist because it has failed to live up to at least three marks of the Church. First, its proclamation fails to call out societal evil in the forms of racism and social injustice; it has failed to preach prophetically and has often failed to preach at all about real evil in the world. For Cone, preaching is never neutral—it must always pick a side. Second, the White Church fails in its service. Having neglected the oppressed and marginalized, it fails to render the very service that Christ requires and that Christ modeled in the world. Finally, it has failed in its fellowship. Cone says the Church must be, in its fellowship, what it hopes to see realized in the world. But the White church has not exercised proper discipline regarding racism within its own congregations. While the Church might impose occasional Church discipline regarding individual moral failings, it rarely exercises discipline in regard to racism. In this way, Cone says, the White Church works against Christ and is therefore antichrist.[30]

If Christ is ontologically Black, then evangelical theologians, pastors, and laity must develop a theological answer to the history of White racism and White defense of racism. A Black Christ personalizes the attack on the Black community in a way a faceless Christ does not. A Black Christ requires a different kind of White Church, if it allows a "White Church" at all. Far from being antithetical to White evangelical theology, a Black Christ might open avenues for a more nuanced and creative Christology to proceed from orthodoxy to orthopraxy. Among the many popular images of Christ across the landscape of the American church, the Black Christ might also be more biblically rooted than any other options. Ultimately an ontologically Black Jesus represents the best hermeneutical equivalent available in North America.

Christ's Kenosis

Given the benefits of embracing an ontologically Black Christ, the understanding of this Christ must include an examination of kenosis. Cone sees White applications of Christ's kenosis as a tool used historically by oppressors to subjugate the oppressed, and his assessments are supported by historical research.[31] But kenosis also remains a means of subordination in contemporary theology.

The biblical motif of Christ's temporal submission to the Father is too extensive to be ignored within an evangelical theological system. To completely lose it would set aside an important point in the biblical understanding of power. There are three ways of understanding kenosis.

First, Christ's kenosis, particularly in Paul's writings, suggests an ethical and sanctifying practice that believers must follow. The emphasis here is Christ's free sacrifice and service, not Christ's subordination. When this emphasis is understood, one can see how the passage has been misapplied to encourage the oppressed to accept their involuntary suffering.

In addition, White theology's use of kenosis seems to focus on soliciting sacrificial, servant-leader behavior from those who hold cultural positions of power, not from those who do not. As already suggested, the household codes make such appeals to kenosis. They imply the need to surrender what one has—power, privilege, position, and status—in the interest of the other and in submission to the power of God.

Finally, this surrender implies a suffering solidarity with those on behalf of whom the surrender is offered. The leader becomes the servant of the servant and thereby relinquishes power in the community's interest. Of course, this reading considers kenosis in relation to its implications for discipleship, apart from any consideration of kenosis purely in relation to Christ's relationship with the Father in the Godhead. But the preponderance of biblical texts points toward the greater significance of the former, in terms of human understanding, and therefore justifies the approach.

Closely related to kenosis is the meaning of the cross. Most evangelical theology looks to the cross as a means to define atonement. This soteriological approach is central to Reformed evangelicalism and cannot be abandoned without rendering that theology hollow. Evangelicalism is also incomplete without the full implications of the cross for the believer's moral and ethical life. Cone is guilty of proposing the opposite. By neglecting the doctrine of atonement in his focus on Christ's solidarity with the oppressed on the cross, Cone comes very close to vacating any eternal, salvific significance of the cross.[32] Again, my intent here is not to parody Cone but to ask whether he brings value to evangelicalism. His work does highlight an aspect of the meaning of the cross that, placed beside evangelical views of atonement and soteriology, can imbue the cross with a further ethical meaning that bears directly on a theology of power.

The idea is not in fact Cone's; it appears in his discussion of Reinhold Niebuhr's ethics.[33] Cone sees Niebuhr, as a white theologian, as racist and therefore lacking in many ways, but he cannot ignore Niebuhr's conception of the "transvaluation of values" on the cross. Cone rightly understands the idea's importance. Niebuhr in turn derives this idea from Nietzsche, who berates Christianity as weak because its God died as a weakling for the weak—although Niebuhr sees a positive where Nietzsche sees a negative. For Niebuhr, humanity's sinful pursuit of self-interested power can only be defeated on the cross by a free, sacrificial surrender on behalf of the other. Christ's death denies the pursuit of power and self-interest and instead upholds the surrender of self for the other. Cone understands how Niebuhr's argument is significant for his own. The oppressor's self-interested power directly opposes Christ's sacrificial act on the cross and is therefore antichrist. The cross of Christ is said to transvalue humanity's value of the self-interested pursuit of power and to create a new value system or ethic that values sacrifice over power and the other over self. This transvaluation has significant implications if it is integrated into an evangelical theology of power.

Power is identified by the cross as alien to Christian sanctification and social ethics. Any justification of systems that perpetuate power, particularly along racial lines, is challenged by Cone's and Niebuhr's broader view of the cross, and any ideas of supremacy are necessarily defeated by it. Again, this ethical perspective does not eclipse the evangelical understanding of atonement; it merely adds to it, an addition that seems justified, per the discussion of kenosis above, because the biblical witness also uses the cross of Christ as an exemplar for the life of the believer.

The Meaning of Christ in a Theology of Power

Thus, direct connections can be traced between an ontological view of Christ's blackness, Christ's kenosis, and the meaning of the cross for a theology of power. All three reject the pursuit of power and affirm an ethic that supports the sacrificial surrender of the powerful on behalf of the other. These understandings of Christ and Christ's work place a specific ethical and moral burden on the powerful and directly oppose individuals and systems who exercise self-interested power, particularly to the disadvantage of the poor and marginalized. Systems of supremacy are particularly antithetical to the person and work of Christ.

Thus, the work of Christ further illuminates God's attributes of love, justice, wrath, and power to deny the believer's exercise of self-interested power. Unrestrained power runs counter to God in God's self. All that remains is a final determination of whether the views put forward above cohere with part III's exegesis of Luke 4, Romans 13, and the household codes toward a constructive theology of power.

NOTES

1. Cone, J. 2018. *A Black Theology of Liberation.* 60–61.
2. Cone, J. 2018. *A Black Theology of Liberation.* 63.
3. Cone, J. 2018. *A Black Theology of Liberation.* 90.
4. Calvin, J. 1993: 110.
5. Hodge, C. 1983: 2:366–67.
6. Hodge, C. 1983: 2:367.
7. Hodge, C. 1983: 2:369.
8. Hodge, C. 1983: 2:373.
9. Hodge, C. 1983: 2:374.
10. Hodge, C. 1983: 2:416–26.
11. Henry, Carl. 1983: 6:402, 406.
12. Henry, Carl. 1983: 6:408–9.
13. Henry, Carl. 1983: 6:410–11; 418–35.
14. Henry, Carl. 1983: 6:405.
15. Henry, Carl 1983: 6:414–15.
16. Henry, Carl. 1983: 5:119.
17. Henry, Carl. 1983: 5:130.
18. Henry, Carl. 1983: 5:132.
19. Henry Carl. 1983: 6:410–12.
20. Edwards, J. 1740. *Writings on the Trinity, Grace, and Faith in Works of Jonathan Edwards Online Vol. 21.* Edited by The Jonathan Edwards Center. New Haven: Yale University Press.
21. See Calvin, J. 1993: 125.
22. Cone, J. 2004: 139–52.
23. Henry, Carl. 1983: 6:402–17.
24. Cone, J. 2018. *A Black Theology of Liberation.* 70–78.
25. Henry, Carl. 1983: 405–6.
26. Cone, J. 1997. *God of the Oppressed.* 122–26.
27. Blum, E., and P. Harvey. 2012. *The Color of Christ: The Son of God and the Saga of Race in America.* Chapel Hill: University of North Carolina Press. 29.

28. Cleage, A. 2017. *The Black Messiah.* Trenton: Africa World Press.
29. Cone, J. 2018. *A Black Theology of Liberation.* 26–130.
30. Cone, J. 1997. *God of the Oppressed.* 63–70.
31. Harvey, P. 2016: 67–92.
32. Cone, J. 2011.
33. Cone, J. 2011: 33–34.

Chapter 16

Toward a Theology of Power

Dialogue with the Biblical Text and Ethical Appropriation

This final chapter places the preceding doctrinal conclusions in dialogue with part III's analysis of Luke 4, the household codes, and Romans 13. That said, the current work's limited scope must be recognized. Placing the previous doctrines in dialogue with different texts, engaging a broader group of texts, or dealing with these texts in combination with other texts might yield a different result.

The intent of this study is to move toward a theology of power. This work needs to be expanded in subsequent research. The aim here is a faithful consideration of the doctrinal and biblical material within the study's limited scope of research. That said, the primary theological motifs arising out of part III—covenant understood in light of reversal, inclusion, kenosis, and civil responsibility—provide productive and substantial materials for final consideration.

COVENANT

Part IIIconcludes that covenant and its restoration are central to the theological cohesion of Luke-Acts and are important for expanding the doctrinal considerations above. Luke's work marks covenant as the restoration of Israel, and the text makes clear that God is making right what Israel has been condemned for. This reading recognizes God at work, through God's justice, both in God's wrath in condemning Israel and in God's love in correcting that injustice by expanding the new covenant community.

Covenant, as seen in Luke, is viewed as relational—not merely, or even primarily, contractual. This relational focus directly critiques federalist theology's hyperfocus on contract and therefore law and order. Henry's prioritization of law and order prevents his full realization of his social ethic. He lacks the understanding of relationality that would allow him to view justice as anything other than equal application of judgment under the law. In turn, adherence to the law becomes humanity's primary ethical responsibility, which weakens any argument in favor of justice and of civil disobedience regarding unjust laws. In Henry, the contractual God of the covenant who administers justice through law has ordained law as the foundation of civil relationship. The federalist perspective often moves theology from the divine right of kings to the divine right of law.

Covenant as the establishment of relationship more directly aligns with Edwards' view of relationality within the Trinity, creation, and providence and connects better with part III's conclusions on Luke 4. God, whose essence is love that exists in mutuality and equality within God's own Triunity, extends God's love to establish a relationship with humanity in and through the new covenant community. God's love becomes expressed in the relationship of covenant, and relationality becomes paramount; even if it does not eliminate law, it certainly subordinates it. This subordination creates the ethical possibility of civil disobedience wherever civil law violates God's self-revealed concern for the poor and the marginalized. It ensures that civil law is not so deified in ideas of covenant that it contradicts God's love for God's creation—particularly when, as stated above, civil law exists to extend the self-interest of the powerful, either individuals or groups, in opposition to the needs of those without power.

The biblical expression of relationality and covenant, or more accurately covenant as relationality, stands as a corrective to federalist legality and as a direct affirmation of God's concern for both the divine-human relationship and humanity's relationship with itself. But covenant in Luke is best understood in light of one condition: inclusion.

Inclusion

The one condition of the new covenant community is inclusion. Luke-Acts reveals the new covenant community in Christ to be inclusive first by breaking down barriers of *ethne* and culture to include the Gentiles, and second, by breaking down social barriers to include those on the margins. In doing so Luke-Acts radically alters the power structure by abolishing the social means for excluding individuals and groups from the social and religious life of the covenant community.

But this inclusion must be understood as existing within a bounded set. Election is not universal; it is limited by virtue of faith in God's own grace. This point speaks directly to Cone's and Henry's contentions that God's wrath cannot be separated from God's love. But one might also understand this idea within the dual relational requirement of the covenant. Both love of God and love of neighbor cohere in a member of the new covenant community, as explained in Edwards' theology of the work of the Spirit drawn from I John and the Gospel of Luke. Those without the love of God cannot be part of the new covenant community or receive its blessings. In this way the poor and oppressed—though they may exist as objects of God's special concern, as Henry acknowledges—are not universally saved by virtue of their poverty.

But the new covenant community does exist as an exemplar of the eschatological community envisioned in Scripture. As such, it mirrors God's ethical social expectations and God's morality and justice as they relate to the larger secular world. Luke reveals three primary ethical practices that respond to the inclusive new covenant community: reversal, kenosis, and civil responsibility.

Reversal

Part IIIhas already elucidated the prevalence of reversal in Luke. That Gospel's call for reversal looks forward to the formation of the new covenant community in Acts and specifically culminate in the communal sharing of goods (Acts 4:32). Luke also seems to recognize that an inclusive community living in covenant relationship, itself reflecting God's Triunity, requires members to surrender status, power, and privilege in favor of a community of mutuality and equality, both before God and in actual human interactions.

Luke also disconnects power, privilege, wealth, and social status from the assumption of God's blessing, so that inclusion in the new covenant community is not predicated on status but requires surrender of status in order to participate in the community. Luke is not suggesting that the rich are, by virtue of wealth, excluded from the community. But the definition of sin as self-interest highlights the connection between power and reprobation and spotlights the difficult path of surrender to God that those in positions of power must walk. The requirements to place no stock in personal position and status and to surrender both in favor of a life lived in service to God and others—particularly others with less status, power, and privilege—place a distinctly heavy transformational burden on those with power, privilege, and status.

Reversal in Luke suggests a divine ethic that values mutuality and equality within human community. If the new covenant community is the ideal, then the social objective cannot support a social condition of "each according to their due" but should embrace instead the principle of "each according to the needs of the other." Thus, surrender to the needs of the other is central to biblical principles of kenosis and also affirms Cone's embrace, by way of Niebuhr, of the transvaluation of values on the cross.

Kenosis

As suggested above, kenosis as an exemplar for ethical behavior has already been discussed in relation to the household codes. The household codes at a basic level inform a mutuality of service that asks the "head" to submit to God and serve the other. This mutuality both subordinates any power to God and obligates them under God to care for the other in God's interest, not their own. They must do this because Christ voluntarily and temporarily subordinated himself to the Father by accepting his incarnation and his death on the cross. The idea of mutual surrender and mutuality of service, as well as the abandonment of self-interest in subordination to God and the other, illustrates how the alien imposition of distributive justice onto biblical notions of social justice distorts Christ's sacrifice. Embracing the kenotic example of Christ means abandoning power, privilege, and self-interest to embrace transvaluation in favor of mutuality and service of the other. This requirement applies equally to relationships within the Church and to the Church's relationship to humanity as a whole.

Civil Responsibility

One problem must be addressed in relation to what is expected of the new covenant community and what the community is expected to do in relation to the greater society. This problem has been the subject of theological works including Richard Niebuhr's seminal work *Christ and Culture*, Stanley Hauerwas' *Resident Aliens*, and a substantial portion of the final book of Calvin's *Institutes*. The interest here is primarily to understand the implications of civic responsibility and social action that derive from part III's analysis and conclusions related to Romans 13 and Luke 4. Four primary considerations arise in relation to both passages.

First, in Luke 4, the clear identification of both the marginalized and the Gentiles as persons of concern in Christ's work is critical in understanding the community's relationship to broader humanity. Christ's admonition that he has come to "preach good news to the poor" (Luke 4:18) makes the marginalized a specific point of missional concern for inclusion in the new covenant community. The church has an obligation to reach the poor and another obligation, by virtue of Gentile inclusion, to reach beyond particular *ethne* to ensure all ethnic groups are included in Christ's community of mutuality and equality. The missional call to inclusion forestalls any attempt to justify isolationism. The Church must be a vehicle of inclusion within its own community and in its encounter with the larger world.

A second consideration is how the Church's role in confronting evil gains even more clarity when sin is defined as the pursuit of self-interest apart from

God. This definition of evil involves the church in the analysis and critique of power—and in opposing it. Assessing the impact of power is central to the prophetic role of the new covenant community. Henry is correct in saying that any cultural engagement must recognize the supernatural and spiritual components of social change. But if sin or evil is the exercise of unrestrained self-interested power, then confronting the social injustice that derives from power imbalance and supremacy does directly attack and reveal the spiritual condition of sin that lies at the core of the world's injustice and suffering. The problem is that Henry sees social action as a mere moral response and emphasizes individual salvation as the real "spiritual" solution to social ills. Henry is not wrong, merely shortsighted. Luke's placement of John's call to repentance (Luke 3:1–14) before Christ's call to salvation (Luke 4:16–30) is instructive. By identifying sin as the abuse of power rooted in self-interest, the Church through social action calls the world to repentance. Missiologically, Luke has it right. The world must see first why it stands in need of a savior.

As a third consideration, Cone must be opposed at this point. His disconnection of liberation from salvation, and his emphasis on the former over the latter, degenerates in many ways into a moral sociology, with limited or no reference to spiritual reality. This study specifically noted this issue with Cone's existentializing of God's omnipotence. As Rowe and Green make clear, Luke-Acts witnesses to both the social and the spiritual. The new covenant community's confrontation of evil constitutes its real engagement against unrestrained, self-interested power on behalf of those such power harms. But the Church cannot simply, like Cone, confront evil out of a moral or ethical social obligation. Through social action, the Church identifies sin, directly confronts it as sin, and proclaims God as the remedy amid its battle. Social action, therefore, becomes a call to repentance as a first step toward a missional encounter with Christ. The clarity with which evangelical theology identifies and engages social imbalances of power as constituent with sin is imperative. Cone's lack of a clear doctrine of original sin weakens his appeal to the Church's responsibility for challenging evil, evil having no connection to a root cause. But evangelical theologians like Henry need also to see social action in opposition to abuses of power as the first step in their missional efforts because it points the world toward its sinful nature and calls the world to repentance in the very real acts of protest, revolution, and the work of social reform.

The fourth and final consideration arises from Barth's instructive analysis of the Church's responsibility in light of Romans 13 and Hodge's affirmation of a just revolution. Barth believes that Romans 13 does not obviate the Church's responsibility to civil government but in fact obligates it. Barth, as illustrated in part III, identifies the Church as a subset of all citizens with a distinct life regulated by God, but he insists that the Church exists as an institution within larger society, with an obligation and responsibility to participate and engage within that society, although larger society has no authority over the Church. Barth highlights the Church's particular obligation within a democratic society, where both the Church and its members have, at least theoretically, a voice, a vote, and the right to dissent, both individually and communally. When the government is the people, then any injustice perpetrated by the government is an injustice perpetrated by the people; as constituents, the Church and its members become implicit in the injustice. Law and order in a democracy cannot be seen as justifying inaction. The right to dissent within democracies therefore becomes part of the Church's continued participation in the secular world, as required by Romans 13.

Likewise, Hodge believes that government can be overthrown and replaced through revolutionary action if it fails in its obligations to the people or proceeds in a manner that violates God's law. Hodge does limit who can rebel and in fact denies slaves the right of rebellion. But understood broadly, Hodge's allowance for revolution creates at least the possibility of dissent that Barth seems to envision in his commentary on Romans 13. Likewise, combined with Barth's view of God's power—particularly his insistence that God's exercise of power is not devoid of morality or rightness—Hodge's argument creates a condition within understandings of power that provides acceptable reasons for revolution. Hodge's allowance of revolution, seen this way, requires not mere objection to government but a moral reason for opposing it. The government's failure to meet its moral obligations to all persons, or its injustice toward particular groups, can justify dissent or revolution.

Far from suggesting Anabaptist isolationism, both Luke-Acts and Romans 13 require continued participation and direct involvement as missional, spiritual, prophetic, and pragmatic acts by the new covenant community in the world. Further, in the relational covenantal act of God in Christ, the Church is called to engage with and bear witness to a bounded inclusivism, abolish status and position in the interest of others, embrace mutuality of service on behalf of others, and totally subordinate self-interest to God in imitation of Christ's kenosis.

Little logical contradiction, then, appears between part III's biblical, exegetical conclusions and the doctrinal conclusions of the current part. Both the biblical exegesis and doctrinal construction point to a view of power that calls for surrender in service to God and the other. Both parts see power as sin when characterized by the unrestrained pursuit of self-interest over the interest of others and God. Both point to God's justice as flowing from God's love—which includes God's wrath toward those who engage in the self-interested pursuit of power, as well as God's love for the marginalized and excluded, love found in the provision of the new covenant community. Both parts affirm the Church's continued participation and, in light of contemporary democratic governments, its exercise of the right to dissent and in some cases to rebel. Finally, both affirm social action as a direct attack on and illumination of sin, making social action a distinct call to repentance and to God. Both parts affirm a missional priority in the inclusion and equal treatment of the poor and marginalized. The doctrinal conclusions of this fourth part, given the limitations noted at the start, can therefore be said, at the very least, not to contradict the biblical theology of Luke 4, the household codes, and Romans 13.

ETHICAL APPROPRIATION

Having suggested constructive ways to understand the doctrine of God (seen in light of a conversation among Cone, Calvin, Edwards, Hodge, and Henry) in the exposition of a theology of power consistent with the biblical analyses of Luke 4, Romans 13, and the household codes, this study now only needs to consider ethical appropriation. The separation of ethics from theology has, as suggested above, weakened both ethics and doctrinal engagement and has disconnected sound doctrine from its implications for both the Church and the world. The stated methodology of this project requires that doctrinal construction be readily appropriable into ethical reflection.

Reconnecting Ethics and Theology

Bernard Ramm discusses this specific problem.[1] He follows Barth in his assessment of Kant, who proposes that ethics can be justified on purely rational grounds apart from any reference to divine command. This proposition effectively severs ethics from theology. The problem has become even more acute with the rise of postmodernism and the subjectification of intellectual rationalism. Ethics, per Kant, requires the application of logical reasoning; but postmodernism challenges the possibility of a universal ethical truth, and neither approach offers an authority or exemplar for human moral or ethical behavior. Christian ethics, separated from any dependence on systematic theology, has adopted either a rationalist or a postmodern perspective on ethical issues. Evangelical ethics in some cases does work within a biblical propositional framework, but propositionalism limits the extent to which any issue can be pursued. This limitation has weakened ethics, which remains disconnected from broader theological discussions and dogmatic theology, which in turn remain disconnected from contemporary concern.

Of course, this is what Cone means when he insists that White theologians fail to consider racism in their theological work. Racism as an ethical and moral issue is absent in systematic theologies that have segregated it from dogmatics and made it a purely ethical concern.

Ramm favors Barth's solution. Ethics must be reconnected to theological work at the point of the doctrine of God. Ramm insists that God and God's self—not simply specific propositional commands, but God in God's very essence—should be the starting point of Christian ethical consideration. He affirms that the doctrine of God speaks directly to contemporary issues. Cone only briefly and reluctantly considers the doctrine of God; he downplays portions of the doctrine, particularly God's person, and makes some aspects significant only as existential encounters in the human spirit. In that way, Cone leaves unexplained a critical doctrine that might have addressed racism within the White theological tradition. This study's doctrinal work on God fills this gap in Cone's work. Per Ramm, it also affords an opportunity to suggest the praxial or ethical significance of the affirmed doctrines. From the preceding doctrinal and biblical study of the doctrine of God, four specific ethical concerns arise: power, justice, community, and responsibility.

Social Expressions of Ethical Concern

Power

The exercise of power in contemporary society must be seen in relation to God's omnipotence and human sin. Power rests with God. Human exercise of power can only be ascribed to God with great critical analysis and hesitation, and human sin—viewed as unrestrained, self-interested pursuit of power—renders most human exercises of power suspect.

Power analysis is central to evangelical theological ethics. Evangelical engagement begins with the assumption, unless demonstrated otherwise, that all human exercise of power is at its base corrupted by sin. Power dynamics must be viewed first and foremost as an exercise in self-interest and as such must be viewed as suspect and in need of confrontation and correction.

This finding also implies that Christians who hold power over others are morally and spiritually obligated to analyze their own motives and actions within these relationships, the objective being to ensure that their individual and group actions are governed by the transvaluation evident in Christ's cross. The abandonment of power—or perhaps its use in sacrificial service to the other—should govern the moral and ethical consideration of Christians. Those in positions of power are uniquely obligated before God to submit to God and serve the other. This service extends beyond the transactional practice of charity toward genuine relationship that establishes real connection. Submission to God requires surrender of self, which includes one's power, privilege, status, and position. It also means committing to everything

God commits to. God's commitment to the poor, the marginalized, and the oppressed means that Christians, in submission to God, must also commit to the poor, the marginalized, and the oppressed—again, not in charitable obedience but in filial love and relationship. Evangelical ethics, pursued in light of this study's understanding of power flowing out of the doctrine of God, must focus on analyzing and correcting power dynamics. This understanding of power always operates in the background of any discussion of justice, community, and responsibility.

Justice

Justice, as determined above, derives from the essence of love in the triunity of God. Thus, it is both retributive and liberative. Love as retribution or wrath ensures that the tyrant and the oppressor do not avoid judgment and punishment. Justice as liberation means that God's justice elevates the poor, the oppressed, the excluded, and the marginalized to equality with the powerful, the privileged, and the rich and offers them the full blessings of eternity.

If God's justice is an exemplar for human justice and grounds the ethical analysis of justice and injustice, human justice must rise to the level of God's justice. It must be prepared to stand in opposition to the tyrant and oppressor. It must actively pronounce God's judgment and seek the end of tyranny and oppression as direct results of humanity's fall.

Further, justice must be seen as the elevation of the poor, the marginalized, and the outcast to mutuality and equality. The standard of justice cannot be distributive if it merely "values" all equally or provides for each only according to their due. To rise to God's standard, justice must be restorative, focused on the elevation of those who suffer the consequences of self-interested power—or put another way, the consequences of fallen humanity. True equality gives to each according to their need. This argument does not prescribe or deify a particular civil political philosophy but provides a standard by which Christianity critiques every political system and work within it to secure justice for the other and to oppose injustice in any form. Retributive justice for oppressors and oppressive systems, and restorative justice for the oppressed and the marginalized, all predicated on understanding God's justice as derived from God's love, should ground Christian assessments of justice and injustice and Christian responses to the same.

Community

The idea of community, rooted in Christ's new covenant community, further engages Christian practice in regard to power. The reversal and submission inherent in Luke and understandings of the new covenant require the elect to surrender power, privilege, and status in the interest of mutuality, equality, and a commitment to serving the other. Christian community, in light of the findings of this study, cannot be characterized by self-interest. Instead, it is a bounded community of inclusion where God has, through the Spirit, brought self-interest back under God's control and infused God's love into believers, whom God's love binds to one another. This act of the Spirit requires the individuals who form the community as well as the community as a collective to extend their love for God into a divinely guided love of neighbor. This love for the other is expressed in service and engagement.

God has revealed the intention that the new covenant community welcome the poor, the marginalized, and those who are excluded by virtue of their race or ethnicity; they all are special objects of Christ's missional concern and compassion. This inclusivity is the mission that the Church has inherited; therefore, the Church has a special concern for the poor, the marginalized, and the diverse people of the world. Inclusion unites all believers in a community of mutuality, equality, and service.

Inclusivity leads to diversity, which requires reversal and surrender. A community that reflects God is a community that exhibits the love, mutuality, and equality evident in the Godhead. Christian community is judged by whether its members, through God's love and grace, have surrendered sinful self-interest in the interest of serving the other. If they are engaged in the missional inclusion of the poor, the marginalized, the outcast, and all peoples regardless of race and ethnicity—and if these individuals then assume places of equality, mutuality, and restorative care within the new covenant community—these praxial concerns, derived from biblical and doctrinal study, can form the marks of the Church.

Responsibility

The missional formation of the new covenant community extends inclusion, service, and love to the poor, marginalized, and racially excluded. But the preceding doctrinal considerations also conclude that both individual Christians and the Church have responsibility for continued participation in civil society. That participation is guided by standards of love, justice, and restoration, defined by the rightness and morality of God. Christians must base all political, social, and cultural actions not on political and social philosophy, but rather on an understanding of God's perfections. Christians, therefore, support or oppose political and social actions not through an appeal to appropriateness and legality within particular political forms or social norms but instead in their conformity to the standard predicated on God's triune being. Any political or social pragmatism that opposes who God is in God's self stands opposed to God and must be opposed by God's elect. The idea of a "necessary evil" contradicts a Christian ethic based on a biblical understanding of God.

Christians, therefore, cannot be passive or dismissive in the face of injustice, abuses of power, systemic inequality, or human need, all of which arise from the unrestricted self-interest of the powerful and privileged. These sins, whether committed by a collective or an individual, are sins nonetheless. Social action and social justice become obligations of evangelicalism. Through social activism, sinners are called to repent: not merely to confess but to cease and reverse their actions. For that reason, Christian social action must also explicitly reference the fall of mankind as the root of all injustice and point to Jesus Christ as the only true answer, while calling on the sinner to cease and correct evil acts of injustice. This understanding distinguishes Christian social activism and ethics from secular social activism and philosophical social ethics, even when the objectives are the same.

Christian individuals and churches within democracies have a special obligation. If democracy means the rule of the people, then the people are the government, and its acts are their acts. Those who have a voice, a vote, and the right to dissent also have responsibility and culpability. The sin of the government is the sin of the people, as both individuals and institutions within democratic societies.

Thus, the doctrine of God envisioned here extends the specific ethical and praxial social obligations relating to power, justice, community, and responsibility. Personal moral obligations that mimic these social obligations also derive from the doctrine of God.

Personal Moral Obligations

Individuals are called to abandon power in humility before God. Personal humility is a focus in the theologies of Calvin, Edwards, and Hodge, so its practice as an ethical extension of a theology of power draws on a long-reformed evangelical tradition. Surrender to God and service to neighbor are not controversial ideas in evangelical theology. But what this study envisions is a humility that draws both on humanity's lowness in relation to God's glory and on a vision of humility as an action not an attitude. When contemplated within the affirmation of hierarchy and distributive justice, humility often references an attitude and determines action based on position, station, and status. Each person should be humble in relation to social position. But here, humility insists on the Lukan principle of reversal, which calls the powerful and the privileged to abandon their power in the interest of mutuality and service. Humility is the actual surrender of the privileges of status. Power is abandoned by the powerful in imitation of Christ's kenotic sacrifice.

Individual Christians are further called to practice justice in opposition to evil abuses of power. They are called into community in solidarity with the poor, the marginalized, and every race of humanity. Finally, they are called to individual engagement in civil society through the lenses of God's standards, evidenced in God's own self.

RACIAL JUSTICE IN EVANGELICAL THEOLOGY

Given these social and personal ethical frameworks, derived directly from a particular view of the doctrine of God, how do these standards speak to and advance racial justice and prevent racism from re-encroaching into evangelical theology? First, the definition of sin as self-interested power places the exercise of power that is inherent in racism and White supremacy outside the acceptable realm of practice of Christians and Christian communities. Second, the degree to which this study insists on the abandonment of power, reversal, and inclusion makes the perpetuation of exclusive, self-interested racial acts antithetical to Christianity itself. Likewise, the affirmation of Christian responsibility for civil society—alongside a redefinition of Christian activism as an evangelistic identification of sin and call to repentance as well as action—stands in opposition to evangelical passivity and dismissiveness around racial justice issues. This book has shown that certain doctrines have been abused in the interest of racist logics, and the study has re-engaged them within the tradition in ways that leave them unavailable for racist appropriation. The historical, biblical, and doctrinal work of this study therefore points to an evangelical vision of power that, when appropriated for ethical and practical ends, logically forestalls the perpetuation of racist logics and their use toward racist ends.

Ultimately what has been demonstrated is that Cone's critique of White reformed evangelicalism's embedded racism is true. Further, understanding this has allowed the author to reimagine evangelical theology in antiracist ways through a methodology that is biblically grounded and true to evangelical ideals.

NOTE

1. Ramm, B. 1983: 144–50.

Bibliography

Alexis, G. "Jonathan Edwards and the Theocratic Ideal." *Church History* 35, no. 3 (1966): 328–43.

Anderson, H. "Broadening Horizons: The Rejection at Nazareth Pericope of Luke 4:16–30 in Light of Recent Critical Trends." *Interpretation* 18, no. 3 (1964): 259–75.

Armstrong, A. "Last Were the Mohicans: Jonathan Edwards, Stockbridge, and Native Americans." *Southwestern Journal of Theology* 48, no. 1 (2005): 19–31.

Baraka, A., and L. Neal, eds. 1968. *Black Fire: An Anthology of Afro-American Writing*. Baltimore: Black Classic Press.

"Barmen Declaration." Accessed November 13, 2020. www.groups.csail.mit.edu/medg/people/doyle/personal/enters/hermann/declaration.html.

Barshinger, D. "'The Only Rule of Our Faith and Practice': Jonathan Edwards's Interpretation of the Book of Isaiah as a Case Study of His Exegetical Boundaries." *Journal of the Evangelical Theological Society* 52, no. 4 (2009): 811–29.

Barth, K. 1954. *Against the Stream: Shorter Post-War Writings 1946–52*. Translated by E. Delacour. London: SCM Press.

———. 1955. *The Theology of John Calvin*. Edited by G. Bromiley. Grand Rapids: William B. Eerdmans.

———. 1960. *The Humanity of God*. 5th printing. Translated by T. Wieser and J. Thomas. Atlanta: John Knox Press.

———. 1968. *The Epistle to the Romans*. Translated by K. Hoskyn. Oxford: Oxford University Press.

———. 2004. *Church Dogmatics II.2*. Translated by T. Parker. New York: T & T Clark International.

Bauckham, R. 2008. *The Jewish World around the New Testament*. Grand Rapids: Baker Academic.

Beale, G. 2008. *We Become What We Worship: A Biblical Theology of Idolatry*. Downers Grove: IVP Academic.

Beck, P. "Edwards and Indians: Inclusion or Evangelism?" *Fides Et Historia* 38, no. 2 (2006): 23–33.

Blount, B. 2001. *Then the Whisper Put on Flesh: New Testament Ethics in an African American Context*. Nashville: Abingdon Press.

Blum, E., and P. Harvey. 2012. *The Color of Christ: The Son of God and the Saga of Race in America.* Chapel Hill: University of North Carolina Press.

Bock, D. 1994. *Luke 1:1–9:50, ECNT.* Grand Rapids: Baker Academic.

Bolton, K. "The Theological Method of James Cone." Doctoral Dissertation, Fuller Seminary, 1986.

Bouwsma, K. 1986. *John Calvin: A Sixteenth-Century Portrait.* Oxford: Oxford University Press.

Bowens, L. 2020. *African American Readings of Paul: Reception, Resistance, Transformation.* Grand Rapids: William B. Eerdmans.

Brueggemann, W. 2018. *Tenacious Solidarity: Biblical Provocations on Race, Religion, Climate, and the Economy.* Minneapolis: Fortress Press.

Burger, J. "The Story of God's Covenants: A Biblical-Theological Investigation with Systematic Consequences." *Calvin Theological Journal* 54, no. 2 (2019): 207–99.

Calvin, J. 1948. *Commentary on the First Twenty Chapters of the Book of the Prophet Ezekiel.* Edited by T. Myers. Grand Rapids: William B. Eerdmans.

———. 1966. *Jacopo Sadoleto: Reformation Debate.* Translated by J. Olin. Grand Rapids: Baker Academic.

———. 1993. *Institutes of the Christian Religion.* Translated by H. Beveridge. Grand Rapids: William B. Eerdmans.

———. 2003. *Commentary on A Harmony of the Evangelists: Matthew, Mark, Luke, Vol. 3.* Translated by W. Pringle. Grand Rapids: Baker.

———. 2005. *Commentary on the First Book of Moses Called Genesis.* Translated by J. King. Grand Rapids: Baker.

———. 2005. *Commentary on the Four Last Books of Moses Arranged in the Form of a Harmony.* Translated by C. Bingham. Grand Rapids: Baker.

———. 2005. *Commentary on the Epistles of Paul to the Galatians and Ephesians.* Translated by W. Pringle. Grand Rapids: Baker.

———. 2005. *Commentaries on the Epistle to the Romans, Vol. 2.* Translated by C. Fetherstone. Grand Rapids: Baker.

———. 2005. *Commentaries on the Evangelists.* Translated by C. Fetherstone. Grand Rapids: Baker.

Camus, A. 1956. *The Rebel.* Translated by A. Bower. New York: Vintage Books.

Carey, G. "Moving Things Ahead: A Lukan Redactional Technique and Its Implications for Gospel Origins." *Biblical Interpretation* 21, no. 3 (2013): 302–19.

Carter, J. 2008. *Race: A Theological Account.* New York: Oxford University Press.

Clark, D. 2003. *To Know and Love God: Method for Theology.* Wheaton: Crossway Books.

Carr, R. "Barth and Cone in Dialogue on Revelation and Freedom: An Analysis of James Cone's Appropriation of 'Barthian' Theology." Doctoral Dissertation, Graduate Theological Union, 2011.

Cerillo, A., and M. Dempster. "Carl F. H. Henry's Early Apologetic for an Evangelical Social Ethic." *Journal of the Evangelical Theological Society* 34, no. 3 (1991): 365–79.

Cleage, A. 2017. *The Black Messiah.* Trenton: Africa World Press.

Coker, J. "Exploring the Roots of the Dispensationalist/Princetonian 'Alliance': Charles Hodge and John Newton Darby on Eschatology and Interpretation of Scripture." *Fides Et Historia* 30, (1998): 41–56.

Cone, J. "The Doctrine of Man in the Theology of Karl Barth." Doctoral Dissertation, Northwestern University, 1965.

———. "Black Theology and Black Liberation." *The Christian Century* (September 16, 1970): 1084–88.

———. 1972. *The Spirituals and the Blues*. New York: Seabury Press.

———. "Black Spirituals: A Theological Interpretation." *Theology Today* 29, no. 1 (1972): 54–69.

———. "The Dialectic of Theology and Life or Speaking the Truth." *Union Seminary Quarterly Review* 29, no. 2 (1974): 75–89.

———. "The Content and Method of Black Theology." *The Journal of Religious Thought* 32, no. 2 (1975): 90–103.

———. "Black Theology on Revolution, Violence, and Reconciliation." *Union Seminary Quarterly Review* 31 (Fall, 1975): 5–14.

———. "God Our Father, Christ Our Redeemer, Man Our Brother: A Theological Interpretation of the AME Church." *The Journal of the Interdenominational Theological Center* 4 (Fall,1976): 25–33.

———. "Sanctification, Liberation, and Black Worship." *Theology Today* 35, no. 2 (1978): 139–52.

———. "What Is Theology." *Encounter* 43, no. 2 (1982): 117–28.

———. "Christian Faith and Political Praxis." *Encounter* 43, no. 2 (1982): 129–41.

———. 1984. *For My People*. Maryknoll: Orbis.

———. 1986. *My Soul Looks Back*. Nashville: Abingdon Press.

———. 1997. *Black Theology and Black Power*. New York: Harper and Row.

———. 1997. *God of the Oppressed*. New York: The Seabury Press.

———. 1999. *Risks of Faith: The Emergence of Black Theology, 1968–1998*. Boston: Beacon Press.

———. "Whose Earth Is It Anyway." *CrossCurrents* 50 (Spr/Sum, 2000): 36–46.

———. "Theology's Great Sin: Silence in the Face of White Supremacy." *Black Theology: An International Journal* 2 (2004), no. 2: 144–50.

———. 2011. *The Cross and the Lynching Tree*. Maryknoll: Orbis Books.

———. 2012. *Martin and Malcolm and America: A Dream and a Nightmare*. Maryknoll: Orbis Books.

———. 2018. *A Black Theology of Liberation*. Maryknoll: Orbis Books.

———. 2018. *Said I Wasn't Gonna Tell Nobody*. Maryknoll: Orbis Books.

Conzelmann, H. 1961. *The Theology of St. Luke*. Translated by G. Boswell. San Francisco: Haper and Row.

Crowder, B. 2007. "Luke." In *True to Our Native Land*. Edited by B. Blount. Minneapolis: Fortress Press. 158–85.

Cummings, R. "Contrasts and Fragments: An Exploration of James Cone's Theological Methodology." *Anglican Theological Review* 91, no. 3 (2009): 395–416.

Danaher, W. "Beauty, Benevolence, and Virtue in Jonathan Edwards's *The Nature of True Virtue*." *The Journal of Religion* 87, no. 3 (2007): 386–410.

De Gruchy, J. "The Revitalization of Calvinism in South Africa: Some Reflections on Christian Belief, Theology, and Social Formation." *The Journal of Religious Ethics* 14, (1986): 22–47.

Delattre, R. "The Theological Ethics of Jonathan Edwards: An Homage to Paul Ramsey." *The Journal of Religious Ethics* 19, no. 2 (1991): 71–102.

Dunn, J. 1998. *The Theology of Paul the Apostle*. Grand Rapids: William B. Eerdmans.

Du Toit, P. "Reconsidering the Salvation of Israel in Luke-Acts." *Journal for the Study of the New Testament* 43, no. 3 (2021): 343–69.

Edwards, J. 1714. *Outline of a 'Rational Account.' Scientific and Philosophical Writings in the Works of Jonathan Edwards Online Vol. 6*. Edited by W. Anderson. New Haven: Yale University Press.

———. 1722. *The Miscellanies Entry Nos. a–z, aa–zz, 1–500 The Works of Jonathan Edwards Online*. Edited by H. Stout. New Haven: Yale University Press.

———. 1723–1729. *Sermons and Discourses in the Works of Jonathan Edwards Online*. Edited by The Jonathan Edwards Center. New Haven: Yale University Press.

———. 1730. "Luke." In *The Blank Bible (The Works of Jonathan Edwards Online Vol. 24)*. Edited by The Jonathan Edwards Center. New Haven: Yale University Press.

———. 1731. *The Miscellanies 68, 557, 702, 754, 815. The Works of Jonathan Edwards Online Vol. 18*. Edited by A. Chamberlain. New Haven: Yale University Press.

———. 1740. *Writings on the Trinity, Grace, and Faith in Works of Jonathan Edwards Online Vol. 21*. Edited by The Jonathan Edwards Center. New Haven: Yale University Press.

———. 1745. *Sermons 75, 87, 179. Sermon Series II in Works of Jonathan Edwards Online Vol. 43*. Edited by The Jonathan Edwards Center. New Haven: Yale University Press.

———. 1750/51. *Sermons 972, 979, 1000, 1003. Sermon Series II in The Works of Jonathan Edwards Online Vol. 43*. Edited by The Jonathan Edwards Center. New Haven: Yale University Press.

———. 1751. *Letters 129, 131, 134, 135, 141. Letters and Personal Writings in Works of Jonathan Edwards Online Vol. 16*. Edited by G. Claghorn. New Haven: Yale University Press.

———. 1980. *The Nature of True Virtue*. Ann Arbor: The University of Michigan Press.

———. 2000. *Charity and Its Fruits*. Carlisle: Banner of Truth Trust.

Eliav-Feldon, M., ed., with B. Issac and J. Ziegler. 2009. *The Origins of Racism in the West*. Cambridge: Cambridge University Press.

Evans, C. "Luke's Use of the Elijah/Elisha Narratives and the Ethic of Election." *Journal of Biblical Literature* 106, no. 1 (1987): 75–83.

Evans, J. "White Evangelical Reponses to the Civil Rights Movement." *Harvard Theological Review* 102, no. 2 (2009): 263.

Fanon, F. 2004. *The Wretched of the Earth*. Translated by R. Philcox. New York: Grove Press.

———. 2008. *Black Skins, White Masks*. New York: Grove Press.
Fee, G. 2005. "Hermeneutics and the Gender Debate." In *Discovering Biblical Equality*. Edited by R. Pierce and R. Groothuis. Downers Grove: IVP Academic: 364–81.
Ferguson, S. 1989. "On the Reformed View of Sanctification." In *Five Views of Sanctification*. Downers Grove: IVP Academic: 57–78.
Frei, H. 1974. *The Eclipse of Biblical Narrative: A Study in Eighteenth and Nineteenth Century Hermeneutics*. New Haven: Yale University Press.
Freudenberg, M. "Economic and Social Ethics in the Work of John Calvin." *HTS Teologiese/Theological Studies* (2009). https://doi.org/10.4102/hts.v65:1.286.
Frye, R. 1990. *John Calvin and the Church: A Prism of Reform*. Edited by T. George. Louisville: Westminster John Knox Press.
Gadamer, H. 2004. *Truth and Method*. 2nd ed. New York: Continuum.
Gentry, P. "The Significance of Covenants in Biblical Theology." *The Southern Baptist Journal of Theology* 20, no. 1 (2016): 9–33.
Gerstner, J. 1991. *The Rational Biblical Theology of Jonathan Edwards, 3 Vols*. Powhaton: Berea Publications.
Gilens, M. "Race Coding and White Opposition to Welfare." *American Political Science Review* 90, no. 3 (1996): 593–604.
Giles, K. 2005. "The Subordination of Christ and the Subordination of Women." In *Discovering Biblical Equality*. Edited by R. Pierce and R. Groothuis. Downers Grove: IVP Academic: 334–54.
Goen, C. "Jonathan Edwards: A New Departure in Eschatology." *Church History* 28, (1959): 25–40.
Goldberg, D. 1994. *Racist Culture: Philosophy and the Politics of Meaning*. Oxford: Blackwell Publishers.
Green, J. 1997. *The Gospel of Luke, NICNT*. Grand Rapids: William B. Eerdmans.
Hafemann, S. 2007. "The Covenant Relationship." In *Central Themes in Biblical Theology: Mapping Unity in Diversity*. Downers Grove: IVP Press: 20–65.
Hahn, S. 2009. *Kinship in Covenant: A Canonical Approach to the Fulfillment of God's Saving Promises*. New Haven: Yale University Press.
Hall, D. "Exegesis and Resistance: The Calvinistic Political Revolution of 1530–1580." *Puritan Reformed Journal* 8 (2016): 51–83.
Hanc, O. "Paul and Empire: A Reframing of Romans 13:1–7 in the Context of New Exodus." *The Tyndale Bulletin* 65, no. 2 (2014): 313–16.
Harvey, P. 2016. *Christianity and Race in the American South*. Chicago: University of Chicago Press.
Hatch, N. 1991. *The Democratization of American Christianity*. New Haven: Yale University Press.
Hendriksen, W. 1978. *Exposition of the Gospel according to Luke*. Grand Rapids: Baker Books.
Henry, Caleb. "Pride, Property, and Providence: Jonathan Edwards on Property Rights." *Journal of Church and State* 53, no. 3 (2011): 401–22.
Henry, Carl. 1964. *Aspects of Christian Social Ethics*. Grand Rapids: Baker Books.
———. 1966. *The God Who Shows Himself*. Waco: Word Books.
———. 1967. *Evangelicals at the Brink*. Waco: Word Books.

———. 1967. *Facing a New Day in Evangelism: One Race, One Gospel, One Task.* Minneapolis: World Wide Publications.

———. 1983. *God, Revelation and Authority Vols. 1, 3, 5, and 6.* Waco: Word Books.

———. 1984. "Liberation Theology and the Scriptures." In *On Liberation Theology.* Edited by R. Nash. Milford: Mott Media.

———. 1986. *Confessions of a Theologian: An Autobiography.* Waco: Word Books.

Herzog, W. "Theology at the Crossroads." *Union Seminary Quarterly Review* 31, no. 1 (1975): 59–68.

———. "Dissembling, a Weapon of the Weak: The Case of Christ and Caesar in Mark 12:13–17 and Romans 13:1–7." *Perspectives in Religious Studies* 21, no. 4 (1994): 339–60.

Hodge, C. "The Integrity of Our National Union vs. Abolitionism." *The Biblical Repertory and Princeton Review* 16, no. 4 (1844): 545–81.

———. "Conscience and the Constitution." *The Biblical Repertory and Princeton Review* 23, no. 1 (1851): 125–58.

———. 1979. *Systematic Theology Vol. 2.* Grand Rapids: William B. Eerdmans.

———. 2011. *Princeton Sermons.* Carlisle: The Banner of Truth Trust.

———. 2017. *Commentary on Ephesians.* E4 Group.

———. 2020. *Commentary on Romans.* Carlisle: Banner of Truth Trust.

Hoffecker, W. 2011. *Charles Hodge and the Pride of Princeton.* Phillipsburg: P & R Publishing.

Holbrook, C. "Edwards and the Ethical Question." *Harvard Theological Review* 60, (1967): 163–75.

Hossenfelder, J. 2015. "The Original Guidelines of the German Christian Faith Movement." In *A Church Undone: Documents from the German Christian Faith Movement, 1932–1940*, by M. Solberg. Minneapolis: Fortress Press. 45–52.

Isaak, P. 2006. "Luke." In *African Bible Commentary.* Edited by A. Tokunboh. Grand Rapids: Zondervan. 1229–1276.

Jennings, W. 2010. *The Christian Imagination: Theology and the Origins of Race.* Ann Arbor: Sheridan Books.

———. 2017. *Acts: A Theological Commentary on the Bible.* Grand Rapids: Westminster John Knox Press.

Johnson, A. "The Prophetic Persona of James Cone and the Rhetorical Theology of Black Theology." *Black Theology* 8, no. 3 (2010): 266–85.

"Kairos Document." Accessed November 13, 2020. www.kairossouthafrica.wordpress.com/2011/05/08/the-south-africa-kairos-document-1985.

Kaplan, M. 2019. *Figuring Racism in Medieval Christianity.* Oxford: Oxford University Press.

Kayayan, E. "Calvin on Slavery: Providence and Social Ethics in the 16th Century." *Koers—Bulletin of Christian Scholarship* 78, no. 2 (2013). https://doi.org/http://dx.doi.org/10.4102/koers.v78i2.2119.

Kimball, C. "Jesus' Exposition of Scripture in Luke 4:16–30: An Inquiry in Light of Jewish Hermeneutics." *Perspectives in Religious Studies* 21, no. 3 (1994): 179–202.

Knight, G. 2021. "Husbands and Wives as Analogues of Christ and the Church: Ephesians 5:21–33." In *Recovering Biblical Manhood and Womanhood*. Edited by J. Piper and W. Grudem. Wheaton: Crossway.

Knox, J. 1994. *On Rebellion*. Cambridge: Cambridge University Press.

Kovaks, F., F. Viljoen, and J. Gosling. "The Lukan Covenant Concept: The Basis of Israel's Mandate in Luke-Acts: Original Research." *Verbum Et Ecclesia* 34, no. 1 (2013): 1–9.

Lee, D. 1971. *Dynamite Voices: Black Poets of the 1960s*. Detroit: Broadside Press.

Lee-Barnewall, M. 2016. *Neither Complementarian nor Egalitarian: A Kingdom Corrective to the Evangelical Gender Debate*. Grand Rapids: Baker Academic.

Levine, A., and B. Witherington. 2019. *The Gospel of Luke, New Cambridge Bible Commentary*. Cambridge: Cambridge University Press.

Lim, S. "A Double-Voiced Reading of Romans 13:1–7 in Light of the Imperial Cult." *Herwormde Teologiese Studies* 71 (2015): 1–10.

Link, C. 2009. "Election and Predestination." In *John Calvin's Impact on Church and Society*. Edited by M. Hirzel and A. Sullmann. Grand Rapids: W. B. Eerdmans. 105–21.

Loader, J. "Calvin's Election Mix in Small-Scale Theology." *HTS Teologiese Studies/Theological Studies* 65, no. 1 (2009). https://doi.org/10.4102/hts.v65i1.337.

Long, C. 1995. *Significations: Signs, Symbols, and Images in the Interpretation of Religion*. Aurora: The Davies Group.

Longenecker, B. 2012. *Hearing the Silence: Jesus on the Edge and God in the Gap: Luke 4 in Narrative Perspective*. Eugene: Cascade Books.

Luther, M. 1959. *Luther's Works Vol. 1*. Translated by J. Doberstein. Philadelphia: Fortress Press.

Maimela, S. 1987. *Proclaim Freedom to My People*. Braamfontein, South Africa: Skotaville Publishers.

Makuka, T. "Reading/Hearing Romans 13:1–7 under the African Tree: Towards a Lectio Postcolonica Contexta Africana." *Neotestamentica* 46, no. 1 (2012): 105–38.

Marsden, G. 2003. *Jonathan Edwards: A Life*. New Haven: Yale University Press.

———. 2006. *Fundamentalism and American Culture*. Oxford: Oxford University Press.

Marshall, I. H. 1978. *The Gospel of Luke: A Commentary of the Greek Text*. Grand Rapids: W. B. Eerdmans.

———. 1988. *Luke: Historian and Theologian*. Downers Grove: InterVersity Academic.

———. 2004. *New Testament Theology: Many Witnesses, One Gospel*. Downers Grove: InterVersity Academic.

———. 2005. "Mutual Love and Submission in Marriage." In *Discovering Biblical Equality*. Edited by R. Pierce and R. Groothuis. Downers Grove: InterVersity Academic. 186–204.

Martin, C. 1991. "The *Haustafeln* (Household Codes) in African American Biblical Interpretation: 'Free Slaves' and 'Subordinate Women.'" In *Stoney the Road We Trod; African American Biblical Interpretation*. Edited by C. Felder. Minneapolis: Fortress Press.

Metzger, B. 2005. *A Textual Commentary on the Greek New Testament*. Grand Rapids: Tyndale House.

Minkema, K. "Jonathan Edwards's Defense of Slavery." *Massachusetts Historical Society* 4 (2002): 23–39.

———. "A 'Dordt Philosophe': Jonathan Edwards, Calvin and Reformed Orthodoxy." *Church History and Religious Culture* 91, no. 1 (2011): 241–53.

Moore, R. "The Kingdom of God in the Social Ethics of Carl F. H. Henry: A Twenty-First Century Evangelical Reappraisal." *Journal of the Evangelical Theological Society* 55, no. 2 (2012): 377–97.

Moorhead, J. "Slavery, Race, and Gender at Princeton Seminary: The Pre-Civil War Era." *Theology Today* 69, no. 3 (2012): 274–88.

Mouw, R. "Carl Henry Was Right." *Christianity Today* (2010). Accessed September 11, 2020. www.christianitytoday.com/et/2010/January/25.30.html.

Naude, P. "Toward Justice and Social Transformation? Appealing to the Tradition against the Tradition." *HTS Teologiese Studies/Theological Studies* 73, no. 3 (2017). Accessed September 11, 2020. https://doi.org/10.4102/hts.v73i3.4350.

Noll, M. 2005. *America's God: From Jonathan Edwards to Abraham Lincoln*. Oxford: Oxford University Press.

———. 2008. *God and Race in America*. Princeton: Princeton University Press.

Nolland, J. 1989. *Luke 1–9:20, WBC*. New York: Nelson Reference.

Omanson, R. 2007. *A Textual Guide to the Greek New Testament*. New York: Hendrickson.

Osborne, G. 1991. *The Hermeneutical Spiral: A Comprehensive Introduction to Biblical Interpretation*. Downers Grove: InterVarsity Press.

Pahl, J. "Jonathan Edwards and the Aristocracy of Grace." *Fides Et Historia* 25 (1993): 62–72.

Palms, R. 1971. *The Jesus Kids*. Valley Forge: Judson Press.

Pederson, D., and B. Owen. 1971. *Jesus People*. Pasadena: Compass Press.

Piper, J., and R. Grudem. 2005. *Recovering Biblical Manhood and Womanhood: A Response to Evangelical Feminism*. Downers Grove: InterVarsity Academic.

Pleins, J. 1992. "Poor, Poverty." In *The Anchor Bible Dictionary*. Edited by D. Freedman. New York: Doubleday. 403–14.

Potgieter, P. "John Calvin on Social Challenges." *Acta Theologica Supp.* 28 (2019): 72–87.

Ramm, B. 1983. *After Fundamentalism: The Future of Evangelical Theology*. New York: Harper and Row.

Ricoeur, P. 1996. *Interpretation Theory: Discourse and the Surplus of Meaning*. Fort Worth: Texas Christian University Press.

Ringe, S. 1985. *Jesus, Liberation, and the Biblical Jubilee*. Eugene: Wipf & Stock.

Roberts, J. 2005. *Liberation and Reconciliation: A Black Theology*. 2nd ed. Louisville: Westminster John Knox Press.

Robison, J. "A Tillichian Analysis of James Cone's Black Theology." *Perspectives in Religious Studies* 1 (1974): 16–30.

Roth, S. 1997. *The Blind, the Lame, and the Poor: Character Types in Luke-Acts*. Sheffield: Sheffield Academic.

Rowe, K. 2010. *World Upside Down: Reading Acts in the Greco-Roman Age*. Oxford: Oxford University Press.

Sailhamer, J. 1995. *Introduction to Old Testament Theology: A Canonical Approach*. Grand Rapids: Zondervan.

Sanchez, M. "Calvin, Difficult Arguments, and Affective Responses: Providence as a Case Study in Method." *The Journal of Religion* 99 (2019): 467–91.

Sandeen, E. "The Princeton Theology: One Source of Biblical Literalism in American Protestantism." *Church History* 31, no. 3 (1962): 307–21.

Shellberg, P. 2012. "From Cleansed Lepers to Cleansed Hearts: The Developing Meaning of Katharizo in Luke-Acts." Unpublished dissertation. Marquette University.

Siker, J. "'First to the Gentiles': A Literary Analysis of Luke 4:16–30." *Journal of Biblical Literature* 3 (1992): 73–90.

Snowden, F. 1970. *Blacks in Antiquity*. Cambridge: Harvard University Press.

Stein, S. "The Quest for the Spiritual Sense: The Biblical Hermeneutics of Jonathan Edwards." *Harvard Theological Review* 70 (1977): 99–113.

Stewart, C. "The Method of Correlation in the Theology of James Cone." *Journal of Religious Thought* 40, no. 2 (1983): 27–38.

Stiver, D. 2003. "Theological Method." In *Cambridge Companion to Postmodern Theology*. Edited by K Vanhoozer. Cambridge: Cambridge University Press. 170–85.

Stroup, G. 1990. "Narrative in Calvin's Hermeneutic." In *John Calvin and the Church: A Prism of Reform*. Edited by T. George. Louisville: Westminster John Knox Press. 158–72.

Sytsma, D. "John Calvin and Virtue Ethics: Augustinian and Aristotelian Themes." *Journal of Religious Ethics* 48, no. 3 (2020): 519–56.

Thiselton, A. 2007. *The Hermeneutics of Doctrine*. Grand Rapids: W. B. Eerdmans.

Thompson, J. "Creata Ad Imaginem Dei, Licet Secondo Gradu: Woman as the Image of God according to John Calvin." *Harvard Theological Review* 81, no. 2 (1988): 125–43.

Torbett, D. "Race and Conservative Protestantism: Princeton Theological Seminary and the Unity of the Human Species." *Fides Et Historia* 37, no. 2 (2005): 119–36.

———. 2006. *Theology and Slavery: Charles Hodge and Horace Bushnell*. Macon: Mercer University Press.

Union News. "In Memoriam: Dr. James Hal Cone." *Union Theological Seminary Press Release* (2018). Accessed January 5, 2018. https://utsnyc.edu/james-cone.

VanderMolen, R. "Providence as Mystery, Providence as Revelation: Puritan and Anglican Modifications of John Calvin's Doctrine of Providence." *Church History* 47 (1978): 27–47. Accessed January 5, 2018. https://utsnyc.edu/james-cone.

Vanhoozer, K. "From Canon to Concept: '"Same' and 'Other' in the Relations between Biblical and Systematic Theology." The Finlayson Memorial Lecture.

———. 2005. *The Drama of Doctrine: A Canonical Linguistic Approach to Christian Theology*. Louisville: Westminster John Knox Press.

Von Rad, G. 1961. *Genesis*. Translated by J. Martis. Philadelphia: Westminster Press.
Vorster, N. "John Calvin on the Status and Role of Women in the Church and Society." *The Journal of Theological Studies* 68, no. 1 (2017): 178–211.
Wallace, R. 1997. *Calvin's Doctrine of the Christian Life*. Eugene: Wipf and Stock.
Ware, B., and W. Linkugel. "The Rhetorical Persona: Marcus Garvey as a Black Moses." *Communication Monographs* 49, no. 1: 50–62.
Washington, J. 1993. "Are American Negro Churches Christian?" In *Black Theology: A Documentary History, Vol. 1*. Edited by J. Cone and G. Wilmore. Maryknoll: Orbis.
Webb, W. 2005. "A Redemptive Movement Hermeneutic: The Slavery Analogy." In *Discovering Biblical Equality*. Edited by R. Pierce and R. Groothuis. Downers Grove: InterVarsity Academic. 382–400.
West, C. 2002. *Prophesy Deliverance: An Afro-American Revolutionary Christianity*. Louisville: Westminster John Knox Press.
Wheeler, R. "'Friends to Your Soul': Jonathan Edwards' Indian Pastorate and the Doctrine of Original Sin." *Church History* 72, no. 4 (2003): 736–65.
White, M. "Charles Hodge, Hermeneutics, and the Struggle with Scripture." *Journal of Theological Interpretation* 3, no. 1 (2009): 64–87.
Williams, G., and A. Mergal. 1957. *Spiritual and Anabaptist Writers*. Philadelphia: Westminster Press.
Yoder, J. 1994. *The Royal Priesthood: Essays Ecclesiological and Ecumenical*. Grand Rapids: Eerdmans.

Index

Baldwin, 31–32
Barth, 36–37, 187–91, 225, 238, 242, 298–301, 317–18
Black Arts Movement, 32–33
Black Power Movement, 17–19, 22–27
Bonhoeffer, 39

Calvin: biblical interpretation, 211–14; racism, 57–80; theology, 86–89, 228–31, 261–62, 280–81, 286–87

Camus, 23–24, 25
Cone: biblical interpretation, 214–16, 255–58; Christology, 20, 304–6; defense of black theology, 16–21; ecclesiology, 12–13; influences, 19–20, 23–24, 31–39; methods, 40–43, 47–50; persona, 21–27; person of God, 285–86; providence, 262–64, 275–78, 279–80; revelation, 240–55
creation, 274–78

Edwards: biblical interpretation, 211–14; racism, 81–101; theology, 86–89, 228–31, 261–62, 280–81, 286–87

Fanon, 23–24, 25

Gadamer, 2, 252

Henry: biblical interpretation, 211–14; racism, 119–39; theology, 236–39, 261–62, 280–81, 288–90
Hodge: biblical interpretation, 211–14; racism, 103–17; theology, 234–36, 261–62, 278, 280–81, 287–88
Household Codes: complementarianism, 197–201; egalitarianism, 201–5; interpretation, 205–7; feminist/womanist/liberationist, 196–97; third way, 205–7

Jones, LeRoi (Amari Baraka), 19, 23

King, Martin Luther, 31–32

Lee, Don, 17–18, 23
Long, Charles, 19–20, 35
Luke 4: biblical theology, 173–75, 176, 211–22; competing views of, 170–73, 176; context, 160–68; exegesis, 148–150, 151–69; interpretation, 168–70, 176–80, 194–96, 207–8; intertextuality, 167–68

Malcolm X, 31–32
marxism, 34–35

333

Moltmann, 39

Niebuhr, Reinhold, 39, 225, 307

person of God: person of Christ, 20, 301–8; work of God, 285–301
providence, 261–82

racism: definition, 50–51; embedded, 47–50; logic, 51–52
Ramm, 225, 258, 267, 317–18
revelation, 227–58
Roberts, J. Deotis, 20, 33–34

Romans 13; 62, 70–72, 148–50, 186–95; interpretation, 194–95; normative view, 187–91; post-colonialist view, 191–94; traditionalist view, 186–87

theological method, 2–6, 9–10, 42–43, 47–56, 54–56, 220, 225–26
Thistleton, 2, 16, 42
Tillich, 37–38, 263–64

Vanhoozer, 2, 16, 42, 185

Wilmore, Gayraud, 20
Womanist, 33, 34

About the Author

Joseph Caldwell (PhD in theology with dogmatics, North-West University; DMIN Fuller Seminary) is on faculty at Memphis Theological Seminary and has served as an associate professor and academic dean at Union University and an assistant professor at Gardner Webb University. His area of focus is the intersection of contemporary ethical concerns with dogmatic theology.

www.ingramcontent.com/pod-product-compliance
Lightning Source LLC
Chambersburg PA
CBHW030259280325
24158CB00002B/12